THE SOVIET
ECONOMIC SYSTEM

THE SOVIET ECONOMIC SYSTEM

by

ALEC NOVE

Professor of Economics, University of Glasgow

London
GEORGE ALLEN & UNWIN
Boston   Sydney

First published in 1977
Third impression 1978
Second edition 1980
Third impression 1984

George Allen & Unwin (Publishers) Ltd,
40 Museum Street, London WC1A 1LU, UK

George Allen & Unwin (Publishers) Ltd,
Park Lane, Hemel Hempstead, Herts HP2 4TE, UK

Allen & Unwin Inc.,
Fifty Cross Street, Winchester, Mass 01890, USA

George Allen & Unwin Australia Pty Ltd,
8 Napier Street, North Sydney, NSW 2060, Australia

British Library Cataloguing in Publication Data

Nove, Alec
  The Soviet economic system. – 2nd ed.
  1. Russia – Economic conditions – 1976–
  I. Title
  330.9′47′085   HC336.25   80–41221

  ISBN 0–04–335041–0
  ISBN 0–04–335042–9 Pbk

Printed and bound in Great Britain by
Billing & Sons Ltd, Worcester

PREFACE TO FIRST EDITION

My textbook on the Soviet economy was written in 1959–60. I amended the text for subsequent editions, but the basic structure remained unchanged. Yet much has changed, both in the Soviet Union and in the author's perceptions. Also the literature available in English has greatly expanded, so the time has come not for a scissors-and-paste updating of the old text, but for a new book.

The main 'structural' change is the partial abandonment of the old division between 'Structure' and 'Problems'. In its place I have endeavoured to cover the basics of structure in the introductory chapter. Thereafter, the specific features of a given sector (e.g. public finance, or industrial management) are integrated in the relevant chapter which also deals with the problems which have arisen in that sector.

The historical dimension is vital, but I have resisted the temptation to enter into the history of the Soviet economy, because my own *Economic History of the USSR* is available, and, for good or ill, represents my thoughts and interpretations on this subject, so there is no point in repeating them here.

I have not gone much into institutional detail. Interested readers can fill the gaps by following up recommendations in the Bibliography. The reason for the omission is that I would like to concentrate on the essential nature of the problems faced by Soviet-type economies, and these are, as a rule, little affected by such details. For example, yet another economic ministry has just been divided into two separate ministries, but no new principles are involved, and our understanding of the nature and functioning of the system is in no significant way affected. Besides, minor institutional changes are going on all the time, and so their minute institution quickly becomes obsolete, and in any event is a bit dull, for author and reader alike. Principles, basic structure and problem areas remain with us much longer.

The study of the Soviet economy has had its ups and downs. As late as the mid-fifties it was necessary to persuade economists to take seriously the fact that the USSR existed and was growing rapidly. Then, in the aftermath of the first sputnik, in the context of the cold war, the attitude of many changed into one of alarm. Khruschev's claim that the USSR would out-grow the West in the process of competitive coexistence was taken very seriously, and works appeared treating 'Soviet economic penetration' as very dangerous. As Soviet growth rates declined, and various weaknesses (which were there all along) became apparent, exaggerated alarm gave way to complacency: it

7

turned out that 'they are not ten feet tall'. (A book under this title did appear.) There was at the same time a notable decline in the attractiveness of the Soviet Union for Western Marxists. Some went beyond the (reasonable) assertion that many aspects of Soviet reality conflict with socialist principles, and refused to see in Soviet planning anything from which socialists could learn. In consequence of all this, as well as of the crisis in university finance, there has been a falling off in interest in the subject, especially in the United States.

However, in the last few years the Western industrialized economies have been shaken by inflation and recession. The Soviet-type economies have appeared to be relatively stable, in an increasingly unstable world. If their centralized economy, with the help of computers, can continue to grow, even at a modest rate, while our own economies decline or are threatened with disintegration, this seems an important advantage, to set against the many micro-irrationalities of Soviet planning. This could well rekindle interest in the subject among students of economics and even their teachers.

There are other reasons for such interest. It is surely of importance to study the Soviet system because centralized planning now affects so large a part of the world, and many spread to more countries. Also, we can understand our own economic theories better if we observe what happens to economic laws in different institutional settings. Can the market be replaced by the 'visible hand' of plan-administrators, and with what consequences? What substitutes can be, or have been, devised for a capital market? Can price and wage control be effective, and at what cost? What consequences follow from the elimination of land rent, and from the highly restricted role of profits and of interest?

Soviet experience must surely tell us something concerning the solidity of old arguments about how a socialist economic model might function, and one must at least consider how far the problems ensolidity of old arguments about how a socialist economic model might function, and one must at least consider how far the problems encountered in Soviet experience must arise in any feasible form of socialist planning. Socialists and others should also consider what aspects are peculiarly Russian or Stalinist, and thus irrelevant to a 'true' socialist model. Then there is the experience of other communist-ruled countries; this will be treated here perhaps too briefly, since the main emphasis will be on the USSR. Almost nothing will be said about China, not because it is either unimportant or irrelevant, but because of lack of knowledge on my own part. Finally, we must bear in mind the relevance of Soviet experience and planning methods to developing countries, and vice versa: i.e. one could interpret the Soviet system in terms of a model of industrial development.

A chapter will be devoted to the evaluation of statistical and other data, but a few introductory remarks are none the less desirable, on the theme of the correct interpretation of critical material. It would be easy to fill a volume, indeed several volumes, with quotations from Soviet sources about things that go wrong. It is also possible to rely on Soviet textbooks and to shrug off critical material as mere examples of local aberrations. In the one case the economy can be presented as an inefficient chaos, while in the other one can paint a far too favourable picture. Naturally, I will try to achieve realism and balance, but, equally naturally, one can be mistaken, and other analysts may legitimately reach a different evaluation. It is, in my view, important to separate *error* from what could be called '*evidence of system*'. Errors can happen, because human beings are fallible. An incorrect investment decision can be due, in any system, to uncertainty about the future. Poor workmanship in construction, a miscalculation of development costs (e.g. Concorde!), failures of inter-departmental co-ordination, can occur anywhere, and tell us nothing very significant about the system, unless it can be shown that these things occur much more frequently in the USSR than in the West, or vice versa. However, the interesting and important 'things that go wrong' are not, strictly speaking, errors at all. Suppose, for instance, a director of a Soviet road-transport undertaking is trying to fulfil a plan in ton-kilometres; his effort to avoid carrying loads for short distances is not a 'mistake', it is a rational response to the system within which he is operating, though this may lead to waste of resources. The same is true of a director who avoids reducing the weight of any product if his plan is expressed in tons. Nor is the behaviour-pattern associated with a sellers' market an 'error'. In other words, the serious and meaningful problems are those which arise out of the nature of functioning of the system, and which can be shown to exist even if the censorship were to eliminate all mention of them from the press.

No system in the real world can fail to generate some form of inefficiency or waste peculiar to itself. Only in textbooks can it be otherwise. This is true of the West also. The *model* of a perfect market economy is perfect by definition, and so is perfect planning. It is plainly illegitimate to compare the messy reality of the USSR not with Western reality but with what our economy is supposed to be. This is what could be called 'comparing model with muddle'. Nor should we lose sight of the fact that efficiency as an abstract concept has certain limitations, that it is proper to ask the question: efficiency for what, perhaps also for whom. We will return to these matters in Chapter 14. There are advantages as well as disadvantages in centralized planning, and the 'weight' one attaches to one or the other is affected by one's priorities, by what it is that one is striving to achieve.

As far as possible, I have tried to mention, or analyse, the factors which bear on meaningful inter-system comparisons, rather than attempting an evaluation. This is because an exact or quantitative analysis is (in my view) impossible, or rather that it does not tell us enough about the *causes* of those productivity differences which can be measured.

This book is not written to prove that the Soviet economic system is no good, or to deny that it has solid achievement to its credit. None the less, the book will tend to be problem-oriented, to stress difficulties, partly because problem areas are more interesting, but also because the difficulties here discussed are also those which worry Soviet economists and planners, and which they themselves discuss. Needless to say, we must also not lose sight of the fact that some issues which worry them are not allowed to be aired publicly, and also that some events are simply not reported in the press.

A brief word about politics and ideology. I tend to adopt the hypothesis that *homo economicus sovieticus* is very like his Western counterpart, in the sense that, if any of us were Soviet managers or planners, subject to the same pressures, rules and incentives, we would behave much as they do. In other words, I assume that there is usually no need to invoke ideological explanations for managerial behaviour-patterns.

More difficult is the identification of ideological motivation in policy choices, not least because the term 'ideology' is itself ambiguous, and because, in the real world, no decision is ever purely ideological, it is always influenced by empirical, 'real' factors. Given the nature of the Soviet system, even the most practical policy decisions tend to be given an ideological explanation or justification, in the sense that appropriate quotations are found in holy writ. (If the opposite decision were taken, a different quotation would be found to justify that!) Probably most analysts would agree that ideology (i.e. Marxism-Leninism) is not a powerful force in the Soviet Union today, but that is not to say that it has become a mere card-index of quotations. The outlawing of private trade, for instance, is scarcely explicable without reference to ideological principle. Ideological principle can be modified, or even ignored. It can also be associated with somewhat different considerations: thus the opposition to private trade can also be interpreted in terms of resistance to all phenomena which are not under the control of the ruling stratum; Lenin also spoke of the necessary 'dominance of politics over economics', but we will return to this theme of the role of politics and of the political leadership in Chapter 1.

Instead I will end this preface with a few remarks about political biases in the study of the Soviet economy. It is too much to expect anyone to approach the subject without value-judgements and sometimes unconscious assumptions. However, there is no point in studying the data selectively, to prove that one's presuppositions were right. As already mentioned, there are plenty of items of evidence which, 'properly' selected and arranged, can prove what the author wishes to prove. Such temptations must be avoided. No cause is served by pretending that Soviet efficiency and output are other than what they are. The evaluation of the economic system and its performance should, as far as possible, be politically neutral. If the Soviets produce 120 million tons of steel or increase their output of oil by 50 per cent, one may, if so minded, deplore the fact that this enhances the USSR's political and economic strength, but if these are the facts, they must be taken seriously. As analysts, we must not copy the Soviet propagandists' regrettable habits of selective omission. For example, if one asserts that the bulk of the low-paid workers are women, it is also necessary to note that women must have been major beneficiaries of the sizable increases in minimum wages. Soviet writers used to be accused (sometimes still are accused) of the sin of 'objectivism' if they analysed the West in an unbiased and scholarly way, without militant epithets. My aim is to commit the sin of 'objectivism', and as far as possible to interest the reader and to stimulate him to study the subject further.

Most of this book was written at the Russian Institute of Columbia University, and at St Antony's College, Oxford. I would like to extend my grateful thanks to both these institutions for their hospitality, and to my own University of Glasgow for giving me a sabbatical year in which to write. I discussed various draft chapters with many colleagues. I would like particularly to thank Igor Birman, Wlodimierz Brus, Alexander Erlich, Aron Katsenellenboigen, Ljubo Sirc, and also some Polish and Hungarian economists, for critical comments on chapters which they were kind enough to read. Martin Myant, graduate student at Glasgow, was extremely helpful in checking references and also in raising questions at many points. Elizabeth Hunter typed semi-legible drafts with admirable speed, accuracy and good humour. Errors and omissions are mine entirely.

Note: In 1961 the Soviet government revalued the rouble in the ratio 10 : 1. Thus 400 pre-1961 roubles became 40 roubles. This *new* rouble has been used throughout this book, and any rouble figures relating to a date prior to 1961 have been divided by ten. For example, the 1940 average wage, 4,068 old roubles per annum, would be given as 406·80. This follows the practice of modern Soviet textbooks.

PREFACE TO SECOND EDITION

As noted in the preface to the first edition, my first textbook, *The Soviet Economy*, was written twenty years ago. Subsequently the original book went through several revised editions, and I then wrote what amounts to a new book during the year 1975–6, and it was published in 1977. There have, of course, been a number of changes in the last four to five years. For this second edition I have written additional material for insertion at the end of the chapter to which it relates, and have updated some of the statistics where new data have a significant bearing on the argument. However, no fundamental changes are needed, because there have still been no fundamental changes in the Soviet economic system. The most recent reform (July 1979), which is summarized at the end of Chapter 4, is essentially a codification of previously introduced or previously attempted measures, all of them variants on the basic theme of centralization. All the problems which have been analysed in the text remain. The statistical report on 1979, published in January 1980, shows alarming shortfalls in plan fulfilment, with significant *absolute declines* in the production not just of grain (explicable by bad weather) but also of coal, iron and steel, cement, fertilizer, tractors, locomotives, paper, an unheard-of conjuncture in peacetime. Serious shortages have developed in many foodstuffs and a wide range of consumers' goods. It may be permissible to speak of a crisis in the planning system. The need for radical reform is profound, yet the forces of conservatism are still very strong, and have doubtless been reinforced by the worsening international situation, following the military intervention in Afghanistan. One must expect greater stress on discipline and central control, stronger priority for heavy industry, but also for agriculture (as a consequence of Carter's use of the 'grain weapon'), and a more cautious approach to East–West trade and to cultural contacts. Yet there is also a clear appreciation of the need for efficiency, for reducing waste of fuel and materials, for improved quality and more rapid technical progress. I hope that the reader will find in this volume a basis for appreciating the strengths and weaknesses not just of the Soviet Union, but also of centralized 'socialist' planning as such.

Since writing the book I have visited China, and it was interesting to note that Chinese economists of the post-Mao period are discussing reforms of *their* centralized system of industrial planning, and that, despite the many differences between the two countries, this visitor had a sense of *déjà vu*: the same problems have given rise to similar proposals. The Cultural Revolution caused disruption, but did not lead to the setting-up of an alternative system. Despite everything, so I was told, the industrial planning system remains in essentials a copy of Soviet planning. (The agricultural situation has its own special features.) A search is going on for a specifically Chinese way forward, and this may give rise to some new form of decentralization and markets, but it is too soon even to try to forecast the way things will go.

GLOSSARY

ASSR	Autonomous soviet socialist republic (national sub-division of a union republic)
Baza (pl. *bazy*)	Supply base, storehouse
Glavk (pl. *glavki*)	Chief department, e.g. of an economic ministry
Gosplan	State Planning Committee (Commission)
Gossnab	State Committee on Material-Technical Supplies
Khozraschet	'Economic' (or 'business') accounting, profit-and-loss accounting
Kolkhoz	Collective farm (literally 'collective enterprise'). The term also covers some fisheries co-operatives
MTS	Machine Tractor Station
Obkom	Party committee of *oblast'* (province)
Obyedineniye (plural: *Obyedineniya*)	(Industrial) association, usually formed by an amalgamation or merger, but sometimes replacing a *glavk*
R.S.F.S.R.	Russian republic (Russia proper)
Raykom	Party committee of *Rayon* (district)
Snabsbyt	Supply and disposal (organs)
Sbyt	Disposals (organs)
Sovkhoz	State farm (literally 'soviet enterprise')
Sovnarkhoz	(Regional) economic council
Tsentrosoyuz	Central union of (retail) co-operative societies
Valuta	(Foreign) currency, usually 'hard' currency
Zayavka	Request (indent), e.g. for supplies

NOTE ABOUT NOTES

All references to *books* are to author and date of publication of the edition used: e.g. Stalin (1952). Details of title will be found in the list of references at the end of the book.

In the case of *periodical and newspaper articles in Russian*, the reference will be in brackets in the text, usually without the title of the article (for instance: *Pravda*, 21 October 1971). The following abbreviations will be used for periodicals:

EkG	*Ekonomicheskaya gazeta* (at present weekly)
EKO	*Ekonomika i organizatsiya promyshlennogo proizvodstva* (usually six copies a year, Novosibirsk)
EkMM	*Ekonomika i matematicheskiye metody*
Kom	*Kommunist*
MSn	*Material'no-tekhnicheskoye snabzheniye*
MEMO	*Mirovaya ekonomika i mezhdunarodnye otnosheniya*
PEG	*Promyshlenno-ekonomicheskaya gazeta*
PKh	*Planovoye khozyaistvo*
VEk	*Voprosy ekonomiki*

The statistical annual *Narodnoye khozyaistvo SSSR* is abbreviated as *NKh*, followed by the date (e.g. *NKh*, 1973).

CONTENTS

CHAPTER 1

INTRODUCTION
TO THE SYSTEM

GENESIS

The centralized or 'directive-planning' system that we know today was born during the period of the first five-year plan, around 1929–32. At the time of the Bolshevik revolution, few socialists had seriously thought about how to plan an actual economy. *Das Kapital,* as the title itself suggests, was an analysis of capitalism. Russian Marxist thinkers had much to say about 'the development of capitalism in Russia' (to cite the title of Lenin's early work), imperialism, the growth of finance-capital. Trotsky had interesting and original thoughts about the relationship of economic-social backwardness and socialist revolution. However, it would not be unfair to say that planning methods, or practical problems of operating a socialist economy, were not seriously discussed by Marxists (or non-Marxists) before 1917, among the few exceptions was the remarkable 1908 essay by Barone (1972). Fully-fledged socialism, or communism, would be a state of affairs in which scarcity would have been overcome, and production would be for use and not for exchange, socially planned for the benefit of the educated and participating working masses. There will be more to say in Chapter 11 about the relationship of Soviet reality to the 'fundamentalist' ideas of Marxism. Of course it was understood that there would be a transition period of unknown length, in which the political 'dictatorship of the proletariat' would be accompanied by transitional economic arrangements of some kind. It was generally assumed that the revolution would occur in a highly developed Western country, in which the concentration of capital would have gone far towards centralizing control over the economy. Understandably, Lenin and his colleagues concentrated on a hard-hitting critique of the system they wished to overthrow, while devoting their principal attention to devising methods of overthrowing it.

Much had to be improvised when the seizure of power presented the Bolsheviks with appallingly difficult problems. 'War-communism' was an amalgam of response to the harsh necessity of civil war and of a naive attempt to leap quickly into socialism. Resources were allocated by the centre, private enterprise was outlawed, peasant produce requisitioned. The chaos that ensued has been described elsewhere (e.g. Nove, 1969a, Chapter 3). The end of the civil war led to the abandonment of this first attempt to plan centrally. In the period known as NEP (the New Economic Policy, 1921 to approximately 1928–9) peasants were left in undisturbed possession of the land, free to sell their produce in the market. Small-scale private enterprise, especially private trade, was legalized. While large-scale industry (together with banking and foreign trade) remained in the hands of the state, most state enterprises also produced for the market, basing their activities on contracts with customers, not on plan-instructions, with due emphasis on the health of the profit-and-loss accounts.

It was the adoption of successive ever-more-ambitious versions of the first five-year plan (in 1928–9), followed by forcible collectivization of the peasantry, that created a new situation. It is not that Stalin and his comrades had a blueprint of a command economy, though the intention to plan in a more thoroughgoing manner had been expressed earlier, and indeed could be said to have been inherent in the basic approach to economic affairs of most Bolsheviks, even though it had not been clearly articulated. But the effort to fulfil overambitious plans, complicated by the consequences of resistance to collectivization, led to acute shortages throughout the economy. To impose the priorities of industrialization, and to ensure that key projects received necessary materials and equipment, there was set up by stages the centralized system of production planning and supply allocation that we now consider the essential feature of Soviet-type economies. The market, and spontaneous forces generally, came to be regarded as phenomena hostile to socialist construction, to the carrying out of plans to transform a backward country at breakneck speed. Each productive enterprise, each collective farm, was henceforth to be instructed what to produce and what to deliver, and to whom, at what prices, and from whom to obtain needed inputs.

This, as Stalin said, was no longer a plan-forecast or plan-guess-timate (dogadka), this was a compulsory, directive plan, with the force of law.

Much has changed, of course. The Soviet economy is much larger, more highly developed. There have been repeated reorganizations of the administrative structure, new techniques of planning have been devised. None the less, the *principles* of its operation were established by 1932 and remain little changed still today. Indeed, one of the best ways of approaching the issues which worry Soviet economists, using Marxian terminology, is in terms of a growing contradiction between the forces of production (modern industry and its implications) and the relations of production (a system of planning and control devised to cope with industrialization at a lower stage of economic development). But we will be discussing these and other aspects of the logic of reform later on.

THE PURPOSE OF THE SYSTEM: POLITICS AND ECONOMICS

The declared objective of the Soviet leadership is to 'build communism'. Socialism, so it is claimed, was achieved already in the mid-thirties. A precondition to a transition to communism is a much greater development of productive forces, leading to abundance, and also the elimination of differences between mental and physical labour and between town and country. Then, in the official view, it will be possible to realize the Marxian objective: 'from each according to his ability, to each according to his needs'. For the present, Soviet socialism is seen as requiring material incentives and therefore unequal distribution of purchasing-power: 'from each according to his ability, to each according to his work'. We shall see also that it is argued that the present stage of development requires the use of money and of value categories, just as, on the political level, the state must be retained (indeed strengthened), though under communism it will have withered away.

At this stage of our analysis, we will confine ourselves only to the question: what effect has the objective of 'building communism' had on economic structure and policy? It could be held to provide the justification of the emphasis on growth ('to create the material pre-requisites of communism'). Khrushchev proposed that actual steps towards free distribution (e.g. elimination of charges for housing, factory-canteen meals, urban transportation) be taken by 1980, as 'instalments' of communism, so to speak, but his successors have not followed up these ideas. None the less, the 'building of communism' remains the declared aim, legitimizing the monopoly rule of the Communist Party, which claims to lead the people towards this objective.

A NOTE ON THE POLITICAL STRUCTURE

The following is a brief sketch of the political framework.

The USSR is a federation of republics, which at present number fifteen. Sovereignty is nominally exercised by an elected body. Until 1937 this was the all-union Congress of Soviets, indirectly elected by lower territorial soviets. The congress elected an 'executive' committee (known as VTSIK). Strictly speaking, this was not an executive but a pseudo-legislature, which elected a praesidium. Since its first meeting in 1938 the sovereign 'parliament' is the Supreme Soviet, which consists of two houses, the Soviet of the Union and the Soviet of Nationalities, both elected directly by adult suffrage. In practice the deputies are nominated by the Communist Party machine, and contested elections are unknown. The Supreme Soviet meets infrequently, often for no more than one week in the year, though its committees, including a finance committee, and an economic committee of the Council of Nationalities, now play a more active role. It elects a praesidium which exercises its legislative powers between sessions, subject to subsequent ratification. In principle at least, laws can only be adopted by the Supreme Soviet, and its praesidium can also issue decrees *(ukazy)* which are supposed to conform to existing laws, but in practice often change them. (Before 1938, laws and decrees emerged from a variety of bodies, including VTSIK or its praesidium, the government and even government committees such as the Council of Labour and Defence.)

The government was known before 1946 by the designation of the Council of People's Commissars, and since that date as the Council of Ministers. In this book, to avoid unnecessary brackets and qualifications, the terms Minister, Ministry, Council of Ministers, will generally be used, and *not* Commissar, People's Commissariat, etc. The Council of Ministers is elected by and is responsible to the Supreme Soviet (or its praesidium between sessions). It is empowered to issue binding orders *(postanovleniya)* within the constitution and the laws. In practice, it can issue *de facto* laws on any subject, since the Supreme Soviet has never used (and is most unlikely ever to use) its formal powers to challenge and revoke the actions of the government.

All the above relates to the all-union government, but the same structure was and is almost wholly duplicated in each of the fifteen federal republics. They have supreme soviets, praesidia, councils of ministers and so forth. Despite the apparently formidable powers with which they are endowed by the constitution, the republics are in fact subject to orders from the all-union government on any conceivable matter, though the amount of autonomy actually allowed them has fluctuated and has recently shown a tendency to decrease as will be shown in Chapter 3. The relationship between centre and republics in particular sectors of governmental activity varies, and has given rise to three different kinds of ministry: there are, first, the *all-union ministries*, which directly run from Moscow the activities of their subordinate units within the various republics. Secondly, there are *union-republican ministries*, which exist both at the centre and in the republics, in which case the republican ministry is simultaneously subordinate both to its elder brother in Moscow and to the council of ministers of the given republic. This is an example of 'dual subordination', which is very commonly encountered in Soviet administration: a local organ is simultaneously an integral part of the local authority and the representative in that area of the appropriate unit of the central government. Finally, there are purely *republican ministries*, which have no direct superior in Moscow, though naturally they have to conform where relevant to central policies and plans. The word 'ministry' does not cover all organizations of ministerial status either at the centre or in the republics: there are a number of state committees, commissions and other bodies, whose heads are members of the council of ministers. One such body, *Gosplan*, has been of key importance in the economy.

The republics are divided into provinces (*oblast'*, plural *oblasti*); there are also large provinces which are called *kray* some of which have autonomous sub-units, including even *oblasti*, but these refinements are hardly worth pursuing here. Finally certain national areas within some of the republics are given the dignity of Autonomous Soviet Socialist Republic (ASSR) and their top officials have the title of ministers; examples include Tartar, Chuvash, Komi and Bashkir ASSR. However, the power of these bodies *vis-à-vis* the authorities above or below them is hardly affected by the differences of designation. Except that the ASSR are represented as such in the upper house of the legislature, the Soviet of Nationalities. In this book, therefore, when the word *oblast'* is used, it may be assumed that the same functions or powers apply to the ASSR and *kray*.

Local government in towns is run by elected town soviets. The big towns have a status similar to the English county borough, in the sense of not being subject to the *oblast'* authorities but depending directly on the republican government. Within provinces, and also within the largest cities, are so-called 'districts' *(rayony)*.

At the very bottom of the scale are village soviets, with only minor powers. When the economic functions of local government are referred to, the village soviet can virtually be ignored.

Underlying all this elaborate governmental structure is the Communist Party of the Soviet Union, the 'directing nucleus' (as the Constitution itself emphasizes) of all state organs and social organizations. In a very real sense, the government at all levels exists to carry out the policies of the party. Its own structure is as follows: party congresses are nominally supreme; they elect a central committee, which in turn elects other committees, of which by far the most important is the Politbureau (known in 1952–65 as the praesidium). The latter is in effect the supreme organ of government. At the party headquarters there are departments which duplicate the various governmental organs. There are also party committees corresponding to the various levels of government below the centre.

It is important to note that the party committees are wholly subordinate to the Moscow leadership, in the fifteen republics as well as at *oblast'* level and below. Thus, for example, the Ukrainian or Uzbek committees of the party have no greater rights *vis-à-vis* the all-union central committee than are possessed by, say, the Leningrad or Omsk *obkom*. Therefore the degree of independence of any federal or local body in the USSR must always be severely limited, in so far as it is controlled by a party committee on its own level, and the party itself is highly centralized.

The party dominates the ministries and the rest of the state apparatus in two ways. Firstly, almost all individuals appointed to posts of consequence are members of the party. Secondly, all posts of consequence are on the so-called *nomenklatura*, i.e. a list of appointments for which the central committee or less exalted committees of the party are responsible. In practice, whoever is supposed to elect or appoint, the appropriate party committee nominates. This applies to deputies of the Supreme Soviet, ministers, editors, trade union officials, directors of important enterprises, heads of research institutes, and so on.

The party dominates the state in the sense that the Council of Ministers and other state organs carry out party policy. However, as we shall see, the functional division of responsibility is often blurred in practice. Thus the government, in carrying out the wishes of the Politbureau, issues orders to its subordinates in the state hierarchy, and it would evidently cause confusion if interference by party officials at lower levels were to obstruct the carrying out of these orders. There is a long series of decrees concerning the need to free various state organs from *melochnaya opeka* (petty supervision or interference); we will return to this issue when we discuss the functioning of economic organs.

A related and difficult point concerns the relationship between politics and economics. The distinction is not easy to draw in any country: when one considers economic policy, is the politician who decides – e.g. on taxation, or a regional investment premium – acting primarily as a political man, or is he reacting to the economic situation as a kind of super-manager? Often the answer is both. It is useful and important to see the process of decision making not on one dimension but as operating on several levels at once. A factory director, let us say, acts in a managerial capacity when he manoeuvres to fulfil plans, or to influence their formulation. There is hardly anything specifically 'political' in this. His party superior, at local level, may also be primarily concerned to ensure that plans are carried out. Somewhat higher in the hierarchy one finds the economic ministry, say the Ministry of Non-Ferrous Metallurgy. Its head, the Minister, holds a political rank. Yet he is effectively the head of a nationalized industry, a senior manager. The official in *Gosplan* whose task it is to ensure that the iron-ore mining and steel-making plans are internally coherent is a specialist technician, no more 'political' than is the input-output table that he is using. Yet, plainly, political choices are being made: on overall economic priorities, on the level of expenditures on housing, steelworks, submarines, secondary education, industrial location, the price of meat, wage differentials, etc. It is *within* these basic political-strategic or 'macro' decisions that technical-economic choices are made in the Non-Ferrous Metallurgy Ministry or in iron-ore mining. Needless to say, these 'political' decisions are not made in a vacuum, they are responses to circumstances, but choices made are in a real sense political choices. The point I am making is that it is the nature of the decision, and not the nominally political rank of the decision maker, which ought to determine how 'politically' it should be regarded. In a centralized economy, the supreme political and economic authorities coalesce, the Politibureau is at one and the same time the supreme arbiter of politics and the board of directors of USSR Ltd, the largest firm in the world. So that even at that level, some decisions of a 'super-managerial' character are taken. Wlodzimierz Brus wrote: 'Economy and politics are so intimately intertwined, especially when considered dynamically, that the continued use of the old conceptual apparatus of [economic] base and [political] super-structure becomes more and more inadequate'. (Brus, 1973, p.88.)

Let us now introduce to the reader in their basic outline the institutions and principles upon which the Soviet economy is founded.

Kosygin has used the term 'directive-planning', to distinguish the system from indicative planning, or from various amalgams of plan and market. The economy is managed by a hierarchy, with the Polit-bureau at its summit, the government (Council of Ministers) being responsible for carrying out the policies decided by the Politbureau. Nominally, the Politbureau is in turn accountable to the central com-mittee, and the central committee to the Party Congress. The govern-ment and its agencies (state committees, economic ministries) issue binding instructions to subordinate units. While of course these sub-ordinate units are expected to make their own proposals, they must carry out the plan-instructions which they receive. These will usually instruct them what to produce, to whom to deliver the product, from whom to obtain inputs, and in what quantities. The plan-instruction will also cover other important operational aspects: payments into and out of the state budget, investments, the wage and salary bill, the value of sales, the size and rate of profits, labour productivity, etc., and many smaller matters, such as material utilization norms. These and other plan-indicators will be discussed in greater detail in Chapter 4. They naturally vary somewhat in different sectors of the economy. Thus trade organizations will receive instructions about the value of turnover and trade margins, transport enterprises have plans in terms of ton-kilometres, farms are ordered to make deliveries of various crops and products to the state, and so on.

The essential distinguishing feature is that the producing enterprises are *told* what to do, whereas in a different model (e.g. Yugoslavia, Hungary) they have much greater power of deciding what to produce through contractual relations with customers. The Soviet system rests on *administrative orders*, not on commercial orders.

This means that the Soviet planning apparatus (and political leader-ship) claim to know what society needs, and issues *instructions* so that the needs of society are met. The primary task of the subordinate managers is to carry out these instructions. As we shall see, the information flows, on the basis of which planners issue instructions, originate with their subordinates, and it would be wrong, even in this introductory chapter, to assert that managers are merely passive executants of orders received from above. However, the fact remains that the Soviet leaders *must* claim that they, and the planners that serve them, know best what needs doing, for only on this basis can one defend centralized directive planning.

The contrary view, which will be analysed in subsequent chapters, rests on the proposition that the centre is *not* usually aware of precisely what needs doing in the micro-economic sphere, and that therefore there should be scope for some form of market relations between enterprises and with the consumer. On this interpretation, planning should, in the main, concern itself with large-scale decisions, especially in the field of investment. However, this line of thought has been rejected in the Soviet Union.

This reduces, without totally eliminating, the role of money, prices and profits. The plan-instructions are often expressed in physical units, or in monetary aggregates (e.g. of furniture or clothing) where physical quantity is not meaningful. Prices at which transactions occur are, with few exceptions, fixed by the state and cannot be varied by management. It therefore follows that, although price relationships and expected levels of profits can affect the decisions of planners, and also the proposals of the managers, the latter must obey instructions even where, at the fixed level of prices, the result is a loss. In other words, the plan must be fulfilled whatever the effect on profits, and the plan-indicators that relate to profits play – despite recent reforms – a subordinate role. This is a logical consequence of a system in which the centre identifies what needs doing and orders that it be done, and within which prices are not seen as information-carriers. This can be contrasted, again, with the underlying principles of the Yugoslav or Hungarian models: prices there are supposed to act as signals, actively influencing the productive behaviour of profit-seeking enterprises. Prices thus play an active role in such models as these, whereas in the USSR their role is more passive. In the language of Soviet economists, the 'law of value' does not determine what is produced, or the distribution of labour and resources between sectors. There will be much more to say about the price system in its various aspects in Chapter 7.

However, the citizens are paid in money for their work, and spend the bulk of this money in the state stores, choosing freely between whatever is available. Here prices do play an active role, directly affecting the decisions of the customer to purchase, and these then have an indirect effect on production plans.

Soviet state enterprises *(predpriyatiya)* operate on the principle of one-man management *(yedinonachaliye)*. The director is responsible to his superiors. He is limited in some of his acts (e.g. hiring and firing), in ways to be discussed in Chapter 4. However, his orders must be obeyed and he is not responsible to his workers or to any committee which they elect. The same applies to the 'associations' *(obyedineniya)* into which many enterprises have been merged.

A state enterprise belongs to the state. From this apparently tautological statement of the obvious flow a number of consequences which are perhaps less obvious. In essence and in law, the enterprise is a convenient unit for the administration of state property. It is a juridical person, it can sue and be sued, but it *owns* none of its assets. The director and his senior colleagues – the chief engineer, who usually acts as his deputy, and the chief accountant – are appointed by state organs to manage the state's assets for purposes determined by the state. This is why there was no charge made for the use of the enterprise's capital, since it belongs to the state anyhow. This is also why the state is entitled to transfer the enterprise's profits to the state budget, save for that portion which the state regulations or *ad hoc* decisions permit the enterprise to retain. That is why it is within the power of state organs to take away any of the enterprise's assets, if they think fit, without financial compensation, though this right is, for practical reasons, now being questioned and circumscribed. It is also important to note that formal state *ownership* can coexist with a high degree of commercial autonomy, for instance in Yugoslavia.

Enterprises are under the authority of *ministries*. At present there are about forty-eight economic ministries, to which productive enterprises of many kinds are subordinated, but their exact number is frequently altered. Sometimes their designations clearly indicate their area of responsibility (Ministry of Coal Industry, or Ministry of Agriculture), but others cover not always clearly defined portions of an industry. For example there is a Minister of Construction of the USSR, but also a Ministry of Industrial Construction, *and* a Ministry of Construction of Heavy-industry Enterprises. Similarly there are numerous ministries engaged in various forms of 'machine-building' *(mashinostroyeniye)*. As we shall see, there can be much overlap and confusion. Also included in the Council of Ministries are chairmen of several state committees of economic importance, such as those concerned with inventions, standards, forestry, supplies for agriculture *(Sel'khoztekhnika)*, and also the heads of the Central Statistical Office and the State Bank. It will be noted that some of the economic ministries have identically named counterparts in Union republics, and others do not. Some enterprises, of local significance, fall under republican ministries with no all-union counterpart, and some operate under the control of local soviets. Ministries are usually divided into 'chief administrations' or divisions, known by the abbreviation *glavk*.

In recent years, many industrial enterprises have been grouped together into 'associations' *(obyedineniya)*, which stand between the industrial ministry of which it is part and the enterprise. Sometimes they have also been known as *firmy*. The *obyedineniye* shares some of the characteristics of the large enterprise and of a *glavk* of an industrial ministry, indeed in some cases it replaces the *glavk*. There has been some experimentation with different types of *obyedineniya*, as we shall see in Chapter 4, but they all differ from *glavki* of ministries in one important respect: they, unlike ministries, are on profit-and-loss accounting, i.e. on *khozraschet*. The enterprises within them may (or may not) be relegated to lower status, with no autonomous profit-and-loss account of their own. The term *kombinat* is also sometimes used to describe an industrial unit, usually a large or complex one.

The organizational forms found outside industry vary considerably. Thus for example the railway administration, under the Ministry of Transport *(putey sóobshcheniya)* is divided regionally. There is an elaborate structure of wholesale and retail trade organs under the Ministry of (internal) Trade, linked locally with the trade organs of city soviets. Rural retail distribution is under 'co-operative trade', which is in fact so strictly regulated as to be *de facto* a part of the state trading network, but there are vestigial elected committees, and a tax is levied on co-operative profits. 'Trusts' *(tresty)* group together construction teams, catering establishments and also state farms in a given area. These designations, which vary between place and time, give rise to no problem of any special interest and seem worth no more than a passing mention.

Until 1961 a small portion (varying from 5 to 8 per cent) of industrial output was the responsibility of *producer co-operatives*. These have been 'nationalized', but some industrial production occurs on collective farms *(kolkhozy)*, including the production for local use of building materials, agricultural tools, electricity and other smaller items. *Kolkhoz* construction teams perform a sizable part of rural building work. Some limited 'industrial' activities, notably food processing, are undertaken by consumer co-operatives. There are also fisheries co-operatives. To this extent not quite all industrial production and construction is within the state sector.

The majority of agricultural production is *not* within the state sector, despite the very substantial increase in the area cultivated by *state* farms *(sovkhozy)*.

Agricultural output was divided between the categories of producers as shown in Table 1.

Private output is insignificant in grain and industrial crops, but is important in the livestock sector (35 per cent of cows were privately owned in 1974), and in potatoes, vegetables, fruit.

Though with less land than *sovkhozy*, *kolkhozy* still exceed them in

Table 1 *Gross output of agriculture, 1973 (millions of roubles, 1965 prices)*

Kolkhozy	39·0
Sovkhozy	29·8
Other state*	3·0
Private**	25·4
TOTAL	97·2

(*Source*: NKh, 1973, pp.469, 456)

Notes.

*The figure for this item, representing farms run by factories and other state non-agricultural enterprises, is derived from the fact that *sovkhozy* as such employ about 90 per cent of those engaged in state agriculture.

**Figure obtained by remainder. It covers household plots cultivated by *kolkhoz* members, state-employed persons, pensioners, etc.

The share of private output was higher in 1973 prices: 29·7% in 1970, 26·5% in 1979 (Shmelev V. Ek. No. 5, 1981).

the value of output, due largely to the fact that they own more of the livestock. The private sector (household plots and privately owned livestock) still accounts for over 26 per cent of the total; this share is gradually declining relatively, though growing absolutely, as the figures in Table 2 show.

Table 2 *Output index 1973 (1965=100)*

All agriculture	138
All state and *kolkhoz*	148
Private	115

(*Source*: NKh, 1973, p.346)
(This implies a weight for the private sector similar to the one calculated in Table 1)

The *kolkhoz* is formally a co-operative, with an elected management committee, headed by an elected chairman. In practice, however, the party appoints, or 'recommends' who should be elected. From collectivization until 1950 the *kolkhoz* was usually coextensive with a village, though in the north it sometimes covered several hamlets. A series of amalgamations have multiplied the average size of a *kolkhoz* five-fold since 1950, and some have been converted into state farms. An average *kolkhoz* today has 6,000 hectares of land, 3,300 hectares of sown area, and a labour force of around 500. (*Sovkhozy*, state farms, on average cover a much larger area.) For many years the *kolkhozy* were subjected to high compulsory delivery quotas at very low prices, and were compelled to buy their inputs at higher prices than those paid by state farms. The latter received subsidies to cover their losses, and were thus enabled to pay regular wages. *Kolkhoz* members were assigned work-day units *(trudodni)* in proportion to the quantity and skill of their work, and the value of each of these units depended upon the amount of money and produce available for distribution in the given *kolkhoz*. It was not until 1966 that the *trudoden'*, widely criticized for its disincentive effects, was abandoned in favour of a guaranteed minimum payment.

The *kolkhoz*, in the form in which it was set up during the collectivization drive, was originally designed as a means of enabling the state to procure farm produce at minimum cost to itself. Hence the peasant was left as a residuary legatee, so to speak, bearing the burden of low prices and excessive exactions in the form of low and uncertain incomes. Things are very different today, and the *sovkhoz* and *kolkhoz* now have much in common, and may eventually merge into one form of agricultural enterprise. They both fall under the authority of the Ministry of Agriculture, exercised through local state agricultural and party organs, the role of the party being greater in agricultural management than elsewhere in the economy. This is symbolized at the top by the continuing habit of the party's general secretary presenting the agricultural report to plenary sessions of the central committee, while the prime minister speaks on industry. The reasons for this will be examined in Chapter 5. As we shall see, obligatory plans often relate not to production but to deliveries to the state.

In the period 1930–58, state Machine Tractor Stations (MTS) provided the tractors and combine-harvesters used by *kolkhozy*, which paid for them largely in produce, particularly grain. The MTS also had important supervisory functions. This mixture of hiring agency and control apparatus was abandoned in 1958, and *kolkhozy* thereafter acquired and operated their own machinery, which the *sovkhozy* had done all along.

The bulk of state enterprises, and more recently the *kolkhozy* too (though in modified form), operate on *khozraschet*. This Russian abbreviation stands literally for 'economic accounting', which could be rendered 'profit-and-loss accounting'. What characterizes *khozraschet* is 'the carrying out of state-determined tasks with the maximum economy of resources, the covering of money expenditures of enterprises by their own money revenues, the ensuring of profitability of enterprises'. (Tyagay, 1956, p.393.) This means that a normally functioning enterprise will cover its operating expenses out of income derived from the sale of goods and services to other enterprises or (in the case of retail establishments) to the population. Similarly it will pay for its material inputs to supplying enterprises, all at prices determined by the planning authorities; it pays amortization (depreciation) charges, also at rates determined from above. Working capital is in part provided by short-term credits obtained from the State Bank; these too are planned, and bear a low rate of interest. Wages paid to workers and employees are likewise based on officially-laid-down scales (see Chapter 8). Note that in this model what is done is laid down in the plan, and the object of *khozraschet* is to encourage the carrying out of instructions with due attention to economy and efficiency.

Khozraschet can be associated with planned losses, necessitating subsidies. This arises partly because of deliberate fixing of certain prices below cost, and partly because prices are usually related to *average* cost (plus a profit margin), in industries where actual costs vary very widely. *Khozraschet* in these cases encourages the minimization of losses. More usually there are profits, and managers are rewarded if they rise, subject to a complex series of provisos to be discussed in Chapter 4.

It may clarify the issue to define the opposite of *khozraschet*. Thus, say, a branch of the post office sells stamps and incurs expenditure on wages, maintenance of premises, etc. However, the revenue goes to headquarters, which issues the sums necessary to cover expenditures. Therefore the branch of the post office is 'not on *khozraschet*'. A workshop within an enterprise is in a similar situation; though it is sometimes the case that a workshop's operations are the subject of profit-and-loss calculations, it is the enterprise which has a bank account, acts as a juridical person and is the effective *khozraschet* unit. As will be shown, there is now some ambiguity in the degree of *khozraschet* applicable to enterprises which are within the more tightly organized *obyedineniya* (industrial 'associations').

In the case of *kolkhozy*, there could be no meaningful *khozraschet* so long as the entire 'remainder' was used to pay the peasants. There could then be no item which could be designated as 'profits'. A successful *kolkhoz* could measure its success by the fact that it paid its peasants well. An unsuccessful one paid them badly. The residual nature of payments to labour also inhibited cost calculations. Some analysts in the USSR tried to overcome these problems by assuming a notional payment to labour (e.g. corresponding to wage-rates in *sovkhozy*) which could be very different from, and usually much larger than, the sums actually paid.

The shift to minimum payments to *kolkhoz* members, the minimum being related to *sovkhoz* wage-rates, has partially resolved the problem, since the use of these wage-rates in calculating costs and profitability now has some relation to reality. However, net revenues are distributed to members in the form of income supplements, and/or allocated to the capital fund, so there are still no profits as such in the *kolkhoz* accounts.

Private enterprise exists in the USSR, though is severely limited. The employment of anyone to make goods for sale, or buying and re-selling for private profit, is illegal. Apart from a handful of heavily taxed private craftsmen, and some individual professional activity (such as private medical treatment), the only significant private activity is in agriculture; as was shown above, the household plots cultivated and animals owned by peasants and by some urban residents still supply over a quarter of total agricultural output. The produce of one's own efforts (as distinct from something one acquires by purchase) may be sold, on a free or *kolkhoz* market (*kolkhozny rynok*, though it is not confined to *kolkhozy* or their members). Markets exist in all cities, in which sales take place at uncontrolled prices, though instances will be mentioned of restrictions imposed both on prices and on the movement of produce. There are also many unrecorded instances of private dealings of many kinds, mostly quite illegal. The extent of this 'subterranean' free enterprise is not known and it may be substantial.

If one views the whole economy as a giant firm, USSR Ltd, it can be said that it finances the bulk of its operations out of profits, i.e. out of the difference between costs incurred by state enterprises and receipts from sales. It is this which provides most of the budgetary revenue, income taxes being relatively small. The state's 'take' of enterprise profits, together with turnover tax, constitutes, as we shall see, the major part of budgetary revenue. One might say that the firm USSR Ltd covers most of its overheads out of the proceeds of its economic operations, 'overheads' here being defined to include investment, research, education, health, defence against the external world, and so on. The close relationship of the economic ministries and enterprises with the state budget and with state banking institutions constitutes, as we shall see, a potent form of control: wages, prices, payments, receipts, must all conform to the various elements of the plan. If not, then the banks, or the inspectors of the Ministry of Finance will want to know the reason why, and can (indeed have the duty to) disallow improper payments – though needless to say improper payments can still occur, in a variety of disguises.

This, then, in outline, is the system we will be examining. Under the leadership of the Communist Party, it claims to be engaged in the construction of communism. It is officially described as socialist, in line with the vision of Marx and of Lenin. It is further claimed that it ensures a high rate of steady growth, free from fluctuations, crises and inflation, that productivity and living standards have risen by remarkable percentages and that, unlike the historically doomed structures of capitalism, it points the way to the future. In the chapters that follow, these claims will be tested and the functioning and problems of this species of economy examined in some detail.

The system in its present form is being given the designation 'mature – or developed – socialism' (*zrelyi*, or *razvitoi sotsializm*), which emphasizes its stable and established nature, though communism remains the declared objective of policy.

CHAPTER 2

PLANNING: THE CENTRAL AGENCIES AND THEIR TASKS

LONG-TERM AND SHORT-TERM

A vital distinction must be made right at the beginning. The word 'planning' in its Soviet context is used to designate several forms of activity which are distinct (though may overlap) and which raise quantitative and qualitative problems of very different sorts.

A medium-term (five years) plan and a so-called 'perspective' plan (fifteen years or more) have two essential features, apart from the obvious one of time-scale, which distinguish them from the current (annual, quarterly) plan: they are aggregated and they are not, or only partially, 'operational'.

They are aggregated not only or mainly because this enables the planners to cope with their task, but above all because they are by their nature developmental plans, which are concerned with the creation of additional capital stock, for the future provision of goods and services. Their operational counterpart will be an investment plan. Questions of product mix do not arise at this point. The aim is to provide the capacity to make or provide a wide variety of goods and services, 'translating' the general objectives of the party and government into a (hopefully) balanced and coherent material plan for a date in the future. At this level of generality it is important to estimate the total requirements for steel of the principal steel-users, and not the precise nature of the types of machinery that will be made in the early eighties. The likely demand for cloth from the clothing industry must be estimated, and related to possible sources of supply, but the assortment of clothing is not a matter to be considered in detail at this point. The objectives of social and economic policy are 'translated' by the planners into their material requirements, and in this process the objectives themselves must be reconsidered in the light of the feasibility of achieving them. Thus if the planners, in working out the investment implications of the leadership's draft policies, find that they cannot be fulfilled within the intended time-period, it is their duty to report this, to persuade their political masters to approve a plan which accords with the possible. But, as already stressed, all this can be done by confining one's analysis to a few hundred aggregated groupings of products. For example, one could have a single heading for 'agricultural machinery', though it is obvious that there are hundreds, or even thousands, of kinds of agricultural machines, and eventually the current or operational plan must ensure that the right kinds are produced. In fact, as we learn from a Soviet textbook, the 1971–5 plan included 'balances' for three hundred product groups, (Yakobi, 1973, p.275.)

The medium- or long-term plan is not operational in the sense that it does not contain specific orders to any industrial manager to produce anything (though the medium-term plan does call for action by the construction organizations). To make it operational it has to be disaggregated, both into a more detailed product mix and into order-instructions addressed to specific executants. As already mentioned, the medium- or long-term plan has evident implications for the investment programme. Let us say that this programme calls for expanding the output of the steel industry by twenty million tons. It will then be necessary to decide what additional steelworks are needed, and of what type, as well as many other related matters (supply of materials, transport facilities, etc.). The current operational plan must then be made to include the 'slice' of the necessary investments which fall into the year (or quarter) to which that operational plan relates, so that the building materials and machines which are needed are in fact made available at the site at which work is progressing.

It is important to bear in mind that, in the real world, any five-year plan is greatly influenced by the consequences of past decisions. Thus those who drafted the plan for the period 1976–80 had to provide the means to complete investment projects which were begun in the previous plan period, and so a sizable portion of resources are already committed.

The statement that the five-year plan is not 'operational' should not be understood as meaning that enterprises do not make long-term plans. They do, and they are fitted into their ministries' plans for the succeeding five years. However, they are subject to many later alterations, and it is the current plan-orders that must be obeyed. In fact five-year plans have never been formally adopted until well after the beginning of the quinquennium. The 1966–70 plan was not in final form until the end of 1967, and this is not the worst example.

The short-term plan must ensure that all the many thousands of productive units throughout the economy actually produce what is needed, and that they are supplied with the means of doing so. This requires the issuance of a very large number of specific plan-instructions. There must be a much greater degree of disaggregation. It is not enough to speak of farm machinery. There must be a distinction made between different kinds of combine-harvesters, harrows, ploughs, cultivators, milking machines and so on. Not just footwear but tennis shoes, heavy-work boots, large sizes, children's sizes. Not a miscellany of components required for making cars, but precisely the radiators needed for making particular cars, and, of course, the means of making precisely these radiators. In other words, from a few hundred aggregated designations one rapidly runs into hundreds of thousands, and in fact the full list of identifiably different commodities (different in type, size, colour, quality, etc.) runs into many millions, as may be seen from the fact that several million prices exist.

This seems complex enough, but only begins to probe the complexities involved. For the multi-thousand list of commodities requires to be produced by many thousands of enterprises, and each of them must in the end receive an instruction telling it what it must produce. Furthermore, the productive process always involves inputs which must be provided by other enterprises, since industrial production is a joint effort by numerous sectors and productive units: materials, fuel, components, transport facilities, spare parts, typically originate in a large number of other productive units. Their plans must include the specific requirements of their customers, and in fact most Soviet industrial concerns produce for other Soviet enterprises. This is what is implied when it is stated that over 70 per cent of Soviet industrial output consists of producers' goods.

Thus there must exist a vast and interconnected body of plan-instructions concerned with output and inputs, organically related plans for production and supply, with most of the production orders being the consequence of supply (input) requirements of the economy itself, disaggregated to ensure the desired product mix, disaggregated too by productive decision-making units and the required pattern of material-technical supply. As we shall see, the task is in fact far too big, so that not all the details of the product mix can be the subject of central orders, and there is much *de facto* devolution. None the less, the logic of centralized 'non-market' planning, based upon the visible as against the invisible hand, requires that from the planning apparatus there must emerge orders about just what should be produced, and orders which ensure the provision of inputs to make production possible. For in the absence of specific instructions the model provides no coherent guide to the actions of subordinate units.

The above does not exhaust the list of operational complexities. There is the time-dimension: supplies must reach the producers when they are needed. Investment plans require the coincidence of the provision of physical means (building materials and equipment, for instance) and finance. Each enterprise's production plan must cohere not only with supplies of materials but also with each enterprise's plans for profits, credits, payments into the budget, and with its 'wages fund', i.e. the amount it is entitled to pay to labour. It is possible, unless financial and quantitative plans are consistent, to have the money without the allocated inputs, or the allocated inputs without the means of paying for them. All this represents a vast challenge to the ingenuity of the planners. It is only by clearly appreciating the objective difficulties which they face that one can understand the nature of the problems with which successive reorganizations and reform proposals have sought to grapple.

One 'functional' necessity arises out of the very scale of the planning operation: this is the division of the apparatus into sub-units. The interdependence of the parts appears to call for their unification, to ensure that the consequences for all the parts of every decision are fully taken into account. However, the vision of a central super-planner is and must be an impossible one. Nor does it matter whether the need to divide various functions is explicitly recognized, whether separate ministries or committees are so named, or whether there is one super-ministry ostensibly responsible for the whole economy. If it is, then its internal divisions will become *de facto* ministries. This does not mean that organizational changes make no difference; they *do* make a difference. One of the key lessons to draw from any study of organization is that what seems important and relevant for a given decision maker depends on his (or her) area of responsibility. If one alters the boundaries of that responsibility, the matters taken into account also alter, and so the decisions taken could be affected. Let me give an example. Let us suppose that the production and supply of certain types of metal components were controlled by the Ministry of Agricultural Machinery. Its supreme management would be well placed to judge exactly what components would be needed, and this would be an advantage. However, similar components are needed by other industries run by other ministries, with the result that there would be duplication, loss of potential economies of scale, etc. An organizational switch placing the production of these components within another ministry, or perhaps into a specialized separate ministry, would affect the outcome, with some advantages and some disadvantages. Presumably there exists some organizational optimum, derived or discovered through a series of structural cost-benefit analyses, in which advantages are maximized and the disadvantages minimized.

The one thing that cannot be, however, is a sort of utopian optimum in which the advantages of central co-ordination are unaccompanied by the strains and limitations necessarily imposed by such considerations as the collection and dissemination of information, the remoteness of decision makers, aggregation, problems of motivation, and above all 'the curse of large numbers', the sheer magnitude of the work of calculating, allocating, evaluating, checking, financing.

Therefore there must be bodies approximating in function to the existing economic ministries, *Gosplan* with its own internal sub-units, the supply agency *(Gossnab)* and its internal sub-units (concerned with supply of different items, or in different areas), state committees and so on. Their precise titles can be altered, they can be re-designated, but they must exist, and in existing they must create problems of co-ordination and coherence – indeed many of the bodies we will discuss exist precisely to ensure co-ordination and coherence.

So it is the current, operational plan that gives rise to the basic practical problems. Needless to say, one can also make wrong long-term decisions, but the task of long-term planning is manageable, in the sense that the amount of information and computation required is within the capacity of the organs charged with the task, with no more (and no less) than the usual difficulties associated with imperfect knowledge of the future (though problems arise at the join between the long-term and the short-term plan). The basic issue to which we will return again and again in discussing current operational planning is that the tasks which the directing organs ought to be carrying out, given the logic of the model, cannot possibly be carried out by them.

THE DRAFTING OF A CENTRAL PLAN: FACTORS AFFECTING

Imagine that one is the head of *Gosplan*, the State Planning Committee. At present the post is held by N. K. Baybakov, who is also a deputy-premier. He calls together his heads of divisions and they consider the next five-year plan. They will have before them some guidelines and priorities which are determined by their political masters, i.e. by the Politbureau. The role of these guidelines is naturally greater when a long-term plan is considered, since many of the physical capacity limits are removable, by investments, within the longer time-period. In the short run, there are more constraints, less can change, and so considerations of balance, of the input-output requirements of past decisions, play a big role, though of course the diversion of resources to priority objectives at the behest of the political leadership can and does occur also in the process of current planning, including amendments to plans already formulated and communicated.

As already stressed, one of the duties of the planners is to inform the political leadership if their requirements add up to too much, or if priority objectives could only be fulfilled at the cost of painful and damaging cuts in some other sectors.

At the same time, a flow of information, requests and proposals reaches *Gosplan* from many organizations. Ministries press their own industry's interests and development schemes. Ministries and managers provide a flow of *zayavki* (indents, applications for inputs) which, as we shall see, are a key feature of the current-planning process. Republican organs and regional bodies put up proposals for developing their areas, these being of particular relevance to the formulation of investment plans in the longer term. The Ministries of Defence, Education, Health, Transport, all add their voices, since all will certainly have projects they wish incorporated in the plan. Local party functionaries press for more resources for their areas. Domestic and foreign trade organs pass on requests for more to be provided to satisfy their respective customers. All these things have their input-output implications. Thus a decision to provide more oil for export may call for immediate additional resources for drilling, laying pipelines, erecting processing plant and perhaps cutting domestic users, and all this in turn has multiple consequences for the production and supply plans of perhaps thousands of enterprises. Then under conditions of rapid technical change, it is vitally important for the planning organs to report on the implications of new technique and its diffusion. The State Committee on Science and Technology drafts plans for new technique, and in recent years there has also been continuous contact with the Academy of Sciences on a wide range of topics.

It is useful to see the various sectoral and regional bodies as competitive claimants on limited resources. This species of administrative competition is of great importance in practice. Needless to say, there is some similarity here to the process by which various ministries in Western countries try to persuade their Treasuries or finance ministries to let them have more for school-building, submarines, hospitals, etc. A similar 'competition' occurs between divisions within large Western corporations. The difference is that, owing to the overwhelming dominance of state-ownership, this process covers the economy as a whole, seen as one great corporation, the largest in the world, USSR Ltd. This question will be further pursued in Chapter 3.

The job of *Gosplan*, acting as the specialist adviser to the Council of Ministers (and in practice also to the central committee of the party), is to achieve balance by cutting the total requests to a level which can be regarded as practicable, as feasible. As we shall see, it does not always succeed in doing this. It must be stressed that *Gosplan* itself, as a state committee, has no productive enterprise under its orders. Although it does have important powers of allocation, formal authority over enterprises rests with the ministries.

The primary method, used by *Gosplan* to achieve coherence, is that of *material balances*. As already mentioned, some three hundred such balances are constructed for the five-year plan. For each major item available sources of supply are estimated (production, import, stocks) and are contrasted with requirements (current industrial utilization, investment needs, consumer demand, exports, possible increase in stocks and so on). In case of a 'misfit', discussion with the ministry concerned might result in a decision to produce more, or else consuming ministries will be told to make do with less, or finally foreign trade can come to the rescue to provide the missing quantity or to dispose of the expected surplus. Needless to say, the ministries and their subdivisions play an active role in this process, since out of it will emerge plan-orders, by the fulfilment of which they will be judged. The process is one of iteration, accompanied by much argument. *Gosplan* carries through 'the complex work of ensuring that resources of the appropriate products are in line with their utilization. This is achieved by partial reallocation of capital investments between sectors . . . by altering the timing of completions of new productive capacity, the volume of output and of consumption and changing other elements in the balance. As the result, at the final stage one has mutually consistent balances of the most important items of production, with the resource potential brought into line with the needs of the national economy'. (Yakobi, 1973 p.279.)

Gosplan is also concerned, along with other ministries, with such a vital matter as ensuring the balance between supply of goods and services and total disposable incomes. If total personal incomes are to rise by (say) 20 per cent in the next five years, then evidently this must be based upon an approximately equivalent increase in output of the items upon which the citizenry spend their income, which in turn affects investment plans and material balances. Indeed *Gosplan* stands at a nodal point of the entire system, since little can be done in any sector or by any ministry which does not have some material requirements calling for allocation or reallocation of a resource, and so for a redrafting of some plan or balance involving *Gosplan*. It should be recalled that planning organs exist also below the centre, and we shall be dealing with them in the next chapter. However, the degree of all-union inter-relationships, and the logic of centralization, reduce the republican, regional and other local bodies to very subordinate status.

Material balances are drawn up on the basis of input coefficients derived from past experience, modified by anticipated consequences of technical change. Here there is scope for the utilization of input-output techniques, but there is an important difference between input-output methods and the material balance. The latter is an administrative-operational tool, designed to reshuffle resources between particular users in the light of priorities and bottlenecks, the operation being conducted mainly in quantitative, physical terms, and related to the administrative subdivisions of the economy, which seldom conform to product designations. The input-output table records (and helps one to anticipate) the sectoral requirements of a given increase in output. It is a help, not a substitute, but it is none the less surprising that this help was ignored for so long (see Leontief, 1960 and Tretyakova and Birman, 1976). In the past, one cause of shortages was the tendency to underestimate the *full* technical coefficients. Let me illustrate this with an example.

Suppose it is decided to expand the output of the oil industry in Siberia. This decision calls for certain material inputs: machinery and equipment, road-making machines and materials, large-diameter pipe, perhaps a new railway line, houses for the workers, and so on. But all of these impose 'indirect' requirements on the rest of the economy: equipment, pipe and railway-lines require steel, which in turn requires iron ore, coking coal, probably additional investments which in turn require building materials, machines (which require more steel), fuel (including still more oil), means of transport, which in turn require . . . and so on. Needless to say the process of planning is not confined to the consequences of a decision to increase the output of oil, which is itself a response to requirements identified in the Soviet economy and outside it. The new techniques, plus hard experience, have helped the Soviet planners to take the material-input implications of their own decisions more fully into account. However, errors and omissions inevitably occur, and amendments have constantly to be made, as bottlenecks emerge. The process is never completed. The various bodies engaged in the process are constantly influencing each other in a variety of ways, and one should not see decisions as being simply passed down the pyramid of hierarchical and/or political subordination.

It is noteworthy that the Soviet planning experts are now more conscious of the consequences of uncertainty. Stalin denounced the notion of 'plan-guesstimate', preferring the view that Soviet plans are orders with legal force. Now, however, the need for incorporating 'prognosis' is explicitly recognized, particularly in the context of technical progress, but also because of *inevitable* imperfection of information. Thus Fedorenko, the head of the Central Economics-Mathematics Institute, has written: 'Economic phenomena can often be better and more accurately described in the language of stochastic models than in determinate models. Therefore probability-theory methods should in the future be much more widely used. . . .' (Fedorenko, 1968, p.211.)

CURRENT PLANS AND THE FIVE-YEAR PLAN

The current plan, covering a year, with a breakdown by quarters, 'fits' into the medium-term plan. In fact it has become the practice to publish the five-year plan with figures for each intermediate year. However, numerous amendments and adjustments occur, as one can readily see by contrasting the annual plan with the figures for the same year in the published five-year plan. Table 3 is an example.

Well before 1974 the published target figures for the final year of the plan (1975) were quietly amended in the light of experience. There is, of course, nothing inherently wrong with that, given that errors happen and new information and new opportunities should be taken into account.

Table 3

	1974A	1974B
Electricity (mlrd kwh)	985	975
Oil (mill. tons)	461	451
Gas (mlrd metres³)	280	257
Coal (mill. tons)	670	679
Steel (mill. tons)	138·1	135·9
Mineral fertilizer (mill. tons)	80·2	80·2
Cement (mill. tons)	116·3	114·9

Λ=1974 plan within the five-year plan, B=1974 annual plan (published at the end of 1973)

CURRENT PLANNING AND MATERIAL-TECHNICAL SUPPLY

Again, the key method used by the planning agencies is the method of material balances. This time the degree of disaggregation is greater. *Gosplan* prepares balances for about 2,000 products, while the Supply Committee, *Gossnab*, prepares some 18,000. A Soviet source pointed out, however, that *Gosplan*'s list covers 80 per cent of the *value* of allocated commodities. (Belyakov, *EKO*, 1975, No. 6, p.133.)

The exact numbers vary, and it is important to appreciate that they do not tell us much about the *coverage* of the centrally administered balances, because they are aggregated. Let the following serve as a clarifying example: let us suppose one position on the list of balances reads 'grain'. If it is decided to distinguish between the principal grains, this can become six positions: 'Wheat', 'rye', 'barley', 'oats', 'maize' and 'other'. The number of balances in this example increases by five items, but the *coverage* is not affected. Grain was and is on the list, but there has taken place a partial disaggregation. In other words, some items are administered and allocated centrally within an aggregated total, with detailed specifications decided at lower levels within the total.

The material balances which we are now discussing are 'operational' in the sense in which the longer-term ones are not. They have to be broken down into allocations of specific quantities for specific uses. The 'balance' of steel for the final year of a five-year plan serves as part of a calculation, intended to ensure plan coherence. The 'balance' of steel for the current year is an integral part of production and supply decisions, which must become actual instructions to particular administrative and production units.

It will have been noted that two separate central organs are responsible. *Gosplan* allocates what is described as 'the most important types of products', while *Gossnab*, together with its local organs, covers items considered to be of lesser importance, but which have a wide 'spread' of users throughout the economy. In addition, economic ministries allocate items which their enterprises produce to other enterprises within their own ministry, which is logical enough, but they also allocate some of their products (which do not figure on the *Gosplan* and *Gossnab* lists) to other ministries. There is created thereby an evident danger: inconsistency could arise between decisions in respect of items 'which are required for the production of the same goods but which are distributed by different organs'. (Yakobi, 1973 p.280.)

Allocation is made in the main to ministries (all-union and republican), which are known as 'allocation-holders' *(fondoderzhateli)*. They sub-allocate to their subordinate units. By this is not meant the physical movement of goods, but the distribution of allocation certificates, which allow their recipients to obtain the items needed in the quantities specified.

One often encounters the use of the term *fondiruyemaya produktsiya* to describe the key items allocated by *Gosplan*, while what *Gossnab* allocates is called 'centrally planned'. (Mavrishchev, 1970 p.420.) However, the former term is sometimes confined to a smaller list of key items whose allocation is approved by the Council of Ministers, which numbered 327 in 1968. (Schroeder, 1972, p.99.) The actual task of handling detailed allocations, of 'tying' customer to supplier, is the task of *Gossnab*, or its republican and local offices, and this happens even if the allocation decisions are taken by *Gosplan*. Indeed the lines of responsibility are extremely difficult to draw or to describe, as is not surprising, in view of the necessarily close links between the various balances and allocation decisions. In her valuable description of the material supply system, Gertrude Schroeder cites sources which show that many of the so-called centrally planned commodities are allocated in a joint operation by *Gosplan*, *Gossnab* and the 'supply-and-disposal' administration *(Snabsbyty)* of *Gossnab*. An example of the latter includes *Soyuzglavmetallsnabsbyt* ('All-union chief office of metal supply and disposal'). Its name shows that it is concerned with the detailed allocation also of items on the *Gosplan* list, which includes metals. There are also *Soyuzglavkoplekty* under *Gossnab*, their task being to supply investment projects with the necessary inputs, especially of machinery. Subject to general guidelines and within the limits set by central allocation, the local organs of *Gossnab* make detailed arrangements for supply, sometimes from warehouses which they themselves administer.

The *Gossnab* network was born in its 'modern' form in 1957, when the industrial ministries were abolished under the *sovnarkhoz* reform (see Chapter 3). Evidently the supply and disposal functions of the defunct ministries, who at that date each maintained separate networks, had to be concentrated in new organs set up for the purpose. A period of trial and error, with no little confusion, followed, as the centre endeavoured to prevent the regional *sovnarkhozy* diverting materials to their own use. When, in 1965, the *sovnarkhozy* were abolished and the ministries reconstituted, it was decided to preserve the supply network which had grown up in their absence, with *Gossnab* as its head, so as to avoid unnecessary duplication: it had indeed been the case, before 1957, that each ministry ran its own network for acquiring and distributing supplies (other than of 'funded' products, which had been *Gosplan's* province, then as now), with much wasteful duplication. However, many ministries have succeeded in retaining their own *snabsbyt* organs, and duplication does indeed persist, as can be seen in numerous published complaints on this subject cited by Gertrude Schroeder in her article. A Soviet source wrote critically of ministries acquiring (indeed 'stealing', *rastaskivat'*) local *Gossnab* installations. (Belyakov, *EKO* 1975, No. 6 p.136.)

The process of allocation, from top to bottom, is based on two sources of information: requests from below or indents *(zayavki)*, and norms or coefficients. As, for reasons to be explained, there is justified suspicion that indents will be inflated, there is much reliance on norms, i.e. the quantities of particular inputs needed to produce a specified amount of a particular output, based upon past experience. One can see that problems must arise in this connection with new methods involving new or different inputs. There is constant pressure to reduce material utilization norms, which should be based upon study not just of past experience but of the real possibilities. In the past the determination, amendment and confirmation of thousands of norms and coefficients was a clumsy, bureaucratic exercise, which rightly attracted criticism. In recent years an attempt has been made to simplify and decentralize the process. Subject to some general norms which are still laid down under the aegis of *Gosplan*, control is exercised by ministries, but the enterprise managers now have greater power to determine the norms applicable in their particular situation, subject, however, to 'a decline on average in the norms of utilization of raw materials, semi-manufactures, fuel and other vital material resources'. (Yakobí, 1973, p.284.)

However, central regulation still extends even to such detail as 'the norm of utilization of wire for pressed hay' (*Gosplan*, 1974, p.188), which suggests a high degree of control. It seems that farms cannot be trusted just to order the wire they need.

A primary task of *Gossnab* and its numerous sub-units is 'the attachment *(prikrepleniye)*' of customer to supplier, a difficult and time-consuming task, as can be imagined, given the multiple thousands of inter-relationships involved. It must be stressed that the enterprise manager can only negotiate about precise specifications after he knows who is supposed to supply him. Luckily for the sanity of Soviet planners and managers, most industrial enterprises supply, and draw their supplies from, the same enterprises or wholesalers as in the previous year. To avoid burdensome and confusing administrative procedures, and to encourage continuous customer-supplier relationships with their evident advantages, there have been decrees on so-called 'direct long-term links' between enterprises, long-term contracts under the authority of the supply allocation organs, but durable, i.e. covering a run of years. In fact many thousands of such long-term arrangements have been negotiated.

This, however, has not worked out very satisfactorily, and the reason is not far to seek: the whole production-and-allocation procedure requires continuous adjustment as shortages develop, or new requirements follow some change in policy priorities. Besides, as we shall see, no current operational plan is ever drafted in time. Therefore the production ministries and/or the supply allocation organs may at any time issue orders which disrupt the so-called 'long-term links', and of course the enterprises concerned have no alternative but to obey. The existence of a contract to supply does not protect from this: one must carry out the order of a hierarchical superior.

This system gives rise to disequilibria, misallocation, mismatching of production and supply, delays in communicating plans and instructions, and repeated changes during the year in these plans and instructions. All this is well known and can be documented by great numbers of quotations from Soviet sources, and we will be returning to the many consequences of this, especially in Chapter 4. Why, then, has the system not been radically altered? In 1965, when Kosygin introduced various reforms, he promised a gradual switch from administrative allocation to wholesale trade in producers' goods. That is to say, enterprise managers would be free to *buy* more of their inputs, from wholesalers, without any allocation certificate. In fact, however, this has grown very slowly. Eight years later, in 1973, in the system of *Gossnab*, there were 740 wholesale stores which sold producers' goods worth 'almost 4 milliard roubles'. (Yakobi, 1973, p.290.) This means that at least 97 per cent of producers' goods do *not* pass through 'wholesale trade' and are therefore 'rationed', administratively allocated.

Why? Perhaps this can best be understood by re-examining the functional logic of the system. The whole annual plan formulation procedure begins when enterprises (or *obyedineniya*) communicate their *input requirements*. This procedure begins half-way through the previous year. They make at the same time their estimates of what they will produce next year, though without yet knowing what their production plan will be. Their requests, and draft production plans, are aggregated by the ministries (local industries deal with their republican organs), and then in *Gosplan* the resultant magnitudes are contrasted with the resources available in the light of policy guidelines and priorities, and amendments made, as material balances can hardly be expected to balance on the first round. Administrative and statistical iterative procedures eventually lead to the emergence of a set of output and material supply plans which are supposed to match. Thus the enterprise manager should be told to produce a batch of goods (by his ministry) which corresponds to the supply allocations, and these may or may not approximate to his original requests. (Chaos is in fact avoided because most enterprises produce this year more or less the same things as they did last year.)

It must be noted that the output plans are to a substantial extent the consequence of the input needs of the economy. Therefore the supply procedures are an integral part of the process of collecting information about what is needed. So long as the current output plan is based upon instructions from the planners, so long must the material-supply system continue in something like its present form. The output of a factory or construction site in fact largely consists of the sum total of its customers' requirements. In a 'market' type reform, say of the limited Hungarian type, the abandonment of allocation of inputs was possible, but only because current output ceased to be the subject of systematic central directives. That is to say, a Hungarian manager negotiated with his customers and based his own plan on this. The Soviet system, as we have seen, is not run in this way. Centralized directives as to what to produce are based, and can only be based, upon the *central organs* collecting information about requirements and then telling the managers to meet these requirements. Thus one cannot have operational control over production without deciding also on supply, since production is mostly for supplying other enterprises, and of course production without the necessary inputs is impossible. Under conditions of full utilization of resources, with little or no 'slack', there is the further danger that important sectors of the economy would suffer from a breakdown in supply, in the event of shortages occurring, unless the 'rationing' system ensures the flow of the needed materials to the priority areas.

A *Gosplan* official, Drogichinsky, contributing to a high-level symposium, reacted as follows to the proposal of 'some academic economists to give the right to enterprises to choose suppliers and customers. This proposal, harmless at first sight, in fact conceals within itself the abandonment of centralized planning, a move towards market relations. What does it mean, to give to the users the right to choose their supplier? This means that the users will choose the supplier who is most advantageous for them . . . This would lead to elemental (*stikhiynym*) search for the best suppliers and customers, would disorganize the work of enterprises and increase their costs.' He insists that the planners can best see what links are in the best interests of the economy as a whole. (Drogichinsky, 1973, p.91.) This faithfully represents the resistance of *Gosplan* to this species of reform. It helps one to see why the references in the 1965 reform speeches to 'wholesale trade in inputs' have had so little effect in practice.

As for consumers' goods, the argument for greater freedom to respond to demand seems on the face of it stronger. Indeed, as we shall see, both trade and industry are repeatedly enjoined to study the consumer market and to produce what is desired by the citizens. However, two obstacles must be mentioned. The first is the evident commitment of the political authorities and economic ministries to the 'directive' or command principle: management shall be told what to do. While these instructions should reflect demand, this need not always be so: apart from potentially poisonous substances, like alcohol or books, there is the belief that priorities are for the centre to determine. The second reason is, again, the link with supply. It is little use authorizing a given sector of industry to make its own market-oriented decisions if the industries which provide its inputs are planned in the old centralized way, since it may then not obtain its means of production. We will return to this point in greater detail in Chapter 11, when reform models are considered.

Thus complexities which 'would overwhelm any apparatus of *Gosplan*, and supply-disposal organs *(snabsbyty)*', to cite the words of Liberman (*Kom* 1959, No. 1, p.89), are inherent in the nature of the centralized system. Yet planners do plan, industry produces, the system does function. We shall be seeing in subsequent chapters how, and at what cost in terms of efficiency.

So far we have been almost exclusively concerned with planning of industrial activity, and particularly with production and supply. Many other planning functions exist, distributed among a number of institutions. *Gosplan* itself contains two kinds of departments: co-ordinating *(svodny)* and sectoral *(otraslevy)*. Chief among the former is the 'co-ordinating department of national planning', which co-ordinates *Gosplan*'s own activities. There are also departments for territorial planning and location, material balance and allocation, capital investments, labour productivity and wages. Sectoral departments concern themselves with planning of particular branches of industry, with agriculture, transport and so on. *Gosplan* is served by a number of expert committees, by a computer centre, a research institute. It is not surprising to learn that it has a complex internal organization, requiring the co-ordination of co-ordinators, given the immense task it has to perform. Its various departments inevitably duplicate the functions of other bodies engaged in the process of central planning: the State Committee on Construction (co-ordinating and guiding the building programme), the State Committee on Prices (which until recently was under *Gosplan*), the State Committee on Labour and Wages, *Gossnab* (whose allocation functions intertwine particularly closely with those of *Gosplan*), the State Committee on Science and Technology, the

Ministries of Finance, of Internal and of Foreign Trade, and of course also the numerous ministries charged with administering the many sectors and branches of which the economy is composed. One must add to this already formidable list the apparatus of the party's central committee, with its own co-ordinating and sectoral departments, whose officials can and do interpose their views – to which much weight must be given – at many points and levels.

There is no need to dwell in any detail on the organizational structure as such. It burdens the memory without adding much to understanding. What is essential to appreciate is that very many departments and organs of government are involved, because it is necessary that they should be. Thus *Gosplan*, in the words of a Soviet textbook, 'must exert its influence on the formation of plans of ministries, departments and union republics, viewing these plans from the overall state standpoint, preventing narrow departmentalist and localist decisions . . . .' (Perov, 1973, p.60.) But it can only do this if it possesses the necessary information, and officials capable of assessing it 'from the overall state standpoint'. Therefore it cannot simply take its ideas on metallurgy from the appropriate ministry, or on the Ukraine from the Ukrainian government or its *Gosplan*. They are likely to pursue their own particular 'departmentalist' or 'localist' interests. It requires to have its own departments covering metallurgy and regional policy, and, as we have seen, such departments it does have. If a major decision is taken on foreign trade, then it must involve at least two of the departments of *Gosplan* itself, probably *Gossnab*, certainly one or more of the production ministries, the State Bank, and so on through the system.

The demarcation of responsibility between various central organs, especially between *Gosplan* and *Gossnab,* is confusing also for those who work in them. A proposal is being discussed to adopt an Economic Code, a Law of Economic Planning, which would clarify who does what. *Gosplan*, so it is argued, should concentrate on planning, and be freed of burdensome operational tasks. Examples cited by a Soviet critic are as follows: 'The question of building houses with electric cooking facilities requires in each separate instance the consent of the USSR *Gosplan*', and 'the all-union Ministry of Agriculture requires the prior agreement of *Gosplan* before deciding on plans for inter-republican transport of eggs for incubation'. (Ivanov, *PKh*, 1975, No. 12 pp.7–10.)

It is essential to bear in mind that no action can be or will be taken unless three elements are present: information (what needs doing), motivation (why should we bother to do it?) and means (financial and material). This is so, needless to say, in all systems and in all branches of human activity. In a centralized economy, with no effective market forces, the administrative system must collect a vast quantity of information, and, assuming for a moment that the motivation to do the best one can is present, the decision as to means necessarily involves a large number of bodies which are, so to speak, means-providers and which must therefore be co-ordinated. Thus even the most well-motivated and well-informed official in charge of saucepan production cannot decide to produce more without seeking agreement from whatever planning offices are responsible for their inputs. Furthermore, the system provides no built-in means of indicating priorities. In other words, information that something needs doing or producing requires to be considered in conjunction with a great many other possible lines of action, which cannot all be pursued at once, since resources are scarce. Each sectoral or regional institution is, understandably, likely to see the urgency of its own needs. For all these reasons, proposals require to circulate around many offices, for comment and reconciliation of views (soglasovaniye).

The bureaucratic problems that arise are common to any large organization, including the Western corporation. They show themselves in acute form in the USSR because of its size and also the vast range of the activities which it covers; it is not only a super-corporation but a super-conglomerate.

PLANNERS' TIME-HORIZON

As already explained at some length, the planning mechanism is heavily overloaded with current detailed work, of ensuring the smooth process of production and distribution. This means that not only is the bulk of the personnel engaged in current work, but also that the pressures from above relate mostly to today rather than several years hence. This is quite understandable. If you are an industrial minister, or the head of a supply agency, or a Gosplan sector chief, you are in trouble if the current programme is threatened, if, for instance, delays in deliveries cause a breakdown in some important production process. In this sense the long-term plan can never be a matter of such dire emergency. True, it ought to be fulfilled, but the consequences of not doing so are not urgent, the plan may be altered anyhow, circumstances change, one may indeed be moved to another official post. Consequently, there tends to be a built-in priority of the short term, at the level of the planning agencies.

This has, on a number of occasions, led to reorganization designed to strengthen those responsible for long-term plans, who otherwise tend to be elbowed out of the way by whoever handles current problems. Thus in 1955–6 the functions of Gosplan were split between two bodies: Gosekonomkommissiya (State Economic Commission), charged with current planning, and Gosplan (State Planning Committee) which was to concern itself with long-term planning. The reason given was that preoccupation with current planning was causing neglect of the longer term. In 1957–60 these functions were reunited under *Gosplan*, which in the first stages of the *sovnarkhoz* reform acquired very substantial additional powers (see Chapter 3). No doubt it was found that the separation of current and long-term had its inconveniences, since one is so closely related to the other, especially with regard to investment planning.

In the late Khrushchev period there were two more reorganizations, only of formal-historical interest in themselves, yet significant as an indication of what kinds of difficulties arose.

In April 1960 *Gosplan* was split again, but this time the designation *Gosplan* was attached to the current planning function, while perspective plans were the task of *Gosekonomsovet* (State Economic Council). There were some differences in detail between this and the 1957–60 division between the two planning bodies, but these are not worth pursuing here.

This proved unsatisfactory yet again. A reform promulgated in March 1963 rearranged things on somewhat different principles: between planning and implementation of plans. No doubt Khrushchev, who was then in control, believed that, as Burns wrote, 'the best laid plans of mice and men gang aft agley', unless they are followed by action and someone is made responsible for ensuring that this is so. In practice 'implementation' meant current operational planning, in a situation in which industrial ministries, abolished in 1957, had not yet been reconstituted. This task was given to a newly named *Sovnarkhoz of the USSR*, while *Gosplan* retained planning, particularly long-term planning. At the same time, anxious to ensure that these and all other co-ordinators were co-ordinated, Khrushchev set up a Supreme Council of National Economy.

His successors dismantled this clumsy machinery, and when the ministries were recreated in 1965 they moved to the division of responsibility that exists to this day, with *Gosplan* in charge of planning on all time-scales. But the issue of long versus short term remains.

It could be pointed out that the Soviet regime is, if anything, obsessed with the future, being ever ready to sacrifice the present to it, as may be seen by the high rate of investment and the priority of producers' goods. In one sense this is so. The strategy adopted is indeed one of building up productive capacity, which certainly means a future-oriented time-preference. But, paradoxically, *given* the adoption of ambitious plans for growth, the choices made and the decisions taken reflect above all immediate concerns. This mainly affects the evaluation of the performance of both managers and officials, up to ministers inclusive: they are in trouble if they do not increase output by the percentage specified in *this* year's plan, and it is easy to see that longer-term considerations can conflict with this objective. Thus, to anticipate matters dealt with in subsequent chapters, the immediate growth of the harvest of grain may be inconsistent with soil-preserving measures (e.g. fallowing) which are needed to ensure a good harvest over a run of years. Technological improvements which do not promise immediate results might be shelved.

The problem arises in especially acute form at the level of enterprise management, as will be seen in chapter 4. The management well knows it is accountable to its superiors in carrying out current operational orders. For reasons to be discussed, these alter frequently: the annual plan is sometimes 'adjusted' in December of the year to which it applies! Then, of course, the manager's (as any official's) time-horizon is affected by the likelihood that he will·not hold that particular job very long.

It is an interesting and puzzling contrast. The traditional socialist view has been that capitalism subordinates long-term economic and social health to the immediate profit motive, and therefore cuts down forests, pollutes, and needs to be 'bribed' by high rates of interest to consider tomorrow. Yet Soviet-type economies have yet to find an effective substitute for ownership. Just as a temporary tenant takes less care of a house than its proprietor, so the temporary chief of a ministerial department or a factory is less involved in its future, with which he will in all probability not be associated. He seems even less involved in it than is the corporation executive in the West, though the executive is usually not its owner. Possibly the reason is that it is easier to identify with the future of even a big corporation, one among many, than with a super-firm which covers the entire USSR. This may be a species of psychological diseconomy of scale. It is analogous to the sense of 'belonging' of a member of a small work-team, which is far more difficult to maintain if one is an individual within a productive unit with 10,000 employees. The point is worth thinking about, though one must appreciate that other factors, political and social as well as economic, affect the attitudes of officials, managers and workers, in Russia as elsewhere.

Another and related issue is one of responsibility. Whose job is it to ensure that plans are correctly drafted and are carried out in line with the original intention? Whose fault is it when things go wrong? Needless to say, responsibility and initiative are qualities both sought and prized. The system does, however, tend to nullify them. When a decision requires to be 'agreed' by five or six administrative instances, who is responsible for it? Can one hold the executant of an order responsible if, for instance, the material means to carry out the order are not provided? There used to be a saying: 'objective causes have a name and address'. This meant that adverse circumstances would not be accepted as an excuse, individuals are responsible. Far too often this simply meant identifying the scapegoat when things went wrong.

As for initiative, the chief obstacle to overcome is usually lack of means or power to act. As we shall see, this is due not just (or even mainly) to reluctance to delegate, but rather to the need to secure the agreement of officials charged with overseeing complementary activities, without which the initiative could not be acted upon. Thus a change in the type or quantity of almost any good or service would involve a change in inputs, in the wages bill, in the financial balance, in the measurement of plan-fulfilment. Without an effective market, it is hardly ever possible simply to order a different material from a supplier; one's ministry, *Gossnab,* possibly even *Gosplan,* and also the supplying enterprise and *its* ministry, may well be concerned with the series of consequential administrative decisions.

It is at this micro-economic operational level that the weaknesses of centralized directive planning are most easily visible.

CRITERIA FOR CHOICE

The planners have a big range of choices, both as to ends and as to means. While the choice of ends may be said to be a political matter, this does not 'exonerate' the planners, since the leadership does not operate in a vacuum and is constantly receiving advice and suggestions. There is a role here, too, for economists. In a conversation in Moscow some years back, a Soviet colleague said, with logic, that the party leadership's aims cannot be the over-riding criterion for economic policy, because the party leadership seeks advice as to what these aims should be, and it is hardly likely to thank those who reply that these aims are right by definition!

This said, it remains true that the leadership does have a programme and priority objectives, and that it takes decisions also on a wide range of more detailed matters. It may appear that the role of the party, and of its central committee apparatus, merely duplicates the state planning machinery and introduces unnecessary and wasteful procedures. Yet things are not so simple, as will become apparent if we examine the criteria for decision making which are available within the system.

There is a considerable Soviet literature on the subject of optimum planning. Consistency, they rightly assert, is not enough, though this too is hard enough to achieve. By consistency is meant the necessary input-output balance: enough iron ore for the metallurgical industry, enough metal for its various intended users, enough sugar-beet for the sugar factories, and so on. However, the structure of production may be sub-optimal, because (let us say) it might be more economical to use different materials, or to produce steel in a different way and in another location, or to shift from hydroelectricity to thermal power generation and vice versa. No material balance, however well balanced, will provide this sort of information. For this one must, in the words of the late V. V. Novozhilov, 'compare costs and results'. (Novozhilov, 1967.)

The problem was formulated as follows: 'The growing scale of production, the speed-up in technical progress, the rapid expansion and growing complexity of economic inter-relationships, call for the consistent realization of the principle of optimality in the development of the national economy, which would ensure maximum results in the use of available resources and the greatest utilization of the advantage of the socialist method of production. The realization of the principle of optimality is possible only in a socialist economy, due above all to social ownership of the means of production, planned development of the economy and socialist forms of distribution.

'These and other circumstances, however, do not only create the necessary conditions for optimizing economic processes, but also substantially complicate the task. Thus the higher level of concentration (of production) is accompanied by the development of specialization, which leads to even more complex linkages between different economic units. The speed of growth and technical and scientific progress gives rise to a great many possible new directions of development. In order to achieve the maximum increase in the productivity of social labour, it is essential consistently to introduce the principle of optimality in the development of the national economy. . . .

'At the present level of productive forces there arise objective obstacles in the way of correct decisions. Today not only the national economy as a whole but also its sectors and even enterprises represent complex human-and-machine systems with an enormous number of interconnections and of factors influencing these. In the process of planning and administration all this needs to be weighed and taken into account. Therefore choices as to the directions, tempos and direction of development of the national economy, changes in its structure, cannot be based just on the intuition and experience of people, however talented they may be.' (Fedorenko, 1968, pp.5–6.)

Optimization in terms of what? What is it that should be maximized? What criteria should be used, at what level and by whom? This too has been the subject of much research and debate in the Soviet Union.

Actual practice is very far indeed from optimization. With 'passive' prices providing an unreliable guideline as to scarcities or real costs, and with state priorities finding little or no reflection in the price mechanism, the planning organs have so far been able (more or less) to reconcile some key priorities with an input-output balance, basing themselves on past performance and acting in a rough-and-ready way on the so-called ratchet principle: whatever you did last year, do more or better this year. To appreciate why this is so we must stress two points. The first is the inadequacy of information received from below, partly for reasons which will be discussed at length in the next chapter (it often does not 'pay' management to tell the truth). The second is, yet again, the impossible *scale* of what needs to be done by the planners. 'Kiev mathematicians have calculated that, in order to draft an accurate and fully integrated plan of material-technical supply just for the Ukrainian republic for one year requires the labour of the entire world's population for ten million years' (Antonov, 1965, p.23.) Allowing for colourful exaggeration, the point is rather strikingly made.

Since the planning organs are overwhelmed and cannot complete their work, despite a great deal of unavoidable aggregation and devolution, they tend to follow above all the objective of consistency, while ensuring a supply of resources to those key sectors or projects by which their political masters set greatest store. 'Manageability' is achieved by basing nearly all plans on past performance.

Investment criteria are a separate – and very important – subject, and will be considered at length in Chapter 6. Here we deal with the current decision-making process, one aspect of which is the so-called 'placing of production orders' *(razmeshcheniye zakazov)*, or who is to do what? A frequently encountered contradiction arises here between profitability and administrative convenience. The *obyedineniye* or the enterprise may be interested in profits, but *Gosplan* and *Gossnab* are not; local branches of *Gossnab*, true, are supposed to be on *khozraschet*, but this simply means that their warehousing and handling costs are covered by the charges they make for their services, not that they gain advantage from supplying a cheaper input to its user.

In other words, an important cause of inefficiency lies in the fact that overworked planning agencies, whose task is to ensure that output instructions are issued and the suppliers supply the necessary inputs, do not and cannot aim at cost minimization. They have for this neither the time nor the motivation. It is like expecting a harassed military quartermaster to send ammunition to a battle unit by the cheapest route; he will normally have other worries on his mind.

Hence there is a sizable Soviet literature on the subject of plan-instructions being issued that cause financial losses to the executants of the instructions, which contradict the emphasis on lowering costs and raising profitability.

There are also numerous complaints arising from the consequences of necessary and unavoidable *aggregation*. Because of the impossibility of dealing at the centre with detail, instructions can too easily conflict with user micro-requirements, with consequences which we will be examining in Chapter 4. Nor can the logic of technical progress or of improved product design be easily fitted into a system so administered. Finally, the existence of many interlocking agencies results in contradictory and inconsistent instructions reaching the managers.

A wide-awake and critical reader might be thinking: so what, so there is no optimization, there never is in the real world. True enough, but the point is that the system too often works, so to speak, against itself. It is not just a matter of imperfect information and failures of foresight, which exist in all systems, but inherent 'systemic' weaknesses which can cause serious distortions, thereby reducing the 'coefficient of effectiveness' below tolerable levels. By 'tolerable' is here meant not textbook optimization, but levels which the Soviet leaders themselves are prepared to tolerate. They all, from Brezhnev down, have been urging greater efficiency, in terms of moving from 'extensive' to 'intensive' methods, a formulation which we will be discussing in subsequent chapters. The fact remains that 'unfortunately we still do not have a scientifically based methodology for determining economic effectiveness', to cite a recent symposium. (Drogichinsky, 1973, p.72.)

In a market model cost-minimization is 'natural', a consequence of trying to make profits. Markets being imperfect, cost is sometimes not minimized, but the propensity is there, in the model. The 'central-directive' model depends on the planners doing the minimizing, and if they do not, no one else will.

The optimization criteria which are sought relate to the general advantages of the economy and society. How can these be determined? What is the Soviet equivalent of a 'social welfare function'? And let us not forget that we in the West find it much easier to talk about a social welfare function than to identify or define it in operationally meaningful terms.

One of the points of principle facing the Soviet theorist is not only what to take as the objective criterion, but also what parameters to choose, what limitations or scarcities to assume. In a current plan, of course, productive capacity can be taken as given, but in a perspective plan the planners' own choices in large measure predetermine the relative scarcities, which their own investment plans can alter. Therefore, as plans change, so do the valuations of factors, in so far as scarcities in relation to plan-objectives change. We will return to this point when we discuss the theory and practice of pricing.

All this is highly relevant to the possibilities and potentialities of improving the planning system through 'optimization by computer'. If we can define an objective, a maximand, there must exist a best route to achieve it, at minimum cost to society.

MATHEMATICAL PROGRAMMING AND OPTIMAL PLANNING

The preceding argument brings out a major limitation in any attempt to achieve an overall optimization exercise at the centre. Let us first dispose of a popular but mistaken view, that computers, being ultra-rapid in their operation, can and will save centralized planning from the consequences of 'the curse of scale', to cite again the phrase used by Fedorenko and which he borrowed from Bellman. It is utterly and totally impossible to collect information at the centre about micro-requirements and then convey the necessary orders to thousands of executant managers. No serious mathematical economist in the USSR pretends otherwise.

What, then, is their approach to a 'computable' optimum? Let us see how a Soviet textbook tackles this question. Here are the 'basics of optimal planning':

(1) The economy is seen as a 'consciously optimized system', based on social ownership.
(2) The unique criterion of optimality is the maximum satisfaction of the needs of members of the society and of society as a whole.
(3) Resources and knowledge are scarce, relative to needs.
(4) There are wide possibilities of substitution in the use of resources in production and also in consumption.
(5) The Soviet economy is viewed as a complex multi-level hierarchical system.
(6) Local, peripheral interests must be organically linked with central objectives, and the evaluation of the activity of subordinate units must cohere with the overall optimality criterion (As presented by Berri, 1973, p.50–1.)

It is taken for granted in the above formulation that the bulk of micro-decisions will not and can not be taken by the centre itself. So of course a major issue becomes one of devising a system in which 'the economic interest of organs at all levels and of their employees *(rabotnikov)* in the solution of a problem faced by the economy as a whole is guaranteed'. (Berri, 1973, p.51.)

Before analysing the obstacles standing in the way of a solution to the problems raised above, let us look briefly at the apparently irrelevant example of chess. The board has sixty-four squares. There are eight pawns and eight pieces per side. The 'objective function' is known and accepted by both players: the loss of the king ends the game. The moves each piece can make are laid down and are not disputed by the participants: a bishop can proceed only on its own diagonal, a pawn cannot move backwards, and so on.

Chess-playing can be computerized, a programme can be and has been written. But the task is burdensome, because the number of alternative moves to be considered grows alarmingly; it is said that in a thirty-move game a computer programmed to examine every possible move has had to consider as many alternatives as there have been minutes since the Pyramids were built. A human grandmaster can beat a computer fairly comfortably.

The Soviet (or any other) economy has many more than sixty-four squares. Its 'pieces' can act in many alternative and unpredicatable ways, and may refuse to obey the rules even if these are unambiguously defined. This applies, for instance, to real-life bishops, not to mention kings, and even to the equivalent of pawns. There is no equivalent in chess of the possibility of strife among pieces of the same colour. Worst of all, in real life there is no agreement about the objective of the game.

This is *not* intended to be an attack on the use of computers in planning or in anything else. Their speed is an obvious advantage, making possible the drafting of several internally consistent alternative plans, from which a choice can be made. Far too often, in the days when calculations were made on abacuses and backs of envelopes, by the time a more or less consistent plan was drafted it was already too late, and there was no chance of drafting another one. (In conversation, a Soviet economist once told me that, though there is a big literature on criteria in choosing between investment projects, there often is only one project and therefore no choice!) Major developments are in progress in 1976 to set up an 'Automatized system of planning computations', abbreviated in Russian as ASPR, which, if experiments succeed, might well greatly improve the informational basis of planning. (For details, see V. Bezrukov, *PKh* 1976, No.5, pp.47ff.) It is also the case that partial optimization solutions, relating to specific problems, are feasible and desirable, in the Soviet as in a Western economy. Indeed, linear programming was developed in the USSR, by Kantorovich, in such contexts as the optimum utilization of machinery or means of transportation, in a situation where there were clear parameters (availability of means) and clearly defined ends.

The Soviet mathematical school is aware of all this. Having listed the six basics of optimal planning, the textbook proceeds to list 'difficulties of both a theoretical and a practical character. These include, first, the determination of the criterion for a national-economic plan; second, the problem of the magnitude *(razmernost')* of the task . . . of aggregation and disaggregation: third, the problem of the normative base'. (Berri, 1973, p.51.)

Let us look at these in turn.

As we have already pointed out, an optimum is more easily discussed in the abstract than defined in practice. Here are some proposals which have been considered in the Soviet literature on the subject. The proposals (and the criticisms) given below, are all summarized from the Soviet literature:

(1) The achievement of a given structure of final output at minimum labour cost, i.e. while maximizing labour productivity. However, it is not clear why this structure of final output, and not some

other, should be chosen. Nor is it related to available resources.

(2) Maximizing the volume or rate of growth of national income. This formulation begs the question of the desired relationship between consumption and investment, and can lead to aiming at maximizing investment and a politically dangerous reduction of consumption at the beginning of the period.

(3) Maximizing material consumption (and 'unproductive accumulation', e.g. housing, hospitals) throughout the period to which the (perspective) plan applies. Defects include the omission of non-material services (which as we shall see, are excluded from the Soviet definition of national income and so of the 'consumption fund'), and also of reducing hours of work. Future growth is underemphasised with this approach.

(4) 'The maximization of total social utility', including non-material consumption, shorter hours, etc. Unsolved problems include 'measurement of social utility', and also the allowance to be made for the time factor. (Berri, 1973, p.51–2.)

There were also theories based upon conscious sub-optimalization, recognizing the existence of several objectives. The supporters of this view urge the drafting of several variants of the plan, each based on maximizing one chosen function, and the one chosen would most closely accord with 'economic policy', i.e. with political preferences. There is even a proposal to adopt 'the criterion of sectoral optimization based upon the existence of multiple objectives and therefore of criteria. An effective plan would be one in which it cannot be improved by any one of these criteria without being by this means worsened in terms of one of the other criteria' (Berri, 1973, p.53), an interesting adaptation to this issue of the concept of the Pareto optimum – though of course with no mention of Pareto. (See also contributions of Malinvaud, Aganbegyan and others in Khachaturov, 1976.)

An interesting and independent approach is to be found in the work of B. Smekhov. He reminds us that simple reliance on 'common sense' is not enough. But he quotes the Polish economist Jozef Pajestka: 'Any (plan) variation requires to be checked by arguments based upon common sense . . . since mathematical models, necessarily simplified, do not enable one to judge precisely which simplifications have what effect on the outcome.' (Smekhov, 1968, p.11.) None the less, some one criterion there must be, even if modified by other considerations. (I once heard the eminent Polish economist Michal Kalecki say: 'The silliest thing to do is not to calculate. The second most silly thing to do is to follow blindly the results of your calculation.') The inflexibility of the models as compared even with inflexible bureaucrats was emphasized in a paper by the Hungarian economist Augustinovics (1975).

Each in their own way, Janos Kornai and V. V. Novozhilov have urged an approach towards efficiency by relating the valuations to policy objectives by a species of mutually affecting iterations. Kornai (*EkMM*, 1966, No. 1, p.39), doubting the existence of an overall welfare function, expressed the view that 'it is sufficient to try to ensure that the system of constraints and objective function of the model together gave a numerical expression to the general tendency of economic policy'. Novozhilov, in a conversation with me, criticized unattainable 'cosmic optima' and thought that it would be sensible to aim at a situation in which managerial incentives and prices were usually consistent with policy objectives (instead of often unintentionally working against them).

Admittedly, as Smekhov noted, there is indeed a serious problem. Kantorovich's 'objectively determined valuations' (see p.176 below) are valuations derived from the plan, which, however, needs them for its own formulation, thus getting one into a vicious circle. On the other hand, he rejects the 'conservative' argument, which A. Boyarsky best represents, which clings to Marx's formulation concerning the non-commensurability of use-values, a formulation to be found in the very beginning of the first volume of *Das Kapital* (more of this in Chapter 12). Boyarsky derives from this the view that one cannot maximize the sum of use-values, i.e. the sum of satisfaction of needs of society. He indeed advanced a very odd additional argument. Suppose an acceptable criterion for an optimum plan were found, 'active planning would from that moment on be liquidated'. (Boyarsky, 1962, p.347.) In other words: planners, beware! If you accept optimal criteria, you are threatened with unemployment!

Smekhov mocks (the word Smekhov actually means 'mocker') the efforts of the Institute of Economics to define optimality in multiple ways: increase in national income; the level of consumption achieved per unit of investment; net output in relation to capital assets; reduction in costs per unit of advanced capital. 'But suppose that different variants of the plan appear more efficient with different optimality indicators. What should be done then?' (Smekhov, 1968, p.15.) What indeed? He rightly points out that the list of criteria would have sense if they were weighted and combined in some way. He again returns, as did many of the others, to social utility, to the level and growth of consumption of goods and services, with investment seen as essential to provide the material basis for increased human welfare, and not as an end in itself. Allowance is, of course, also made for military expenditures, regional policy and so on.

Existing criteria have an element of arbitrariness. Smekhov gives as an example the plan for 1970, which provided, *inter alia*, for an increase in dry-cleaning by 550 per cent and of hospital services by 12 per cent, dairy produce by 15–18 per cent, and so on. Probably such enormous differences are due to failure to see the totality of the desired consumption pattern. Whatever Marx (or Boyarsky) may be alleged to have said about non-commensurability of utilities, the fact remains that, in the words of Smekhov, even such different items as dry-cleaning and fruit 'compete with each other, objectively, as investment resources are limited and, secondly, in long-term planning the redistribution of resources can materially alter the proportions of consumption'. (Smekhov, 1968, p.33.) Clearly, it is essential to calculate how different possible patterns of consumption of goods and services affect social welfare. It is also essential, in planning, not to operate exclusively with global aggregates, such as national income, since there must be some proportionality between sectors (thus it matters whether one expands hospital services, dry-cleaning, dairies, or housing-space in this or that proportion, and the 'right' answer would not be indicated by monetary demand even if prices were more 'rational' than they in fact are). It is as if one sought to optimize food consumption in terms of an aggregate figure in calories, regardless of what the foods actually were.

There is a cogent argument against using any given pattern of final outputs as a criterion, if these are to be seen in micro-economic terms. Not only are there too many final products, but it should be the task of the *central* plan to provide means, not determine detailed ends. One must agree here with Smekhov's formulation: 'central planning should be confined to that nomenclature of output, which if it were altered would call for changes in the distribution of the accumulation fund', in other words for changes in investment. (Smekhov, 1968, p.40.) Detail should be a matter for negotiation between customer and supplier, and indeed this is so to some extent today. In a lecture he gave in Glasgow in 1966, Kantorovich made the same point as follows: We do not know what women's fashions will be in three years' time. Consequently, in planning investments in the clothing industry, we should ensure as far as possible that the machines be not too specialized, so that they can be adapted to the required pattern of production (I quote from memory). Those, in West and East, who criticize the 'traditional' Soviet planning system for planning intermediate goods, materials and fuels instead of final output are mistaken. Or rather, their criticism should be of a system which subordinated the production of consumers' goods not to consumer requirements but to the capacity available, which in effect treated consumption as a residual, giving priority to producers' goods and armaments. The 'correct' solution Kantorovich implied, is not to derive the plan for cloth from a central plan disaggregated to the level of skirts, blouses and overcoats, but to provide the capacity, in equipment and materials, to meet the demand for clothing as this shows itself in the consumer market, where the citizens express their taste and choice. In other words, centrally determined disaggregated final output is *impossible,* except for a short priority list (which could include nuclear submarines, the collected works of Brezhnev and meat, but to be enforceable the priority list must be short). Furthermore, centrally determined final output is in principle *undesirable*, because it obstructs the micro-adjustments which have both economic and social-political significance; one must recall that doing exactly what one is told from a remote centre is not a socialist ideal, nor is it conducive to the stimulation of necessary local initiative.

The future general pattern of final consumption, in the opinion of most Soviet analysts, must be estimated by some mixture of 'normative' and 'market' analysis. Examples would be studies of medically desirable dietary patterns or climatically determined demand for heavy woollen goods on the one hand, and, on the other, analysis of actual supply-and-demand patterns reinforced by research on income-elasticities. The *existing* market cannot provide sufficient information, if only because some goods which people plainly want are not available, and considerable changes in demand for these and other goods (and services) will occur when and if they are provided in greater quantity. Thus a large increase in output of private cars will be accompanied by a relative fall in their price, and will lead to demand changes (both higher demand for items connected with car ownership, and a transfer of purchasing-power away from other things). Such calculations, for reasons already explained, would have to be in terms of aggregated groups (e.g. 'meat', 'pharmaceuticals', 'clothing', etc.), leaving for subsequent micro-adjustment the (very important) operational-current decisions which will disaggregate down to cleaning mops, aspirin and blue shirts actually produced by specific units and supplied to Tashkent or Archangel. We shall see how important this distinction is when we discuss economic reform.

There must also be included in the process of optimal plan formation data on technical coefficients, i.e. material and labour requirements for various kinds of output, modified as necessary by estimates of technological progress, the appearance of new methods and materials, changes in relative costs and so on. Also defence expenditures are given from outside the 'optimization' exercise, and foreign trade too must be included (at this stage of analysis we will abstract from foreign trade).

An important unsolved problem is that of the role of prices in the exercise. There is a wide range of opinions on this issue. The plan depends on relative prices which depend on the plan. Is it a matter of mutual interaction, to be handled, as Novozhilov argued, by a series of 'iterative approximations' as both plan and prices are modified and modify each other? Or is this a verbal evasion of the recognition that this is a vicious circle?

We cannot pretend (it would be arrogant to do so) to resolve perplexities which continue to attract some first-rate minds in the Soviet Union. High-level mathematical analyses have been undertaken by eminent men such as Shatalin, Volkonsky, Pugachev, Lurie, and Belkin, and also Konyus, which cannot be analysed here. Some Western scholars, notably Michael Ellman (1973) and Alfred Zauberman (1967 and 1975) have written at length on Soviet mathematical modelling. My object here has only been to acquaint the reader with the perplexities and also to give some sense of the ongoing debate, which does highlight real problems of both theory and practice.

A final consideration, of great practical significance, is the attitude of the party leadership to the new possibilities opened up by the mathematical school. Fedorenko heads not only the Institute of Mathematical Economics but also the entire economic 'sector' in the Academy of Sciences, which suggests high political support. At first it may have been due to the false idea that 'traditional' centralized planning could be preserved by computer. It seems clear that this cannot be so. However, Fedorenko's notion of optimal organizational structures, designed to ensure greater efficiency in carrying out policies which in the last analysis will still be the subject of political choice, must have attractions for leaders whose own political career can be made or broken by efficiency or inefficiency, and who may wish for their own reasons to identify with modern techniques. Some of Fedorenko's colleagues had for a time emphasized the need for a micro-economic market. This has to some extent been implied in the analysis of the last few pages, and this point will again be discussed in the context of reform models. But the 'market' concept is unpopular at the political-ideological level, and has been de-emphasized in recent years.

A decree published in July 1979, as well as making a number of changes in plan indicators (see addendum to Chapter 4), reformulated the procedures for the drafting of five-year plans. Gosplan is to submit outline proposals one and a half years before the start of the next quinquennium. When these are approved, Gosplan sends 'control figures' to ministries. These disaggregate them and send them down to 'their' *obyedineniya* and enterprises. These then put forward their own draft proposals as to their five-year programme, broken down by years. They then enter into preliminary discussions with the supply organs about prospective supply/delivery contracts. These plans go back to the ministries, which process them and send them back to Gosplan. The latter drafts a fuller and more detailed plan and submits it to the government at least five months before the plan is due to come into operation. This goes back to the ministries, and in the end the producing units are supposed to have stable plans for each year of the quinquennium, and are encouraged to make higher counterplans (*vstrechnye plany*). However, this timetable is already being ignored, since Brezhnev stated (*Pravda*, 28 November 1979) that Gosplan is to submit its outline proposals to the *Central Committee* in January 1980, for the 1981–5 plan.

CHAPTER 3

'CENTRALIZED PLURALISM': MINISTRIES AND REGIONAL PLANNING

WHAT IS 'CENTRALIZED PLURALISM?'

In the preceding chapter it was shown that centralized decision making in a large, modern industrially developed economy sets up an unmanageably large number of micro-economic inter-relationships. None the less, the economy functions, and this is only possible because the central planners do not in fact take the bulk of detailed decisions. We shall be seeing that many of the essential weaknesses of the Soviet-type economy arise because, within the logic of the model, the central planners *should* be taking them. Be this as it may, we must now consider how the inescapable delegation (devolution, decentralization) in fact occurs, and with what consequences.

One must distinguish between the planning organs as such and the management of nationalized industries. *Gosplan* is at the heart of the plan co-ordination process, along with *Gossnab*, *Gosstroy* (the State Committee on Construction) and other committees already referred to. They do not themselves command any productive enterprise. When we speak of 'the central planners', it is they and their analogues in the party's central committee apparatus whom we should have in mind.

The management of specific industries, as these are defined and de-limited for purposes of administrative convenience, falls to the economic ministries. We have already outlined their nature and functions in Chapter 1. Let us look more closely at their role. Let us take as examples say the Ministry of Coal Industry, or the Ministry for Construction of Oil and Gas Enterprises. The Minister and his deputies are super-managers, they are in formal charge of production in the sectors for which they are responsible. Just as they are not 'politicians', so they are best seen not as co-ordinator-planners but as the objects of planning-co-ordination. There are, however, a number of deputy-premiers in charge of groups of ministries, who can be said to act as sectoral co-ordinators. In a book of memoirs, an ex-minister refers to a deputy-premier who was supervising (the Russian word was *kuriruyet*) his ministry, and he mentions that he needed his permission if he wanted to leave Moscow to visit one of his ministry's enterprises (Smelyakov, 1975, p.170.)

It is important to note that the 'boundaries' of ministries seldom accord precisely with their designation. Thus some output of 'their' product will fall within enterprises subordinate to other ministries. (Indeed, a Soviet critic argues for giving the relevant ministry 'influence over the development of productive capacity of its sector in enterprises under other ministries'). (Drogichinsky, 1973, p.76.) We shall see why this is so in a moment. Conversely, a ministry is likely to have under it some productive activities which might be expected to fall under other ministries. Thus enterprises of almost any ministry might be making spare parts for tractors; some farm machinery is made in enterprises subordinate to the Ministry of Armaments; many consumers' goods, especially durables, are made in workshops (which used to be known as *tsekhi shirpotreba*, mass-consumption workshops) within heavy-industry enterprises whose principal output is something totally different.

It is surprising, but a fact, that 'metal-cutting machine tools and forging and pressing equipment are made in enterprises of twenty ministries, equipment for the food industry in eighteen, equipment for livestock in fourteen. . . . The share of specialized ministries in the production of many items covers 60–80 per cent, but for many products it is much lower: for washing machines only 38 per cent, refrigerators 37 per cent, plastic glass 38 per cent' (Dunayev, 1974, p.120.) The same source points to lack of component specialization. Only 1·5 per cent of the output of machinery and metal-working consists of components made at specialized enterprises, and the proportion is falling. (Dunayev, 1974, p.114.) No wonder so many items are made in small quantities within almost every industrial ministry. Enterprises within a construction ministry are often engaged on contract work erecting a factory, a hospital or a housing scheme which have nothing to do with the designation of the ministry, because they have spare labour and capacity in the given locality. As input statistics tend to follow administrative boundary-lines, the information necessary for input-output tables is often incomplete, and this is a frequent cause for complaint. (The same problem arises in the West also, but of course input-output data are of less operational significance there.)

However, despite all this 'untidiness', ministries do usually manage the bulk of the activities implied by their names. They play an important role in devising investment and technological change. They press the interests and problems of 'their' industry upon the central planners. The latter, in turn, can use the ministries as a means of reducing their own otherwise impossible work-load. Thus it is possible to allocate materials and other inputs *(fondy)* to the ministry, which, as we have seen, becomes the 'fund-holder' *(fondoderzhatel')* and sub-allocates to its enterprises. A production programme agreed with a ministry can also be further broken down by that ministry. Inputs made within a ministry for the use of its own enterprises can be omitted from the allocation schemes of *Gosplan* and *Gossnab*.

In practice things are not so simple. An allocation decision which 'attaches' *(prikreplyayet)* a supplier to a customer contains within itself an instruction to produce as well as to deliver, and this can originate with *Gossnab*, or in some cases *Gosplan*. This follows logically from the task of the central planners in allocating scarce inputs to 'the most important users: but who is most important? This must be decided by the planner who allocates the *fondy*.' (Petrakov, 1971, p.48.) Obviously, if several ministries 'consume' the allocated item, the ministries cannot be left to decide. The ministry's responsibility for plan-fulfilment implies that its enterprises receive the supplies necessary to fulfil the plan, yet the *snab* function belongs to *Gossnab*. It is not surprising that, as we saw in Chapter 2, ministries have tried to retain their own supply organs, and they and their enterprises continue to produce a variety of items, especially components, the supply of which from outside their own area of control cannot be relied upon. There are also many complaints about the limitations placed on ministries with regard to altering the plan targets of 'their' enterprises: for example, if (as we shall see) unfortunate consequences follow from expressing a plan target in tons, it is usually beyond the powers of the ministry to alter this, as its own plan is confirmed in such units, and a change would require the approval of *Gosplan*. The ministry is also bound by financial plans which the Ministry of Finance could be unwilling to alter. So critics speak of the need to 'increase the rights and responsibilities of ministries', that too often the ministry 'merely administers the enterprises under its control' instead of 'planning the sector so as to satisfy fully the requirements of the national economy for its output'. (Drogichinsky, 1973, pp.74, 76–7, 84.)

There has been discussion of making the economic ministry subject to *khozraschet*, in the sense that its own revenues, and money at its disposal for distribution among its enterprises (all within or for the purpose of the national-economic plan) becomes a percentage of profits made in its enterprises. This would interest the ministry in so exercising its powers as to make profits (or at least not issue orders which cause financial loss). The possession of financial resources linked with profits could increase the means by which the ministry could operate autonomously. This, however, is still at an early stage: in 1973 the Ministry of Instrument-Making, Automation Equipment and Control Systems was on this type of *khozraschet* on an experimental basis. (Drogichinsky, 1973, p.87.)

So, for the present the typical ministry has only limited authority and is *not* on *khozraschet*. Both these characteristics are explicable by the ministry's situation in the hierarchy. Being charged with administering a segment of a complex interconnected whole, in a largely non-market context, its production and allocation decisions must be systematically geared in to the requirements of the users of its products. But the users are mostly within other ministries, and these communicate their requirements and requests to the planning organs. So these organs must constantly 'interfere' with the ministries. The latter may be primarily super-managerial, but they operate within state plans which, though they participate in their drafting, they must enforce on their subordinates even if the financial consequences are adverse, and this can contradict the *khozraschet* principle, which applies to the managerial rather than the governmental-planning role.

In practice the sheer volume of work and of decisions in *Gosplan* places very considerable powers in the hands of the ministries. They are more likely than the planning agencies to have information about the existing situation and future possibilities. Their proposals, and their reaction to proposals made by 'their' enterprises, affects the plans and instructions which they receive. Those with experience of these matters speak of a constant tug-of-war between the ministries and *Gosplan*.

Ministries become interest groups. The motive may be aggrandizement, or empire-building, a motive familiar in Western writings both with regard to corporation executives and government officials. The head of a division, be it of a private concern or a ministry, can usually see very good reasons why more resources should be allocated to the sector for which he is responsible. Nor is he necesarily insincere. This principle extends to all kinds of Soviet ministries. Under conditions of relative scarcity, and with investment allocations virtually free, demands for more such allocations, combined with pressure to obtain them, cause *Gosplan* and the government many problems. Cuts have to be made. We shall see, when we discuss Soviet-type inflation, that these cuts are sometimes insufficient, in the sense that the total planned demand exceeds the means available. Since problems so often arise with supplies, the ministries tend to over-indent, and also, as we have seen, to set up workshops and procurement agencies to provide inputs for their enterprises, which causes duplication and also inefficiency, since these workshops are, as a rule, much less well equipped than the more modern units situated within the ministry responsible for the mass-production of the item in question. Costs would be lowered, labour productivity increased, if only there were sufficient supplies reliably available from the modern producing units. But, as will be repeatedly shown, reliable availability of supplies of inputs is very untypical of the Soviet system.

Ministerial empires, and upward pressures originating with them, are facts of economic and political life, and it is this which could be called 'centralized pluralism'. If the balance between economic ministries and the plan-co-ordinating agencies tilts too far in favour of the former, plans go seriously out of joint. It was Khrushchev's contention, in 1957, that this was the case, and he took the drastic step of abolishing the ministries.

However, before analysing the causes and consequences of Khrushchev's liquidation of ministries, we must examine regional planning.

REPUBLICS, REGIONS

The USSR is a federation, containing fifteen union republics. Each possesses a Council of Ministers, a number of economic ministries, and its own *Gosplan*. However, these union republics range in size from the giant Russian Federation (RSFSR), which stretches from the Baltic to the Pacific, to the tiny Estonia. The boundaries of the republics were drawn for reasons which have little or nothing to do with economics. Thus the Donets industrial and mining complex is divided between the RSFSR and the Ukraine.

Republics are represented as such in the central government, and a republican *Gosplan* drafts a plan which influences the central plan in some degree. They too, like the ministries, can and do act as pressure groups. Thus the government of Uzbekistan urges greater attention to the need to provide employment because there is rural overpopulation and also a high birth-rate. The influence of the republics over the content of plans is not easy to determine from the outside. The formal position is that, under the system of dual subordination, a republican *Gosplan* is simultaneously under 'its' Council of Ministers *and* under the all-union *Gosplan*. One surmises that the all-union *Gosplan* is firmly in charge, but there may well be room for argument and manoeuvre. The republican party machine can doubtless influence the centre, especially as their respective first secretaries are high in the all-union party hierarchy. As for the ministries, one must recall that three types exist: all-union (with no republican equivalent), union-republican (identically named ministries at the centre and in all or some of the republics), and republican. According to an official textbook, 'union-republican ministries . . . draft perspective and current plans . . . with the direct participation of the appropriate ministries of the union republics. All-union ministries . . . submit their draft perspective and current plans to the Council of Ministers of the appropriate union republics, examine their proposals and present their conclusions upon these, along with the draft plans, to the Council of Ministers of the USSR, copy to *Gosplan USSR*'. (Perov, 1973, p.61.)

Evidently the all-union ministries are in a stronger position to bypass the republic level, since there is no ministry (and therefore no expertise or 'power-point') at that level. It is therefore significant that the bulk of the economic ministries have been becoming all-union, and this trend continues. For instance in the interests of administrative streamlining, connected with the creation of industrial associations (obyedineniya), the Ministries of Chemical Industry and of Oil Industry were transformed into all-union ministries (Drogichinsky, 1973, p.76.) The Soviet source clearly suggests that the elimination of the republican rung on the hierarchical ladder was rational. As we shall see, there is some solid reason for this.

The task of allocation at republican level is largely carried out by the republican *glavki* ('chief departments') of the *all-union Gossnab*, and in practice many of the actual allocation decisions are made by sectoral chief departments of *Gossnab* at all-union level (e.g. *Soyuzglavmetall, Soyuzglavkhim, Soyuzglavpodshipnik*, respectively concerned with metals, chemicals and ball-bearings, and so on). Republican organs, in the words of a textbook issued in Minsk, 'allocate products of local significance with a restricted circle of users. In Belorussia, for instance, such products include peat, clay, chalk, quartz sand, etc.' (Mavrishchev, 1970, p.420.)

The USSR is also divided into eighteen 'large economic regions'. There are ten in the RSFSR and three in the Ukraine, and for purposes of regional planning the smaller republics are grouped together. For reasons of geographical location plus (one surmises) a sense of its own dignity, Moldavia is neither a 'large region' (it is too small) nor part of its neighbouring large region, which is one of the Ukraine's three. These regional planning bodies have no executive authority. Where they are not coextensive with republics there are advisory expert commissions, but their chief purpose is to act as a basis for regional planning at the centre. As we have seen, *Gosplan* contains a regional planning division. Its task is to consider regional specialization, economies of scale arising from complementarities, the bringing into use of the natural resources of regions, and so on. This is primarily a central responsibility, for several cogent reasons. Firstly, the centre is the only significant source of investment funds. Secondly, only there can one compare the relative advantages and costs of alternative regional development schemes. To give an example, there are major (indeed immense) mineral deposits in Yakutia, north-east Siberia. Naturally, any local authority or party secretary would extol the virtues of developing these resources and would seek to do so. (For example, see G. Chirgayev, Secretary of the Yakut Party, *EkG*, 1974, No. 32, p.5.) However, this area is climatically very unpleasant, largely empty of population, lacking means of transport, and extremely expensive to develop. Who is able to compare the costs of this and of other alternatives, and decide on the appropriate strategy for the complex development of Yakutia? Plainly not the Yakuts, it *must* be the centre.

Similarly, a great oil company cannot delegate a decision as to what resources should be put into developing the Alaskan oilfields into the hands of its Alaskan manager. Of course, these are big decisions.

Under more 'normal' Western competitive conditions, micro-decisions can very frequently be left to local commercial calculation: it pays to locate in West Lothian or Delaware, rather than in Argyll or New Jersey. We know from the ample Western literature on regional policy that this simple statement does not resolve the problem, but at least the model (and often the reality too) does resolve it, with no more imperfections than have to be tolerated in an imperfect world. But in the Soviet case, with capital resources allocated by the centre and price-and-profitability calculations playing a subordinate role, we can be certain that every local administrative authority will be seeking to press its own claims, and this cannot be left to its own adjudication, even in relatively small matters. In practical terms, it is not possible to delegate the micro-decisions and maintain control only over the big items: to adapt a Scottish saying, many a micro makes a macro, many a big magnitude is the sum of mini-decisions. Of course, there are various ways of delegating: thus one can (and does) allow expenditures of certain categories to be authorized by lower-level organs, subject to an overall 'ceiling' and to reference upwards if any single item exceeds so many thousands of roubles. But even this has to be limited very severely in the Soviet case, because monetary 'limits' have to be reconciled with the materials allocation system: thus the mere possession of the right to spend 100,000 roubles does not ensure that a local planning body or a management can acquire (say) steel pipe, ball-bearings, coal, plastics: it would in all probability need an allocation certificate from the appropriate *Soyuzglavsnabsbyt*.

Attempts are being made centrally, in *Gosplan*, to calculate regional inter-sector balances, as part of the endeavour to plan regional development, but, as might be expected, this runs into 'immense difficulties', since the available statistics fail to catch the 'imports' and 'exports' across regional boundaries and do not give sufficient data on material costs. (Dzarasov, 1974, p.83.) It is clear that any regional analysis, if it is to have practical consequences, must involve the joint activity of numerous economic ministries. At present, plans are formulated by the ministries, which put up their proposals to *Gosplan* and to the government and party. The ministries do not first discuss their ideas with regional organs, and nor do the latter discuss with the ministries. A Soviet critic urges that 'the *Gosplany* of Union republics and the local planning organs . . . should put their proposals for the development of enterprises of all-union and union-republican subordination to the appropriate ministries of the USSR, before their [the ministries'] plan projects are confirmed by the USSR *Gosplan*'. Also it is proposed that 'the complex plans for the development of the economies of the republics and large regions elaborated by the [central] planning organs be considered and decided in the USSR *Gosplan* with the participation of ministries and other all-union organs. This would facilitate fuller and more concrete reconciliation *(soglasovaniye)* with the ministries . . . of questions of developing this or that sector in its territorial aspect'. (Dzarasov, 1974, pp.89–90.) It would indeed! This passage suggests, or confirms, that the regional aspect, being detached from sectoral decision making, is not adequately considered. Other evidence, as we shall see, points in the same direction.

NATIONALITY POLICY

An important aspect of regional policy arises out of the multi-national aspect of the Soviet Union. In varying degrees, the nationalities are politically and socially conscious, and, while the formal rights of the republics are largely fictional, it remains the case that the Soviet leaders have to take into account the nationalities, if only to avoid a potentially dangerous sense of grievance. Furthermore, the ideology and policy of the regime proclaims the objective of evening out disparities between nationalities and regions, and also town and country. For historical-cultural reasons, as well as because of uneven resource endowment, there are wide differences between national republics. In terms of productivity or *per capita* income, Latvia and Estonia come out top, and the Central Asian republics are far behind.

Government policy affects the situation in a number of ways: through zoning of wage- and salary-scales, through fixing of prices of farm products, through budgetary redistribution to finance social services. By the above three routes, on balance, it can be said that resources have been redistributed towards the more backward areas. Thus wage-rates in Central Asia are similar to those in Central Russia, the prices of cotton, citrus fruits, grapes, tobacco, have been relatively favourable, the social services provided in Central Asia have been on the standard 'Soviet' scale, and budget statistics show that additional sums are earmarked for the budgets of the backward republics. (See Nove and Newth, 1967.) It can, of course, be argued that this is to the detriment of the more advanced republics, just as in Yugoslavia one frequently hears criticism from Slovenes and Croats about the diversion of resources to the backward south.

Less clear, however, is the issue of the location of investment, and of interpreting the trends in relative industrial growth. The available statistics are somewhat inconclusive. Thus huge percentage increases in industrial production of the most backward republic of Turkmenia are based on a very low starting-point and relate to few industries. By contrast, the low percentage increases recorded by Azerbaydzhan are explicable by a relative decline (through resources exhaustion) of what was by far its biggest item of industrial production – oil. The fact remains, as can readily be seen from the statistics, that the Central Asian republics are still largely rural and lack heavy industry; indeed, most of their textile raw materials are utilized in factories in Central Russia. The biggest new investments in major industrial complexes seem to be within the RSFSR, or to a lesser extent in the Ukraine.

Soviet regional and nationality policy could be the subject of long books, and here the object is simply to draw attention to some of the key factors involved. One that is familiar in other countries with regional problems is the contradiction between economic advantage and the 'regional' objective, a contradiction which partially explains the inequalities which it is the 'regional policy' objective to diminish. Thus the Central Asian republics lack fuel (except gas), they are remote from the principal consuming centres, transport costs are high. Economies of scale and complementarities are more readily to be found in or near existing areas of industrial concentration. Planners must also take the location of natural resources into account, and these point (for instance) to Siberia rather than to Tadzhikistan as priority areas for large-scale investments. It is true that Central Asia and Azerbaydzhan are noteworthy for high birth-rates and for having larger potential labour reserves, much of them in rural areas, than the industrial centres or (especially) Siberia. The Central Asian nationalities are unwilling to move out of their areas, and, paradoxically, there is some Russian migration into Central Asia, not, it appears, because of deliberate 'colonialism', but because in terms of climate and supply of vegetables and fruit it is better to live there than in Siberia, where labour is urgently needed. It should be added that, according to some sociological surveys, factory jobs in Central Asia sometimes go to Russian immigrants because of the reluctance of traditionally minded natives to leave their rural society, to move to strange cities where the language is likely to be Russian, so that new industries are 'staffed in the main by people from other republics', as referred to, *inter alia*, by Kostakov (*PKh*, 1974, No. 7, p.77.)

In analysing or criticizing the Soviet record in this field, it is important to adopt reasonable criteria. This is sometimes forgotten by enthusiastic nationalists. In their eyes, the centre cannot do right. If investment in their area does occur, it is in order to exploit the inhabitants and to take away their resources. If investment does not occur, then the area is being deliberately left underdeveloped, as a backward appendage. If *per capita* income is below average, this can be cited as proof of ill-intentioned policy. If it is above average, as in the Baltic states, then they are dragged down by their association with a more backward Union. Some of these arguments may be correct, of course. Thus it may well be that Latvia (say) suffers disadvantages from being subject to 'all-Soviet' wage- and salary-scales. However, one should recall that nationalist aims can, and often do, contradict economic advantage. Thus the Lodz area of Poland benefited from being a relatively advanced part of a vast Russian-imperial market before 1914, and it is certainly arguable that, economically speaking, the peoples of the Austro-Hungarian empire, for instance the Czechs, would have benefited from its retention as a big free-trade area. None of this affected the desire of the Poles, the Czechs, etc. that their countries be independent. It may be possible to demonstrate that Turks would be better off materially if they joined the USSR, or Mexicans if they were part of the United States. It does not follow that either Turks or Mexicans desire, or should desire, any such outcome.

An interesting issue is raised by mineral rights. Let us imagine that the Bashkir ASSR were an independent state. It happens to produce oil. If it joined OPEC, charged high prices and utilized the resultant revenue wholly within Bashkiria, no doubt its inhabitants would gain. So the fact of membership of the USSR, and the transference of oil revenues to the all-Union budget, *could* be presented as evidence of the exploitation of Bashkiria. However, this argument has weaknesses. Most of us would probably agree that the huge revenues of Kuwait and Abu Dhabi, arising from their sovereignty over oil-bearing areas, are disproportionate, and unfair to the majority of Arabs who live in other countries. Where does one stop? Should Scotland keep all the oil revenue from off-shore installations? Should the oil-bearing district of Venezuela retain all the oil revenues of Venezuela? If some identifiably different nationality or tribe inhabits the area in question, does this change the answer? If so, why?

All this is not to say that Soviet nationality policy is good, let alone optimal. There can indeed be strongly felt grievances especially of a non-economic sort (on cultural matters, say), and economic-political protests may relate not mainly to the question of the content of decisions as to the fact that they are taken in Moscow, i.e. the issue can be one of autonomy, of independence. The extent of centralization, the by-passing of the republican 'level', has undoubtedly increased since 1964. There may also be loss imposed by being cut off, except where Moscow allows it, from foreign markets and foreign sources of supply. One must, however, discuss these and similar matters in the knowledge that nationalist economics, and regional economics too, raise issues in all societies which are controversial, contradictory and too readily the subject of propagandist assertion. This is so in 'capitalist' countries. It is even more so where almost every investment decision is taken by political authorities. In *every* multi-national or multi-tribe state, issues of economic 'rationality' can conflict, and often do conflict, with national aspirations, especially if the state plays a major role in the economy.

REGIONAL PROBLEMS: THE SOVNARKHOZ EXPERIENCE

It is possible to reinforce generalizations about the problems of regional planning in the USSR by studying the years 1957–64, in which an attempt was made to 'regionalize' the entire system.

This reform was apparently touched off by the errors contained in the sixth five-year plan (which was to have covered the years 1956–60). It had been adopted by the party Congress in February 1956, but was found to be unbalanced, overambitious, unworkable. At the Central Committee plenum of December 1956, it was decided to revise the plan. To ensure more effective co-ordination, it was also decided to alter the administrative planning structure, by placing the economic ministries under the authority of the body which at this time was in charge of current operational planning, *Gosekonomkommissiya* (see page 46, above), whose head at this time was M. G. Pervukhin.

This had its political aspect, as we shall see, but it was felt that the errors of the plan were in some sense due to the separate existence of powerful ministries. It also can be surmised that Khrushchev's power to interfere in matters economic was being undermined. Indeed in the first published version of the proposals even agriculture was placed under Pervukhin's aegis.

In the spring of 1957, Khrushchev defeated his party enemies (the so-called 'anti-party group', whose leaders were Molotov, Kaganovich and Malenkov, but with which Pervukhin was associated). But he faced the same problem, that of ensuring co-ordination in the face of ministerial particularism and empire-building. He argued that there was excessive duplication in component manufacture and supply organization, there were unnecessary cross-hauls (as when ministries moved parts and components all over the country to 'their' enterprises, instead of utilizing local capacity which happened to fall under another ministry). We were told of river steamers owned by ministry A sailing empty on their return journeys, instead of carrying loads for factories under ministry B. The weaknesses of regional policy making, to which we have already devoted attention and which are a consequence of sectorial-ministerial organisation, were duly stressed. The point was also made that utilization of by-products was impeded by ministerial boundary-lines. Finally, the concentration of authority in Moscow was held responsible for bureaucratic delays in taking decisions.

To overcome these weaknesses, Khrushchev adopted a radical solution: he abolished the economic ministries. With minor exceptions, they vanished. Their administrative functions were transferred to 105 (later 103, still later 47) regional economic councils, *sovety narodnogo khozyaystva*, or *sovnarkhozy*, and these in turn were subordinated to the union republics. In the case of the smaller republics, their boundaries were coextensive with a *sovnarkhoz*. Their functions were confined to industry and construction; thus they were not concerned with agriculture, transport and retail trade, save in so far as these were auxiliary to industry (e.g. farms run by industrial concerns, factory canteens, etc.). The *plan* was to be determined centrally with *Gosplan*, the key body (*Gosekonomkommissiya* was abolished). The *sovnarkhozy* would exercise their authority over the enterprises in their region to see that the plan was fulfilled, utilizing to the full the advantages seen in regional co-ordination.

The diagnosed weaknesses of the ministerial empires certainly existed, and indeed they exist today. It seems likely that co-ordination was, in those days, weaker than it had once been, under the impact of two events. One was the arrest of the senior planner, Voznesensky, in 1949, followed by his shooting, and accompanied by the weakening of *Gosplan*, which had been his power-centre. The other was the reorganization already undertaken under Khrushchev. Be this as it may, it is the unanimous view of Soviet and foreign commentators that the *sovnarkhoz* experiment was a failure. It was a failure from which much may be learned.

Let us recall that the *sovnarkhozy* were supposed to implement plans adopted by the centre. However, their functions included the drafting of plans (which inevitably affected their content), organizing their fulfilment, supervising supply contracts and deliveries and many other matters, which were not covered by precise instructions – and we have seen repeatedly that many matters are not and cannot be covered by precise central instructions. What could guide them in taking decisions? In an article written only two months after the adoption of the *sovnarkhoz* reform, this author argued that distortions were certain to occur and so they did (Nove, 1957a.)

Sovnarkhozy were judged by the fulfilment of plans, and their officials were bound, therefore, to seek so to administer their fulfilment as to ensure success by this criterion, i.e. to divert to their region's needs any resource not earmarked by the centre for outside customers. Their own draft plans, especially investment plans, concentrated on the given region's needs, neglecting other considerations, and this for several predictable reasons. Firstly, the *sovnarkhoz* officials were held responsible for their region, not for others. Secondly, they knew their own region's needs best. Thirdly, ministerial empire-building was bound to be replaced by regional empire-building. If Khrushchev hoped that the provincial party officials would impose the all-union as against the regional view, then he was doomed to disappointment: local party officials were also judged by the success of their area of responsibility, and were as likely as any *sovnarkhoz* official to divert resources to local needs if no directly contrary order prevented it. This 'deviation' became known as *mestnichestvo*, 'localism' or 'regionalism'.

The trouble can be simply explained. Each of the original *sovnarkhozy* covered on average 1 per cent of total Soviet industrial production. The factories controlled by any *sovnarkhoz* drew their supplies from dozens or even hundreds of factories or mines located outside the given region, and supplied products to numerous factories and wholesalers similarly located. *Gosplan* decided major inter-regional deliveries and these were incorporated in the plan. But even then *sovnarkhozy* gave priority to deliveries within the region, necessitating in April 1958 a decree requiring them to give priority to customers outside their region, with threats of punishment in case of non-compliance. Yet innumerable press complaints about the disruption of supply links across regional borders did not cease. And, of course, many items and transactions were not covered by precise central instructions.

An assemblage of examples would fill many closely printed pages. They show that 'regionalism' was a built-in deviation, which required to be repressed by invoking non-economic weapons. The weapons themselves were sometimes irrational. For, given that some material was unexpectedly short, it is no more logical to give priority to customers situated outside the given area, so that the entire burden of shortage falls on users within the region, than to do the opposite. (*PEG* 19, September, 1958.) However, the 'regionalist' deviation was not cured by the 1958 decree, as the same complaints reappeared again and again.

There were many other instances. *Sovnarkhozy*, like enterprises, were guided by their success indicators, rather than the requirements of the customer. After 1957 a wide range of consumer goods was not subject to central allocation, and *sovnarkhozy* issued orders to curtail their production if local needs were met, since they could have no idea about the needs of outside users and had no incentive or interest to supply them. This explains the numerous complaints about *sovnarkhozy* which 'on various excuses stop production of much-needed cultural-domestic consumer durables', mentioned in decisions of the Central Committee of the Communist Party (*Pravda* 17 July, 1960 and *Pravda* 6 September, 1958) and also in many other sources. What mattered it to (say) the Tula *sovnarkhoz* that its hammers or tin-openers were in urgent demand in Orel and Voronezh? If any plan was more easily fulfilled by the use of the productive capacity for some other purpose, then it was used for some other purpose. In fact, it proved necessary to *forbid* the *sovnarkhozy* to cut production of consumers' goods without special permission from superior authority, in the decree published on 9 August 1960.

In putting forward development plans, the *sovnarkhozy* were equally unable to take into account the impact of their plans on the economy as a whole. For example, while economists published articles seeking to prove that the lignite in the Tula area was high-cost and inefficient, the chairman of the Tula *sovnarkhoz* attacked this view, and urged the adoption of a plan which envisaged a large increase in production of this lignite (*Pravda* 17 August, 1957; Somov, *VEk* 1957, No. 2, pp. 29–33; Chukhanov, *VEk*, 1958, No. 9, pp.42–4.) This was an aspect of the autarchic tendencies, or 'empire-building', familiar among the former ministries, but now transferred to a territorial rather than industrial-sector basis. The built-in tendency towards 'regionalism' necessitated the preservation or reinforcement of strict centralization. The right of *sovnarkhozy* to redistribute resources between different industrial sectors was in fact severely limited, in order to prevent any initiative which was inconsistent with centralized resource allocation. This led, for example, to complaints from the Karaganda *sovnarkhoz* that it was forbidden to shift funds from coal to building materials, and from non-ferrous metals to coal, although this was needed to fulfil plans. (*PEG*, 30 March, 1958.) By a decision in 1959, *sovnarkhozy* were strictly forbidden to issue allocated materials to their enterprises without a *naryad* from above. (Baranov and F. Liberman *PKh*, 1959, No. 6 pp. 39–40 and Podgorny, *Pravda*, 12 January, 1961 concerning the disposal of some of the products of local – i.e. non-*sovnarkhozy* – industry by the republics.)

This in turn led to complaints about 'excessive centralization' of the supply and disposals system, which in fact predetermined much of the enterprises' activities over the heads of 'their' *sovnarkhozy*. The representative of the Estonian *sovnarkhoz* complained that only 0·2 per cent of the production of his republic was allocated by republican organs; all the rest was under the control of Moscow. (*EkG*, 5 January, 1962.) In this respect recentralization continued steadily, especially after 1960. A number of all-union bodies had production and supply functions, and this gave rise to much administrative overlap and confusion in the localities.

The consequence of a regional structure of this character must be, and was, a reconcentration of effective decision making (above the level of minor details) at the centre. But, since the ministerial form of centralization was abolished in the reform of 1957, this means a recreation of central planning and administration on a new basis. This process led to a proliferation of central agencies.

Further difficulties arose because the enterprise management faced several masters. Nominally its 'master' was the *sovnarkhoz*, but in practice the central planners expanded their functions to fill the vacuum created by the abolition of the ministries. Yet as the planners' own divisions were based on *products*, and many enterprises produced several different items, there was no central authority which could view the enterprise's output and potential as a whole. There were a great many complaints from confused and frustrated managers, who received orders from any different quarters.

Finally, there was another and very important weakness. In the original 1957 reform decree, no provision was made for the consideration at the centre of the common problems of each industrial sector. Again, nature abhors a vacuum, and so the task at first fell to sector divisions within *Gosplan*. Soon there were set up a number of industrial-sectoral state committees, which had the task of devising technical policies and investment schemes. However, such bodies had no operational control over enterprises. They were in a much weaker position than were ministries to administer the steel industry or the agricultural machinery industry, say, in the light of all-union requirements for these products. Experience showed that, given the nature of Soviet-type planning, the gain which accrue from a form of organization which stresses the common problems of one region is notably inferior in its effectiveness to one which is based on the common problems of industrial sectors. In both instances there are bound to be difficulties with boundary-lines, with empire-building, with co-ordination. But because the entire logic of the system is based upon conscious decisions about needs, *and* because a modern industrial economy is an interconnected whole, the regional control model must break down. Only the centre can identify need, only the centre can attempt to ensure that these needs be met by a complex co-ordinated effort of production units located in many regions.

In other words, if there is to be decentralization, the periphery must have a criterion for decision making other than the central plan. The reform discussions, which we will be analysing later, return to this point again and again. These discussions hardly mention the role of regional-territorial authorities. There are sound reasons for this. Either *management* can discover through negotiation and market research what its customers need (this is the Hungarian model in essence), or the *central* planners must do so and tell the management. Investment decisions of any major kind, involving supplies to the whole country, must be the responsibility of a national authority (even in Hungary, as we shall see), but we are here discussing current planning, concerned primarily with the utilization of existing capacity. The object of so long an apparent digression into the now-abandoned *sovnarkhoz* experiment is that it affords living proof of the snags and disadvantages of regionalization as a solution to the problems posed by the impossibility of centralization. If a reader feels that such conclusions are disproved by Chinese experience, the answer is that China's decentralization is based upon a much less developed economy, in which resources within a province are used mainly to satisfy the requirements of that province. This can be and is done in the USSR too. If timber in the Archangel area is used to make wooden toys for children in the Archangel area, there is no need for all-union organs to be involved at all. However, in a modern industrial economy these local industries producing only for the local market with locally produced inputs are a minor segment of the whole. In China too, the output and allocation of products of large-scale industry of national significance are centrally planned.

EXTERNAL ECONOMIES AND COMPLEMENTARITIES

One of the traditional claims made for a socialist economy is its ability to surmount considerations of micro-profitability and to view decisions from the standpoint of the common weal. Such claims have been made in the USSR, by Stalin and by lesser mortals.

We must recognize that external economies and diseconomies are important, and also that contemporary orthodox theory tends either to disregard them or to underestimate their significance, probably because they disrupt the picture of a free-enterprise, market-based optimum. We shall see that some Soviet reformers have also been guilty of neglect of this factor.

However, when we examine the Soviet record, we find that the advantages of central consideration of the interest of the totality are seldom realized. It is worth inquiring into the reasons.

Some of these have been indicated already earlier in this chapter. The evidence is clear. Externalities can arise whether or not there is private ownership, they can arise because of the fragmentation of decision making, between firms and organizations and also *within* large firms and organizations (as between sub-units and departments). This is so in West and East alike. It is an inescapable diseconomy of scale, which it is a struggle to mitigate or minimize. The motivation of the individuals concerned is a factor, but the problem would still be there even if all the human beings involved were angels (or the Marxist equivalent of socialist angels).

The theory of centralized marketless socialism requires that all be considered in the context of all, yet this is physically impossible. Hence 'centralized pluralism', i.e. a division of the centralized economy into quasi-autonomous units. Each of these must be given objectives, and be judged by whether, and how, these objectives are realized. Each administrative unit – sectoral, functional, territorial – knows its own needs, has a sense of their importance and priority. The needs of others, the consequence for them of action or inaction, are outside its line of vision, or seem of lesser significance. It is only very partly a matter of motivation. Even if one were to assume a universal tendency towards unselfishness, which is not too realistic, the fact remains that on one's own level one is usually unable to judge what are by definition *external* effects. To take an example, many an action can benefit some and harm other enterprises, regions, citizens. It is at higher administrative or political levels, in the light of information collected and assessed at these levels, that a cost-benefit analysis can be made. It is unreasonable to expect more of management at any level than that it should seek to fulfil plan-instructions received, keep its customers or consumers reasonably satisfied (though we shall see that this may conflict with the goal of reporting the fulfilment of plan-instructions) and to put forward proposals and requests based upon its intimate knowledge of its own area of responsibility.

Evidently, externalities can arise howsoever the performance of enterprises, ministries and other economic organs is evaluated. Whether it is profits, gross value of output, sales, net product or whatever, it is always possible to achieve these objectives without regard for externalities, these being precisely the effects which do *not* show up in the given unit's performance indicators. A naive reader may say: but surely the correct criterion for evaluating performance should take into account the external effects, the good of society. To this there is a simple answer: of course it should, but the whole problem is how to, and who should, define and identify these things. We shall have much more to say about this in Chapter 4.

The Soviet record on pollution, for instance, has been as bad as that of most capitalist countries, since industrial enterprises and planners pursue plan-objectives (produce more at minimum cost), which make anti-pollution measures as 'unprofitable' as for any Western corporation. The cutting down of the most easily accessible forests, in the interests of fulfilling short-term plans, is another (much-criticized) consequence of the way the system operates. Local soviets have as many difficulties with reconciling factory-building with the needs of town planning as any Western local authority. Ministries planning new investments are reluctant to locate them in small towns or in new and remote areas, because they see economies of scale, and economies also in social overhead capital, in erecting new plant in already highly developed areas. This contradicts regional planning objectives, and arises from familiar reasons: the ministry tries to present a project that minimizes those costs which it can identify, those that accrue to it. The longer term problem of (say) the development of empty spaces in Siberia, or the provision of employment in small towns in the Ukraine, is not its responsibility.

Here is a powerful indictment by a Soviet critic. 'Natural resources are still wastefully used . . . . Often up to 40–50 per cent of reserves of coal, oil, potash, remain in the workings. Much gas is wasted or burned off. A significant portion of non-ferrous and precious metals is lost during mining, enrichment and processing.' Heaps around mines, enrichment plant and factories contain so many valuable materials that they are sometimes called 'ores lying on the surface'. In some regions systematic over-cutting of timber [takes place, which affects climate, causes soil erosion . . . . Wasted timber] rotting or burnt and almost unutilized as materials, amounts to half of the annual value of cut timber. The reserves of pure water diminish; in many industrial regions there is a grave shortage. At the same time rivers are intolerably polluted: three quarters of industrial liquid waste *(stochnykh vod)* pour into waterways without any cleaning. The pollution of water leads to the destruction of fish . . . and so on. (Krasovsky, 1970, p.9.)

Needless to say, the centre takes corrective action. Thus regulations are passed banning new industrial construction in the largest cities, requiring smoke-abatement, or limiting river pollution. But such measures are taken in the West also. The Soviet source went on to point out that fines, when levied, are paid out of enterprise funds, i.e. by the state to iself, and that the guilty managers in practice suffer no effective penalty when rules designed to stop pollution are ignored. (Krasovsky 1970, p.9.) The point being made here is that there is as yet no evidence that the system is *better* able to cope with these problems by reason of its centralized nature and of public ownership. This is a consequence of the pluralist aspect of centralized pluralism.

Paradoxically, this can create problems of co-ordination which are easier to overcome under Western imperfect competition even though Western orthodox micro-economics neglects all this. (Nove, 1973.) This can be seen if one compares the West Siberian oil development with that of Alaska. The practical questions to be solved had a good deal in common. The area was remote and largely uninhabited. To develop oil production the co-operative effort of a great many sectors and production units was necessary. Mining machinery, building materials, pipe, many kinds of construction, workers' housing, means of transportation, fuel and heating equipment, road construction, retail-trade establishments and much else besides had to be provided. Many of these things were required in a particular sequence, dictated by technical necessity. In the Western case, a large oil company would plan the operation, carry out some of the tasks itself, place orders for the many inputs required and employ large numbers of sub-contractors. Once the initial decision to proceed with the project has been taken, the subsequent decisions are 'consequential'. By this I do not mean there are no choices, as there may be many choices. But they are made in the context of, and by reference to, the project as a whole. The criteria by which they are judged relate to the project, and the judging is done by the corporation which acts as principal.

In the Soviet case, however, the ministerial system impedes these arrangements. This was pointed out in several articles published in the journal of the Economics Institute of the Siberian branch of the Academy of Sciences. Its director, A. G. Aganbegyan, set out the issue with clarity. 'Construction work must be looked at not in terms of its own effectiveness (*effektivnost'*), but from the standpoint of total efficiency in the context of those projects which are being constructed on the basis of the given investment programme . . . . Unfortunately this elementary principle . . . is by no means always observed. . . .' He went on to argue that 'a second requirement of systems analysis consists in examining not each item separately, but within a group of interlinked multi-sector objectives. The investment programme must ensure the systematized and balanced completion of projects. Often this does not happen, especially in Siberia, in the case of large economic complexes, because, as a rule, each project belongs to its own department.' (*EkO*, 1971, No. 6, p.7.) Another economist, V. Krasovsky (*EkO*, 1971, No. 6, p.22), gave an example of a timber complex which is the 'responsibility' of eight different departments or ministries, and that 'therefore departmental demarcation lines, the absence of a complex inter-departmental construction programme, of complex regional plans, is a cause of serious losses in the implementation of large-scale investment projects'.

Why the contrast with Alaska? Because with the exception of construction ministries there is no principal-and-contractor-subcontractor relationship. The oil development is the primary responsibility of the Ministry of Oil Industry, timber of the Ministry of Timber Industry. But they do not command the numerous enterprises which are subordinate to other ministries and whose collaboration is essential if the projects are to be completed. These other ministries have other urgent tasks, and are answerable for their overall plan objective to the government and party. Whatever success criteria they have for 'their' enterprises, they are not related to the total oil or timber project. Nor can they be so related, unless they are, so to speak, under command of whosoever is the principal *responsible* for the project in question. Contractual relationships are not enough, because in the Soviet system they play a subordinate role, being derived from, made by reference to, plan-obligations. So the practical conclusion of the critics is to recommend the setting up of an authority charged with the project (e.g. Siberian oil) with power over the other enterprises involved, regardless of their ministerial subordination. (This presents its own difficulties, as the enterprises may have other duties, unconnected with *this* project.)

Some reader may reach the conclusion that this is a plea for the creation of regional bodies with power, a species of neo-*sovnarkhozy*, and that this contradicts the argument advanced earlier in this chapter. However, this is not really so. A West Siberian oil trust with power over its contractors and subcontractors is a very different thing to a territorial economic authority with power over all economic activities in West Siberia.

This example shows, yet again, how nominal all-round centralization can frustrate itself by its own, administratively inescapable, fragmentation. *Ad hoc* arrangements have to be made, in particular cases, to cope with the resulting problems. In Stalin's time, and sometimes since, this has taken the form of sending Central Committee plenipotentiaries, and there exists a procedure to keep a special eye on projects of especial importance *(osobo vazhnykh stroyek)*.

THE OBYEDINENIYE

This word, as we have seen, means industrial 'association' or 'union', and a possibly better term is 'corporation'. Since none of these are really adequate, we will go on using the Russian word. The more so because the word covers a wide variety of bodies. At one extreme we are dealing with the equivalent of a ministerial department *(glavk)* with all-union responsibilities. Or it may be a very large enterprise (sometimes known by that designation, *predpriyatiye*, sometimes as a *kombinat*). Finally it may be a merger of a number of small enterprises in a particular republic or region. There are other types too.

This makes generalization a difficult task. It is best to begin by explaining why the *obyedineniye* was brought into being, and why it has appeared in so many different guises.

One reason is *administrative economy*. The existence of numerous enterprises of very diverse sizes contributed to the existence of a complex 'ladder' or hierarchical subordination. It also complicated the task of operational planning. It is necessary to 'reduce the number of economic links. . . . Enterprises entering into an *obyedineniye* had previously to be administered by higher organs. . . .' A merger 'reduces several-fold the number of units which have to be planned and administered from the centre, and frees ministries and departments from a vast number of petty operational questions.' (Dunayev, 1974, pp.228–9, 231.) The same point is made more emphatically in this way: 'The number of links grows rapidly with the expansion of production and acceleration of scientific-technical progress. It has been shown that the number of economic links increases, other things being equal, at least to the square of the rate of output. Therefore, a twofold increase in total output would correspond to a four-fold increase in economic links. [This] leads to an increase in the number of administrative levels, and of the size of the administrative-managerial apparatus . . . The most effective way is to concentrate production, increase the size of enterprises and reduce their number.' (Drogichinsky, 1973 pp.77–8.)

A second reason is to secure the advantages of *economies of scale*, especially through specialization. Sometimes this could be achieved by placing successive processes under the same management, so that, for instance, one small factory makes heels for shoes which are assembled in another nearby factory. Alternatively one factory can specialize on the production of one type of shoes.

A third objective is to *facilitate technical progress,* by linking research and production more closely together, which is hardly possible if enterprises are small, and by creating 'scientific-and-production' *obyedineniya.*

Fourthly, it is a means of promoting the status and enhancing the powers of management of *very large enterprises* by giving it the functions performed by the ministerial chief department *(glavk),* which brings one back to administrative economy, since the *glavk* can then be abolished.

Fifthly, it was hoped to achieve 'the consolidation of the given sector', in those numerous instances in which output of some products was scattered among different ministries as was mentioned by Dunayev (1974, p.120).

Last, but not least, one must consider that *obyedineniya* disturb the existing ministerial system and could alter the distribution of economic power between ministerial departments, managers and party officials. It is therefore not surprising to learn that this reform has been obstructed, delayed, resisted, and that the 'old' system may survive in spite of it.

Let us now look at the different types of *obyedineniya,* bearing in mind that changes may still be in progress.

There is, first, the *production obyedineniya,* also known as 'primary' *(pervichnogo zvena),* distinguished by being in charge of production processes. These in turn can be subdivided into:

(a) Very large enterprises or *kombinaty* 'promoted' to *obyedineniya* status. Example: the great nickel enterprise at Noril'sk.

(b) A large enterprise which absorbs other and smaller enterprises in its own area, which then become its branches *(filialy).* In these instances, the director of the large enterprise, redesignated 'general director', assumes authority over the smaller ones. Example: *Elektrosila* (electrical machinery) and *Skorokhod* (footwear), both based in Leningrad but both with *filialy* factories in other towns as well as Leningrad itself (Dunayev, 1974, pp.150–1), so that *Skorokhod* now includes all the footwear factories in northwest Russia.

(c) A merger of numerous small enterprises. This was sometimes designated by the term *firma,* which was used in 1961 when small footwear factories in Lvov were joined together. In practice these three types cannot always be clearly distinguished. Thus in type (c) one enterprise was usually designated as the principal one *(golovnoye).* All three types are usually 'serviced' by research institutes.

These 'production' or 'primary' *obyedineniya* can also differ from one another in two other respects. The first is in the degree of autonomy of their constituent parts. Sometimes there remain 'enterprises' *(predpriyatiya)* within it, still operating on *khozraschet* and with juridical status and somewhat reduced powers. Sometimes they are reduced to the status of mere workshops *(tsekhi)*, with authority and bank balance more strictly centralized in the *obyedineniye* management. Again there are variations within variations: thus one Leningrad *obyedineniye* treats its *filialy* as mere workshops if located in the city, but grants more autonomy to those in Pskov or Vologda.

The second difference relates to the position of the *obyedineniye* in relation to 'its' ministry. It may be so large as to acquire the status of a ministerial *glavk*, as in the case of Noril'sk. More usually it is under the command of either the *glavk* or of the other species of *obyedineniye*, which may be called 'administrative' to distinguish it from 'productive', and to which we will now turn.

There are many sub-species of the administrative type.

(a) *The all-union obyedineniye*, which may replace the *glavk* and take responsibility for the production of all or most of a product nationally. Some are being set up within the Ministries of Automation Equipment, Chemical Industries . . . Another instance is *Soyuzbumaga*, within the Ministry of Pulp and Paper, responsible for paper production. (Dunayev, 1974, p.159.) An early example of the all-union type is the well-known gramophone-record firm *Melodiya.*

(b) *Republican obyedineniya*, in charge of production within a republic under the authority of a republican ministry, or as a subdivision of an all-union ministry or an all-union *obyedineniye.*

(c) *Territorial obyedineniya*, for instance within the coal or electricity industries.

All these types may have under them either the production *obyedineniya* or old-style enterprises. One should also bear in mind that at the time of writing (January 1976) within many ministries the 'normal' enterprise and the traditional lines of subordination have survived with little alteration. As late as March 1976 *obyedineniya* of all types still produced less than a quarter of total industrial output. (Brezhnev, *Pravda,* 25 February 1976.)

The Ministry of Pulp and Paper has published a reorganization scheme, which reduces by merger the number of 'enterprises and (production) *obyedineniya* from 186 to 103, sets up four all-union *obyedineniya*, but over 20 per cent of output will continue to be undertaken in enterprises directly under the ministry'. (Galanshin, *EkG* 1976, No. 19, p.6.) This seems an exercise in streamlining rather than a change in principle.

The decree of 1973 stressed the need for diversity – but ordered all ministries to prepare and submit reorganization schemes, and we are told that some of these have been rejected. (*Pravda*, 31 July 1974.) There is an inter-departmental commission in *Gosplan* studying experience and making recommendations in the light of this. (*Pravda*, 23 May 1975.)

The bemused reader may be asking: why all this detail? It is not included here for its own sake, but for two reasons: firstly, the 'traditional' presentation of the role of the ministry and of the enterprise requires to be re-formulated in the light of changes now in progress, changes which have their analogy in earlier and also current reforms in East Germany, Poland and elsewhere. Secondly, and surely more important, these reforms, which are still very much in the formative stage, are a response to real problems and perplexities, and represent the Soviet leaders' chosen alternative to market-type decentralization. The bewildering variety of organizational forms reflects – and *should* reflect – the variety of planning and operational problems. One valid criticism of the Soviet system has been a tendency to standardization of administrative structure. It is inherently improbable that the right way to run the steel industry is also suitable for clothing, cabbages or children's toys, or, for that matter, nickel mining. In the West there is a great variety of types of corporations, with widely differing hierarchies and degrees of managerial autonomy.

The idea, certainly, is to give to these industrial complexes, at various levels, a flexibility, and a means of responding to user requirements and to technical progress, which the traditional 'ministerial' system lacks. The varied forms in which smaller factories and establishments are related to the large ones, have their analogue in the Western corporation: subcontractors, wholly owned subsidiaries and the like. It is also hoped to reduce the work-load on the central planners by giving them fewer units to plan for: economy of planning effort through merger.

These changes are still in progress, and may be successfully resisted. Ministerial *glavki* may simply be re-labelled all-union *obyedineniya* and continue to operate as before, with the same personnel. Many reforms have in the past caused little change. This is what *Pravda* (editorial, 23 May 1975) described as a 'tendency to confine it all to changing of name-plates', i.e. to altering labels on the doors of the same officials. Some *obyedineniya* have been abolished because of (real or alleged) physical difficulties. Nor has their status been properly established.

'*Obyedineniya* up till now have insufficient rights. . . . In their legal position they almost in no way differ from any enterprise, even the smallest. Ministries and departments usually utilize towards big *obyedineniya* the same methods of control as towards enterprises, usually subordinating them to *glavki*. Nor do the *obeydineniya* differ in any way from other enterprises in respect of the indicators centrally planned. Their material and financial resources do not reflect such specific features of the work of *obyedineniya* as specialization and reconstruction of production. Directing personnel of enterprises are not interested in the creation of *obyedineniya*, since salaries do not differ from those of directors of ordinary enterprises, despite the sharp increase in volume of work and degree of responsibility.' (Fedorenko, 1973, p.112 and Drogichinsky 1973, p.82.) Judging from various discussions about the rights and obligations of *obyedineniya* published since the appearance of the book from which the above quotations are taken, there seems to have been little change in this situation.

So it is far from clear just what all these changes entail in practice. For purposes of the analysis that follows, the word 'enterprise' will be used to cover also those firms and 'primary *obyedineniya*' which are in effect large enterprises, i.e. which actually produce something. The all-union and other intermediate *obyedineniya*, though they share the same designation, are in fact basically different: they are part of the command structure over actual producing units, albeit with a greater admixture of *khozraschet*.

The reform has left unsettled the inconvenient problem of many ministries making the same product (see page 61, above), and also the division between ministries of complementary production and investment tasks (as in the case of Siberian oil, already cited), but there is evidence that such matters are being carefully considered: 'it is particularly important that administrative boundary lines and departmental subordination should not be obstacles to the introduction of more effective forms of control' (CPSU Congress, 1971, p.68.)

A new development, designed to cope with such problems as these, is the 'Territorial-production complex', an idea supported in speeches at the 25th party Congress (February–March 1976). The only functioning example so far encountered is based on Pavlodar-Ekisbastuz, where there is cheap open-cast coal which is to be used to fire power-stations, local bauxite plus cheap electricity as a basis for aluminium production, crude oil piped from Omsk provides for oil-processing and petrochemical plants, and there are also large projects for railway extensions, a new river port at Pavlodar, housing etc. All this is to be jointly administered, to ensure maximum use of by-products (A. Dikarev and E. Kozlov, *EkG* 1976, No. 19, p.24.) It is too soon to see whether this idea will spread, and how such 'complexes' will be fitted with the ministerial structure. It may be that this organizational form will be used only or mainly when there is an integrated set of new investment projects in a previously under-developed area.

One final comment is called for, with regard to economies and diseconomies of scale. The object of the *obyedineniye* reform seems to be to wipe out the small enterprise:

'Small factories as autonomous units should not exist'. (Drogichinsky, 1973, p.82.) It is argued that small is inefficient – though a percipient Soviet critic noted that this is not the case in developed capitalist countries. (Dunayev, 1974, p.107.)

This argument can be contrasted with the view of Ya. Kvasha. He pointed out that Soviet industrial establishments are big:

Table 4 *Numbers employed per enterprise*

	All industry (except power stations)	of which: machinery and metalworking
USSR	565	2608
USA	48	74
West Germany	83	139

Kvasha's point is that there is great advantage in modern industry to have numerous independent *small* firms, which in practice work closely with the industrial giants. Thus (he wrote) General Motors has 26,000 supplying firms, Renault obtains from subcontractors 20,000 items. Small firms can also make a variety of minor consumers' goods. However, Kvasha notes, small-scale autonomous enterprises are inconsistent with state ownership, 'because of high administrative overheads'. He proposed the revival of producers' co-operatives, (Kvasha, *VEk*, 1967, No. 5, pp.26ff) (which had been liquidated in 1961).

His was a lone voice. But it reminds one of diseconomies of scale, and of the fact that, howsoever decision making is devolved or deconcentrated, the system is still basically centralized. Perhaps the *obyedineniya* will provide a less clumsy method by which central orders will be obeyed and plans implemented. But the chronic defects of 'directive-planning', which we have only begun discussing, will not thereby go away.

In a speech (*Pravda*, 28 November 1979) Brezhnev made critical remarks concerning the effects of *Vedomstvennost* and *mestnichestvo* ('departmentalism' and 'localism'), and the insufficient powers of Gosplan to deal with them. This reinforces the arguments advanced earlier in this chapter on the importance of interest groups and sectional pressures.

An important development in the field of regional planning is the emergence of Territorial Production Administrations (*Territorial'no Proizvodstvennoye Upravleniye*, or TPU). This is in response to the need for an authority to supervise the carrying-out of a regional development plan, involving numerous enterprises owing allegiance to several separate ministries. It is not yet clear how these administrations will relate to the industrial ministries and to other local authorities.

Their plans will be drafted by Gosplan, and it seems possible that the task of co-ordination on the spot may be carried out by a plenipotentiary of the Council of Ministers. These new bodies are being introduced in areas where the need for them is particularly urgent, particularly in connection with the big investment projects in Siberia.

The difficulties so frequently caused by interministerial 'boundaries' cannot be resolved by the creation of *obyedineniya*, so long as these are within separate ministries. We may therefore see a reform which creates regional industrial complexes which, like the TPUs, group together enterprises under a number of different ministries, accompanied by a major reorganization of the entire ministerial structure. These new bodies would not resemble the *sovnarkhozy*, in that they would be differentiated by sector (e.g. food processing and distribution, building materials, consumer durables, oil and petrochemicals, and so on). This, however, is no more than a possibility at present.

The reform decree of July 1979 also envisaged the designation of 'head ministries' (*golovnye ministerstva*) to take charge of production and design of those (numerous) products which are made within a number of different industrial ministries.

The number of *obyedineniya* has been rising steadily, and it is intended that they cover the bulk of industrial output within the next two to three years. In 1978 they were responsible for 46·3 per cent of total output (*NKh*, 1978, p. 115).

CHAPTER 4

INDUSTRIAL MANAGEMENT
AND MICRO-ECONOMIC PROBLEM S

WHAT IS 'MANAGEMENT'?

At the cost of repetition, let me again stress that many of the functions of government ministers and senior party officials can be regarded as a form of senior management, in some respects analagous to that of the senior directors of a big Western corporation. In this chapter we will be concerned with more junior levels, that is to say with the executants of plans, who run actual productive units. In the previous chapter we have noted that various intermediate bodies, e.g. the all-union *obyedineniya*, combine in some measure the task of plan-administrator and that of managerial-executor of plans handed down. While the reader should be conscious of this, what we will now be concentrating on are the issues and problems that arise in *carrying out plans*. The content of the plans will not be our concern as such, not in this chapter, except in so far as this gives rise to ambiguities and contradictions, and also in so far as the management can affect this content by its own action or inaction.

THE BASIC PROBLEM: COMMUNICATION AND EVALUATION

Given that the centre knows (or is supposed to know) what is to be produced, how can it issue the necessary instructions and encourage management to carry out these instructions with maximum attention to economy and the avoidance of waste? There is then the further question of what incentives should be provided, how they should be calculated, *what* should be rewarded. Given that one must evaluate the performance of management, how can one define a good performance? With this is linked the issue of managerial autonomy. Thus it is easier to allow freedom of decision to management if one can define the parameters within which it can exercise it, and one can define what actions qualify for reward, material or moral. A phrase that frequently recurs in the works of many different kinds of reformers, from Liberman to Fedorenko, is a variation on the theme: what is good for society (or optimal for the economy) should be advantageous (or profitable) for each unit of which the economy is composed. Management at all levels would then exert its efforts in conformity with the objectives of the planners. This, however, has not been achieved, for a number of reasons the discussion of which will occupy many pages of this chapter and also will be tackled again in Chapter 11.

How can the centre issue instructions in a form which does not give rise to ambiguities and contradictions? How can it encourage initiative, new techniques, the flow of desired and undistorted information? By what standards and in what way can we evaluate performance? Around these issues one finds grouped many of the most serious weaknesses of Soviet micro-economics. This is where many things go wrong.

Some critics consider that these problems arise primarily out of the lack of common interest between planners and managers (and workers too), that the hierarchical-bureaucratic form of the society prevents communication and understanding. Such considerations are important. This, however, misses the essential point, which is that in most instances *the centre does not know* just what it is that needs doing, in disaggregated detail, while the management in its situation *cannot* know what it is that society needs unless the centre informs it. Despite all talk of reform and direct links, the fact remains that in a basically non-market model the centre must discover what needs doing, and the centre *cannot* do this in micro-detail. At the same time, the centre pursues its own priorities, including growth. To encourage growth it sets objectives, goals and rewards their attainment. These targets are expressed in aggregate terms, inevitably. The attempt by management to obey plan-instructions, which gives rise to many distortions, is not evidence of lack of common interest; if anything it is the reverse. The trouble lies in the near-impossibility of drafting micro-economic instructions in such a way that even the most well-meaning manager will not be misled. It is no use asserting that he should satisfy his customers by making the things they want. If he did that, he would be producing for his customers and not to the orders of his superiors, in other words output would be determined by the market. It is precisely this type of reform that has been rejected. Yet, paradoxically, the Soviet planners *do* want output to match user requirements. The whole contradiction of the reform measures to date is herein contained.

The behaviour of management of factories and of industrial complexes makes a profound difference to the efficiency of the Soviet (as of any other) economy. The Soviet *model* appears to cast management for the role of simple executants of orders. They are told what to produce, from whom to obtain inputs, they have no control over prices, they cannot exceed the prescribed wage and salary bill. Orders which they must obey pour down from above on a variety of topics, including many which, according to the 1965 reform, should be within their own competence to decide. This picture suggests that they are there to supervise the technical operation, to ensure the machinery is oiled, so to speak. If one notes that certain decisions (e.g. over dismissals, welfare funds, etc.) require the consent of the trade union, and that they are subject to the supervisory role of the party and of several other controlling and checking agencies, not to mention the bank, the manager's status seems to decline still further.

Yet this would be quite wrong.

However, it seems clear that the situation has only marginally altered since 1965. The much-publicized reform decree of that year should not be underestimated; but, no prescriptions about the range of topics left to managerial discretion can make a decisive difference, so long as: (a) the management is a subordinate unit in a hierarchy and therefore must obey orders from their superiors on whatever topic, including even (as in a Western corporation) on the hiring of a red-haired secretary; and, (b) the model upon which the economy is based still assumes that the primary duty of determining what is to be done rests not with the management but with the planners, and so long as the 'standard' plan-indicators do not cover various eventualities which give rise to further orders from above.

THE 1965 REFORM AND ITS LIMITATIONS

The context of the 1965 reform was the abolition of the *sovnarkhozy*, inherited from Khrushchev. It was decided to return to the 'ministerial' system, based on industrial sectors, but the vigorous debate on managerial autonomy, and the greater use of 'commodity-money relations' (including the use of profitability as a criterion) had its effect. The efforts of Liberman, whose personal importance was much overstated in the West, were a small part of the flood of proposals, which had pointed out the many micro-economic irrationalities of the system, the need for a greater degree of decentralization. The mathematically minded economists (Kantorovich, Novozhilov, and later the talented young men of the Central Economic Mathematical Institute) urged the use of programming techniques, computers, optimization, but this did not make them (or most of them) ultra-centralizers, because of their recognition of the impossibility of including micro-economic detail in any feasible central programme.

One point in common between all the critics was that the number of compulsory plan-indicators was far too large, too narrowly constricting managerial freedom of action. Thus, to take an example utilized by Kosygin in his speech introducing the reform, there were four standard indicators for labour: productivity, number of workers, average wage and wages fund. Henceforth there would only be one: the wages fund. In addition, the following indicators would be obligatory: value of sales (*realizatsiya*), 'the basic nomenclature of output' (interpreted as the main items to be produced, often expressed in physical units); total profits; profitability (*rentabel 'nost'*, i.e. the rate of profit on capital, expressed as a percentage); contributions to and receipts from the state budget; centralized investments and introduction of new productive capacity; 'the basic tasks for the introduction of new techniques'; and finally material supply obligations. (Kosygin, 1965.)

A large number of other compulsory indicators were declared to be abandoned, not only the much-criticized 'gross output' but also cost reduction, which stood in the way of quality improvements. However, as we shall see, this still left the field open for many detailed instructions from above, including on matters not on the list, or later added to it. As was pointed out, the enterprise (or *obyedineniye*) has no protection against orders on any topic issued by its hierarchical superior.

Some of the above indicators were described as *fondo-obrazuyushchiye pokazateli*, i.e. on their basis payments into incentive funds were to be calculated. These were:

(a) Increase in sales *(realizatsiya)* in the given year, over the previous year.
(b) Per cent increase in profits.
(c) Profitability *(rentabel 'nost')*.

These three indicators are often reduced to two, consisting of (a) and (b) *or* (c). The *planned* increase in the indicators must be achieved for sums to be paid into three *incentive funds,* out of retained profits:

(a) The material incentive fund.
(b) The social-cultural and housing fund.
(c) Fund for the expansion of production (i.e. investment fund).

Managerial bonuses are, in the main, financed out of the material incentive fund. (Most of the bonuses paid to workers form part of the wages fund, but they also share in the incentive fund.) To encourage enterprises to adopt ambitious plans, payments into the incentive funds are reduced by 30 per cent in respect of overplan sales, profits and/or profitability. This provision has been ineffective, and has been reinforced by a so-called 'counterplans' scheme (*vstrechnyye plany*, see p.106, below).

Payment in respect of those indicators can be made conditional upon the fulfilment of other elements of the plan, for instance carrying out of delivery obligations in the required *assortiment*, increasing labour productivity and various other requirements. The payments into the incentive funds are calculated in a manner so bewilderingly complex that both author and reader would be reduced to paralytic boredom if the rules were here reproduced. The essential point is that norms are laid down, which can differ as between enterprises (or *obyedineniya*) and sectors. The norm in the case of the first two of the funds is given as a percentage of the wages bill (e.g. for fulfilling a sales plan of a 5 per cent increase over last year a sum equal to 2 per cent of the wages bill, say, is paid out of profits into the material incentive fund). The norm in the case of the investment fund is a percentage of the planned value of basic capital. The investment fund also benefits from a portion of the depreciation (amortization) fund, and from proceeds of sales of surplus equipment. The norms, though differentiated, were supposed to be stable, save that those enterprises with high profits 'for reasons outside their control' were to have their norms reduced. As we shall see, the norms have in fact been frequently altered.

Rather than going further into detail, it may aid clarity if we were to see the logic of the scheme. Management was to be rewarded not just for fulfilling quantitative plans (though the amount specified in the plan had to be produced) but for increasing sales and for profits. However, the simple solution of rewarding increases over some previous period was rejected, in favour of rewarding the fulfilment of plans. Since enterprises differed greatly in the level of their profits, often as a result of the level of fixed prices, a sense of fairness led to a differentiation in norms, to even things out. An increase in profits due to change in product mix was regarded as illegitimate, so norms were manipulated to eliminate extra payments into the funds from this source. As the size of the work force in relation to profit varied greatly, the percentages paid into those funds which benefit labour (i.e. the incentive and social-cultural funds) were calculated as a percentage of the wages bill.

One method of reducing variations in profit rates was the introduction of rental and other 'fixed payments' (under the general heading *fiksirovannyye platezhi*), which are paid into the budget by favourably situated enterprises, e.g. those mining a particularly rich and cheaply worked seam. But this practice has not been so systematic and widespread as to eliminate the need for norm differentiation, and has in fact been largely confined to mining. Its extension, to 'even out the calculations of profitability' in different enterprises is advocated. (Rotshteyn, 1971, p.262.)

The basic problem could be defined as follows. The authors of the reform were not too clear about what the incentives they were discussing were for. Were they to encourage managers to use more initiative in deciding what to produce and how to do it? Some of the more radical reformers thought so. But then a management that selects a more profitable product mix ought to be rewarded, providing always that prices serve as an indication of what the customers, or society, most need. But this was too radical a view. The planners insisted that the primary task of management was to obey their instructions, which covered what they had to produce, where they were to obtain inputs, and the prices at which all these transactions were to take place. In that case the level of profits, and to some extent also the value of sales, were the result primarily of orders received from the ministry or the planning organs. But this, plainly, made it irrational to reward (or penalize) managers or other employees for the financial consequences of decisions which they did not take.

All kinds of anomalies emerged. Thus suppose that profit goes up as a result of a reduction in numbers of workers employed. The wages bill goes down. Therefore, since the material incentive fund is calculated as a percentage of the wages bill, it could well turn out that payments into the incentive fund actually fell as a result of the economy! Then, of course, the existence of *several* indicators imply that they could contradict one another.

An important disincentive to the making of profits is the severe limits placed on their retention. After paying the capital charge (see Chapter 7) and other fixed payments, and transferring sums to the incentive funds in accordance with complex, ever-changing and quasi-incomprehensible formulae, all that remains of profits ('free remainder') also goes to the budget, unless the planners authorize retention for specifically indicated purposes, such as finance of centrally planned investments. Why not allow the enterprise to accumulate reserves, asked Bunich (*VEk*, 1967, No. 10, p.49.)

The answer to this question, as Bunich himself must know, is that the planners have difficulty already with unplanned demand. The various incentive funds combined equalled 16 per cent of total profits in 1972. This was almost 14½ milliard roubles. Part of this is distributed as personal incomes, but a large part represents a claim on productive resources: for example materials and furniture for a crèche, or a new kitchen, or machinery and equipment needed to complete a decentralized investment project. Provision of the necessary material counterpart for decentralized investment funds is already difficult, as numerous comments show. The existence of reserves which the management could use when it suited them could hardly commend itself to the planners.

The change wrought by the reform is none the less noticeable, as Table 5 shows.

This does not mean a proportionate increase in enterprise autonomy. Retained profits may only be used for authorized purposes. Nor has interference from above diminished, though it is certainly true that certain plan-fulfilment indicators have been dropped, even they sometimes reappear in a new guise. Thus the gross-output *(valovaya produktsiya)* indicator is 'dead' as such, but the labour-productivity indicator (subsequently introduced) requires that the number of labourers

THE SOVIET ECONOMIC SYSTEM

Table 5   *Utilization of profits of industrial enterprises**

	Per cent of total	
	1965	*1972*
TOTAL PROFITS	100	100
of which: *To the budget*	71	60
(Deducted from profit)**	(71)	(2)
(Capital charges)	(—)	(19)
(Fixed rent charges)	(—)	(4)
(Free remainder)	(—)	(34)
Retained	29	40
(Incentive funds)	(6)	(16)
(Investment financing)	(9)	(13)
(Other purposes)	(14)	(11)

Source: NKh 1972, p. 698. Figures relate only to enterprises that made profits.
**See Chapter 9 for explanation of this term.

be divided into a total that looks very much like gross value of output. 'Sales' is also a 'gross' measure, as we shall see.

Labour productivity was not on the original list of centrally planned indicators, but by 1970 it proved desirable to insist on it. Then there was added quality, material utilization, and some other sectoral indicators. The list of such indicators for the 1976–80 period, which looks formidable, is appended at the end of this chapter. Nor is this all. The Siberian branch of the Academy of Sciences sent a questionnaire to 1,064 directors. Eighty per cent of them 'replied that their superiors lay down compulsory indicators (such as the costs of specific products, the number of employees by category, etc.) which, according to the provisions of the economic reform, ought not to be imposed from above. Breaches of *khozraschet* rights established by existing rules occur on a mass scale'. (Aganbegyan, *Pravda*, 12 November, 1973.) Matters are clearly not improving when, in his speech presenting the 1976 budget, Finance Minister Garbuzov instructed ministries to save materials to a specified value and to distribute to their enterprises *(dovesti do predpriyatii)* what must obviously be compulsory indicators. (*Izvestiya*, 3 December 1975.) No exception is made for *obyedineniya*. All this plainly contradicts the need for managerial flexibility in the use of their material inputs.

So the reform has not given the managers firm powers they did not formerly possess. (The typical response of Hungarian or Polish economists, on being asked what they think of the Soviet reform is: reform? what reform?) It is still the case that anything *could* be the subject of a detailed order, but many things cannot be, for reasons abundantly explored already.

Managerial *de facto* powers arise from the following circumstances.

(a) Output plans being in some degree aggregated, their decisions partly determine the product mix.

(b) Both output plans and inputs, though 'decided' above, are often decided on the basis of information and proposals submitted by management. This is what the late Imre Vajda, of Budapest, once described as 'commands written by their recipients'. Even when, as often happens, the actual plan/order differs from what is proposed, it is still influenced by management, which knows best what the plant is capable of doing.

(c) A variety of innovations, in product design and in methods of production can be initiated at enterprise level, and so it matters greatly what the managerial incentives (and disincentives) are.

(d) Because of 'centralized pluralism', orders which reach the management from different quarters can be contradictory or mutually exclusive. In these instances, management has some choice thrust upon it as to what orders to obey.

(e) Particularly in matters relating to supply of inputs, there is much scope for semi-legal (or even downright illegal) initiative. Indeed, a good deal depends on a whole network of informal links, which supplement the official hierarchy and channels.

(f) Management seldom meets opposition from the trade union (the manager is himself a member), save on a narrow range of labour issues, which point will be further discussed in Chapter 8. The secretary of the party group within the enterprise is not, as a rule, a problem: again, the manager is himself almost always a party member, and a more influential one than the secretary at that level (the *gorkom* or *obkom* secretary is quite another matter).

A MAXIMIZING MODEL?

Can one express in formal terms what it is the Soviet manager is seeking to maximize? What are his goals? It is tempting to devise a model in which the manager seeks to maximize his income, i.e. the bonuses he receives, for fulfilling whatever are the bonus-determining elements of the plan (as we have seen, some determine the magnitude of the bonus, others are a precondition for receiving any bonus). One must at once introduce a modification, which, however, applies also to any intelligently presented profit-maximizing model in the West: one must have a time-dimension, and take into account that too vigorous a pursuit of current advantage (e.g. *this* year's bonus) might cause difficulties in the next years. This, in my view, is still nowhere near sufficient. The Soviet manager must obey many orders. which have no effect on his bonus, and in some circumstances might even reduce it, because his chances of promotion (and avoidance of demotion) depend on his reputation for discipline and obedience to orders.

Then he must avoid trouble which could arise if he annoyed influential customers, or the regional party secretary, or anyone on whom he depends for supplies, or if he so altered the product mix in a bonus-maximizing direction that it would cause a public inquiry – for example if he made all raincoats the same size. The kind of behaviour which might earn a medal or a commendation – such as completing or delivering some item in time for a revolutionary anniversary – may or may not earn a bonus. Of course, if one wishes one could subsume all of this under maximizing behaviour, subject to various constraints. But if one did that, there is some danger of saying, in a rather round-about way, that the manager behaves in a manner which advances his material and career interests as he sees them, while minimizing the risk of reprimand or other troubles. This is doubtless true, but is of very limited analytical use.

THE SUCCESS INDICATOR PROBLEM

Let us examine in some detail the troubles that arise from defining, or failing to define, the product mix. As is laid down in the text of the 1965 reform measure, the 'most important' items to be produced are usually specified as well as delivery obligations. But there is still the question of expressing the desired total output target in some way: tons, square metres, length, thousands of units, or pairs, kilowatt-hours, etc. This is additional to the duty of fulfilling plans in terms of sales (realizatsiya), profitability, etc. The survival of aggregate totals in non-monetary units is in considerable part due to the fact that ministries continue to have targets expressed in such units; as may be seen from a glance at either a five-year or an annual plan, targets for many products are given as 20·5 million tons, 200 million square metres, 600,000 units and so on. Not surprisingly, the ministries concerned subdivide such figures among 'their' productive units.

The difficulty arises from the fact that no measure is adequate, whenever there is any sort of product *mix*. In some instances this is not a problem. Thus there is that rare totally homogeneous commodity, electricity, which is supplied in kilowatt-hours which cannot vary in size, shape or colour. The second, and very different, exception concerns items which (in all countries) are ordered with detailed prescribed specifications from the centre, and for which no managerial 'choice of product mix' arises: say a nuclear submarine. One might add to this list certain minerals: given the content of the mine or well, what is extracted is, so to speak, predetermined by nature. But most products are quite unlike electricity, minerals and submarines, in the respects with which we are here concerned. Even so apparently simple an item as ball-bearings in fact is produced in eight hundred varieties. Farm machinery, dental equipment, clothing, dyestuffs, radios, etc.

etc., are produced in many shapes, sizes, qualities and designs. This is why Soviet price-lists fill such heavy volumes: identifiably different products need to be separately priced, and there are literally millions of them.

A logical parallel to the problem may be adapted from Chapter 2, when we mentioned the inadequacy of calories as an 'optimizing' measure for food consumption. This too is an aggregate, and it matters greatly to the consumer what the composition of a given total number of calories is. A more or less appropriate balance is found in a market economy because the preference of the consumer for a particular food can be expressed in the price he is prepared to pay. But we are not dealing here with a market economy.

Of course, no one plans output in calories. But tons have analagous defects. Let us imagine that the output of any metal goods is planned in tons. Then it *must* 'pay', for plan-fulfilment purposes, to make heavy goods. To reduce weight may economize materials, but threatens plan-fulfilment.

The literature on distortions due to plans being expressed in tons goes back at least twenty years, and served me as material for one of my first articles. Criticism of this abounds. The aircraft designer Antonov devoted many pages to citing examples of the waste to which it gives rise. (Antonov, 1965. See also Kornai, 1959.) Long ago *Krokodil* published a cartoon showing an enormous nail hanging in a large workshop: 'the month's plan fulfilled', said the director, pointing to the nail. In tons, of course. It is notorious that Soviet sheet steel has been heavy and thick, for this sort of reason. Sheet glass was too heavy when it was planned in tons, and paper too thick. Khrushchev mentioned that chandeliers were also planned in tons. This is perhaps the best known of all Soviet micro-economic deviations from rationality, and it may be sufficient to confine oneself to documenting the fact that the disease is still rampant, and then discussing why, since the defect of 'tons' as an indicator has been known for decades, it has not been abandoned.

In 1974 *Pravda* published an article under the title: 'How tons defeated metres'. The story was a simple and sad one. Water-pipes were being made that were heavy and dear. A lighter and cheaper variant would have contradicted plan-fulfilment. A conscientious management, with the support of a sympathetic ministry, fought hard to get the plan-indicator changed to metres. After much effort they succeeded, only to find that light, cheap pipes contradicted the plan-indicators of the wholesaling, project-making and construction organs, who proved very reluctant to handle or to lay these pipes, 'preferring' dear and heavy ones. The author of the article comments: 'What isn't planned in tons! Pipe, rolling-mill and other equipment and even in one instance plastic dolls! Yet everybody knows that this contradicts the national-economic interest'. (*Pravda*, 22 August 1974.) It is worth noting here that 'output' of trade and construction organizations is often measured in such a way that economy is penalized; thus the handling or use of a cheaper material can affect the computed value of the work done.

Why cling to tons? Two reasons suggest themselves. The first is concerned with the planning of inputs. As was pointed out in Chapter 2, the planners try to crosscheck the often excessive requests of enterprises and ministries by reference to norms, coefficients. They know from experience that to produce X tons of some metal goods requires specified quantities of materials. It would be much harder to make such estimates if the figures were (for instance) in roubles, since clearly a thousand roubles' worth of metal goods would be a much less precise guide to inputs, as some metal goods are much dearer than others. The second reason is that, in many cases, no obvious alternative exists which does not have its own specific deficiencies.

Take the two examples of sheet steel and plate glass. If the measure were not in tons but in square metres, i.e. in terms of area, the temptation would be to make them thin even if they ought to be heavier. One could use an aggregate monetary measure, but this also need not lead to the production of the desired product mix. Of course, ideally the plan should specify the 'right' quantities, weights and sizes of all glass, metal goods, sheet steel, nails, etc. . . . But the problem arises precisely from the impossibility of doing this. This is just what is meant by saying that the centre does not and cannot know in detail what needs doing. This *is* the problem of disaggregation.

All quantitative aggregates have their distorting effects, though doubtless some are worse than others. When cloth was planned in *linear* metres, it gradually became narrower, as harassed managers strove to fulfil plans with a given quantity of raw materials and labour. The shift to square metres corrected this 'deviation', but can obstruct improvements in quality, in that they may well depend on additional inputs of labour and machine-time, or a greater density of threads, within the same square-metreage. Antonov told the sad tale of how it proved impossible to shift footwear production from a type that was not wanted to one that was acutely scarce, because the change would lead to a reduction in the number of pairs of boots and shoes produced, and not even the ministry would sanction this, because *its* plan was millions of pairs. (Antonov, 1965, pp.43–5.) The matter called almost for a summit conference. Another well-documented instance concerns a road transport undertaking, whose lorries ran to an aggregate plan expressed in ton-kilometres. Several writers have pointed out that such a plan encourages long and even useless journeys, so as to 'clock' up the tons and the kilometres (or even kilometres only, if tons are lacking), so that they can multiply out to the prescribed figure (tons carried times kilometres run). This contradicts any attempt, with or without computers, to *minimize* transport costs. (Antonov, 1965, p.70.)

We should, however, not delude ourselves into thinking that irrationalities of this sort occur only in Soviet-type economies, even with lorries, indeed particularly with lorries. The following example happens to be American:

'A trucker carrying chickens from Delaware to New York is unregulated because Congress created the so-called "agricultural exemption". But he is not allowed to pick up any manufactured goods in the city to carry on the return trip. The cost of this "deadheading" is naturally figured into the cost of the chickens.

Many business firms own their own fleets of trucks in order to assure themselves of speed and flexibility in delivering their products. The ICC does not permit these so-called private carriers – as distinguished from common carriers that serve all businesses – to lease their vehicles and drivers to outside truckers when not needed for their own use. This restriction creates a double inefficiency since the private carriers cannot make maximum use of their equipment and common carriers cannot expand their services in temporary peak periods without investing in the purchase of additional trucks'. (*New York Times* editorial 16 November 1975.)

The Soviet lorry example illustrates one familiar principle and raises a new one. The familiar one is the disaggregation problem: the *logic* of the system would require the planners to specify the journey of every lorry every day, and because this is plainly impossible they present the road transport enterprise with an aggregated target in what appears to be at first sight a sensible measure, ton-kilometres. The second, and new, point concerns the whole principle of minimizing the input of materials and intermediate goods and services. To achieve a given output of any assortment of products, common sense suggests that expenditures be low rather than high. But the final product, by the time it reaches its final user, has been the product of a joint effort of many enterprises. If all of them are rewarded and praised for fulfilling (or worse still, overfulfilling) an output plan, and if in addition this output is expected to increase year after year, then inevitably one is sometimes providing a direct incitement to waste. This is because a change in the intermediate good or service provided, if it makes possible a reduction in its measurable quantity, threatens the plan-fulfilment of the enterprise providing the good or service. Hence the ton-kilometre absurdity. Hence also excess tonnage, and so on. Brezhnev spoke of this problem in general at the 25th party Congress by deploring 'the chase after intermediate results' (*Pravda*, 25 February 1976.)

It is easy to say yet again: surely only those lorry journeys which are necessary should be made, and this is what the aggregate plan should express. Yes, of course, it should. But since the planners who issue the orders do not know which journeys should be made, they can only talk in aggregate terms. The only level at which a plan can be made up of its journey-constituents is at the level of local management, in negotiation with customers. But again this is – as we shall see – the Hungarian quasi-market solution. It is rejected in the USSR, where much store is placed upon the principle that the primary task of management is to obey planners' instructions.

But to return to the issue of performance evaluation. Refraining from the temptation of quoting still more anecdotes about tons, square metres, etc. – and they could fill a book – let us look at various forms of monetary indicators.

The one which predominated for a generation and more was gross output (*Valovaya produktsiya*, or *val*). This was simply the total value (at the fixed prices) of the entire output, including unfinished production, regardless of whether it found a purchaser. Commonly plans specified a percentage increase in the *val*, and attached bonuses to success and reprimands (or worse) to failure to achieve the increase.

There were three major deficiencies in this measure. In the first place it was 'gross' in the sense that it included the value of inputs produced in other enterprises. Therefore it paid the management to propose dearer inputs (provided these found their reflection in the fixed cost-plus-based prices) and to resist proposals for cheaper inputs. Secondly, it also discouraged enterprises from switching their output towards cheaper items, since this would affect their gross value of output, even though this created contradictions with the pattern of consumer demand. Thirdly, the inclusion of products made and not sold failed to penalize what is sometimes called 'output for the store-room' *(na sklad)*, of items which were simply not wanted, but which 'clocked up' roubles in terms of *val*. Conformity between the product mix which added up to the planned total in thousands of roubles and what the users actually needed would be purely coincidental. Despite much criticism, the *val* survived as the principal criterion until the middle sixties, and is not dead yet.

Its survival can be explained by the deficiencies of the most obvious alternative measure, that of *net* output, or value-added. On the face of it, this seems the right measure: after all, we want to know what contribution *this* enterprise made to the provision of goods and services, and one arrives at this by subtracting inputs purchased from other enterprises. Yet this measure contains yet another source of distortion, which doubtless explains why it has not been adopted. In the case of gross output, the actual goods produced are expressed in official prices. Thus if 5000 square metres of wool cloth cost an average of 10 roubles per metre, then the factory's output is 50,000 roubles in terms of *val*. In pursuit of this target, at given prices for inputs and output, it would certainly not pay the management to undertake unnecessary operations, as these do not add anything to the monetary measure of *val*. This is not so in the case of net output, for there is now no fixed price; what is being measured is value-added, the work done, and value can be added in order to fulfil a plan even if the work done is wasteful. It is interesting to note that the attempt to introduce the value-added indicator in Poland in 1975 has given rise to just such a criticism.

To obtain the advantages and avoid the defects of the value-added criterion, Soviet planners have experimented with so-called 'normed value of processing'. The idea was that the enterprise would be credited for the amount of value which it *ought* to be adding. That is to say, various operations were 'normed', and that contribution to the productive process would be measured as the sum of the value of these norms. To illustrate, if to make 5000 square metres of cloth required operations valued at 4 roubles per metre, then the 'normed value of processing' of this quantity of cloth would be taken as 20,000 roubles, regardless of how much processing the enterprise actually undertook.

This scheme suffered from two defects. The first, and the most important, is that it required a very large number of calculations to determine what the norms should be, and this additional to the already very burdensome task of deciding the prices of the goods produced. Second, there quickly developed a bewildering variety of ratios between the 'normed' and the actual cost of processing, which caused anomalies and distortions. (See article by P. Malyshev, *VEk,* No. 6, 1965.) So this indicator was abandoned, save for some calculations connected with labour productivity.

However, 'from 1973 . . . mainly in the machinery sectors, experiments are being conducted in the evaluation of enterprises' activities in terms of net output. The volume of net output is calculated by the so-called normative method, utilizing stable norms ("prices of net output") for each product'. It seems that these calculations are made by taking the official wholesale price and subtracting from it the level of planned material inputs. (*Gosplan*, 1974, p.63.)

Finally, among monetary measures, there is the indicator of *sales* (or strictly 'disposals', *realizatsiya*). This differs from *val* by excluding unsold production and work in progress. It suffers from one major defect, which it shares with *val*: being a monetary aggregate, inclusive of the value of inputs, there is a direct inducement to maximize, not minimize, the cost of inputs, always provided these can be included in the prices at which output is computed. In other words, it incites management to propose expensive variants. In some branches of the economy, notably construction, the incitement is even more direct: 'to this day in computing labour productivity in construction the decisive element is the cost of materials. The dearer they are and the more of them are expended, the "better" is this indicator'. (*Pravda*, 22 August 1974.) The same is true in both wholesale and retail trade: turnover statistics benefit from handling items of high value, especially if they require no processing. Thus it is notorious that catering establishments can fulfil plans in roubles very conveniently by selling bottles of vodka; much more 'profitable' than tea, which is not only cheap but needs labour to make and serve.

Thus *realizatsiya* has deficiencies. It has also two advantages, as against *val*. One is the obvious one that unsold and perhaps unsaleable products cannot be counted, which does represent some discouragement to the production of things no one wants. The other is that nothing can be counted as sold unless it is paid for. This gives some additional leverage to the customer-enterprise, which can cause difficulties in plan-fulfilment by delaying payment. This can at least marginally increase its influence over the product mix.

None the less, 'one still continues to see the fulfilment of plans in aggregate terms; some users are undersupplied, others receive too much'. The required product mix is amended in the interests of the supplier. 'The indicator of sales, though it has played a positive role, does not solve the problem of ensuring supplies that the users need. . . . Very often one finds that the sales plan is fulfilled, but contractual agreements are not observed.' (Drogichinsky, 1973, p.93.)

It must also be made clear that the 'sales' indicator does not replace, but is additional to, the requirement that the enterprise (or *obyedineniye*) fulfil the plan in terms of the 'main types of product', which could be in tons.

In general, we can note that, while no success indicator is without deficiencies, some are more suitable, or less noxious, than others, depending on the sector and the alternative techniques, models and variants that one wishes to encourage. Anomalies can arise quite unexpectedly. Thus even the apparently 'perfect' and unambiguous measure of electricity output in kilowatt-hours can give rise to a nonsense: when I was in Leningrad, I was told that *Lenenergo*, the Leningrad electricity undertaking, was reprimanded, in that it failed to fulfil the plan. This, however, was due to the weather in winter being unusually mild, so less heat was needed!

One could go on. But perhaps enough has been said to show that evaluation of performance presents serious practical problems and gives rise to unintended distortions, irrationalities and waste.

CONTRADICTION AND INSTABILITY OF PLANS, AND CONCEALMENT OF POTENTIAL

Seen from the standpoint of management, a major difficulty arises from the fact that different elements of the plan fail to cohere, and that when the current plan is amended (which is often) this is not done systematically, so that, for instance, the output plan may be changed without analogous changes in the supply, finance or wages plans.

That this is so can be easily documented, using a multitude of printed sources. In quoting a small selection of these, we will try to identify the causes, as well as considering remedies tried and remedies that could be tried.

The commonest 'disease' is the failure of the supply plan to match the output plan. 'The necessary interlinking (uvyazka) of production tasks with material-technical supply is not ensured.' One reason is the need to make provisional application (zayavka) for material inputs '6–8 months before the beginning of the plan-year', on the basis of what they expect the plans to be. Yet at this time there are not yet any detailed contracts with the requisite technological documentation.' Details, as to type of product and date of delivery, are 'most often made known in the first quarter of the plan-year'. Furthermore, 'in the course of this the production programme is significantly altered, and consequently so is the need for material inputs. The result is numerous changes in plans, difficulties in technical and organizational preparation of production, breakdown in supply, the creation of excess stocks, disruption of productive process. . . .' (Tsarev, 1971, p.246.)

Repeatedly one hears of another cause of supply breakdowns: the adoption of over-optimistic investment plans, so that inputs ought to be flowing from new productive units that are not in fact completed in time. Similarly, planners and supply organs are blamed for assigning supply obligations to factories which exceed these factories' productive capacity. Again, quotations could be assembled which would fill a sizeable volume. Let us confine ourselves to one article which mentions both these deficiencies, and then consider the causes.

The article was headed: 'How long will the tolkach live?' The tolkach, literally 'pusher', is a breed of unofficial supply agent, whose job is to agitate, nag, beg, borrow, sometimes bribe, so that the necessary materials, components and equipment arrive. Since the supply plan is supposed to match the output plan, and to be in turn consistent with the output plans of the supplying enterprises, the existence of the tolkach is evidence in itself that something is seriously amiss.

The Pravda article points out, quite reasonably, that 'it is only possible to get rid of the tolkach if supplies are properly planned, and for this one must take into account the real possibilities of the supplying enterprises'. Citing an example concerning a breakdown in the supply of cement, the author quotes the director of the cement works as saying: 'We cannot help you. Our enterprise has received delivery obligations *(naryady)* in this quarter which are almost 70,000 tons above what we can produce.' The *glavk* responsible, *Soyuzglavtsement*, 'seeing the unreal nature of its own instructions', improvised a priority list. 'In this situation the fate of cement and of other materials fall into the hands of *tolkachi*. Utilizing all permitted and more often non-permitted methods of "persuasion", they ensure supplies to their enterprises.' This causes confusion in production, at the supplying enterprise as well as at the customers, 'the allocation certificate is devalued, so is responsibility for and planning of supply'. The planners pass the responsibility on to the management, especially that of the enterprise which 'has failed to obtain the necessary materials and components and has thus caused the plan to break down'. A proverb is cited: 'He is to blame who has failed to obtain'. Not, it seems, who has failed to supply. The author goes on to cite complaints about material supplies of the wrong type and quality.

There are indeed provisions for financial penalties for failing to observe contracts, but they are ineffective, which, if it is physically impossible to observe them, is scarcely surprising. Fines, if levied, are paid out of the enterprise's bank account, and do not damage any living person. Finally, the author begs for:

'a stable plan, linked with material-technical resources. A real one, soundly based and not requiring telephone calls for help. How can one even speak of scientific labour deployment and long-term prognoses when, for example, the Urals automobile plant received in the first quarter of the current year forty amendents to its [output] plan? Nor can one regard as normal that consumers of, say, metal, are attached to enterprises whose new capacity is not yet operational. The supply organs argue more or less as follows: yes, the plans are unreal, but the users will compel the *glavk* or the ministry to take all possible action. . . .' (G. Yakovlev, *Pravda*, 4 August 1972.)

Among many ways chosen by managers to avoid these difficulties is unofficial barter. This too is a field for *tolkachi*. But it can be con-ducted openly, by advertisement. The following, for instance, appeared in the central committee's own economic organ: 'WILL EXCHANGE sweeping machine KO-304 for chassis of a GAZ-53 [lorry], a new LA3 bus or a GAZ 51-52 or 53 lorry. Dnepropetrovsk oblast repair and construction trust'. (*EkG*, 1975, No. 43, p.23.) Needless to say, such exchanges are useful, as they serve to correct errors and omissions in official allocations. But the errors are, evidently, all too common.

Why all this? Firstly, it is a consequence of the sheer impossibility of completing the planning and supply work in time. So to speak, one iterates and iterates, and meanwhile the plan-year is already beginning. By this time the task is still far from completed, and amendments require to be made repeatedly during the currency of the plan-quarter or year. Hence no possibility of a 'stable plan', which adversely affects the efficacy of any plan-related incentive scheme, as well as disrupting production planning. Hence also the frequency with which disaggregated supply arrangements fail to match the desired output mix.

Secondly, such strains are (in my view) the inevitable consequence of aiming at the highest possible growth rates, with full utilization of resources. For reasons to which we will return in Chapter 9, this is bound to lead to micro-imbalances, under conditions in which micro-detail cannot be adequately covered by the production and supply plans. In particular the investment plan is always in excess of the availability of investment goods – of which more in Chapter 6.

Thirdly, there are the psychological consequences of the sellers' market, the general atmosphere of shortage. Selling is easy, procurement difficult. This gives rise to a take-it-or-leave-it attitude, which weakens the customer's influence over his supplies.

Fourthly, there are the success indicators applicable to the supplying enterprise, plus the fact that its responsibility is primarily to its own hierarchical superiors, not to the customer, which inevitably weakens the significance of the contract, as against fulfilling the plan in terms of whatever indicators are applicable. (True, these indicators are now increasingly accompanied by injunctions to fulfil the delivery plan in accordance with the approved product nomenclature, but the overall target figures still have priority for the manager and the ministry alike.)

Uncertainty of supply has many consequences: excess stocks immobilized at the enterprises just in case, overapplication for supplies in the hope of obtaining what is needed, striving for a modest plan in case there is a breakdown in the flow of inputs, work stoppages when this breakdown has occurred, irregularity and rush periods if supplies arrive late, and so on. The combination of supply delays and the need to fulfil a plan by a given date cause the phenomenon of *shturmovshchina*, 'storming', which adversely affects the quality of anything made towards the end of a plan period, including the last days of any month. There is widespread evidence that this is still a major problem.

One can also appreciate the difficulty, in the face of forty amendments of the output plan in one quarter, of keeping pace with these by making the consequential amendments to the financial, labour and other parts of what ought to be an integrated and internally consistent *tekhpromfinplan*, an abbreviation standing for 'technical-industrial-financial-plan'.

One can readily see why this state of affairs leads to concealment of productive potential, thereby adversely affecting the flow of information to planners. This is reinforced by a number of other disincentives, which we will now consider one by one.

The first is quite fundamental: if one is to be judged by plan-fulfilment, and penalized for not reaching the prescribed target, it evidently becomes important that the plan, or target, be modest enough to be safely within reach. This would be so even if one could be sure that supplies would arrive, and that superior authority will not alter the plan. It is doubly so because these risks exist.

It is trebly so because superior authority knows all this, and therefore assumes that the enterprise will conceal and that it is not telling the whole truth. This helps to explain the apparently irrational behaviour of planners who seem to allocate more than there is to allocate: there must be something hidden, they reason, and pressure will compel it to emerge. Speeches and articles often refer to the need to *vyyavlat' reservy*, – cause reserves to appear. But if this is so, it is very dangerous indeed for management to tell the whole truth about its productive potential, for it will not be believed and the plan will be set higher than is feasible. For the same reason, it will seem dangerous to over-fulfil the plan by too much, as the authorities might then fix an impossibly ambitious goal for the next plan-period.

Soviet economists have laid great stress on the need to overcome the tendency to opt for low plans *(zanizhennyye plany)*. This was one of the chief arguments used by Liberman in urging changes in the system. The 1965 reform was intended to encourage management to bid high at the stage at which they themselves propose and inform. The importance of this stage cannot be sufficiently stressed. Let us again recall the words of the Hungarian economist: 'most orders are written by their recipients'. Much of the information on the basis of which orders are issued comes from below.

However, the 1965 reform failed in achieving this objective, for one essential reason: although since 1965 the rewards payable for planned achievement are higher than for exceeding a more modest plan, it still pays to aim low, 'which is explained by the survival of stimuli for the adoption of insufficiently taut plans, which exceed the additional reward for aiming high'. The Soviet source puts first on the list the fact that non-fulfilment is penalized, that 'engineer-technical and managerial personnel of enterprises and *obyedineniya* are wholly deprived of bonuses if planned incentive-creating indicators *(fondo-obrazuyushchiye pokazateli)* are underfulfilled even by an insignificant fraction. They also injure their standing, their chances of promotion. Whereas in the event of an easy plan, bonuses for these categories of personnel are guaranteed'. (Bunich, 1973, p.57 and F. Veselkov, *VEk*, 1973, No. 10, p.12.)

Similarly, any bonuses paid for economy of materials, fuel, etc., are calculated in relation to the plan. 'Thus the higher the planned norms of utilization, the easier they are to fulfil, to show a saving and to get bonuses. This still more strengthens the stimulus to get high-cost plans adopted. . . .' (Bunich, 1973, p.51.) Indeed it is quite logical, within such a system, for management to understate its output possibilities and overstate its input claims, as well as its costs.

The same source goes on to refer to the notorious habit – amply documented elsewhere – of increasing not only the plans but also the financial burdens of the successful, so that in the end no additional advantage accrues, and 'it is clear that these anti-stimuli encourage concealment of reserves rather than their mobilization. . . . Finally, the moral evaluation of the production unit and its managers is often based on plan-fulfilment regardless of the tautness of the plans, since precise determination of tautness has not been devised. This interests the managers in plans . . . whose fulfilment and overfulfilment is assured, thus getting onto the prize list in socialist emulation. . . .' (Bunich, 1973, p.52.)

One cause of frequent changes in plan has not yet been mentioned. It is that the ministries wish to report not only that they have fulfilled *their* plans, but that most of their enterprises have also. This has various aspects: 'formal', physical and financial. If, for instance, enterprise A looks as if it could produce 110 per cent of its original plan and enterprise B only 94 per cent, then, without actually changing anyone's output, it is possible to alter the plan (even in December of the year to which it applies) so that both are at or just in excess of 100 per cent of the revised plan. This could be labelled 'formal'. 'Physical' would be a late change in the plan, designed to compensate for a shortfall at enterprise B by placing additional production obligations on enterprise A. A variant of this is the so-called *vozdushny val*, literally 'gross output of (or made of) air', which is an additional obligation to produce something, anything, so as to enable the ministry to reach its aggregate plan target. (Veselkov, *VEk*, 1973, No. 10, p.7.) Finally, finance. The ministry has financial obligations written into its plan. If enterprise A seems able to exceed its expected profits, which need to be paid into the budget, and enterprise B is in financial difficulties, a rearrangement of profit plans is a way out. However, all these changes upset the whole basis of the incentives of the 1965 reform, which requires stability of plans and of norms on which bonuses (and payments into the various incentive funds) are calculated.

According to a sample survey covering ninety-five enterprises in the Novosibirsk area, it turned out that in an average year they received a total of 1,554 amendments to the annual production plan, without any consequential amendment in the financial indicators! (Aganbegyan, *Pravda*, 12 November 1973.)

The non-stability of norms is notorious, and represents yet another reason for not aiming too high: the advantages of doing better will be removed, if not by a change in the plan then in an amendment of the rules governing the payments into incentive funds and therefore of the bonus entitlements, in a downward direction.

Why *these* amendments? Reasons are given in an article devoted to this topic, as follows. Firstly, some improvements in measured performance, profits, etc., arise for reasons unconnected with the quality of that enterprise's work (e.g. changes in prices or product mix, the installation of new equipment, etc.). Secondly, ministries were given 'limits' (maximum sums) for incentive funds, and then cut back the rights of enterprises to allocate money into these funds to fit into the prescribed limits. Thirdly, bonus payments to management and workers had to keep within bounds set by availability of goods and services. (Veselkov, *VEk*, 1973, No. 10, pp.4, 5.) It should be added that the more is allocated to these incentive funds, the greater the demand for non-centrally-planned investments, and the greater also the likelihood of shortages of investment goods.

The net effect is that neither 'stable norms' nor stable plans could survive.

Conscious of the inadequacy of their knowledge of productive potential, of hoarded stocks of materials and of the degree of tautness of past and present plans, the ministries and *Gosplan* tend to rely heavily on the one set of data in which they have confidence: past performance. This method of planning is known in Russian as *po dostignutomu urovnyu* ('on the achieved basis'), which is sometimes rendered as 'the ratchet principle': whatever it was (output, profits, productivity, etc.), do more of it this year than last – unless it is the percentage of spoiled work, materials utilization or costs, in which case it should be less. Numerous Soviet criticisms of this practice have not changed matters, for it is grounded in necessity: one can only plan on the basis of what one knows, which is what happened last year. This has 'conservative' implications in other respects, which will be further explored in Chapter 6.

It is worth noting that an experienced top manager (who had also been an *obkom* secretary and an industrial minister) had very sharply critical remarks to make about the impact of compulsory 'economy of materials' indicators on the work of industry. Repeatedly, in his experience, it led to improvisation to the detriment of the quality of the product, and also to the impossibility of satisfying customer requirements in the desired assortment, especially of spare parts and components *(komplektuyushchiye izdeliya)*. (Smelyakov, 1975, pp.175–6.) Yet, as we have seen these indicators are being yet again enforced in 1976.

Amendments introduced in 1971 have had as their object the overcoming of the reluctance of management to be ambitious in putting forward taut plan proposals: this is the so-called *vstrechny plan*, or 'counterplan'. The idea is as follows: *after* the ministerial organs have confirmed the plan, the fulfilment of which is obligatory and is the precondition of receiving any bonuses, the management is encouraged to put forward a more ambitious 'counterplan', and this is rewarded by additional bonuses in the event of success (i.e. by being higher, in terms of sales, physical output, profits, etc., than the directive plan), but bonuses are not lost if the 'counterplan' is not quite fulfilled, provided the lower 'directive' plan is fulfilled. The *vstrechnye plany* are submitted for approval to the appropriate ministry, bearing in mind the need for additional inputs which they might imply. This, at least, is my reading of the very complex explanatory document, published in *EkG*, 1974, No. 4.

The weakness of this scheme to overcome weakness is well described by a Soviet critic: 'enterprises are still interested in concealing their productive potential right up to moment of receiving their "directive" obligations, since the lower these are, the higher can be the counterplan and the rewards. . . . Some ministries may try to understate their five-year plans, and then put forward easily fulfillable (additional) undertakings and then obtain larger incentive funds to reward their "initiative" in elaborating higher annual and five-year plans.' (Veselkov, *VEk*, 1973, No. 10, p.7.)

Worse still, ministries treat the *vstrechnyye plany* as evidence of successful concealment of potential: 'ah, so you have so much under-utilized reserves? Right, we will add half of your proposed increase in output to the obligatory plan. . . .' Matters got worse, since 'in the last few months of the year there were eight more upward amendments of the plan'. Indeed 'the ministry does not respect *vstrechnyye plany*' when some of its enterprises were falling short of their obligatory targets. 'Therefore the habitual procedure was followed: reduce the plan for the laggards, increase it for the successful. After these arithmetical procedures, not a single enterprise in the [ministerial] sector has underfulfilled the plan' but, 'in the interests of departmental arithmetic the enterprise was deprived of reward for its initiative'. (*Pravda*, 27 November 1974.) Note the word 'habitual' in the above quotation.

One can appreciate how the management is harassed by a flood of orders, plans which are changed and which may fail to match supplies, and an incentive scheme of great complexity and subject to frequent amendment. One must also mention the limiting effects of the wages-fund. This, let it be recalled, set a limit to the total wage and salary bill. Surveys conducted by the Siberian economics institute showed that this limitation is particularly felt. (*Pravda*, 12 November, 1973.) It is linked with another indicator, that of labour productivity. Let me illustrate the negative effect of all this by an example. Suppose that a factory making a machine finds that it can notably improve its quality and productivity, but on condition that it employs an additional dozen skilled workers. If, as is usually the case, this requires a sum additional to the planned wages fund, it cannot do so without seeking permission, and this may or may not be granted, since the organs responsible for the wages fund are interested in avoiding inflationary increases in personal incomes, and not in the quality of a particular machine made in some factory perhaps a thousand miles away. Furthermore, the effect of taking on the extra workers on labour productivity statistics is, at best, problematical. In one instance, the plan specified that 97 per cent of the growth of output should be due to improved labour productivity. Taking on extra labour reduced this to 81·5 per cent, and so a necessary improvement in quality involving some additional input of labour led to a shortfall in a plan indicator. (Bunich, 1973, p.53.)

Some may think that these numerous instances of indicator-distortions, instabilities and arbitrary switches in plans and in incentive-norms are an untypical catalogue of critical material gathered by someone devoted to proving that the system cannot operate. It may then be argued that the system does operate, that it grows, and that therefore the analysis distorts by overemphasizing negative phenomena.

More will be said in later chapters about the strength of the system. However, these weaknesses in its micro-economic operation are real, well known to Soviet economists and constantly discussed in print. The citations given here could be multiplied a hundredfold. Above all, these are not 'mistakes', they are not instances of individual stupidity. They have their purpose. Given the institutional structure, given the objectives (growth, combating 'routine and inertia' by 'pressure' – to quote the title of Grossman's excellent article (1960)), given that the plan can *never* be completed or fully balanced in time, given that prices (and therefore profitability) are not related to scarcity or need, given finally that the basis of the Soviet model requires that the centre tells the production management what needs to be done, the complexities and distortions follow as the night follows day. Not, of course, that each individual irrationality (seen here as an *unintended* departure from what the economy really needs) is inevitable. Rules can be changed, but, if they are, other irrationalities follow. Antonov (1965, p.41) quotes the instance of electric lamp factories whose plan was expressed in terms of aggregate watt-power, and which therefore produced hardly any low-power lamps. If the indicator ever changed to thousands of lamps, hardly any high-power ones would be made. Or, using another Antonov example, women unloading bricks from a lorry smashed many of them. But if the unloading were done more carefully, they would 'produce' less and be paid less, the driver of the lorry would make fewer runs in the day, and finally his enterprise would clock up fewer ton-kilometres. (Antonov, 1965, p. 59.) In every case, the essence of the problem is that the centre is trying to set up an incentive system designed to achieve more efficiency, but, because it does not *and cannot* know the specific circumstances, its instructions can frequently contradict what those on the spot know to be the sensible thing to do. If the needs cannot be identified in time, and bottlenecks and shortages appear, the planning and supply organs *must* alter the plan, it *cannot* be stable, and nor can the incentive norms, and so on. Seen from below, of course, it is confusing and disorganizing. The moral effect of all this on the management and on the workers cannot be other than negative.

It may be thought that the *obyedineniya* at least would have greater leeway to take their own decisions freely. Yet the famous Leningrad *Elektrosila*, 'receives from the ministry an annual plan in which it is laid down in what month this or that machine-complex should be made. . . . Based on this plan, economists aided by the factory's computer centre made up a production programme for workshops and sectors. It then became clear that, if the ministry's plan were to be followed . . . there would be bottlenecks and overstrain, while in other months work would be lacking. To avoid this it seemed sensible to alter the order in which the machines are made . . . It would present no problems to agree this with the customers. But, says general director Fomin, the *obyedineniye* has not the right to decide how best to organize the fulfilment of the plan. No arguments have any effect. . . .' Proposals to spend the last month of the year preparing for the following year, instead of delivering completed machines, are rejected, because the ministry wants every *month* to show good indicators. (*Pravda*, 7 August, 1974.) The same author cites complaints that specialized equipment at the factory in Leningrad has to be used for making parts for meat-mincers and vacuum-cleaners, instead of high-class electrical machinery, and an effort to transfer these activities to a *filial* located near Pskov ran into opposition from the Leningrad authorities, because *their* (regional) consumers'-goods indicators would suffer! Finally, *obyedineniya* are severely limited in their rights to invest in new capacity, but, it seems *are* allowed to extend existing premises. Thus the *obyedineniye* 'Salyut', which makes clothing, has put up new workshops as an 'extension' to a half-ruined barn: 'This is like the proverbial action of sewing the trousers onto a patch.' But otherwise 'we would have to obtain permission from many higher organs. Imagine how much time would be lost on all the necessary agreements *(soglasovaniya)*. . . . This picture is typical for *obyedineniya* in light and local industry and in consumer chemicals.' (*Pravda*, 7 August 1974.) Note that again it is 'typical' and *not* exceptional.

Experience will show whether this species of critical material will lead to enhanced powers of *obyedineniya vis-à-vis* ministries and planning organs. Past experience gives one strong grounds for doubt.

CONTRACTS, INFLUENCE OF CUSTOMERS, INFORMAL LINKS

The study of the law of contract and the functioning of the arbitration tribunals *(Gosarbitrazh)* is a specialized area which I am not qualified to discuss and can only recommend the relevant portions of Hazard et al. (1969). We must, however, consider the *role* of contracts, especially in the context of the influence which the user can exert upon what he obtains and when he obtains it. Leaving the problems of consumer demand aside for the moment, let us look at supply contracts involving two state enterprises (one of them could be a trade organization, and so indirectly reflecting what the ultimate consumer is prepared to buy).

Arbitration tribunals do not interfere with the relationship between superior and subordinate within the same hierarchy. They have, however, an important role at two stages. Firstly, they are involved in what are called *pre-contract disputes*, i.e. if the parties cannot agree on the detailed terms of a contract which, under the plan, it is their duty to conclude. Supplier and customer are designated by (say) *Gossnab*, so there must be a contract.

The second kind of dispute concerns *non-compliance with the terms of the contract*. For instance, goods are supplied late, or of the wrong specification or quality. In both cases, the arbitration tribunals endeavour to enforce the intention of the planners.

Judging from a massive Soviet literature on the inadequacy of contract enforcement, this is a weak spot in the system. The problem seems to be two-fold. Firstly, in many cases the contract becomes physically unenforceable, as when, as already shown, the supplying enterprise cannot supply that which it cannot make. Secondly, there are numerous cases in which the terms of the contract (e.g. product specifications) conflict with the enterprise's other success indicators. Thus to supply cloth or leather of the required quality might involve non-fulfilment of a plan in tons or in roubles. In these cases, it 'pays' the enterprise to incur fines, which in any event hurt no individual. So long as the primary duty of management is to their hierarchical superior, and to the indicators which this superior determines, rather than to the customer, this difficulty will and must persist, no matter how often books and articles stress the necessity of reliable contractual links between enterprises. Indeed the argument in favour of the large *obyedineniya* is that they can enforce delivery obligations within a vertically integrated production structure.

This raises the more general point of the influence of the customer. Abundant evidence shows that many difficulties arise for directors because his supplies cannot be relied upon; even if they arrive on time, the quality or specifications are unsuitable, so that he, in his turn, cannot make his products measure up to the quality or durability requirements of *his* customers. In this connection, an effort is made to enforce standards, and indeed there exists a state standards committee, which defines *Gosstandarty*. We shall be saying more about quality considerations generally. Right now it is sufficient to stress that no Soviet critic is happy with these minimal *standarty*, although sums may be deducted from the value of sales, for delivering sub-standard goods. (See *EkG*, 1974 No. 19, p.14.)

A key factor here, additional to those already mentioned above, is the sellers' market plus monopoly. In an economy of shortage, the supplier is powerful. He can insist on his own terms, knowing that he can cause great inconvenience. This attitude is frankly analysed by one Soviet critic, who roundly says: 'the producer, the supplier, dictates'. (A. M. Birman, *EkO*, 1975, No. 1, p.57.) He goes on to cite Western views to the effect that this is inherent in the system, which he denies, while admitting (indeed stressing) that it is indeed so as things now are. The monopoly element is provided not merely by the fact that the state owns all of industry, since within state ownership one would still have a competitive situation, but particularly because the customer enterprise has, as a rule, no choice: it is tied to a particular supplier by the plan. It is simply not allowed to go elsewhere.

As we have repeatedly seen, the centre cannot in fact deal with detail. It can push through priorities. This, while helpful to the priority sectors or projects, can lead to many difficulties. Thus one critic points out that the enterprise's plan will usually contain indicators 'of plan fulfilment . . . for the production of the most important *(vazhneyshy)* types of product. Therefore the production and delivery . . . of all other "less important" types of product drops out of the incentive system', and management can be rewarded 'whether or not they carry out their contractual obligations in respect of the product mix'. (Tsarev, 1971, p.247.)

In my view, there is involved here a point of great significance for the health of the system. Anticipating the discussion of agricultural problems in Chapter 5, let us take the following examples: farms need fertilizer and the means of transporting and spreading it, they need tractors and tools to maintain and repair tractors. The farms, as customers, ask for all of these things. Notoriously, they can obtain some and not others. It appears that they receive 'the most important' ones, that is to say the tractors and the fertilizer. Unfortunately, these are of little use if they cannot be, respectively, spread onto the fields and kept in repair. What, after all, *is* 'most important'? Who judges? How far is it an accidental function of the rank or responsibility of particular officials charged with this or that sector? Or the importance or definability of some plan-indicator? In the case, say, of a car, no one in his right mind would say that the wheels are more 'important' than the engine. But it is certainly possible, indeed it happens, that some product is given priority, while goods and services essential for its proper functioning turn out be some other department's responsibility and are perhaps regarded in that department as 'less important'.

One cannot quantify the extent of micro-economic distortion and confusion. Some critics (including Soviet citizens speaking off the record) lay great stress on these negative characteristics. Things sound so chaotic that it is indeed a wonder anything gets produced at all. The weaknesses discussed throughout this chapter are, I am convinced, real. Yet life goes on. They explain the existence of various forms of waste and inefficiency, but they are consistent with a functioning system. How can this be?

One reason, already mentioned, is that most of the time the various units of which the economy is composed go on doing whatever they were doing in the previous plan-period (only more so). This is a source of inefficiency from the standpoint of innovation, but it makes it possible for the system to cope with an otherwise intolerable burden of planning work.

Secondly, *priority* projects can be 'expedited' through the bureaucratic jungle under special *ad hoc* arrangements. This is why the system can claim spectacular successes from time to time, in carrying out big and ambitious plans, for instance in the oil industry: to build up the output of West Siberian oil to above 100 million tons in a very few years is a great achievement, and no doubt the relevant department of the party's central committee exerted pressure on the various planning and ministerial organs to ensure that supplies did arrive. Similarly, one hears of a military-industrial committee within the planning agencies, and no doubt in the central committee also, whose job it is to ensure that parts for ICBMs or nuclear submarines arrive punctually wherever they are needed. Quality control by representatives of the Defence Ministry is said to be very strict. Only, of course, this downgrades non-priority items.

Thirdly, there exists a complex network of informal relationships. Management know 'their' party secretaries, ministerial chiefs, suppliers, customers, engineers, accountants, and make arrangements with them. These things are difficult to document in the nature of things, but references can be found in Soviet press and literature and evidence has been gathered by Andrle (1976). This is not the same as the *tolkach* type of relationship, it is more like mutual aid. It includes exchanges of materials urgently needed by one enterprise which happen to be in surplus in another, on an informal barter basis. Managers know well that they could get one another into difficult situations, or out of them. One can 'exchange' promises of punctual payment for some modification in product specification. Ministry officials have their own plans, and management can help or hinder their fulfilment. Workers at the plant could make it known, quite informally, that extra payments are a precondition of the extra effort needed to meet plan delivery schedules. Numerous adjustments at a personal level 'cover' gaps and shortages, and a great many unofficial bargains are made; indeed the discussions between ministries and management, about what the plan-orders are to be, can be described as a form of bargaining. In a situation in which, for reasons abundantly explored, the directive-plan *must* be full of gaps and riddled with petty (and not so petty) inconsistencies, the informal network of relationships becomes a matter of considerable significance.

THE PARTY AND MANAGEMENT

This section could be entitled: the micro-economic role of the party, i.e. of its committees and officials at all levels. We have seen that the party central committee and Politbureau play the dominant role in the formulation of economic strategy and in a wide range of planning decisions. Party organs appoint key personnel, including managers. They can also dismiss them. But logic and good order would seem to require that, *given* the plan and given also the party's role in appointing those who execute the plan, the latter should be allowed to get on with their job, without lines of responsibility being confused by a political commissar at their elbow.

Indeed the manager of the enterprise or the 'general director' of the *obyedineniye* is in command. It is also the case that he is superior to the secretary of the party group at the productive unit. One can find numerous instances of secretaries of such groups being criticized for failing to restrain a wilful director, but I have encountered no case in which they are accused of interfering too much.

However, it would seem that pressure from above has been exerted in the direction of greater activity by party groups within enterprises. An example is a long statement issued by the central committee on the role of the party committee in 'building trust No. 36', evidently intended as a model for others to copy. The party committee is shown as 'ensuring coherent and well-aimed *(tseleustremlonnoy)* work of the collectives of construction workers, erectors, project-makers. . . . [and so on]. The party committee pays constant attention to the strengthening of *khozraschet* at all levels, the improvement of planning and supplies of construction sites'. After a number of other paragraphs in the same spirit, the central committee notes deficiencies in party work, including the fact that 'the party committee, while taking decisions on eliminating weaknesses in the work of the trust, does not always sufficiently insist on the implementation of these decisions'. (*Pravda*, 21 August 1974.) One is left wondering what is left of directoral powers if this approach becomes typical. (One's impression is that it is not.)

It may seem odd, in a textbook, to cite a film as evidence, yet it seems worth noting that in the Soviet film *Premiya* (The Bonus) a decision to reject a bonus ('earned' through having persuaded the ministry to lower plan targets) is taken by the *party committee* of the construction enterprise by four votes to three. It is taken for granted that the decision is binding on management; indeed it is suggested that the manager will resign or be dismissed.

There have also been a series of articles on more effective party activity within ministries and their sub-divisions, but these imply that this activity is not effective. One article gives as an example various bureaucratic deformations in the Ministry of Electricity Generation. A local manager in Kostroma complained that essential work could not be undertaken because 'a paragraph was missing from the plan'. Appeals had no effect. 'This was, so to speak, an elementary instance, frequently noted in the sphere of administration: the wires of irresponsibility often complete their circuit and have no end. If anyone is accused he replies: not my fault, it is Ivan Ivanovich, who blames Ivan Petrovich. . . .' But what does the party committee do? They reprimand 'for losing a party card, for illegally obtaining a car, for not paying dues . . . But has anyone been punished for bureaucratism?'. (*Pravda*, 2 December, 1974.)

What, then, *ought* to be the role of the party at intermediate and lower levels? This has been the subject of confusion and unclarity since earliest times. In the twenties, it was understandable that the manager was liable to be a 'bourgeois specialist', who needed a party commissar to watch him. But today the manager is a reliable party member, and a party superior or 'chaser' *(podgonyala)* seems unnecessary. One well understands the remark of an American scholar, commenting on the post-1965 situation, about 'grave problems in the functional definition of the party's proper role'. (Conyngham, 1973, p.273.) And yet a role it certainly has, best defined in Jerry Hough's well-known analysis of the role of local party secretaries (1969). There are bureaucratic tangles to be unravelled, there is point in having a line of appeal upwards other than via the governmental-ministerial pyramid. There are routine and inertia to combat. The party is supposed to mobilize the workers and managerial-technical staffs, to stimulate their faith and enthusiasm, to impose the general interest (defined by the party leadership) as against bureaucratic or local particularism, and to help – along with other inspecting and auditing agencies – to identify wrongdoing or failures in plan-implementation. It would scarcely be proper, as some do, to call these roles 'parasitic', or the equivalent of a fifth wheel to the bus. But problems of demarcating the relative functions of management and party remain.

The key level is not in fact the enterprise party unit but the local, i.e. territorial, party secretariat, which for industry will be the *gorkom* (city committee) or the *obkom* (oblast' committee).

We have seen in Chapter 3 that the *sovnarkhoz* reform, while it lasted, enhanced the role of republics and of *oblasti*, and therefore also of their party secretaries. Khrushchev learned, however, that the secretaries, far from combating 'localism', themselves encouraged it. The reason is clear enough: they were judged by the achievement of the locality for which they were responsible, and exhortations to concern themselves with the (vaguely defined) all-union interest did not have much operational significance. In 1962 he caused confusion by two measures, which were doubtless designed to shake up the party apparatus in the localities: firstly, he reduced the number of *sovnarkhozy*, in a manner which caused their boundaries no longer to correspond (as most of them had done) with *oblast'* boundaries. Secondly, he divided the party apparatus into two: industrial and agricultural, apparently to concentrate them on economic matters. This arrangement could not have worked well, especially as many party functions were neither industrial nor agricultural, while some (e.g. transport, or spare parts for farm machinery) clearly concerned both industry and agriculture. It was no surprise that it was abandoned after Khrushchev's fall in 1964.

The local (city or *oblast'*) secretaries do have real power, *vis-à-vis* the director. He is likely to be affected in his career by the local party's recommendations, positive and negative. So he sometimes finds himself under pressure to produce extra items – for instance spare parts for agriculture – at the behest of the party, or to release labour and transport for the harvest rush, or some other local need. True, his primary duty is to fulfil the plan received from his superiors. The party secretary cannot, unless this is cleared with higher officials, simply order the director to use his resources contrary to plan-instructions. The party secretary can also be of help to the director, in so far as he has a line to Moscow through party channels and this can provide extra priority for supplies. For example, when the first secretary of the Krasnoyarsk *gorkom* discovered that a textile factory was not fulfilling the plan, because it did not receive the necessary materials in time, 'We consider it our duty to interfere. . . . It is necessary sometimes to make representation on such questions to the *kraykom* of the party, and to the party organs of those enterprises which failed to deliver, and to the departments to which they are subordinated.' (*Pravda*, 21 June 1975.)

A multiplicity of inconsistent orders, or of channels of requests for supplies, must surely be a cause of difficulty.

The party organs of the town and *oblast'* also receive plans or instructions which can give rise to confusion, especially now that many *obyedineniya* have branches *(filialy)* outside the area of that local party's responsibility. Thus in the already cited article on the Leningrad *Elektrosila*, the general director complains of pressure from the local organs of Leningrad, in cases in which he finds it convenient to transfer some activity to a branch *(filial)* located in Novgorod. From the standpoint of *Elektrosila*'s indicators, and probably also of efficient specialization, the general director was doubtless right. But it would have adversely affected the Leningrad indicators, because Novgorod is in another *oblast'*. *(Pravda,* 7 August, 1974.) This case, and the publicity given to it, suggests that at least a group at the centre would like to limit the interference of the local party organs, or to confine it to exhortation, inspection and checking on the fulfilment of plans which the local party should treat as binding.

THE REQUIREMENTS AND LIMITS OF REFORM

The whole question of alternative models will be gone into at length in Chapter 11. At this point it will be sufficient to pull together some of the threads. What is it that is wrong? None can doubt the need for change in the direction of greater efficiency. How can this be achieved? Can it be achieved at all without major structural and perhaps political changes? Will the *obyedineniya* make a decisive difference?

As already pointed out, it is too early even to attempt an answer to the last question. There could well be some improvement achieved by deconcentrating more decisions to the level of a smaller number of larger units, formed in most cases by merger. But present indications are that the planning organs will continue to retain their powers, and, because there are fewer recipients of orders, may gain time to make these orders more detailed. In this case there will be little improvement.

Let us take an example gleaned from the pages of *Ekonomicheskaya gazeta.* (V. Volodarsky *EkG,* 1975, No. 33, p.7.) Ouput of machinery, in this case rolling-mill equipment, is still planned in tons, and, despite repeated criticisms, this is still to be so in 1976-80. The factory in question makes complex equipment requiring much skilled labour by hand. Its plan is expressed not only in tons, but also sales *(realizatsiya)* in roubles. Its machines go to factories at home and abroad. New and better equipment needs more skilled labour and more time and trouble to make. The author calculates that, to fulfil *Soyuzglavtyazhmash*'s instructions (this is the all-union heavy-machinery *glavk*) would be impossible: it would require the factory to operate for '32-5 hours a day'. A modified version of the plan would be feasible, but only on condition that the machines be of inferior quality. The home and export orders of *high-quality* equipment would imply a feasible production of 6,400 tons or 13·6 million roubles of output. This would mean, respectively, 59 per cent and 57·6 per cent of the plan. Here is a direct and plain disincentive to the design and output of *productive* capital goods, and this, as the author points out, could even lead to the loss of valuable hard-currency export orders. The reader might suppose that the fault lies with pricing, at least so far as the plan in roubles is concerned, but this (according to the author) is not the main point. By this presumably he means that profit rates are satisfactory, but the plan is in 'gross' roubles, i.e. inclusive of inputs, and so does not sufficiently reward labour inputs (value-added) at the enterprise.

This is indeed reflected in another of his complaints. He points out that it is supposed to be the planning organs' duty to decide who is to be supplied in the first instance, when circumstances make it impossible to produce and deliver all that is ordered. In practice, however, they seem unable to do this, and the enterprise management is left holding the baby. Since there is a labour shortage, this provides an incentive to concentrate on the least labour-intensive machines (labour-intensive in their production, not in their use), although this may well not accord with national-economic goals.

If one examines the causes of the situation here described, one sees the now familiar picture of the ill-informed centre trying to issue directives in aggregate terms, and unintentionally stimulating an inferior or ill-adapted product mix. One gets the same picture in an article on a footwear factory: the plans include a target for economy in materials, and this contradicts consumer demand (e.g. for boots as against shoes, which require more leather per pair), and in any case good materials may be unobtainable, whatever the prescribed quality of deliveries ('can we refuse? Under no circumstances. We take what we are sent, otherwise we will get nothing') (Shutyak, *EkG*, 1974, No. 3, p.6.) Note the importance here, as so often, of the sellers' market, i.e. the consequences of taut plans, of shortages.

What difference would it make, so long as the system remains in other respects unaltered, whether the authors are referring to a production *obyedineniye* or an 'enterprise'? The planning organs and ministries retain their powers regardless, as may be seen in the list appended to this chapter of indicators applicable to the new (1976– 80) five-year plan period, a list which is laid down as applicable to the *obyedineniye* too.

What is decisive is the right of management to make up its own production programme in the light of customer requirements. Only thus can these requirements exert the necessary influence on the product mix. Only then can the wasteful distortions illustrated repeatedly in this chapter be eliminated or reduced. It is important to note that these distortions are usually unintentional. The planners *desire* that footwear should fit to customers' tastes and feet. They most certainly desire that rolling-mill equipment be modern and of high quality. If the opposite occurs, this is *not* due to conflict between planners' preferences and users' preferences, but to a malfunctioning of the system. Enough has been said to show that this is a *systemic* malfunctioning, not due to errors of individual planning officials or managers.

However, before jumping to the conclusion that the 'market' solution is all that is needed, one must remember the existence of large Western corporations, whose internal interlinks are *administered*. This suggests that the problem is more complicated. Let us take as an example the American chemicals corporation, DuPont. Its turnover is analagous to that of the Soviet Ministry of Chemical Industry, and they make many of the same things. What is the decision-making power of a manager of a plant within DuPont, or of the top man in one of DuPont's divisions in charge of particular groups of products or activities (*glavki*? all-union *obyedineniya*? These are possible analogies). Is the manager within DuPont the possessor of greater powers over output, investment and price decisions than his Russian opposite number? Very little empirical research has been done on this, but I suspect from admittedly inadequate evidence that the answer is: there is not much difference in the two situations. If DuPont is more efficient, if it is able to ensure that its component parts perform in line with the intentions of its top management, this is not achieved by market-decentralization within the organization.

But if this is so, why should we expect the correct solution to be the granting of more powers of decision to the Soviet manager – in the chemical industry at least?

It seems that an essential point is in danger of being overlooked in such discussions as these. There is the problem known as 'sub-optimization': junior levels of management in any corporation may well be unable to judge what impact their activities might have on the corporation as a whole. Decisions require to be taken at a level at which the necessary *information* is available, and, as already pointed out, there must also be *means* and *motivation* to act. We have seen that the centre is frequently without the necessary disaggregated information on the basis of which to issue unambiguous and uncontradictory instructions. But it does not follow that the factory manager is the right decision-making level. It depends on the type of decision and the sector with which we are concerned. If a micro-decision is taken by reference to relative profitability, this can only be rational on certain assumptions concerning not only prices but also competition: in the absence of competition, profits can be increased by worsening quality, for instance. It must also be assumed that there are no appreciable external diseconomies, and that indivisibilities and complementarities do not substantially distort the picture: thus one recalls the example, cited above, of the oil complex of north-west Siberia. Plainly the *separate* profitabilities, howsoever defined and computed, of each segment of the interconnected sectoral development pro- gramme could not form a 'rational' basis for operational decisions. These would need to be taken by reference to the development pro- gramme as a whole, which (let us assume) is profitable from the stand- point of the whole economy. The decision as to whether north-west Siberian oil is necessary for the economy as whole could scarcely be taken in north-west Siberia, since this requires information – about other sources of supply, domestic needs for oil, foreign markets, etc. – which the centre and only the centre is likely to possess.

But these arguments, which could typically apply to oil, many chemicals, electricity, steel, copper and similar industries, are much weaker when one turns to such things as farm machinery, clothing, footwear and technological innovation generally, not to mention agriculture. There is also an important difference between major investment decisions and operational questions affecting the product mix. The centre clings to control over means and tries to process information, but in fact is unable to issue meaningful instructions. To repeat the words used long ago by Liberman, the task simply 'over- whelms any apparatus of *Gosplany* and *snabsbyty*'.

These questions will be reopened in Chapter 11. But the evidence points to the need for diversity, the unlikelihood that any *simpliste* decentralized market solution would or could be a satisfactory, universally applicable remedy.

APPENDIX (TO CHAPTER 4)

The following is part of the *tipovaya metodika* (basic rules) for drawing up plans for the five-year period 1976–80, as laid down by the USSR *Gosplan* and reported by *Ekonomicheskaya gazeta* No. 3, 1975. Re- produced here is only the part described as 'indicators confirmed by superior organs', i.e. those which the enterprise or *obyedineniye* is not free to determine, which can be the subject of instructions from higher levels.

Volume of sold *(realiziruyemoy)* output
Output of the most important *(vazhneyshikh)* types of product in physical terms
Share of top-category output in total output
Growth in labour productivity
Total wages fund
Profit
Profit rate *(rentabel'nost')*
    Total

Accounting [i.e. net of capital charge]
Receipts from budget
Payments to budget
    Turnover tax
    Charge on basic capital and on normed working capital
    Fixed (rental) payments
    Free remainder of profits
    Total
Capital investments: Total volume of centralized** investments of
                       which: building and installation work
Completions (vvod v deystviye) of centralized capital works
                       Basic capital
                       Productive capacity for the most important
                       products
Tasks for introduction of new techniques
....
Tasks for reducing utilization norms for important economic
resources***
....
....
Norms for payment in respect of capital assets and normed working
capital
Norms for payments into fund for developing production and the
economic incentive funds.
(NOTE: The multiple dots are in the original, implying the existence
of other compulsory indicators applicable to specific sectors. The
above list is followed by a longer one of indicators which are compulsory in the sense that the *obyedineniye* or enterprise must report
them, but which, according to the rules, they are free to decide for
themselves.)

[i.e. centrally planned]
***[i.e. norms for use of materials, fuels, etc., per unit of output]

NOTE

Important changes in the system of plan indicators are being introduced following the decree of July 1979. Its full text may be found in
Ekonomicheskaya gazeta, No. 32 of 1979. The following is the briefest
sketch of the proposed changes (many of the details have yet to be
elaborated):

(a) *A reassertion of principles* which were supposedly in existence
     before, but which were frequently disregarded: thus plans were
     to be implementable ('assured of the necessary material, human
     and financial resources'), balanced and stable, and should 'not be
     corrected downwards to the level of their actual fulfilment' (!).

(b) *Normed net output* (normed value-added) is to be used 'in the majority of sectors as the basis of planning production, labour productivity and the wages fund'. This requires the separate calculation of a normed net output for every product, including a notional rate of profit, so that there will in practice be variations as between the normed and actual cost of processing, the normed and actual profits, in every productive unit. There will in effect be two 'prices' to fix for every product, and these number many millions. A detailed description of the complex procedures to be used appeared in *Planovoye khozyaistvo*, 1979, No. 11. It must be added that it is *not* clear whether growth-rate plans will be expressed in terms of normed value-added, or whether *val* will be in practice preserved for this purpose. The object of using normed value-added is to remove the incentive to use dear inputs. But this is only one indicator among many.

(c) *Volume of output* of the most important products in quantitative terms, with some modification of volume measures to take *quality* into account (how?).

(d) *Total value of sales*, to ensure that delivery contracts are fulfilled in total.

(e) *The fulfilment of planned delivery contracts:* great stress is being placed on this.

(f) *Increase in labour productivity.*

(g) *Maximum numbers employed*, and within this total also maximum number engaged in unmechanized work (*ruchnoi trud*).

(h) *Norm of wage payments per unit of net output* (which may make possible increases in wages if labour is economized).

(i) *Total profit* (the profit *rate – rentabel 'nost'*) apparently disappears as a compulsory indicator.

(j) In some sectors, *cost reduction.*

(k) *Investment* objectives.

(l) '*Tasks for the introduction of new technique.*'

(m) (In the construction industry) *net value of work completed* (an improvement on a system which expressed output as moneys expended, which stimulated waste of materials and was unrelated to completions).

Such indicators as payments into the budget, norms of utilization of various materials and probably also the wages fund will presumably survive.

The only comment called for is to draw attention to the complexity and probable internal inconsistencies) of this multiplicity of indicators, and the increase in the burden of the already greatly overburdened central planning mechanism. This reform will surely not cure the chronic ailments from which the system suffers.

CHAPTER 5

AGRICULTURE

WHY A SEPARATE CHAPTER?

Agriculture deserves separate consideration for a number of reasons.

Firstly, as already shown in Chapter 1, it is unique in having three major categories of producers: state, *kolkhoz* and private.

Secondly, it has a special history of its own with regard to prices, incentives, relationship with party officials and also planning (e.g. of procurements rather than production).

Thirdly, the agricultural process is highly specific: 'it is concerned with live organisms, affected by many natural, including biological factors, and also organizational-economic and social conditions'. (Dobrynin, *VEk*, 1974, No. 11, p.38.)

Fourthly, it can be said that the very nature of the productive units is unique to the system. Thus a steelworks, or clothing factory, or transport undertaking, is more or less similar, given the techniques used, in any country. However, the size and internal organization of *kolkhozy* and *sovkhozy* have few parallels elsewhere, and the 'private plots' are mini-enterprises whose growth is deliberately obstructed by state policy.

Therefore, while other sectors of the economy certainly have problems of their own – transport, for instance – they will not be separately considered in a book intended to introduce and analyse the Soviet type of economy, while agriculture does merit separate consideration.

THE THREE FORMS OF PROPERTY: THEIR SIGNIFICANCE

Picking up again the thread of an argument just made, the basic organizational arrangements in agricultural production bear the imprint of revolutionary change, indeed imposed change. Whereas a factory and its productive methods were not significantly altered when it was nationalized.

The *kolkhoz*, as was pointed out in Chapter 1, was originally set up as a pseudo-co-operative, designed to ensure supplies of agricultural produce to the state at minimum cost to the state. Everything was subordinated to 'procurements' as described in the excellent paper by M. Lewin (1974). In the Stalin period, the income of the peasant for collective work was minimal; most families could subsist only because of the produce of the household plots and privately owned livestock. Work for the collective became the equivalent of work for the lord on a mediaeval manor, and was sometimes (unofficially!) known by the old Russian word describing serf labour-service: *barshchina*. *Kolkhozy* were 'exploited' in all kinds of ways: not just low prices for compulsory deliveries of produce, and overcharging for the equally compulsory services of state-owned tractors, but also by overcharging for inputs: unlike state organs, *kolkhozy* were compelled to pay high retail prices, but in many cases could not obtain inputs at any price, being considered low-priority. For example, in the late Stalin period they were denied electricity supplies, having to generate their own or do without – which did not prevent official painters from showing Stalin against a background of electric tractors! (There were no such tractors anyhow! But what do such details matter? Socialist realism is not vulgar naturalism.)

Sovkhozy, being *state* farms, were better treated. Even if they were paid low prices, the resultant deficits were met by the state by way of subsidy, so that wage payments were guaranteed. *Sovkhozy* were better provided with inputs, operated their own tractors, and were supplied at state wholesale prices. Evidently, for as long as the object of policy was to exploit agriculture for the benefit of industrialization, the *kolkhoz* form was preferable, because cheaper for the state.

After Stalin's death there was a change in policy. The condition of agriculture was deplorable, as Khrushchev pointed out to the September 1953 plenum of the central committtee. A series of measures were taken to remedy matters. Prices were repeatedly increased, so farm revenues rose. So did pay for collective work, and (by a lesser percentage) so did wages in *sovkhozy*. Investments, financed by the state and by the farms themselves, increased, as did output of farm equipment and of fertilizer. The gap between rural and urban incomes has been greatly narrowed. Indeed, it may no longer make sense to speak of the 'exploitation' of agriculture, if by this is meant the pumping out of resources for the benefit of industrial investment. The evidence for this will appear when we discuss agricultural prices (Chapter 7).

By stages the administrative and operational differences between *sovkhozy* and *kolkhozy* began to diminish. Prices of most farm products were equalized. The same supply organization, *Sel'khoztekhnika*, was set up to provide inputs for both types of farms at the same prices. In 1958 *kolkhozy* were allowed (indeed compelled) to acquire tractors and combine-harvesters, with the abolition of the state Machine Tractor Stations. Finally, in 1966 the *kolkhozy* shifted to a guaranteed-income basis: instead of the work-day units based on the residuary-legatee principle, payments to labour of a specified minimum became a primary charge on the *kolkhoz* revenues, as already explained in Chapter 1. There will be more to say about labour incentives later in the present chapter.

This has left in being the following significant differences between *kolkhozy* and *sovkhozy*: firstly, the juridical fact of co-operative as against state ownership. Secondly, the formally elective nature of the *kolkhoz* chairman and management committee, as against the appointed *sovkhoz* director. Thirdly, the degree of autonomy, legal and to some extent real, of a *kolkhoz* is greater, in that a *sovkhoz* is directly subordinated to a territorial *sovkhoz* administration (Bronshteyn, *VEk*, 1973, No. 10, pp.10ff and the decree on *Sovkhoz* trusts in *EkG*, 1975, No. 45.), whereas the nominally co-operative nature of *kolkhozy* gives them greater leeway. Fourthly, the *kolkhozy* finance the bulk of their investments out of revenue, while *sovkhozy* receive more grants from the state, though with the spread of 'full *khozraschet*' among *sovkhozy* (see below) this element of difference is diminishing. Finally, despite the changes introduced in 1966, there is greater dependence of incomes in *kolkhozy* on the financial results of that *kolkhoz*. That is to say, subject to a minimum, there is greater variation in payment to labour than in *sovkhozy*. There is at present a clear trend towards 'bringing closer together' the two types of property, as a number of party pronouncements bear witness, above all by involving them in joint enterprises and other activities.

In the interests of accuracy, one must mention that there are farms in the state sector which are not *sovkhozy*. These are normally auxiliary farms operated by non-agricultural enterprises, for example to supply factory canteens.

In the analysis that follows, there will be few occasions to contrast the economic effectiveness of *sovkhozy* and *kolkhozy*. The problems and difficulties of Soviet agriculture in the seventies appear, in the large majority of instances, to apply in equal measure to both.

PRIVATE PLOTS: A CLOSER LOOK

Before discussing these, it is necessary to consider the still very considerable 'private sector'. To designate it by this name is to depart from Soviet statistical practice: they treat the output of this sector as in some way socialized. There seems no basis for this. The land of what will have to be called private plots is not privately owned, but is cultivated by peasants (and also many state-employed persons in rural and suburban areas) with the authorization of the *kolkhoz* or state organ concerned. Livestock is genuinely private property, but is usually pastured on collective or state land. These are facts to be borne in mind. However, the individuals concerned work for themselves and own the produce. The fact that many of them are also engaged in collective work introduces a tension, arising out of the division of work time between private and collective (or state), which has several times affected official policies.

The 'auxiliary household plot', for reasons already given, was for decades not auxiliary at all, but vital to the survival of the peasant family. From it came the bulk of foodstuffs other than grain, and from sales in the free market came most of the average *kolkhoz* family's cash income. As far as cash is concerned the situation has radically altered, but to this day the plot is the source of most livestock products and vegetables consumed in peasant families. One important reason for this is the poor development of retail trade in foodstuffs in rural areas.

Thus a book published in 1966, using data from a sample survey carried out in three *oblasti* in the Ukraine, showed that *kolkhoz* peasants obtained 96·5 per cent of their potatoes, 84·6 per cent of their vegetables, 98·9 per cent of their milk, 99·8 per cent of their meat and lard, from their household plots and private animals. (Dmitrashko, 1966, p.46.)

Just as the Soviet type *kolkhozy* and *sovkhozy* have no analogy in the Western world, so nowhere in the West is there a parallel to the private plot. Of course, the cultivation of vegetables (for instance) on allotments by workers and their families is to be found in many countries, but their contribution to total output is insignificant. Whereas we are dealing with a sector which, as we saw in Chapter 1 still contributes over 25 per cent of total agricultural production, and is still vitally important as a producer of potatoes, vegetables, eggs, fruit, meat and dairy produce, though its share has been in steady decline for decades.

This sector is still mediaeval in its techniques. The little plots are cultivated with spade and hoe. Fodder for animals has to be collected by hand, sometimes in fact stolen (on the occasions when fodder was short or priority was given to collective livestock). In assessing the efficiency of this type of cultivation, other factors must be taken into account: thus much of the work is done in the spare time of *kolkhoz* members, or by pensioners and other dependents; the small area of the plot (most often 0·25 hectares) receives a disproportionate share of manure from the privately owned livestock, as well as a disproportionate amount of care and attention from those who cultivate it. So the yield per hectare is, understandably, higher, crop for crop, than on collective or state land. Furthermore, there is a concentration on high-value crops on the resticted area (e.g. onions, not rye), so that the *value* of output per hectare is *much* higher. This, plus the fact that the private livestock derive their food from collective or state land, helps to explain the apparently remarkable fact that '3 per cent of the sown area produces 25 per cent or more of the produce'.

It is worth mentioning that, in the process of criticizing the 50 per cent bonus for over-quota deliveries, it was stated that both *sovkhozy* and *kolkhozy* purchase livestock from households, and without bothering to fatten it simply deliver it to the state, 'which permits without trouble to increase over-plan sales and the consequent material rewards'. (Shainov and Kharchenko *EkG*, 1976, No. 3, p.9.) The extra money can then be quietly shared out with the peasants, who, of course, cannot get the over-quota delivery bonus if *they* sell to the state, since they have no compulsory quota! Note that this probably means that the share of the household plots in total output may be understated in the official statistics.

The neglect of the needs of the private plot has from time to time attracted critical comment in the USSR. Thus: 'Let us look how the houshold plot is cultivated? In the main by means inherited from the distant past. Up till now there is no organized production of mechanical tools for market-gardening. Yet such equipment is produced in other socialist countries, for instance Czechoslovakia. This is the so-called "hand-operated tractor" run by a petrol engine with various attachments capable of doing up to twenty kinds of operations, including ploughing, cultivation, transport of small loads, pumping water, sawing logs and spraying trees' (*Pravda*, 9 January 1975.) If these things were available, argues the author, 1½ to 2 milliard man-years [mostly in fact woman-years] would be saved.

However, as the author well knows, a major cause of low productivity in the *kolkhoz-sovkhoz* sector is lack of what the Russians call *malaya mekhanizatsiya*, or mechanization of auxiliary tasks. Amid all the other national priorities, including agricultural priorities, the needs of peasant private plots have in fact been ignored. There have been difficulties too in supplies of pesticides, good seeds, fodder. Indeed the peasants have at times been denounced for buying bread to feed to chickens and pigs, or even to cows. No doubt these are irrational and wasteful practices. However, if other and more 'rational' sources of fodder were unavailable, what was a peasant to do?

The other source of inefficiency associated with the private plot concerns the marketing of its products. Untold millions of days are lost as peasants set out for town, and it may be a very distant town, with whatever they can carry, and they may spend several days away. Transport facilities have somewhat improved in recent years, and there also exists a system of co-operative commission sales: the peasant can avoid going to town and leave it to the co-operative to market his produce for him. However, the co-operative organization in rural areas is often absent or inadequate (Dmitrashko, 1966, p.51), and journeys to town are due partly to this cause, and partly to the peasant's age-old belief that he can strike the best bargain.

On several occasions in Soviet history the authorities have intervened to limit peasant private activities, since the time in the early thirties when, in the bitter aftermath of collectivization, the rights of the peasants to have household plots, animals and access to a free market were recognized. This interference has taken many different forms: denying adequate fodder or pasture facilities, heavy taxation, cutting the size of the allotments, administrative pressure to sell livestock, obstructing journeys to market, and attempts to impose ceilings on market prices. (Dmitrashko, pp.46, 49, 50–2.) The motives behind such policies seem to be a mixture: to combat distraction from collective work, opposition to so-called 'speculation', ideologically inspired objection to private enterprise. This despite a good deal of evidence collected by Soviet sources to the effect that it can be counter-productive to restrict private activities: not only is it bad for morale, but peasants simply spend more time in seeking out fodder and otherwise evading the restrictive regulations, still further reducing the quantity and quality of their labour inputs for the collective. This is revealed in the famous story by Abramov (1963). From time to time such restrictions and tax burdens are denounced. Thus Khrushchev criticized Stalin for imposing them, and yet he himself acted similarly in his last years, and this in turn was criticized by Brezhnev in 1965 at the March plenum of the central committee.

The present situation is not too clear. On the one hand, there is recognition in official documents, including the revised *kolkhoz* charter, of the rights of peasants in this matter. None the less, the greater burdens of collective work, with the formal right of the farm management to require attendance to such work whenever it is deemed necessary, can cut into the time available for looking after private activities and travelling to market. In the late Stalin period there was a compulsory minimum of collective work, but under Khrushchev this was left open-ended. The transfer of several millions of *kolkhoz* peasants, along with their farms, to the *sovkhoz* (state-farm) category led to reduction in private activities, both because state-farm labour is to a greater degree full-time, and because the rules specify a smaller size of household landholding (though the peasants were promised that existing plots would be retained). Finally, occasional references are still encountered to price ceilings in free markets and to obstruction of movement of produce, e.g. out of Georgia (see also Chapter 10).

It is an interesting instance of official psychology to note the reaction to high free-market prices. After all, they obviously reflect the gap between supply and demand in state stores, a measure of shortages which the free market exists to fill. Yet the official response can be negative: high prices mean profiteering and speculation. True, the law allows sales of own produce, but it is suspected (not without reason) that some may be selling other people's produce.

It is important to note that a slow decline in the role of private plots can be due to causes other than administrative restrictions. Thus the improvement in pay for labour on collective and state fields makes some peasants less willing to devote time to private activities, especially to the time-consuming journey to market, unless prices there are very much above official levels. It is interesting to note that recent surveys have shown that peasants have very little spare time, after their collective and private activities (see Perevedentsev, 1975, p.142.) It must be stressed that the vigorous efforts devoted to the private sector in the past were due in some degree to sheer necessity: the *kolkhoz* was plainly unable to pay enough on which to live. Many, especially young people, prefer leisure to milking cows and hoeing cabbage-patches, once they can earn enough to enable them to spend time on more amusing pursuits. Many also prefer to migrate to towns.

So the household plot and animals were a necessity for survival for most peasants until comparatively recently, and remain an essential source for many foodstuffs still. However, they are no longer an indispensable source of cash, and their role may steadily diminish as rural incomes and rural retail trade improve. They are, however, a good way of using the labour of older women in particular. Given that material inputs (other than manure) are few and primitive, the productivity of labour compares well with the much more highly capitalized state and collective sectors.

SPECIFIC FEATURES OF AGRICULTURAL PLANNING

The 'objects' of agricultural planning are *kolkhozy* and *sovkhozy*. There was a time, before 1958, when state procurement quotas were levied also on private plots. But no longer.

Agricultural planning developed the following features, for reasons many of which require a historical explanation.

Firstly, the primary concern was for *state procurements*. In the case of *sovkhozy*, the produce belonged in principle to the state. The *kolkhozy*, however, owned their produce, and could divert it to the use of their own members, or to feed animals. This, indeed, is one of the special features of agricultural products, at least of foodstuffs: they can be eaten. Factory output can, it is true, be stolen, but that is not quite the same thing. Thus it is evident that the output of a typical factory is for delivery to customers, i.e. for sale. Whereas even in recent years only a third of the grain harvest was purchased by the state, most of the crop being retained for seed, fodder, peasant consumption, etc.

Secondly, procurements were seen for a generation at least as a form of tax, unremunerative, a duty. Hence, of course, the need to make them *compulsory*. As we shall see in Chapter 7, prices paid to farms are now much more favourable. However, the price relationships between products remain 'irrational', in the sense that the desired product mix is seldom if ever stimulated by price relativities. Hence the need to maintain the compulsory element in procurements.

Thirdly, it is a characteristic of agriculture that land has large numbers of alternative uses. A steelworks or a radio factory makes steel or radios; admittedly there is still a problem of what kind of steel or radios, but at least there is not likely to be a switch to producing women's blouses or nitric acid instead. Land can grow many crops, or be left for pasture for the livestock. Also, as we have seen, it can be diverted to grow things which the producers can themselves consume. Given the fact that for a generation the prices paid by the state were very low, it became 'traditional' for party and state officials to interfere to ensure the desired cropping pattern and livestock numbers.

Fourthly, in the early stages the 'interference' was in fact a continuous necessity, to maintain collectivization; hence the use of political officers (or party secretaries) based upon the MTS (Machine Tractor Stations, until their abolition in 1958) as a species of political commissars. The combination of lack of incentives and the existence of numerous alternative uses for land and its produce created tensions unique to agriculture, and these in turn led to a much more systematic supervision by party officials than was the case in industry. The main reason seems to have been the following. Whereas, given an order to fulfil a plan, it was in the interests of management and workers alike in industry to fulfil it, in agriculture this was not the case. The farm was very likely to be more prosperous if the (procurements) plan was *not* fulfilled. Many normal farm operations – even ploughing and harvesting – had to be (and still are) the subject of national party-inspired campaigns, because the 'automatic' desire of any individual peasant or farmer to make a success of his enterprise was absent. It had in fact been killed by collectivization and its harsh aftermath as was declared to have been the inevitable consequence of the struggle against private property instincts (Motyashov, 1968). After all, no one needs a national publicity campaign to persuade American or French farmers, or even Russian peasants on their household plots, to undertake routine agricultural operations.

Hence the repeated 'campaigns'. Some were built around much-publicized projects, or methods. The list is a long one. The introduction of an alleged rubber-substitute plant, *kok-sagyz*, occupied space in the press in the thirties, as did the raising of rabbits, and the *travopolye* (ley grass) crop rotation scheme. Then after the war came Stalin's 'plan for the transformation of nature' (forest shelter-belts). More recently, under Khrushchev, there was a whole series of campaigns: the ploughing up of virgin and fallow lands, expansion of acreage under maize, 'overtake America in the production of meat and milk', reduction in area under sown grasses, the introduction of two-stage harvesting, the use of 'peat-compost pots' *(torfo-peregnoynyye gorshochki)*. All had as their motive the improvement of agriculture. All were distinguished and indeed disfigured by the administrative methods used, primarily through the use of the local party machine, whose response to orders of the above kinds was to impose them regardless of local circumstances. This 'planning' (really anti-planning!) by set pattern *(shablon)* was repeatedly criticized, and as repeatedly committed again and again. The resultant losses are hard to compute, the more so because some local party officials and farm managers became adept at reporting obedience to orders even while evading them. Khrushchev, himself more guilty than anyone of imposing campaigns from above, explained how he had successfully resisted, while in the Ukraine, orders from Moscow to expand the acreage under spring wheat, instead of the higher-yielding winter wheat. It is odd that he failed to draw the moral when it was his turn to issue orders. Apparently he knew of no other way to get things done in agriculture.

Let us look briefly at the consequences of such 'campaigning' methods.

In many instances a basically sound idea was distorted by *shablon*. Thus it was sensible to plough up the little-used lands in West Siberia and north Kazakhstan, as *(inter alia)* it spread the risk of drought: often, when it rains in the Ukraine it is dry in Kazakhstan and vice versa. Khrushchev also hoped that more wheat from the east would release land for fodder crops in European Russia, including his favourite, maize, which he dubbed 'Queen of the fields'. But what in fact happened was that party officials also ordered the ploughing up of lands which were unsuitable for cultivation, so as to overfulfil the virgin lands plan, and then (not without encouragement from Krushchev himself) resisted agronomically sound measures to conserve the soil by increased fallowing. As for maize, it was spread by order to areas in which it could not flourish, or would only do so if more fertilizer and equipment were available than in fact existed. Examples were cited (while Khrushchev was still in power) of party officials ordering the ploughing up of growing clover so as to be able to report a reduction in sown grasses, even though no seed was available to sow any other crop. The 'meat' campaign led one party secretary, Larionov of Ryazan', to such expedients as over-slaughtering, and the delivery to the state of meat obtained from other areas and from peasants' own livestock. Methods of cultivation and breeding developed by the notorious Lysenko were taken up by party officials and thrust down the throats of farm management.

The provincial and local party secretaries were at once the enforcers and the victims of these methods. The best 'catalogue' of 'campaigning-planning' and of its ill-effects may be found in the stenographic report of the March 1965 plenum of the central committee, held after Khrushchev's fall. For example, the reader may be referred to such speeches as that of Gustov, secretary of the Pskov *obkom*.

Brezhnev undertook to abandon such methods, and indeed matters have improved since 1964, with much more freedom given to local party and state officials – though little more to farm management – to choose what is most suitable for the area. Since officials do not (and did not) desire to harm agriculture, and behaved as they did because of pressure from the centre, the relaxation of this pressure has had a positive effect. It used to be said that the villages suffered from the effects of *vodka i svodka*, the latter term meaning the report to higher party and state authority (e.g. reporting the fulfilment of some unsound campaign-plan). There is now less emphasis on *svodka*, judging simply by the disappearance of most of the much-publicized campaigns.

Most, but not all. What remains, very significantly, is precisely that which should be routine: sowing, repairs to equipment, harvesting, deliveries to elevators. Every year it is the same. Thus the central committee and council of ministers issued a decree 'on measures to ensure the harvesting and procurement of farm produce in 1975'. (*Pravda*, 18 May 1975.) Similar decrees were issued in previous years and another appeared in 1976. This, it is true, concerns also such matters as mobilizing people and means of transport from town, a procedure of which more will have to be said. But around the harvesting and procurement the party and state machine is annually mobilized. Thus, to give one of many examples, a secretary of the Kustanay *obkom* tells how '*we* attach lorries, wagons (trailers) and storage capacity to each harvesting group', and the *Pravda* correspondent comments that 'party organs must take under the strictest supervision *(kontrol')* the preparation for the harvesting. . . .' (*Pravda*, 9 August, 1975 – my emphasis.) In another article, significantly entitled 'direction of the harvesting' *(upravleniye zhatvoy)*, the secretary of the Nikolayev *obkom* speaks of '*our* having to take charge of the reorganization of the direction of all branches', especially those concerned with harvesting and transport detachments. 'Much of the responsibility falls upon the *rayon* level', and the party secretary points to the operational role of the *rayon* agricultural department *(raysel'khoz-upravleniye)*, which is the lowest rung of the ladder which stretches upwards to the Ministry of Agriculture.

Presumably the reader is convinced by now: the farm management, whether the elected *kolkhoz* management or the appointed *sovkhoz* director, is subject to detailed operational supervision, qualitatively different from the supervision over industrial managers, who usually do not require to be told by superior officers to oil machinery and to fuel the boilers. And yet no mention has yet been made of the annual 'sowing campaign' *(posevnaya)*, the publicity and exhortations around autumn ploughing (a regular subject for a *Pravda* editorial every autumn), and there has only been a brief reference to the annual procurements *(zagotovka)* drive, designed to ensure that the state gets its share of the produce. The much better prices now paid by the state have diminished the relative intensity of the *zagotovka* drive, which used in the Stalin period to be most ruthless, as described in detail by Lewin (1974). None the less, as the columns of the Soviet press bear witness, pressure to deliver to the state is still present, and publicity is given to party officials and farms undertaking to make over-plan deliveries.

On repeated occasions, the most solemn being perhaps Brezhnev's speech to the March 1965 plenum of the central committee, it was promised that delivery quotas would be fixed for years in advance, so that management could confidently plan ahead. Thus no crop-rotation scheme, or livestock expansion programme, could be safe if state exactions were arbitrarily varied. And arbitrarily varied they were, as Brezhnev, and Khrushchev before him, admitted with regret.

Yet the practice continues, though in modified form: it seems that the delivery quotas are not frequently altered, but over-quota deliveries have become compulsory. Indeed this was built in to the 1965 decision, which fixed the quotas to add up to an amount below known procurement needs. Also one must bear in mind the effects of weather variations: in some areas damage to crops by drought or frost can make it impossible to meet even the quota, so that it must be made up by other areas. To reward over-quota deliveries, a bonus of 50 per cent over the procurement price is paid for most products. More will be said about the logic and illogic of this when we discuss prices.

Despite all the above, it must not be thought that the *kolkhoz* chairman and the *sovkhoz* director are powerless. On the contrary, they have great powers over their subordinates, especially because of the living conditions in rural areas: rural trade is still weak, and many elementary facilities (from firewood to transport, from fodder for private livestock to building materials essential for repairing the peasant's hut) are provided – and can be withheld – by the management. Leisure facilities are equally dependent upon the allocation of funds and space by management. As in all real-life situations, management is also in some degree dependent on its subordinates, especially as go-slow and absenteeism are difficult to check and poor work difficult to prevent. (Semi-fictional examples of this are in Abramov (1963) and Mozhayev, 1966.)

Vis-à-vis his superiors, the chairman or director, just as his industrial equivalent, has the important advantage of knowing his own local circumstances best, and thus being in a position to supply or withhold information. Much therefore depends on his initiative. Yet much has been done by spasmodic interference from above to penalise initiative, and in particular to penalize the long view. This is particularly dangerous in agriculture, where, after all, it is evident that crop rotations take many years to complete and soil preservation and improvement are of necessity long-term measures. It has been a feature of partystate intervention, often carried out through plenipotentiaries *(upolnomochenyye)* whose normal job is not in agriculture, to impose the fulfilment of current plans to the detriment of longer-term considerations. However, especially since 1965, much more attention has been paid to soil improvement.

It is impossible to measure the negative effects of the planning system as it affects agriculture, since it is inextricably tied in with other material and organizational inadequacies, to which we will turn in a moment. All that need be said at this stage is that the specific features of agricultural production, plus the habits formed at a time when coercion predominated and incentives were minimal, have together had a negative impact. Along with other factors, these features of Soviet agriculture help to explain why, despite much effort and heavy expenditures, productivity and efficiency remain at levels which the Soviet leaders know to be unsatisfactory. Nowhere is the Soviet Union further behind the developed West than in agriculture. The rest of this chapter will be examining the causes of this relative inefficiency and also the actual and potential effectiveness of various remedies.

In making comparisons, however, it is essential to bear in mind the unfavourable influence of natural conditions: whether measured in terms of soil fertility, rainfall, liability to drought or frost damage and length of growing season, the United States is greatly superior. This means that the same inputs, the same effort, the same skill, would yield less in the Soviet Union – though we cannot know how much less – and that therefore the inefficiencies ascribable to the system do not account for all the differences of productivity. Nor can we assume that Russian peasants would have been as enterprising and productive as American farmers under identical natural conditions if private farming had not been eliminated in the USSR. Inter-system comparisons will be discussed at greater length in Chapter 14.

SOURCES OF AGRICULTURAL INEFFICIENCY: MATERIAL INPUTS

A feature of the recent history of Soviet agriculture has been the energetic and evidently sincere effort to repair past neglects. Thus total investment in agriculture rose from an average of under 3 milliard roubles a year in 1951–5 to 7·27 milliards in 1961 and then to 23·7 milliards in 1973. The latter represented over 24 per cent of total investments in that year.

Astonishingly, the proportion of US total civilian investment devoted to agriculture in recent years is less than 4 per cent. There is an element of statistical non-comparability about these percentages, in that some activities which are considered 'agricultural' in the USSR are provided by various specialist-auxiliary industries and services in the United States. However, the fact remains that any under-capitalization of, and under-supply to, Soviet agriculture is hard to reconcile with the very substantial sums which have been devoted to investments.

Large increases have also been recorded in deliveries of fertilizer to agriculture: a more than seven-fold increase in the period 1960–72. (*Nar. Khoz.*, 1972, p.367.) In the same period, delivery of tractors almost exactly doubled. It must also be emphasized that output of farm produce has risen appreciably. Comparing the three years 1959–61 with 1970–2, for example, there is a rise in gross agricultural output by over 35 per cent. The bad harvest of 1975 is explicable very largely by poor weather, the 1976 record by very good weather. Nevertheless, proportionately to effort and to inputs, and to plans and needs as these have been defined and accepted by the leadership, performance has not been adequate. The fact that yields remain well below those of adjoining East European countries is a source of concern, and demonstrates *(inter alia)* just how low was the Soviets' starting-point, after a generation of neglect.

Past neglect is, indeed, an explanation in itself. Thus the supply of electricity to agriculture has risen rapidly, but it had been so small that very large percentage increases still leave the farms poorly supplied, with one tenth of the electricity available per worker as compared with industry (Dobrynin, *VEk*, 1974, No. 11, p.39.) The contrast in this respect with Western countries is particularly striking. In addition, evidence exists of frequent power cuts, which can hardly be a sound basis for electrification: thus milking machines cannot be used if no power is available, and this necessitates keeping milkmaids on call, thereby negating the labour-saving effect of mechanized milking.

A powerful indictment of unbalanced and often self-defeating planning of inputs was published in *Voprosy ekonomiki*. It is worth citing its arguments in some detail. The points the author makes can be conveniently classified as follows:

(a) Far too little investment in industries and sectors serving agriculture.
(b) Far too small a range of machinery and equipment to ensure 'complex mechanization'. Of the 2350 types that ought to be produced, less than a thousand are made. 'In the last five years

the purchase-requests *(zayavki)* of *kolkhozy* and *sovkhozy* for agricultural equipment were satisfied in various regions only to the extent of 50 to 80 per cent (Dobrynin *VEk*, 1974, No. 11, p.40.) (This presumably relates to requests for the kinds of machinery that were available.)

(c) Costs of new machines are high, building materials, oil, lubricants, fodder concentrates, have gone up in price.

(d) Mechanization is inadequate even as regards tractors: thus one tractor per 100 hectares of arable land, or 1 tractor utilized for every 180 hectares of grain, 'exceeds the optimal load factor 1·5 – 2 times'. Yet in fact the equipment available per worker in livestock farming 'is 10–12 times lower than in fieldwork'. Livestock farming is under-capitalized, but unevenly so. 'Thus the level of mechanization of fodder distribution is 7 times lower for cattle, 3–4 times for pigs, 2·1 times for poultry, than is watering'. Consequently, 'as a result of lack of complex mechanization of livestock farms, labour economised in one process does not lead to a reduction in the numbers working. Thus from 1965 to 1972 the numbers engaged on livestock farms in *sovkhozy* increased by 19 per cent.' (Dobrynin, *VEk*, 1974, No. 11, p.41.) The bulk of the workers are engaged in 'work by hand', i.e. unassisted by machines.

(e) Fertilizer supplies remain inadequate. The author claims that a further 10 million tons are needed 'as a minimum', which requires an increase of 50–55 per cent over existing levels. Without this, other measures are ineffective on the soils of the so-called 'non-black-earth zone' of the RSFSR. (Advance in this sector has been rapid; the USSR has overtaken the United States as a fertilizer producer. But US soils are naturally more fertile.)

(f) However, output of fertilizer must be accompanied by the production of the means of transporting it and spreading it. Yet fertilizer-spreaders increased by 35 per cent in a quinquennium during which fertilizer production rose by 70 per cent. This must lead to waste and to 'irrational utilization', to use the author's words. Another source states that in 1971 the farms requested 42,000 fertilizer-spreaders, but the plan specified the production of only 14,000 of them, 'which had to lead to losses of fertilizer and its irrational use'. (Lemeshev, 1973, p.249.)

(g) Then there is lack of *malaya mekhanizatsiya* ('petty mechanization'), the subject of a *Pravda* article among others, (9 January 1975) and its consequence: 'loading, unloading, transport, storage and other work is carried out by hand'. The number of auxiliary workers, even on large-scale specialized livestock complexes, often exceeds those engaged on the primary tasks. This, argues the author, creates social and labour problems: there are fewer who are willing to undertake physical unskilled labour. We shall see how important is the labour bottleneck. Clearly, lopsided mechanization contributes greatly to it.

(h) Still another aspect of what Dobrynin calls 'lack of *kompleksnost'*, i.e. of complementarity, is the supply of tractors without adequate backing in the form of spares, workshops, covered garage space, maintenance equipment and trained staff. Dobrynin points out that a tractor costs two to three thousand roubles, but that the necessary additional expenditure per tractor should amount to ten times more. Evidently these expenditures, and their material equivalents, are not made. (No doubt this is why we so often hear complaints about tractors and combine-harvesters not being in working order.) Similarly, argues the author, the acquisition of a cow calls for expenditures on construction, equipment, fodder provision and labour (including, he insists, on adequate housing and cultural services) several times higher than the cost of the cow. Again, the implication is that the cost is not paid, and that this has adverse consequences.

(i) Fodder supplies are inadequate overall, the deficit being estimated by the author as 20 per cent of the total, but the animals' ration is unbalanced, suffers from lack of protein, making the use of fodder economically ineffective. Incredibly, 'the share of fodder grains and pulses in the sown area under grain in the country as a whole is lower than it was in 1913, by 1·7 per cent (Dobrynin, *VEk*, 1974, No. 11, p.43.)

Much more could and should be done, he asserts, to improve the yield and protein content of natural pastures and hayfields (which, as the statistics show, are indeed very low by any standard).

The common denominator in all this is failure to ensure the kind of inter-relationships which, one might have thought, is precisely what good planning is about. It requires no great thought to appreciate that tractors need to be repaired, that repairs call for parts, skilled mechanics and a workshop. Or that it makes no sense to double the supply of fertilizer but not the means of moving it to the fields. Or to mechanize one process and create a bottleneck at the next related but unmechanized stage, e.g. livestock feeding or loading or drying grain. The pattern of crops and livestock prescribed ('recommended') for the farms seems to pay little attention to the problems of peak demand for labour, and the attempts by management to acquire equipment which would help to overcome these labour bottlenecks all too frequently fail, for lack of availability. There is also the general question of the quality of farm machinery, which is widely criticized.

The whole question of maintenance of machinery is partly linked with another matter: the consequences of the abolition in 1958 of the

MTS (state-operated Machine Tractor Stations). At the time the measure seemed sensible. The uneasy mixture of supervisory agency and machine hire centre seemed unsuitable, and there were frequent conflicts between the interests of the *kolkhozy* in the use of the machinery and those of the MTS which 'served' them. This conflict had two causes: firstly, the MTS were expected to maximize the payment in kind for their services, which were an important source of state procurement of grain. Secondly, the MTS had plans in tractor-work units (expressed in terms of 'soft ploughing'), and their desire to fulfil such plans could and did lead them into conflict with the interest of the *kolkhoz* to minimize the amount of such work (or rather to relate it to what really needed doing).

However, I met a Soviet farm manager who declared (off the record!) that the abolition of the MTS was a grave error. He explained that before 1958 *kolkhozy* were *forbidden* to acquire tractors and combines, and this was bad. After 1958 they could not hire them and were *compelled* to buy them, and that too was bad. The correct solution (he said) was to allow them to choose. Some would have derived advantage from ownership. Others had no workshops or skilled maintenance personnel, and for them hiring was much more sensible. After all, many American farmers hire combine-harvesters.

This is an illustration of the ill-effects of bureaucratic inflexibility, based on fear of spontaneity (in Russian *samotyok*, which in Soviet planning-language is a pejorative term).

Sel'khoztekhnika has acquired considerably more powers in recent years over maintenance and repairs, with 'special departments for production and agrochemical servicing of *kolkhozy* and *sovkhozy'*, including 'storage and application of mineral fertilizer, liming, etc.' (Borchenko, *PKh*, 1974, No. 7, p.86.) This can make sense if flexibly administered. Much less likely to be satisfactory is a decision, which led to protests, to stop selling motor vehicles and buses to *kolkhozy* and *sovkhozy*: 'they are concentrated at the *sel'khoztekhnika* bases. This is considered to be economical. Can it be always so?' There are, apparently, difficulties with intra-farm transport: in every instance the farm management has to apply for it to the *Sel'khoztekhnika* regional office. Some farms can still get vehicles all the same, but 'the requests for means of transport are only 50 per cent satisfied'. (Sergeyko, *Pravda*, 13 January 1976.) The increase in *sel'khoztekhnika*'s functions should be watched with care.

But to return to the explanation of unbalanced planning which fails to deal with predictable complementaries. Why?

Dobrynin explains it by the lack of 'a single governing system'. By this he means that the bulk of inputs are produced in numerous other branches of the national economy, and their output is 'insufficiently co-ordinated with the needs and requests of the [agricultural] sector'.

This is certainly one cause of the trouble. Thus farm machinery and spares are produced by enterprises owing allegiance to numerous bodies, even, as Brezhnev told us, armament ministries. It is inevitable that many ministries are involved. Obviously the plans for fertilizer will concern primarily the chemical industry, but responsibility for fertilizer-spreading equipment will lie elsewhere. The task of collecting, collating and passing on the requirements of the farms rests with *Sel'khoztekhnika*, the supply agency for agriculture. However, it is plainly unable to exercise sufficient influence over industrial production programmes. Judging from numerous critical remarks made about it at the March 1965 plenum, its efficiency was a subject of doubt to put it mildly. If plenum proceedings of more recent date had been published, there might well be evidence as to its performance in more recent times.

It may be said: but surely *Gosplan*'s job is to co-ordinate just such things as these. However, let us recall how overburdened it is, and how inevitably it concentrates on 'key' or 'especially important' items. Here, in my view, lies a vital part of the solution to the puzzle; and this brings one back to the logic and frustrations of industrial planning. We have seen that the plan specifies the output of 'the most important products in physical units', and that this implies that officials and managers will regard items not so listed as less important or even unimportant. As we have also seen, output of equipment of all kinds for agriculture is widely scattered among various ministries. In many of them the equipment in question is a sideline, classified therefore as 'less important'. Under conditions of strain and shortage, this inevitably affects the fulfilment of plans. Nor is priority given within these ministries to the design of new and better equipment. The leadership has tried to resolve the problem by setting up specialized ministries: thus there is now a Ministry of Machinery for Livestock and Fodder. This gives greater weight in the administrative competition for resources. This is evidence, if any is needed, of the importance being attached to correcting the distortions which have been described above. None the less, past experience can offer no optimistic conclusion. For example, articles, cartoons, speeches, have for decades drawn attention to shortages of spare parts. Admittedly it is more 'news-worthy' to produce X thousand tractors than Y rouble's worth of miscellaneous spares, but, since any child knows that a tractor or a lorry needs spares, surely the system could and should have taken cognizance of this decades ago. Yet the problem remains acute. Brezhnev referred to it in his speech to car workers. (*EkG*, No. 19, 1976, p.4.)

One of its many aspects is the relative weakness of the customer. The farms will usually know best what they lack, what kind of modifications and attachments are needed to existing equipment, where they most suffer from bottlenecks. Yet their requests *(zayavki)* channelled through *Sel'khoztekhnika* are far too often frustrated. Indeed there are cases of deliveries of *unordered* equipment, described wittily by Antonov as 'burglariously imposed supply' *(sbyt s vzlomom)*. Obviously the wholesalers were fulfilling their plan regardless of customers' needs.

The supply organs are sometimes not to blame. Thus agricultural machinery is frequently supplied in parts, which have to be assembled on the actual farms, yet half of the farms do not have adequately equipped workshops, and trained personnel is scarce. Some parts then turn out to be missing. Apparently one reason for the practice is to simplify loading up railway wagons. (Putov, *MSn*, 1976, No. 4, p.42.)

LABOUR SUPPLY AND INCENTIVES

When the MTS were abolished in 1958, their employees were converted from privileged state workers into *kolkhoz* members. True, they were (at first) assigned special status within the *kolkhoz*, and their pay rates were well above the average. However, a contributory cause of the troubles of mechanization has been the departure from the villages of young skilled men, who are not attracted to the status of *kolkhoz* peasant.

This problem of migration out of the villages of younger skilled manpower is a constant source of difficulty. This is not so everywhere, but in many districts the shortage of skilled labour is acute. Since there are also large seasonal variations in demand for labour, the general picture seems to be one of shortage, which might appear to be paradoxical, given the high percentage – by the standards of developed countries – of the total labour force engaged in agriculture: 26 per cent in 1972, a figure that omits part of the labour input on household plots (*NKh*, 1972, p.501 and p.788n), so that the actual number may be over 30 per cent.

The movement of young people from the villages to the bright lights of cities is a problem familiar in many countries. It is exacerbated in the USSR by the wide gap still prevailing between style of life and amenities in town and in country, and also by the primitive nature of rural retail distribution and the inferior educational opportunities. Peasant incomes have been substantially raised in the past two decades, relative to urban incomes, but the opportunities to spend the money are much more restricted. We shall see in a moment that material incentives are also ineffective for other reasons. An excellent survey of the problem and its causes is given by Perevedentsev (1975).

The attempts to restrict migration by denying internal passports to most rural residents was counter-productive, in that it labelled such residents as second-class citizens and still further enhanced the desire to acquire a higher status by leaving the village. In 1975 it was finally decided that passports would be issued to all citizens, by stages. However, even without them a determined individual could get out, e.g. after completion of military service.

Some areas appear to have a more balanced labour force. Estonia, for example, with the most prosperous agriculture in the Soviet Union, has an adequate supply of skilled labour: one is left wondering whether success and high incomes are the causes or the consequences of the presence of good-quality labour in the villages. Probably both.

Central Asia is supposed to have a labour surplus in the villages. Yet peak demand for cotton-pickers is far from satisfied. A report from Turkmenia speaks of schoolchildren 'annually taken from their studies for three months' (!). The author criticizes the conditions under which they work, and goes on to ask why their mobilization is necessary (along with 'workers, employees and students'). It turns out that out of Turkmenia's 5,000 cotton-harvesting combines, 1,000 are out of action at harvest time, and far too little is done to use the labour of the peasants, especially of women ('owing to the bad work of crèches, chronic inadequacies in trade and services in rural areas'). (*Pravda*, 7 January, 1975.) Many millions from the towns help with the harvest in many parts of the USSR annually. A Soviet source had stated that the number of persons so mobilised more than doubled during the 1970s and reached a figure of $15\frac{1}{2}$ million in 1979! (Manevich *V. Ek.* No. 9, 1981).

There is, of course, nothing inherently wrong with seasonal labour to cope with harvest peaks. What is wrong is the *extent* of the import of labour from the towns, the ineffective use of existing rural labour, and, last but not least, weaknesses in mechanization and in maintenance of existing equipment.

However, it is time to turn to the organization of the use of labour on the farms, and to incentives. An essential aspect of the problem is the size of the farms. The average *kolkhoz* is a complex enterprise with 500–600 able-bodied member-labourers, 6,200 hectares of agricultural land, (3,200 hectares sown), and many thousand head of livestock; and *sovkhozy* are substantially larger in every way except in the average size of the labour force. (*NKh*, 1972, p.388, 399–400.) There is comparatively little specialization (though increasing talk of it), and nearly all farms cultivate a wide variety of crops and keep all the main categories of animals. These big farms are usually based upon several villages. These are very seldom connected by hard-surface roads, and can be cut off for months at a time by the notorious Russian *bezdorozhye* ('roadlessness'), i.e. spring and autumn mud. The damage done to rural life as well as to agricultural efficiency by poor roads, and therefore poor and frequently interrupted transport links within and without the farms, is immeasurable in the figurative as well as the literal sense.

The management of these large and very mixed farms faces acute difficulties, which could best be seen as diseconomies of scale. For a generation the basic unit of field work was the brigade. headed by a brigadier, and assisted by 'mechanizers'. The field brigade used to number seventy to a hundred, though now the figures are often much lower. In the large multi-village farms, some brigades organize the labour of one village and separate groups work on livestock rearing, dairying, etc. (for some reason, the livestock complexes are known as *fermy*, and this word is never used for any other agricultural units).

Kolkhoz and *sovkhoz* managements must try to link the efforts of their peasants with results, to stimulate efficient work. However, sheer size is an obstacle, since there is too wide a gap between the work of any individual and the final outcome. Let me use the following frequently quoted illustration: tractor-drivers are rewarded primarily on piece-rates, and the 'pieces' are the area they plough. They are also encouraged to economize on fuel and to avoid mechanical break-downs. To achieve these objectives, it is evidently desirable to plough shallow. Yet deeper ploughing may be desirable if the harvest is to be increased. True enough, the pay of tractor-men (along with that of others on the *kolkhoz* or *sovkhoz*) also benefits if the harvest is a good one, but the predominant element is the piece-rate. Therefore inspectors need to watch carefully to ensure that ploughing is deep enough. The Soviet critic cited a common saying among tractor-men: *zaglublyay direktor yedet* ('plough deeper: I see the director coming'). (Rebrin, 1969, p.156.)

It can be seen from this example that the improvements which have occurred in the *level* of pay are, in *this* context, irrelevant. The problem is to link reward with final outcome. On the huge multi-purpose farms this link is at best tenuous. One does not have to tell a Western peasant to plough to an adequate depth, because he is directly interested in the final outcome, in the size of the harvest. If he employs a few labourers, the link between effort, pay and result is still much easier to define than in Soviet large-scale agriculture. Yet: 'Who does not watch the work of the ploughman: the accountant, the supervisor, the brigadier, the representative of the People's Control, the rural Soviet, the agronomist, the agitator-political-organizer, and even a volunteer-quality-controller. Yet what sort of a peasant is it, if it is necessary to follow him about to ensure that he ploughs and harrows properly.' (Rebrin, 1969, p.156.)

The present trend is towards ever larger units, in agriculture as in industry. There is publicity being given to 'agro-industrial complexes', to *sovkhozy* and *kolkhozy* pooling resources in joint activities. Like so much else that is proposed in the USSR, there are important elements of sense in all this. There could be valuable links with industrial processing – canning vegetables, for instance, or processing sugar-beet, grapes or milk. Indeed activities of this type are already under-taken in a number of areas, Moldavia being one prominent example. There is also the 'industrial' production of eggs and broiler chickens, which has its own national centre, *Ptitseprom*, and some specialized modern enterprises for the production of pork, vegetables and a few other items. This trend is certainly developing faster following a long decree of the central committee of the party on 'kolkhoz-sovkhoz co-operation and agro-industrial integration' (June 1976). This directs the party to encourage the creation of joint enterprises in which *kolkhozy* and *sovkhozy* collaborate and in which they will be shareholders *(payshchiki)*, to undertake specialized production, by modern methods, of meat, fodder concentrates, wool, vegetables, fruit, and also joint arrangements for storage, transport, construction, and production of building materials. While the decree warns against excessive haste and against the creation of 'unadministrable' units, and states that the *kolkhozy* and *sovkhozy* would retain autonomy and that their collaboration should be 'voluntary', there is every sign that this is now party policy, and therefore that it will be imposed, creating in the process still more large units and still more bureaucratization in a sector where flexibility is particularly urgently needed. It is also significant that the decree speaks of 'gradually creating the conditions for bringing closer together kolkhoz-co-operative property and state property, their merging in due course into all-peoples *(obshchenarodnaya)* property'. (*Pravda*, 2 June 1976.) Thus perhaps by the time this book requires a new edition, it may be necessary to devote much space to production by joint *sovkhoz-kolkhoz* enterprises (still in the formative stages in 1976) and to discuss the stages by which *kolkhozy* as such will wither away. It is too soon to tell.

This still leaves the problem of relating performance to end-result; of interesting the *sovkhoz* worker or the *kolkhoz* peasant in his work. As already suggested, this does have aspects specific to agriculture, though, of course, incentives present some difficulties in any branch of the economy, and indeed not only in the USSR.

A solution to excessive size is decentralization. One form of this, which has a long and controversial history, is the *zveno*, literally 'link', better rendered as 'team'. As such it has existed for almost as long as *kolkhozy,* at least as a subdivision of a brigade. It can consist of a small group of six to twelve individuals, set up to carry out tasks which a small group can best carry out. With the growth of mechanization, most tasks do not require anything like the old field brigade (which at its primitive heyday often consisted of eighty to a hundred women hand-hoeing a field, strung out in a huge long line). In this form the 'team' is not controversial. True, the use of the *zveno* was the subject of sharp attacks in the late forties. This, however, apparently related to its over-use, to political orders in grain-fields, where in the interests of combating 'irresponsibility' *(obezlichka)* the advantages of large-scale mechanized harvesting were lost. For other crops the *zveno* never disappeared. Its use is not now controversial, if the *zveno* is regarded simply as a way of getting a specific task performed to the order of the management.

The trouble is that, in this form, the *zveno* does not solve the problem. Responsibility for the final outcome will still be lacking. Thus, for example, suppose a team is assigned to cultivate or weed a field; it will have been ploughed by others, and will be harvested by whosoever is assigned to that task. Furthermore, the burden of actually organizing the work and handing out the assignments still belongs to the *kolkhoz* or *sovkhoz* administration. To resolve both these difficulties, the idea was put forward to have an *autonomous zveno* (known as *beznaryadnoye*, i.e. without work-assignments). The idea is simple: the growing of barley, onions or whatever, on a particular area of land is assigned to a *zveno*, or team, which is then responsible for the whole group of tasks from ploughing to harvesting and is paid by results. The team has under its control the necessary equipment and arranges its own work schedules (hence *beznaryadnoye*). In one of its versions, all members of the team were paid equally.

This idea was experimental to begin with and attracted some support. Its advocates pointed to the large saving in supervisory labour: since the team is very interested materially in increasing final output, there is no need to ensure that they plough deep, weed properly, etc., as they would do it themselves. They also become more willing to work longer hours at peak periods. The advantages seem very great. An article praising the experiment pointed out that the savings in supervisory labour were *not* its most popular feature among local officials, who felt their jobs to be threatened. (Rebrin, 1969, p.159.)

Flexible arrangements with small groups of peasants are a feature of the successful Hungarian collective farm system, and would seem to represent the way forward in the USSR also. This need not exclude the development, where feasible, of agro-industrial complexes, nor of joint arrangements to manufacture various inputs, or to process farm produce. There is room in any agriculture for infinite variety, of size, of degrees of specialization and of incentive arrangements. Unfortunately, the autonomous *zveno* has run into trouble. The difficulty is partly that this degree of autonomy upsets the conventional lines of control and authority, affecting the role of management and of the local party and state officials. It smacks of spontaneity *(samotyok)* and can easily be made to look like a step towards decollectivization, especially if members of the *zveno* are relatives. There are also practical problems. What happens to labourers and machines when they have no work on their crop? Is there not some advantage in their being disposed by management where they are most needed? What of bad feelings and jealousies if a particular *zveno* earns very much more than others in the *kolkhoz* or *sovkhoz* who may have worked equally hard? There is not enough machinery to equip everyone adequately.

What of the unskilled peasant women, who do not easily 'fit' into a mechanized *zveno*? One should not see the opposition as due only to some mixture of ideology and vested interest.

Despite the frustrations experienced by this brand of reformer, changes in this general direction seem inescapable, as the authorities cannot but seek ways out of the obviously unsatisfactory situation in agriculture, especially with regard to labour productivity. So there are signs of a renewal in interest in the small team. Thus *Pravda* (20 September 1974) sharply criticized local management (in a grape-growing area) for 'killing an important experiment' of this type and even more recently publicity was given to a 'detachment' *(otryad)* of seventeen persons which worked 'without work-assignments' *(bez naryadov)*. (S. Atryganyev, *EkG*, 1975, No. 43, p. 18.) Of course the name does not matter. Call it a 'detachment', or even a 'small brigade'. The essential is its right to organize its own work and to be paid by *results* (as distinct from piece-rates, such as hectares ploughed).

As already mentioned, *kolkhoz* pay now approximates to a wage, replacing the ineffective work-day unit *(trudoden')*, which had reflected the peasant's status as a 'residuary legatee'. There used to be extremely wide variations between pay in successful and unsuccessful *kolkhozy*, and in the same *kolkhoz* in years of favourable and unfavourable weather. Some variety persists, because, subject to the minimum, payment still depends more on final financial results than is the case in any state enterprise. In the republic of Estonia, where agriculture has done well, one consequence is that pay on *kolkhozy* rose for a time above those in *sovkhozy,* since in the latter it was tied to a national wage tariff, though this difference disappeared during the seventies. (*NKh*, Est. SSR, 1972.) However, on average in the USSR *kolkhoz* remuneration is still lower, and an important distinction is that the *kolkhoz* pays only for days worked, while *sovkhoz* staffs are on a monthly basic rate.

While pay rates are far higher than they were twenty or even ten years ago, the effectiveness of incentives is affected by lack of things to buy in rural areas, and also by the modest requirements of culturally underdeveloped peasant families.

KOLKHOZY: PROBLEMS OF MANAGEMENT AND CALCULATION

The status of a *kolkhoz* as a co-operative does give, as already stated, a greater degree of formal autonomy. It is limited in practice by constant outside intervention, especially in the 'election' of the chairman. To cite one example among many, some recent memoirs by a former *ôbkom* secretary spoke of the 'defects in the selection *(podbor)* of *kolkhoz* chairmen', for which he puts the blame on the party's *raykomy* and *obkomy*. (Smelyakov, 1975, p.273.)

The leaders have vacillated in their approach, between administering *kolkhozy* and *sovkhozy* jointly, and associating *kolkhozy* in some species of unions which would deal with the specific problems and interests of *kolkhozy* as such. After a long delay, a *kolkhoz* congress was convened in 1966. Out of it emerged a new organ at national, republican and regional levels: the *kolkhoz* council *(sovet kolkhozov)*. What at first sight might have seemed to be a representative institution in fact conformed to official patterns: thus, although representatives of farm management attend, control is firmly in the hands of party-state machine. Thus, the national chairman is the Minister of Agriculture. An all-union congress held in Moscow in March 1975 stated that there were 2,417 councils at local, *oblast'* and republican levels. The Congress 'elected' the all-union council. The *Pravda* editorial and report mentioned how 'the party organs direct the activities of the *kolkhoz* councils to . . . carry out the complex programme of the development of agriculture approved by the 24th party congress'. (*Pravda*, 11 March and 15 March 1975.) It does not appear that the councils have either executive authority or an effective representative function.

There is an exception: Moldavia. There the *kolkhoz* council carries out administrative functions. Decisions on repair of equipment were addressed to various republican ministries of agriculture, and to the *sovet kolkhozov* of the Moldavian republic. (Denison *EkG* 1976, No. 13, p.19.) This may be an interesting experiment. But such a trend runs counter to the policy of joining *kolkhozy* and *sovkhozy* together. As this book was going to press, a new Moldavian experiment has been reported: the creation of what amount to local machine tractor stations (under the name of mechanisation and electrification associations (*EkG*, No. 1, 1977)) servicing the *kolkhozy* in the area and operated by the district *kolkhoz* council (the separate *kolkhozy* would retain only motor transport). These are co-operative and not state property. It will be interesting to see if the idea will spread.

But to return to the management of the *kolkhoz*. The chairman's salary is linked with plan-fulfilment, especially what is still described as the 'basic *(osnovnoy)* indicator of the plan of agricultural development – the volume of state procurements'. (Gosplan, 1974, p.160.)

So long as the *trudoden'* was the basis of peasant remuneration, the *kolkhoz* faced the gravest difficulties in computing its costs. The reason was simple: if labour absorbed the residual, there was no profit. Unsuccessful production expressed itself in the low value of a work-day unit, successful production in a higher value. If labour was wastefully used, this led to no addition to cost, as would be the case in any state enterprise which had to pay tariff wages; additional labour inputs merely increased the divisor. Let me illustrate: suppose that the total available for distribution, in cash and kind, was represented by 100,000 roubles. Suppose that the total work done totalled 20,000 work-day units. Then every peasant would receive 5 roubles. But suppose, through wasteful labour deployment, the same tasks required 40,000 work-day units. Then the pay would be 2·50 roubles; the total paid out would still be 100,000 roubles, this being the residual available for distribution. This fact, as well as the disincentive effect of not knowing what a given amount of work would in fact earn, contributed to the demise of the *trudoden'*. However, the substitution of minimum pay-rates, in 1966, required not only higher revenues for the *kolkhozy*, and therefore higher prices for state procurements, but also credits from the state bank in the event of shortage of funds; until 1966 no credits were available for the purpose of paying peasants. Also it was necessary to change the procedure by which not only production expenses but also a mandatory allocation to the so-called 'indivisible fund' (capital fund) took priority over payment to members.

The present position is more satisfactory. The accounts distinguish between:

(a) Gross output (total value of output, prices being those at which transactions take place. For the rules governing the valuation of unsold produce see *Gosplan*, 1974.)
(b) Gross revenue *(valovoy dokhod)*. The above, less cost of material inputs.
(c) Net revenue *(chisty dokhod)*. Gross revenue less the 'fund of payment to kolkhoz members', pay of hired labour and contribution to state social insurance fund.

Net revenue covers expenditures on taxes (levied as a percentage on a sliding scale), allocation to the capital fund, social security payments to members, cultural expenditures and bonus payments, plus any allocation to reserves. The ratio of net revenue to the total costs incurred in producing output for sale *(tovarnaya produktsiya)* is the profitability rate *(rentabel'nost')*. (*Gosplan*, 1974, pp.205–6.)

Sovkhozy are in most respects state enterprises that happen to be engaged in agriculture, but a comment is called for in connection with a switch towards 'full *khozraschet*'. By this is meant not only doing without state subsidies, but also financing the major part of their investments out of retained profits or by bank credits. However, owing to high costs and unfavourable natural conditions many *sovkhozy* still operate at a loss, or their profits are insufficient to finance investments or even to provide the minimum of incentive funds. In these instances budgetary aid continues to be given, either as subsidy or as investment grant. In addition, as part of much-needed land improvement schemes, the state budget pays for much drainage, irrigation, liming and so on. (Prosin and Rapetsky *EkG*, 1974, No. 3, p.18.) *Kolkhozy* also benefit from land improvement grants. But much the larger part of *kolkhoz* investment expenditures continue to be financed out of revenue, plus bank credits.

LINKS WITH URBAN MARKETS

As already mentioned, 'roadlessness' is among the major causes of inefficiency, both within farm complexes and in obstructing links with the cities. This is exacerbated by lack of suitable vehicles, and the high proportion that remain in disrepair for lack of spares. An *obkom* secretary wrote: 'Many roads are notorious . . . The most "famous" of them are such that one has the feeling of travelling on square wheels.' (Smelyakov, 1975, p.250.)

It is evident that this must adversely affect economic performance. Fresh milk and other products cannot reach cities, and the flow of equipment, fuel and consumers' goods to the villages is frequently interrupted.

Means of transport are often short, and, as already mentioned, unsuitable. Even grain, a priority product, is often transported to state elevators in open lorries, and some of it simply blows away en route. (I once saw a dirt-track in the steppes 'sown' thickly with grain for this reason, and the grain was being eaten by geese and other less economically useful birds.)

There has also been a serious lack of packaging materials, and also of storage space (for grain, vegetables, etc.). The newspapers very frequently report complaints from farm management as to their inability to dispose of perishable products, which are in fact scarce in many cities but which the procurement and trading organs refuse to handle. Sometimes the cause is, again, lack of physical facilities: thus if fresh milk cannot be stored, there is nowhere to keep tomatoes or apples, and the capacity of a canning plant is fully utilized, then there is little the enterprises concerned can do, except to report the situation and to ask for additional investment funds. The fault then is that of under-investment in these facilities in the past. However, there are also 'economic' reasons: it takes trouble to cope with perishables, the inevitable losses through spoilage have a negative effect on profitability (trade margins are treated as a cost to be minimized). So there are some evident weaknesses. Efforts are being made to overcome them; thus *kolkhozy* and *sovkhozy* often sign direct contracts to deliver vegetables with the retail network in nearby cities. Also some farms sell direct to the customers in the free market, though limits are imposed on their doing this until they have carried out their delivery obligations to the state.

Much more could be done by the rural co-operatives, which run the retail trade network in rural areas and have other duties too: They could improve the quality of life by making more available in the shops, and they also have a function of purchasing many kinds of foodstuffs (in addition to deliveries to the state) and marketing them in urban areas. One of the ways they do this has been mentioned already: sales in the free markets on commission, on behalf of peasants or *kolkhozy*. Judging from frequent criticisms, there is ample scope for improvement in all those activities, though turnover statistics show that retail sales in rural areas have been rising steadily.

SPECIALIZATION AND RENT

For decades the farms were in effect not allowed to specialize. This was because state procurement quotas were imposed for a wide variety of products, so that management could not avoid growing or producing them. There was even a quota for goats'-milk cheese *(brynza)*. The most probable reason for these practices was that for a generation and more a delivery quota was in effect a tax in kind, since prices were so low, and it seemed simplest and fairest to distribute the burden (*razverstat'* is the Russian word for this procedure) to all the farms in the given area. There was a shortage of almost anything, and so even farms operating in unfavourable soil and climatic conditions were ordered to deliver products which, for them, were a very high cost. This did not matter to the procurement officials, the burden falling either on the peasants (in *kolkhozy*) or on the state budget (in the case of *sovkhozy*).

In denouncing these practices, a Soviet critic cited the following: a *kolkhoz* in the Krasnodar *kray* 'was compelled to sell annually to the state not only basic items such as grain, sunflower seed, sugar-beet, milk, meat and eggs, but also twenty other items: 200 tons of castor-oil plant, 75 tons of cabbage, 11 tons of cucumber, 54 tons of tomatoes, 8 tons of other vegetables, 36 tons of hay, 70 tons of miscellaneous fruits, 250 tons of grapes, 73 centners of wool, 35 centners of honey, 1042 centners of selected vegetable seeds (including specifically seeds of cucumber, carrots, onions, pumpkin and water-melon), 150 centners of root-crop seeds, $1\frac{1}{2}$ centners of perennial grass seeds, 25 centners of silk cocoons, 30 centners of fish.' (Dmitrashko, 1966, p.118.) So much for specialization! Admittedly, this report dates from 1966.

Things appear to be (slowly) changing. Prices are much higher, and tend to be particularly high in high-cost areas, which affects the financial performance of the procurement agencies. The advantages of specialization are better understood, and delivery obligations reflect this. Thus, for example, the Baltic states are, as a rule, exempted from central delivery quotas for grain, to facilitate concentration on livestock and on fodder crops. The much-discussed 'agro-industrial complexes' are expected to encourage specialization within the complexes, just as in industry an *obyedineniye* could concentrate some activities in this or that factory within it. It hardly requires proof that mechanization will be more effective if there is greater specialization. As things are (as the author has himself witnessed) many of the urban labourers and students drafted in to help with the harvest are engaged in coping with a wide variety of vegetables and fruit grown on many farms.

Who is to decide about specialization? Is it consistent with a system of compulsory deliveries? There has been some debate on these topics. In 1966 arguments appeared in print to the effect that *compulsory* procurements be abandoned. Then farms would adopt the product mix which is economically most suitable for them, given the level of prices, the natural conditions, labour supply and available mechanization. (Terentiev, *VEk*, 1966, No. 4, pp.42ff.) However, this was firmly rejected and the discussion has not been resumed. The all-union planning organs determine all-union needs, and the local authorities add their requirements, and in the end the farms are still ordered what to deliver, and also what to produce, what and when to sow, etc.

Among the reasons for the prevalence of compulsion one must mention price relativities. Although the general level of prices is now much higher than twenty or even ten years ago, profitabilities vary widely and irrationally. Of course, 'rational' prices for agricultural products are rarely encountered anywhere; any citizen of a member country of EEC should be acutely conscious of this. The word 'irrational' is used only to indicate that there is a very wide disparity between the desired pattern of output and the existing pattern of prices. The prices themselves will be discussed in Chapter 7, as will the limited issue of land rent. It is sufficient at this point to stress that the abandonment of *compulsory* procurements would require a very considerable change in price relativities, *and* would be a large step towards a greater reliance on the market than the present generation of leaders are prepared to tolerate in any branch of the economy.

The problem of land rent has been much discussed. This will be taken up in Chapter 7 in conjunction with a closer look at farm prices.

ASSESSMENT

The reader will have obtained from this Chapter a picture of a weak sector in the Soviet economy. No one, certainly not the Soviet leadership, doubts that it *is* a weak sector, though it is only proper to repeat that its performance has been showing a steady improvement, albeit at high cost. Indeed the high cost of agricultural production is in itself a worrying feature, imposing as it does a major burden on the rest of the economy – a contrast indeed with the days when agriculture was exploited for the benefit of industrial investment. A key element in the high cost is the excessive use of now much-better-paid labour. This is a consequence of a complex series of causes: lopsided, expensive and incomplete mechanization, lack of motivation within excessively large and clumsily administered farms, too many detailed orders from above about what and how to produce. As an illustration of the economic effectiveness of recent advances in output, let us take the relatively successful republic of Belorussia. There, we learn, output in the period 1970–4 had risen by 29 per cent but costs by 44 per cent: 'in other words the *kolkhozy* of the republic spent 1·15 roubles to obtain 1·00 rouble's worth of produce'. The financial situation was saved by the fact that the state pays higher 'bonus' prices for over-plan deliveries. (*Pravda*, 30 January, 1975.)

What chances of reform? Do not the party leaders see what harm is done by constant interference from above? Many a story has appeared in print, for instance about orders, issued by distant officials, that sowing be completed when it is evident to farm management that local conditions require (say) a week's delay. *Why* cannot farms be allowed to decide such things for themselves? And might not an ambitious party leader find that it pays politically to support major reforms in agriculture, including the autonomous *zveno* or small team?

More probable, at the time of writing, is that the party leaders will seek a way out through higher inputs: more fertilizer, more and better machinery, a greater degree of planned specialization, all this within the existing planning and control structure, under the slogan of intensification and 'industrialization of agriculture'. Progress there can be, even on these lines, but it will surely be very costly progress.

Further evidence has accumulated about rising agricultural costs. Thus V. Tikhonov (*Pravda*, 4 August 1978) pointed out that in recent years the price paid by farms for one h.p. of tractor-power has increased by 70 per cent, mineral fertilizer by 20 per cent, concentrated feeds by 100 per cent, the construction of cowsheds 2·3 times (per cow), of pigsties no less than fourfold (per pig). 'As a result, material costs per unit of output rose in the ten years 1966–76 by 77 per cent, payments for inputs from outside agriculture by 2·1 times.' Khachaturov, in *Voprosy ekonomiki*, 1980, No. 7, deplored heavy losses of produce due to lack of elevators, storage, processing facilities, roads, the needed assortment of attachments to tractors.

The idea of the autonomous work-unit, which had apparently been rejected, has reappeared in the press. *Pravda*, 25 December 1979, published an article praising this method, which was being used in a *kolkhoz* in the Kolinii province. The authors also bitterly complain about lack of spare parts, losses due to lack of transport and storage, and the disincentive effect of lack of goods to buy in village shops.

There has been no move to increase the autonomy of *kolkhozy* or *sovkhozy*. On the contrary. The press repeatedly prints decrees instructing party and state organs to interfere more (e.g. *Pravda*, 20 January 1980). One specialist complained that in his area no head of cattle can be slaughtered without the personal signatures of the local party secretary and the head of the provincial agricultural office! (*Pravda*, 16 January 1980.)

There has been a substantial increase in the number of *joint enterprises* of various kinds, in which *kolkhozy, sovkhozy* and sometimes also other state enterprises join together for such purposes as construction, producing building materials, lumbering, providing feed concentrates, processing farm produce, running modern and mechanized piggeries, broiler and egg production, and so on. These enterprises numbered 8,906 in 1978, 515,600 persons were employed in joint livestock enterprises, 1,175,000 on construction and on making building materials. They operate, *inter alia*, over 16,000 bulldozers. Industrial production by these joint enterprises included 1·3 million tons of cement, 4·1 milliard bricks, 59·7 million cans of foodstuffs. So they must be seen as a significant and growing factor in rural life.

A record grain harvest of 237 million tons in 1978 was followed by a weather-affected harvest of only 179 millions tons in 1979, and by the American decision to reduce grain deliveries. This may be making the leadership more willing to listen to reform proposals, of which the autonomous work-unit (*beznaryadnoye zveno*) is one of the most promising.

CHAPTER 6

INVESTMENT AND
TECHNICAL PROGRESS

INVESTMENT CRITERIA

It has been argued, with a great deal of truth, that modern ideas on 'developmental' investment criteria were born in the Soviet Union in the twenties. (Collette, 1965.) However, Stalin closed the debate and imprisoned most of the debaters. Investment decisions became a function of politically determined priorities and their material-balance logic. Thus, *given* a decision to enlarge the steel industry by 50 per cent, consequential investments would be required in iron ore, coking coal, railways, electricity, forging and pressing machinery, etc. etc. Of course, the decision to increase the output of steel by 50 per cent also had its cause, based upon an estimate of the needs of expanding metal-using industries, such as heavy machinery, construction, armaments and so on. The point is that the calculations were quantitative and based upon priorities. To introduce objective *criteria* seemed like providing an objective basis for judging whether the decisions of the state and party were right, and under Stalin this would be regarded not as reasonable but treasonable.

However, already in the thirties the practical men who actually drew up investment projects were faced by the need to choose between different ways of achieving a given objective: for them a problem would be defined as 'not what but *how*'. Given that one needs X million tons of steel, what kind of steelworks should be built, located where? Given the need for Y million kw of electricity-generating capacity, should the power stations be thermal or hydro, large (with long-distance transmission) or small (with less costs for transmission), and so on.

I have argued elsewhere (Nove, 1973) that many (not all) investment decisions in the West are also of this type, that they are taken within larger decisions, are consequential upon them, and that these larger decisions are also sometimes based upon a quantitative (or partially quantitative) analysis. Thus a British or German analysis on choosing what steelworks to build will commonly take as given a calculation as to the future need for steel, and the expansion of French generating capacity will be based largely upon estimates of demand for electricity made in terms of quantity. This is not what Western textbooks tell us. There we find a discussion of internal rate of return *versus* discounted cash flow, and students learn to give reasons for preferring the latter to the former. However, this approach plays down the decisive importance of uncertainty (we do *not* know the future), and also of the distinction, already stressed, between 'what' and 'how': are we deciding whether to invest or choosing between alternative ways of achieving a given result? I stress this point right at the beginning, because one should not judge the errors and inadequacies of Soviet investment planning by unreal textbook criteria, inapplicable also to a Western economy.

In real life, of course, the distinction between 'what' and 'how' becomes blurred. Thus for instance, given the need for more fuel, the fuel could be coal, gas, oil, peat or firewood. For given purposes there can be multiple choices: many materials other than (say) steel could be used. There are choices between natural and synthetic materials. In all these instances, one is not simply deciding the best means of expanding the output of a given product, one is choosing between products, which (in the examples given) fulfil the same basic need. A further logical step leads one to the proposition that, in a sense, all goods are substitutable. Thus a consumer can choose between buying shoes, cabbages, trousers, radios and a visit to a theatre. At least in the area of consumer demand, therefore, it can be argued that there should be a generally applicable criterion of choice, not separate criteria for footwear, vegetables, clothing, etc. We shall see that some Soviet critics have generalized this into the proposition that the entire economy requires one common criterion, i.e. that, just as in Western conventional theory, a rational price system should indicate where investment resources should go, on the basis of calculations of relative profitability (whether these are to be of the rate-of-return or discounted-cash-flow type is a detail which need not trouble us in the present context).

In any real economy, there are several obstacles to the practical application of the apparently rational principle that the incremental rate of return on investments in all branches of the economy should be equal, i.e. that identical criteria should apply throughout a system in which, at the margin, all is substitutable for everything. It may seem evident that it is irrational to forgo any opportunity for a higher rate of return at the margin, and yet there are important modifying factors. The first of these is *indivisibility*, or the existence of subsystems within which many marginal decisions are in fact taken. An example already used is the West Siberian oilfield: it is essential to invest in pipelines, because failure to do so would imperil the entire West Siberian operation. The *separate* consideration of the 'marginal' investment in pipelines becomes irrational and meaningless, save in the context of possible alternative ways of moving oil, i.e. the question becomes 'not whether but how'. If, however, one discovers that the cost of any variant proves prohibitively high, then one might have to re-examine 'whether'.

Secondly, some investment decisions are, of their nature, not incremental. In a way this is a variant of the first point. A decision to quintuple the output of mineral fertilizer, to develop Alaskan oil, or East Siberian minerals, or the Brazilian interior, is a different *kind* of decision to one aiming at expending the output of one firm in the footwear industry. The latter decision is authentically incremental, marginal, rightly taken by reference to the anticipated financial results flowing from that decision itself, visible at the level of the footwear firm. Of course *any* decision should be such that a better opportunity is not forgone. None the less, different considerations in fact apply, and should apply, to these different *'types'* of decision.

The third point relates to uncertainty, and to the time factor. If a project takes five years to complete, one ideally requires to know the prices of the output, of inputs, the level of demand (including the plans of one's customers), changes in technique and much else, as they will be in five years' time. The use of present prices can, obviously, mislead. The theoretical answer is that one uses shadow prices, which can be obtained from a computerized programme. This, unfortunately, evades the issue. This is simply another way of saying that we should use the prices which will rule in five years' time rather than those of today. But the whole problem is precisely that we do *not* know them! The computer cannot provide this information unless the answers to the unknowns are fed into it. It is for this reason, to diminish the area of uncertainty, that planners (in Western corporations as well as the USSR) frequently analyse future requirements in quantitative terms. If their calculations are correct, *then* the future rate of return (and the shadow prices) will also be correctly estimated. These problems of uncertainty and error are sensibly discussed by Malinvaud and Stojanovic (in Khachaturov, 1976.)

Fourthly, even in a Western economy current prices can mislead about the current situation, because of distortions due to government intervention, monopoly and externalities. In a Soviet-type economy prices are fixed arbitrarily, altered infrequently, and do not even in theory reflect either scarcity or demand (see Chapter 7). While ideally, as already mentioned, one needs to know the future, it is certainly useful to have the information provided by current output and input prices. If, for instance, demand is not satisfied for wool cloth, this should be an indication that more is needed. In a market economy, demand *would* be satisfied, but at a price which would yield a higher-than-average rate of profit, and therefore investments in wool textiles would yield an attractive return. In the Soviet case, if price is *below* the level at which demand and supply balance, obviously the financial rate of return need not be higher than average, and so it is likely that the investment decision would be based on information concerning shortages of cloth and not on financial results. However, since other items are also short, the planners are deprived of a useful indicator of the relative intensity of consumer demand for the different items. A customer who cannot buy what she wants, and must perforce turn to substitutes, has not made her requirements known to the planners by any *economic* means (she can, of course, write to *Pravda* to complain).

The same is true of the distorting effect of prices of inputs. These are utilized in cost calculations at all levels. No doubt one would like to have the 'correct' shadow prices, but in their absence one makes do with the current ones (with perhaps some modifications to take known trends into account). But suppose that current prices are below (or far above) cost, or have been deliberately tampered with – as for instance when it was decided to encourage the production of Moscow-basin brown coal by reducing freight rates. Then the calculation will be wrong, and so will the investment decision, for reasons unconnected with lack of information about the future.

Another consequence of Soviet pricing is as follows. Suppose that one makes a *correct* prediction of rising demand for a given product in five years' time. The Western manager could deduce from this a future profitability based upon the higher prices which would follow from the expected expansion of demand. But in the USSR prices are unlikely to be altered for such a reason, and calculations in shadow prices have no economic purpose at the level of the enterprise or even ministry, where targets are in terms of real financial flows, or set in physical terms.

After prolonged and inconclusive discussion among Soviet economists, the following is the 'state of the arts' in the USSR. There is widespread agreement that measurement should be in terms of a 'norm of effectiveness' *(norma effektivnosti)*, or 'recoupment period' *(srok okupayemosti)*, these being two ways of looking at the same thing: the relationship between capital expenditure and its result. Depending on the nature of the choice being made, this could be either the savings made on current costs (compared with the actual situation, or alternative variants), or the profits yielded by the proposed new investment. Many economists argue for a minimum norm of effectiveness, i.e. a rate of return below which no investment project should fall (without some very strong special reason). The introduction in 1965 of a capital charge could be regarded as a species cf minimum: the charge averages 6 per cent per annum, and it may be argued that the outcome ought at least to ensure that this can be paid without loss.

No one supposes that the rate of 6 per cent has any serious

economic basis, and a number of economists have urged that a much higher rate be used as a 'cut-off' for investment projects. For example, Petrakov urges that investments should be largely financed by bank credits, and the rate of return should be sufficient to pay the interest on these as well as the capital charge, and he assumes each of these to be 6 per cent. (Petrakov, 1971, p.52.) (His proposal was linked with one urging the bank to pay 4 per cent interest on enterprises' reserve funds, to discourage their instant use for investment purposes.) Other economists have named other, sometimes higher, figures. There has been a debate about further criteria (additional to, or perhaps replacing, the 'norm of effectiveness'), and also about the appropriate *level* of investment. We shall first turn, however, to the problem of whether the norms should be the same throughout the economy. Needless to say, the supporters of this idea link it with a price system which would eliminate various existing irrationalities. Among the 'mathematicians', this proposal is connected with optimization on the basis of a programme, from which are derived the prices appropriate to that programme, which Kantorovich has called 'objectively determined valuations', and which others have labelled 'prices of the optimal plan' (more about this in Chapter 7). Such prices would form an integral part of the process of plan-formation, as successive versions of the plan-programme would imply investment decisions which would modify scarcities and therefore the price-valuations of materials, fuel and final products. It would also imply an effectiveness norm, but, as Khachaturov pointed out (1968, p.35), it is not clear whether this is 'the outcome of the optimal plan or used as an indicator in its formulation'. (Both?)

Khachaturov himself opposes a single norm of effectiveness (1968, p.23), because 'there is no free movement of resources between sectors, conditions for investment vary in different sectors, there are differences in tempos of technical progress, there exist non-economic factors . . . and there is the nature of the present price system'. Others have argued the contrary. They do not dispute the legitimacy of priorities, but the deliberate introduction of priorities into the process of calculation could lead to waste. The debate continues.

In the Soviet system the differences by sector in 'norms of effectiveness' can be very great indeed, reflecting the priority of some branches, and the neglect of others. Thus in the early sixties Khachaturov had calculated that this norm varied from 0·14 in electricity and 0·17 in oil and gas to 0·73 in light industry. Commenting on these figures, another Soviet economist remarked that 'with such large differences in effectiveness . . . the situation could exist (in the event of structural shift towards sectors with low effectiveness) in which the coefficient improves in each sector but on a national-economic level effectiveness may not rise or could even fall.' (Shuster, 1968, p.174.) Even allowing for pricing distortions, these figures certainly suggest that highly advantageous investment opportunities have been forgone in non-priority sectors of the economy.

As already argued, decisions about investment in the real world must take into account many factors other than prices. As Kornai has pointed out, in a fascinating work (1971a) prices nowhere contain all the information required for decision making. Thus, apart from considerations of priority, there are questions of regional policy, and also shortages of labour. So where there is acute labour scarcity, investments which release labour for other purposes have an advantage which does not find its full expression in comparative effectiveness calculations if these are based on actual (or even prospective) labour costs. Some economists argue for multiple criteria, others for a single coefficient of effectiveness, though not decrying the relevance of other considerations. However, as we shall see, the principal troubles of Soviet investment performance have causes other than failure to agree about appropriate criteria for choice between variants.

There is not and cannot be a simple solution, even if Soviet prices were drastically reformed. It is true that the present confusing price system can cause wrong decisions to be taken. To take one example, if the price of a material known to be acutely scarce does not reflect this fact, its use in proposed investment projects is likely to be in excess of availability, and so administrative guidelines or a rationing scheme would have to be introduced. Or to use another example, which introduces an important principle. Let us suppose that prices are based on costs. Let us further suppose that two machines exist, which cost the same to produce, yield the same profit, but one machine is notably more productive in use than the other. Unless the fact of its greater productivity is reflected in price and profit, a decision based upon the 'norm of effectiveness' of the producing enterprise (or *obyedineniye*, or ministry) might well be less effective from the standpoint of the national economy. (In reality, as we shall see, there is often direct contradiction between the quality-in-use of a machine and the success indicators of its producer.) These are instances of the importance of value-in-use and user demand as a factor determining price, and will be further discussed in that context.

The practice of Soviet planners remains anchored in quantitative, material-balance analysis, and, given the nature of the system, it is logical that this should be so. It must be stressed that for many large-scale decisions this has its advantages. Any major investment must be based on estimates of future demand for the product in question. For many materials, fuels, semi-manufactures, demand is a function of the perspective plan itself. To repeat a point made earlier, this is valuable information, from which calculations of future rates of return (profitability) can be derived. Needless to say, the Soviet planners can err in their picture of the future, they sometimes achieve input-output consistency rather than efficiency, and even consistency eludes them. We shall be discussing the reasons for this in a moment. But the main reason is not the unavailability of 'rational' prices or the appropriate shadow prices, which are in fact not available anywhere in the imperfect real world. Adapting a saying of the mythical poet Kozma Prutkov, 'one cannot attain the unattainable'.

HOW MUCH INVESTMENT?

What should the *volume* of investment be? What proportion of the national income should be accumulated? In the Stalin period the answer was almost: the maximum feasible. The constraints could be seen as the level of consumption necessary for subsistence and incentives, and also defence expenditures (these are, strictly speaking, ·neither productive accumulation nor − except for pay and subsistence − consumption). In the post-Stalin era, the emphasis on consumption greatly increased. It could no longer be regarded as a species of residual. Indeed, one now encounters formulations such as this: 'accumulation is the diversion of resources from current consumption, or from shortening of the working day, in order to increase consumption or reduce the working day in the future, and it recoups itself by the future flow of consumers' goods, or a future shorter working day'. (Val'tukh, 1969, p.141.) The objective being rapid growth, the creation of 'the material basis of communism', greater abundance, or the satisfaction at the earliest date of many needs and demands of the citizens, the potential investment programme exceeds the feasible. It is the task of the planning organs to cut it down to the appropriate size. This still leaves one in the dark as to what the criterion of 'appropriateness' is, or could be. Linked with it, indeed related organically to it, is the proportion of investment in, and output of, producers' goods as against consumers' goods, since the proportion of investment in national income must affect the composition of present and future output, the 'proportions' of the economy. One approach, used by Kantorovich and Novozhilov, is to take the volume of investment as given and to seek to optimize on this basis. Val'tukh disputes this, while praising the originality and talents of these distinguished economists. It is necessary, he asserts, to introduce time-preference, the comparison through time of use-values. He rejects the subjective time-preference theory, and seeks to prove that 'the utility of a given set of consumers' goods is a function of time, it being obvious that the earlier a given level of welfare is reached, the more effective [is the solution]'. Therefore the postponement of the achievement of a given level of welfare requires to be compensated by a future rise in this level. (Val'tukh, 1969, p.145 and p.161.)

This is a more promising approach to a theory of time-preference than Strumilin's effort. He based it on what seems to be a crude application of Marxian values. If productivity rises, he argued, then the value (labour-content) will go down. Therefore the same goods in the future will have less value than at present (*VEk*, No. 8, 1962.)

None of these theories can in practice determine, or even explain, why a given proportion of the national income is accumulated. This proportion, and indeed its division by main sectors, is a political decision, based at least in some degree on investing as much as possible, but with a greater sense than under Stalin of the need to increase current consumption. This, at least, seems a reasonable way of interpreting present policies in this regard.

'PROJECT-MAKING', CHOICE OF TECHNIQUE AND TIME-LAG

Only very large and key projects can be considered at the top of the economic planning hierarchy. For potent administrative reasons the choice between variants usually takes place *within* a branch or ministry, and the question is usually 'not whether but how'. Alternatives which might be more advantageous but which exist within other sectors run by other ministries (or are the responsibility of a different department of *Gosplan* or of the central committee apparatus) can seldom be considered. It is also important to note that one can only choose between those alternatives which are in fact prepared and costed, and this is a time-consuming process. Quite often some potential alternatives are not considered at all, because those whose task it is to prepare investment variants do not prepare this one, and so it is not on the agenda. It therefore becomes important to look closely at the 'project-making' *(proyektnyye)* organs, for many an error or weakness originates there. They too have plans, success indicators, they can suffer from overstrain. Thus if there is time to draft only one project, the process of choice is frustrated from the beginning, and this does happen. Investment efficiency also depends on the construction industry, and on the design and production (and import) of capital equipment, so in due course we will discuss these matters also.

The *proyektnyye* organs (project-making, design bureaux including research in this field) number 1500, they employ 706,000 'project-makers' *(proyektirovshchiki)*, and they have been growing much faster than the volume of investment: from 1950 to 1970 investment rose 6·5-fold, but the volume of project-making work 11·5-fold. This alarms the Soviet critic who quotes these figures: most construction takes place to standard designs, new projects are delayed for lack of blueprints, so there must be some inefficiency. He also criticizes the project-making organs for not being sufficiently in touch with technological innovation. (Krasovsky, *EKO*, 1975, No. 1, p.18, 19.) He is also appalled by the clumsy and unnecessary documentation prepared by these apparently overstaffed offices, 'which is measured now not in sheets, pages or volumes, but in lorry- and wagon-loads. The documentation for a new petrochemical plant was so enormous that it required two rail wagons to transport it'. (Krasovsky, *EKO*, 1975, No. 1, p.20.) At the same time the project-makers have few powers, as against the 'customer' (i.e. the organ for which the work is to be done); the latter sometimes underestimates the cost and the task, and then even when the plan is apparently fulfilled the new capacity is not in fact operational.

This is one reason among many for long delays in completions: there are many others. Quite recently, according to this reliable Soviet source, 'the construction period was double the planned norm, the period of running in *(osvoyeniye)* 1·5 times as long. In turn, our construction-period norms are double the actual periods of construction abroad . . . The investment process with us drags on for 8–12 years, which causes heavy loss in the economic effectiveness of new enterprises, makes for unintended obsolescence of equipment, causes the project-designs to be out of date, sharply worsens the planned technico-economic indicators of newly created capacity, impedes the rapid recoupment of capital investments. . . .' (Krasovsky, *EKO*, 1975, No. 1, p.22.) This quotation deserves to be re-read, for within it is contained evidence of a major source of inefficiency of the entire economy. Note that if construction takes twice as long as planned, and the plan-norms are already double the actual time taken in the West, it follows that the period of construction is *four times* greater than in the West. Evidently, this is accompanied – is caused by – a large increase in the volume of unfinished construction. We will have to examine the reasons for this. The *normed* 'running-in' period *(osvoyeniye,* the time between the formal completion of the investment project and it becoming fully operational) averages one-and-a-half to two years. The actual period is much higher 'and reaches three to four years, sometimes even five'. It may be reasonably surmised that the vast resources 'frozen' in unfinished investments, plus lacunae in the work of the project-making bureaucracy, are far more important explanations for investment inefficiency than the failure to agree upon criteria for choice between variants, or even the misleading effect of irrational pricing. One might even say that it is a typical *déformation professionelle* of economists to concentrate on 'economic' categories like price and calculations of rate of return, rather than on other and probably more significant matters.

Another Soviet economist points to the tendency for the capital-output ratio to rise *(fondo-otdacha,* capital productivity, to fall). He notes that this helps to explain the persistent tendency of producers' goods output to increase faster than consumers' goods: if more investment is needed per unit of final output, this naturally affects the structure of production (Ivanov, *VEk*, 1974, No. 11, p.26.) He identifies the main causes as the high cost of new investment, the fact that new machinery is often not more productive (or more labour-saving) than the obsolete machines they replace, and also the large proportion of the existing stock of machines that should have been retired through old age. He, like Krasovsky, criticizes investment delays: how can one avoid obsolescence if 'the preparation of the project takes 2–3 years, construction 5–7 years, and the so-called *osvoyenie* 3–5 years and more. Therefore the new basic capital becomes fully operational 10–15 years after it has been projected, i.e. often the machines are already obsolete'. (Ivanov, *VEk*, 1974, No. 11, p.281.) He advances as a reason for this the separation of the complex investment process into organizationally distinct stages, particularly the processes of *production* (utilization of production equipment, and the production of this equipment) and *capital investment*, and each are further split between different planning organs and ministries. For many years the volume of project-making work was planned in the rouble value of the projected investments, which was a direct incitement to designing dear factories. This at least has been dropped, but there remains insufficient incentive to save resources both in the project-making process itself and in the investment variant proposed, or indeed to avoid major miscalculations. Worse still is the position of construction enterprises, whose plans and rewards are geared to the quantity (value) of work done. Not only are delays insufficiently penalized, not only are the enterprises interested in dear materials (see example cited on page 98, above), but the cost-estimates can be exceeded without effective penalty; 'capital construction has to all intents and purposes an open account in the bank, and without great difficulty can exceed the original projected cost of the construction by 1·5–2 or even 4 times. No other sector of material production in the USSR is in this position'. (Ivanov, *VEk*, 1974, No. 11, p.27.) The *average* overspending as against the cost-estimates has been calculated by *Gosstroy* at 24·5 per cent (or 30 per cent in extensions to existing enterprises). The costs go up by 10 per cent a year. The only solution, asserts the author, is to fix a firm final price for construction and to pay on completion. He adds that the cost-estimates themselves are sometimes very crudely calculated. Urgent improvements are evidently necessary here.

Attempts to alter the success criteria of construction enterprises has not eliminated the problem. 'For decades we counted [as output] cubic metres of earth-moving, or completed concreting, or bricks laid, or square metres of finished wall surface or metres of pipe. Everyone fulfilled the plans and received bonuses, but the facory might remain unfinished for years . . . Now the output of construction is interpreted as meaning finished buildings. But in fact so-called 'stages' of construction are counted as output, . . . and in consequence the indicator of sales *(realizatsiya)* still includes unfinished construction. . . .' The author ends by urging that output should be counted only when buildings are completed and operational. (Komzin, *Pravda*, 12 January, 1976.) Experiments on these lines are continuing, for instance in Belorussia, as described in detail by Rotshteyn. *(PKh, 1975, No. 12, pp.76ff.)*

No sensible choices can be made if the costs of various alternative projects are very different from what they will be in reality. Also the financial provisions (budgetary grants, retained profits, credits) are bound to prove inadequate. This also helps to explain why the financing of investment projects ensures that they will not be completed in time: when the authorities find that investment demand exceeds available physical resources, one of their defence-mechanisms is to limit financing to the planned level, and this is insufficient to finance speedy construction, reflecting also the fact that the materials would not be available. The combined 'rationing' of money and materials means that, in any one year, only (say) a sixth of the total work can be 'funded', which in the given example means a construction period of six years.

WHY OVER-INVESTMENT?

This brings one to a matter of fundamental importance, independent (or part-cause) of the organizational-administrative failings just discussed: the investment plan as a whole seems to be too large. By 'too large' is meant that it is not balanced by (or with) the material resources necessary for its implementation. The volume of unfinished construction is growing, despite repeated exhortation to 'concentrate resources on completions'. Year after year the Minister of Finance deplores what he calls 'the scattering of resources in construction' *(raspyleniye sredstv v stroyitel'stve)*. Even if the various planning organs were working with optimum efficiency, even if project-makers and building organizations were performing perfectly, the fact remains that if the requirements of the investment plan as a whole exceeded the supply of building materials, there would be delays and frustrations. As Bukharin remarked as long ago as 1928, criticizing by implication the 'hurrah-planning' which was then developing, one cannot build with bricks that are not there. Of course, plans are now less unrealistic than in those early days, but the tendency to overstrain is certainly present, as shortages of materials repeatedly bear witness.

Part of this shortage could be ascribed to errors in micro-planning, and also to large stocks of materials and building equipment which are at any given moment not in use. The first of these points can be best made as follows. Imagine that, by some sleight-of-hand, there is an exact equivalence between total investment and the total supply of investment goods, at established prices. Even if the global plans and estimates were correct, it is likely that some micro-imbalances would show themselves, because, for reasons abundantly explained, the central plan cannot cover the micro-detail, and so some non-substitutable items would be short, others available in excess of requirements, and there would be lack of spare capacity, under conditions of full resource utilization, to adjust for errors once they are discovered. Therefore there might be a shortage of roofing materials (say) and a surplus of prefabricated cement blocks. The tendency for excess stocks to accumulate at enterprises is not peculiar to the building industry: we have seen that it is a disease to which the whole economy is prone, a consequence of supply uncertainties. This is exacerbated by the nature of construction organizations. These are in principle of two kinds: *podryadnyye* ('contract'), and *khozyaystvennyye* (literally 'economic'). The former are permanent enterprises or trusts, the latter are created for a specific task. The 'contract' type predominates. However, as Krasovsky pointed out, some of these enterprises, after completing some large project, may have insufficient work, and considerable building capacity may be idle. (This is bound to happen to some extent, but better planning, according to the Soviet source, can reduce the losses arising from this cause. (Krasovsky, *EKO*, 1975, No. 1, p.24.)

However, there is still the need to explain the apparent excess of the *total* investment programme. This has been the subject of some discussion in Eastern Europe, with papers by Goldmann of (1964) and K. A. Soos (in Hungarian) among others. These and other authors identify a strong 'political' pressure to over-invest. The resultant exhaustion of resources gives rise to cyclical fluctuations in some countries; Poland has been a recent example. The ambitions of the political leadership are reinforced by the competing claims of sectors (defence, agriculture, steel, Uzbekistan, East Siberia, etc. etc.), all urging their own claims. It has been repeatedly noted that capital seems to them free: either it is a non-returnable budgetary grant, or it is an authorized retention from profits of sums which would otherwise be transported to the state budget. This ensures over-application for investment, and, given the nature of managerial incentives and enterprise finance, one cannot envisage this tendency being effectively combated by a capital charge: the charge finds its way into the determination of state-fixed prices, and can even add a little to the gross value of sales (*realizatsiya*, see page 88 above). Because it is easier to obtain central funds for a project already started, there is a tendency to start far too much, rather than concentrate on completing work in progress.

Of course, it is the task of the central planning organs to cut down

excessive requests to a level which corresponds with available resources. They do cut, but the total in the end seems too high. One
reason is the commitment of the political leadership to high growth
rates. A further reason, already mentioned, is persistent underestimation of actual cost of projects. A motive for this is familiar. As a
Soviet economist put it, in conversation: 'if we showed the full cost
at that stage, the project might not be approved!' A Soviet émigré
informed me that a local party official said (under the influence of
drink): 'there are clear advantages in maintaining a flow of central
funds and materials to the area, some of which can be diverted to
other purposes, and so there is no sense of urgency about completing
a large project' (or words to that effect). These are causes of inflationary pressure. (As we shall see in Chapter 9, there is a parallel here
with the impact of 'excess demands' in Western countries. And, needless to say, cost estimates are often exceeded in 'capitalist' economies.)

THE DIFFUSION OF NEW TECHNOLOGY

As all Soviet commentators, from Brezhnev down, both admit and
repeat, this is now a period of 'intensive' growth. A large proportion
of the increase in national income must come from improvements in
labour productivity, and these in turn must be made possible by
labour-saving devices, by technical progress. At the same time, there
is an urgent need for higher quality, not least in the key machinery
sector, which makes the labour-saving devices. So we are here concerned both with new techniques and with new products embodying
new techniques.

It is important to distinguish between several aspects of the problem.
There is *research*. There are *inducements to innovation* at managerial
level. There are *innovation plans*. Finally, there is the production and
supply of *modern machinery*, technically and economically suitable.
There is widespread agreement among Soviet commentators that all
is far from well in this whole area, and this is particularly serious not
only because of the universally recognized need for 'intensification'
(not more labour into more factories, but more productive labour with
more modern equipment), but also because of the speed-up of technical progress itself; indeed the words 'scientific-technical revolution'
are used so often that they have come to be abbreviated into the
Russian initial letters NTR *(nauchno-tekhnicheskaya revolyutsiya)*.
Hence the danger of falling behind in technology. Hence the importance now attached to this whole field.

Research as such is not our subject. It is enought to mention that
expenditures and the size of research staffs are very substantial, and to
refer interested readers to existing valuable studies (e.g. OECD, 1969).
There can be criticism of their effort, as of scientific research any-

where, but no one can doubt the intensity of the effort. Criticism sometimes centres on the secrecy (and large size) of defence-oriented research; its isolation inhibits the 'fall-out' into the civilian sector of the results it achieves. Perhaps more important is the effect of a different kind of isolation: Soviet scientists and specialists still have very restricted opportunities to meet and discuss with their opposite numbers in other countries. But when all is said and done, the weakness lies not in the research effort as such, but with its link with practical applications. This has been partly the consequence of another kind of relative isolation: of research establishments from productive enterprises. Only a small proportion of research staffs were actually at the enterprises, and these were underpaid and undergraded; the bulk were in research establishments under the Academy of Sciences or one or other of the economic ministries and state committees. They were remote both from the life and problems of the factory and from the economic consequences of their designs and their advice. An effort by some research organs to create 'science-industrial associations', in which research institutes and individual scientists extended their activity into engineering and management consultancy work, has been largely frustrated. Such enterprise did not fit the central control system, and despite some promising results, few still exist: all this is usefully described by Löwenhardt (1974, pp.113ff). As we have seen, the creation of *obyedineniya* has as one of its principal purposes the establishment of closer links between research and production, and it does seem that progress in this direction has been made.

Yet results are likely to be disappointing unless management is interested in innovation and has the practical possibilities for action. Far too often there are in fact (unintended) *dis*incentives. These we must now examine.

First, it is necessary to establish that the role of management (whether of enterprises or the basic *obyedineniya*) in this field is crucial. The Soviet model implies, indeed is based upon, the proposition that the central planners know what needs to be done. We have seen how often this is in fact not the case. Particularly is this so in the area of technical progress. The central planners desire it, and appropriate exhortatory orders flow downwards. But new designs of machinery, improved quality or durability of the product, the utilization in factories of new production techniques, the upward flow of suggestions and proposals, these are very often decisive in the real world, in the USSR or elsewhere. A classic instance of the helplessness (combined with good intentions) of the planning organs is: 'the plan for the introduction of new techniques in the Ukraine envisages 2900 measures'. (Petukhov, *Pravda*, 17 July 1960.) Innovation is desired, but a quantitative plan of this sort can only lead to nonsense (in the given instance, some of the recipients appealed for a reduction in the number of planned innovations!). The example cited above is admittedly fifteen years old, but the problem and the practice remain: plans for innovation are still passed down the hierarchy; they are on the list of compulsory indicators for the 1976–80 plan, in the appendix to Chapter 4, above. Yet those who draft them cannot know, in most instances, just what it is that needs doing, what is most economical in the circumstances.

High ·on the list of snags listed in an authoritative article by Aganbegyan is lack of managerial power. Far too many indicators, including, as we have seen, indicators which formally speaking should be determined by management, are imposed from above. (*Pravda*, 12 November 1973.) The smaller the area of effective responsibility of the management, the more likely it is that innovation will either conflict with some indicator (e.g. cost per unit, or material-utilization norm), or it may simply be impossible to obtain or reshuffle the necessary resources without prior authorization from higher planning organs.

The system in fact discourages management from even trying, because:

(a) Management is judged above all by fulfilment of current plans. Almost any innovation entails some temporary disruption of productive processes. There is the likelihood that the current plan will suffer, and so will the incomes of many employees, as well as the standing of the manager himself. The 'evaluative time-horizon' of his chiefs tends to be short.

(b) All innovation entails risk. Yet risk as such is not rewarded.

(c) If the innovation requires a change in the plan – e.g. additional investments, different materials or whatever – the planning organs are very likely to alter the compulsory plan-indicators, so that the new plan, containing the innovation, will be at least as difficult to fulfil as the old, with the added element of risk mentioned above. (Of course the necessary materials may not be available).

(d) Even if no authorizations or formal changes of plan are needed, a successful innovation which fits into the established indicators positively is quite likely to be followed by an arbitrary upward change in these indicators, or downward amendment of the norms applicable to payments into the incentive funds.

(e) Actual plan-targets sometimes directly stand in the way of improvements in quality, and this affects particularly the production and design of new and better machines. Readers are referred back to the stories of the conflict between labour productivity measurement and tonnage and value of sales on the one hand, and the production of higher quality machinery on the other (see Chapter 4). By adversely affecting the design and production of efficient machinery, these 'distorting' indicators make it harder for the users to obtain what they need.

(f) Improvements in quality and durability are seldom rewarded, as these often fail to find reflection in the inflexible price system. There is little or no opportunity for the customer to persuade the producing enterprise to make improvements by offering a higher price. Indeed, one high-level Soviet critic stressed the 'lack of the necessary link between the production of machinery and the requirements of sectors and of customer-enterprises. . . . The plans for output of new kinds of equipment are drafted without the needed participation of the users, which inevitably has a negative effect on technical progress and its effectiveness.' (Gatovsky, 1967, p.59.)

This critic also commented on the excessively large number of designs of similar machines, the allocation of highly specialized equipment to factories which cannot adequately utilize it, and also on the fact that the various 'funds' and payments designed to encourage new techniques are usually less important (and smaller) than the frequently negative effect of innovation on the standard success indicators of the enterprise. He also deplores the insignificance of the role of economists in the whole process of deciding on technological innovation, which leads to decisions taken 'from a narrowly technical angle'. (Gatovsky, 1967, pp.57, 59, 60, 65.) Indeed we do often read of instances when the net effect of the innovations was to *increase* and not to reduce costs. For example in agriculture costs rise because, *inter alia*, 'new machinery costs much more than the old'. (*Pravda*, 20 August, 1974.) No doubt this is partly the consequence of the administrative allocation scheme, which restricts, when it does not eliminate, the user-enterprise's choice as to what equipment it can purchase.

Machinery design, production and standardization are all impeded by the multiplicity of producing enterprises, scattered among many ministries, a point already stressed in Chapter 3. To cite one more example, the deputy-chairman of *Gosplan* (who should know!) complained that 'materials-moving *(podyomno-transportny)* equipment is made by 380 factories, under 35(!) different ministries . . . Over 140 organizations of various subordinations are brought into project-and-design work in this field'. Many types of machines are not in the centrally confirmed plan (i.e. they are covered by some global total), and too little is devoted to so-called minor mechanization, though much labour could be saved by it. The author calls for a 'complex approach'. (Lebedev, *PKh*, 1975, No. 11, p.12.)

In all these circumstances, it is not surprising that many modern machines require to be imported from the West.

There remains one other major source of inefficiency, which has not yet been mentioned. This concerns the grossly excessive expenditures in money and labour-time on repairs. The Soviet critic already cited (L. Gatovsky), after deploring the 'extremely long period between the design of new machines and their use in production', which causes them to be obsolete already when introduced, stresses the extreme slowness of replacement of old machinery by new: far too much is spent on repairs: 'as is well known, the repairs sector (sfera remonta) is enormously inflated with us', and 'in the guise of capital repairs there takes place on a huge scale so-called reconstruction repairs, which several times resurrects obsolete equipment on an antique technical basis. Such reconstruction repairs artificially increase the requirements for additional repairs, and the diversion of large resources to repairs reduces the amount available for developing new equipment, and the shortage of new equipment makes it necessary to increase the volume of repairs.' The work of repairs is scattered among large numbers of workshops and is largely done by hand. Spare parts have to be made in a primitive (kustarnym) fashion, or repeatedly patched and repaired, for lack of supplies of spares. (Gatovsky, 1967, pp.63, 64.)

Another author cites figures which help to explain the survival of obsolete machines. Assuming a desirable average of ten years of service, derived from US experience, he shows that production not only falls short of replacement needs, but that the situation has been getting worse.

Table 6 *Relation of production to replacement needs, per cent*

	1962	1965	1968
Machine-tools, metalworking	75·0	67·4	63·7
Forging and pressing machines	67·7	59·7	61·0
Spindles	72·5	66·8	47·8

Repairs absorb huge resources: 'one third of all the machine-tool park and 3 million skilled workers'. Replacement of machines by new ones is three to four times faster in the United States. (Val'tukh, 1973, pp.236–8.)

Another source, the deputy-chairman of *Gosplan*, deploring the number of old and obsolete machines still being used, notes that 'for the time being industry cannot fully satisfy the requirements both of replacement of obsolete equipment and the supply of new equipment to factories under construction'. In consequence he too deplores the large expenditure on repairs. His figures are somewhat lower than Val'tukh's cited above: 2½ million skilled workers and 800,000 machine-tools (under a fifth of the total) are engaged on 'repair-reconstruction' (remontno-vosstanovitel'ny) work (Lebedev *PKh*, 1975, No. 11, p.12.) There is probably no contradiction, as Val'tukh referred to *all* repairs, whereas the deputy-chairman of *Gosplan* may have had capital repairs only in mind.

Evidently, all this points to an excess of new construction, as against replacement of existing equipment, though there is some improvement: retirements of out-of-date machinery and equipment doubled in number between 1969 and 1972. (*NKh*, 1972, p.144.) The reliance on repairs is partly explicable in terms of financing as well as allocation. Enterprises finance 'capital repairs' out of their share of the depreciation (amortization) fund. It is therefore simpler to spend money which is already earmarked for this purpose than to go through the complicated procedures for securing authorization for investment in new machines. Especially if the new machines cannot be obtained.

This last point is vital. There exist funds designed to compensate for losses in the initial period of the manufacture or adoption of 'new technique'. However, apart from the already mentioned difficulty of 'fitting' them into the standard set of success indicators, which stress quantitative short-term targets, there is the simple point that a good new machine cannot be installed unless it is available. All the most ingenious inducements to user-enterprise management will not help, and nor will the finest calculations of investment criteria, unless machines of the right type are made and supplied. One must emphasize again the importance of the plans and success indicators of enterprises making machinery and equipment. Hence the comment of yet another Soviet critic: 'Measures directed towards the further improvement of the existing system of planning and stimulating scientific-technical progress must be organically related to the national-economic planning system. Only on this condition will they have noticeable results.' The authors stress the importance, *inter alia*, of ensuring the observance of contracts to deliver, in respect both of punctuality and of the delivery of the types ordered. Managerial initiative could be encouraged if they were able to obtain credits for innovation, but, although the regulations provide for them, they remain insignificant: in 1970 they were a mere 0·86 milliard roubles, which should be compared with centralized state investments of 82·0 milliard roubles in that same year. (Fedorenko, 1973, pp.122, 123.) They might have added that some revision of success indicators is vital. As another critic pointed out, it is deplorable that output plans for many kinds of machines are still being planned in tons in 1976–80! (Volodarsky *EkG*, 1975, No. 33.)

It must be stressed that the planners and the political leadership are aware of all these deficiencies and are devoting much attention to putting them right. While some are inherent in the nature of the centralized planning system, one cannot deny that there is room for improvement within the system, and that innovation can speed up, especially if more of the 'machinery and metalworking' sector can be devoted to civilian, and not military, equipment.

The reader again needs warning against implicitly assuming that wasteful methods and delays are to be found only in Soviet-type economies. Construction can fall behind schedule anywhere, and sometimes does. Cost-estimates are often exceeded; blueprints have to be submitted to authorities to obtain planning permission, which in some cases is accompanied by public inquiries and the hearing of objections, which can impose both expense and several years' delay (the Alaskan pipeline, and oil-linked industrial development plans in Eastern Scotland, are two examples among many). And a recent article showed that American cement-making technique uses twice as much fuel as the West Europeans per ton of cement. (Carr, 1975, p.60.) All this is not meant to imply that the Soviet economic system is no worse in these respects than ours. I believe the contrary to be true; there will be more to say on 'systems comparisons' in Chapter 14. But it remains important not to compare model with muddle, to use a phrase from the preface.

BALANCE BETWEEN SECTORS AND 'INPUT-OUTPUT CONSERVATISM'

It is not enough to assert that the allocation of investment resources between sectors is deter .ined primarily by state priorities (and their input-output implications). One has also to ask: what determines these priorities? It is necessary briefly to return to the 'centralist-pluralist' model developed in Chapter 3. Decisions are influenced by pressure groups; ministries, republics, *oblasti*, exert pressures designed to influence decisions on priorities.

This must have the effect of making investment allocations in some degree a function of the relative influence of the various sectors and groups. This introduces a rigidity into the system: by definition, anything that is new and ought to be rapidly growing is not yet big and powerful.

This same trend is reinforced by what could be called 'input-output conservatism'. The planners, themselves divided into departments, work with material balance tables, or input-output coefficients, which inevitably reflect the past. Thus experience has taught them that to produce X tons of item A required given quantities of items P, Q, R and S. The supply system is geared to ensuring the allocation of physical quantities of P, Q, R and S from factories and mines which produce or extract them. All concerned are overworked, and, as we have seen, tend to plan 'on the basis of past performance'. This too has conservative implications: orders go out which have the effect of telling the recipients to go on doing what they were doing before, only more so. A change in input coefficients, or in the material or fuel used, means a lot more work for harassed planning officials.

Yet changes must occur. There are several possible case studies of how they do occur.

The first concerns fuel. During the Stalin period there was overwhelming reliance on coal, and an almost total neglect of natural gas. It needed the intervention of the political leadership, including Khrushchev personally, to order a change towards non-solid fuels, based upon a realization that the fuel balance was totally different in the United States, and on the fact that immense opportunities to expand oil and gas existed. In other words, routine, vested interest plus material-balance methodology held the Soviet fuel balance to an obsolete pattern until the situation attracted the notice of the topmost political authority.

The second example relates to chemicals. This was a notoriously backward industry in virtually all its branches, from mineral fertilizer to plastics and synthetics. Again, no effort could be generated to transform the situation until the top political authority – Krushchev again – appreciated the need for urgent action. Indeed Khrushchev specifically accused the planners of conservatism and complained about 'metal eaters', i.e. those who went on expanding the metal industries along well-established lines regardless of other needs.

Having done this, he proceeded to launch corrective campaigns, which caused a lurch from one extreme to the other. He did the same in yet another instance of 'political overcorrection': he demanded less bricks and more prefabricated cement, and this caused a serious shortage of bricks. An excessively rapid shift of resources away from solid fuels created a temporary shortage of coal. The great drive to expand chemicals caused overstrain and waste through the adoption of unrealistic investment plans, as anyone can see by constrasting the targets announced by Khrushchev for 1965 with the actual output data for that year, for such items as fertilizer, plastics, synthetic resins, etc. One could not, in the space of a quinquennium, build so many factories, design (or import) machines, train engineers and workers and generally make up for generations of neglect.

There is a basic 'systemic' logic about the role of the supreme political leadership in the process of changing the proportions and shape of the industrial structure, indeed economic strategy generally. For who else can take the necessary decisions?

The total picture is only visible at the top. Beneath it, sectoral, departmental, ministerial blinkers are worn. There we have the iron and steel industry, the chemical industry, the textile industry, the armaments industry and other organs which can best see only their own sectors plus those directly related to them. In the Western model, new and unexploited opportunities visible (say) to the bosses of firms in the chemical industry should lead to their adopting ambitious investment programmes and seeking capital, machines, materials, in the market. But in the Soviet model even if the Ministry of Chemical Industry were powerfully motivated to expand (which perhaps it was and is), there is nothing it can do autonomously, except to make representations, to submit plans and projects to higher authority. It has no *means* of just going ahead and acquiring the necessary resources. If its proposals are to be acted on, they have to catch the ear of leaders powerful enough to rearrange in a major way the allocation of investment, which must mean cutting allocations to some other sector(s). Theoretically, *Gosplan* ought to make the necessary calculations and submit appropriate plans to the political leadership, which can issue orders that they be enforced. However, we have seen that *Gosplan* is itself split into sectoral departments, and is overwhelmed with the task of ensuring balance, and above all balance in the short term.

Needless to say, efforts are constantly being made to modernize the industrial structure and to combat the kind of conservatism here described. New materials and new techniques are developed in research institutes, and such bodies as the Academy of Sciences, the State Committee on Science and Technology, as well as the sectoral ministries, make their reports and recommendations. A list of innovations of major significance is included in the national-economic plan: for example, in 1976 there are to be 4,000 new types of machinery and equipment, of which 650 appear in the plan (*Pravda*, 3 December, 1975), i.e. presumably are individually listed. But here, as in so much else, there is a penalty to be paid for over-centralization.

Attempts to devise macro-criteria for allocation between sectors sometimes founder on another difficulty, not yet mentioned, only remotely connected with pricing, where conventional investment criteria become simply perverse in their effects. To illustrate this point, let us briefly turn to the services sectors, particularly retail trade. It must be stressed that the very serious neglect of generations is being corrected, as can be seen from the large increase in the past decade in a very wide range of services provided for the population. As we shall see, many services are excluded from the Soviet definition of national income, and so their expansion does not fit one of the proposed indicators for allocating investment resources: the increase in national income yielded. It is sometimes argued that the past neglect of so-called unproductive services is due to their omission from national income, but this proposition cannot be very convincing, given that 'unproductive' activities in this sense include (among other things) the party and state apparatus and the armed forces.

However, trade *is* regarded as productive (for reasons set out in Chapter 12). So it might be thought that expansion in the retail trade network must have a positive effect on growth statistics. But this is not necessarily so. The total volume of goods sold is limited by the volume available, at established prices, and the effect of having more and better shops is not to increase turnover but to increase the convenience and save the time of the customers. But convenience and time-saving do not figure in national income statistics, and in fact the effect of increasing the number of shops faster than the volume of goods sold might be to 'worsen' the trade 'efficiency' indicators: costs are minimized and productivity per employee is at its highest when there is a constant line of customers waiting to be served.

As will be pointed out again when we discuss the logic of various reform proposals, good service is seldom 'worth' providing, by conventional 'commerical' criteria, unless the existence of competition makes it possible for bad service to be punished by the customer going elsewhere.

INVESTMENT AND TECHNICAL PROGRESS: RECAPITULATION

The evidence, I suggest, supports the view that the deficiencies of pricing, and their effects on calculations of recoupment periods or coefficients of effectiveness, are not the most important on the list of problems. Far more important appear to be the long delays in completions, the shortage of good-quality equipment, the resultant practice of devoting massive resources to patching up and repairing old machinery, and also many instances of failure to meet the detailed needs of the purchasers of capital goods, notably the frequent inattention to complementarities (the lack of *komplekstnost'*). The overblown 'project-making' organs do not have a close enough link with the planning of the output and design of capital goods, the success indicators of machinery-producing enterprises fail to encourage the production of the types of machines most needed by their customers, and there is about the whole system an unintended discouragement of both innovation and quality, because of the priority given to the fulfilment of short-term quantitative plan-objectives. All this is part of the now-familiar cost of micro-economic centralization and its reflection in the field of investment and innovation.

All these factors combine to give an unnecessarily low 'coefficient of effectiveness', which expresses itself in an unnecessarily large volume of investment and of intermediate goods in relation to the end-result, i.e. to the volume of final consumable output. In the end, inefficiency and waste are 'paid' for by the consumer, in terms of living standards. The Western economies doubtless also generate waste and can misuse resources (an inevitable consequence of errors due to uncertainty about the future, to mention no other causes). None the less, the disparities between living standards in East and West do appear to be wider than the disparities between aggregate totals such as national income or industrial output, which does suggest that the Soviet system is better at 'extensive' provision of inputs than at using the resources so created to good advantage.

Some readers might demur, and point out that in the *military* and space fields the Soviet achievements have been impressive. So they have. (They have been impressive also in some civilian sectors.) The military sector is special, however, not only because it is given priority, and can expect the best of management, materials and attention from planners and central committee officials. It is also a case in which *the state is the customer.* Of course, it may be said that the state is also the customer if any state enterprise purchases anything: a plough or a ton of sheet metal, for instance. Formally speaking this is so. But we have repeatedly had reason to note that at the level of the enterprise (or *obyedineniye*) the customer is seldom right, the supplier of scarce goods and scarce inputs has the whip hand. Not so if the 'commodity' is, say, a nuclear submarine. The quality of its design depends on the quality of scientific research. The detailed specifications (in Russia as elsewhere) are determined centrally in the nature of things. The state, or its defence establishment, places these orders and ensures their fulfilment. Here at least the customer is always right.

It may be asked: if the system works well in the military goods field, why not extend the same methods to the rest of the economy? The answer is: the deliberate concentration of resources, under close central supervision, to any sector of the economy works only on condition that only a few sectors are affected, and that the rest of the economy is non-priority. The advantages which this gives to the key, priority sectors makes of them likely centres of resistance to any economic reform which weakens their exclusive position. But more of this in Chapter 11.

In his speech reported on 28 November 1979, Brezhnev referred in strong terms to the continued *raspyleniye* (scattering) of investment resources over too many projects, criticizing officials who divert (perhaps 'steal', *rastaskivuyut*) these resources for unauthorized purposes. In a vigorously critical article, the economist V. Krasovsky pointed to a continuous fall in the rate of return on investments in recent years: while accepting that many expenditures in Siberia, plus the cost of combating environmental pollution, are part of the explanation, he laid particular stress on the rapidly rising *cost* of both machinery and construction, casting very severe doubt on the official price indices which pretend to show reductions in prices of machinery and of costs of construction.

According to an article in *Pravda* (19 December 1979), waste of resources in inefficient and costly repairs has reached enormous dimensions: repairs plus the needed production of spare parts employ 7 million workers and employees, and one-third of all machine-tools. Often repairs cost more than a new machine or vehicle would cost!

CHAPTER 7

PRICES
IN THEORY AND PRACTICE

PRICES IN THE 'STALIN' MODEL

In analysing the actual and potential nature of prices in the USSR, or anywhere else, it is always important to ask oneself the question: what practical role are they intended to play? What operational purpose do they serve, or should they serve? Let me begin by concentrating on *industrial wholesale prices*, defined as the prices at which the producing units (enterprises, *obyedineniya*) deliver (sell) their products to other state enterprises. The latter may be other industrial units, or some part of the state trading network. We will leave consideration of retail prices, and also the special case of agricultural prices, until late in this chapter.

The discussions on the role of prices necessarily involve consideration of the role of market forces, and also of the 'law of value', the latter being widely used as a shorthand way of referring to the economics of purchase-and-sale, of exchange relationships and, therefore, of the market. In discussion in the twenties concerning the role of the law of value in the transition period to socialism, several participants counterposed state planning and the market, the expectation being that, as deliberate control by society over resources spread, the function of the 'anarchic' and unplanned market would diminish, indeed wither away.

The elimination of the private sector in the 1928–32 period, collectivization of agriculture, the adoption of the 'command' planning model, led to the assertion of the total dominance of the plan. The party and state, the planners, decided what to do and how to do it. The 'law of value' was irrelevant. Prices were what the planners decided they should be. Many basic industrial materials and fuels were priced far below cost (in 1933–5, for instance) and large subsidies were doled out from the state budget to cover the difference. (For an excellent historical account see Malafeyev, 1964.)

This was associated with the view that the state was omnipotent in economic affairs: 'there is no fortress the Bolsheviks cannot take', to cite a slogan of the time. Since, however, objective limitations did exist, and some attention had to be paid to efficiency, this downgrading of economic laws was in due course challenged, and 'the law of value in transformed form' was born. Later on, in 1951, Stalin contributed his own reformulation: the 'law of value' applies where a genuine sale takes place (e.g. in retail trade, or when a *kolkhoz* sells its produce). It does not apply to what are in effect transfers within the state sector. The theoretical issues will be discussed in Chapter 12.

Stalin did not deny that these transfer prices have significance: 'Such things as cost accounting and profitableness, production costs, prices, etc., are of actual importance in our enterprises. . . . It is really not a bad thing, as it trains our business executives to conduct production on rational lines and disciplines them. . . . It teaches them to count production magnitudes, to calculate real things in production precisely . . . to lower production costs, to practise cost accounting . . .' (and so on). But 'the law of value can be a regulator of production only under capitalism'. (Stalin, 1952.)

Prices, then, in this conception, have no allocative role, but encourage fulfilment of plans with due regard to economy, and serve also an *evaluative* purpose: they enable the supervisory organs to judge how effectively the management functions.

The implied model was as follows: the centre decides what is to be done and how to do it, and prices and profitability do not play an active role at any level in the allocation of resources. Nor do they affect the incomes of either workers or management; thus if the price of coal was below cost, or above it, it made no difference to anyone concerned with mining, whose incomes were determined by wage and salary scales and whose bonuses related to norms and output plans, and not at all to the profit and loss account. Nor do changes in the price of coal affect the use of coal by industrial enterprises, since coal is allocated to them administratively and they are not free to change to some other fuel. But the fact that transfer to and from other state enterprises took the nominal form of *sales* was useful: *khozraschet* accounting meant that one could calculate costs and therefore reward economy and identify waste in the fulfilment of the obligatory plans.

For this purpose, i.e. for evaluating performance, the actual level of prices did not seem to matter, but there was a clear advantage in their being stable. If either output or input prices changed frequently, the task of using them to evaluate performance was made more complex. Stable prices enabled one more easily to assess the information that costs had been reduced by 2 per cent, or the gross value of output had increased by 10 per cent, over the preceding period. If at the prices ruling there was a book-keeping loss, a subsidy would cover it.

This 'Stalin' view was deficient in several important respects, even in terms of the highly centralized system of his day. It is not surprising that it was challenged within a few years of his death.

Firstly, prices were in fact used by the planning organs when they considered alternatives. They had at various times to say: to produce or invest by this method is *cheaper* than by some other method. Whenever they did so, prices affected resource allocation.

Secondly, management affected the plan-orders received from above by their own proposals. Such magnitudes as gross output, or costs, were computed in roubles. Therefore prices affected these magnitudes, and through them the plan-fulfilment indicators and the management's proposals about both output and inputs.

'VALUES' AND COST-PLUS

The debate which opened in earnest in 1956 raised issues concerned with Marxian 'values' which will be treated in greater detail in Chapter 12. The essential point on which agreement was widespread was that Stalin's formulation left the field open for arbitrariness in pricing, that prices should be rational, because otherwise errors in allocation were bound to occur. But what is 'rational'? Should they accord with 'values'? What, for practical purposes, *are* 'values'?

Wholesale prices, according to the textbooks then in use, were based upon average costs (*sebestoimost'*), including depreciation (*amortizatsiya*), plus a profit margin, usually described as 3–5 per cent of costs. In reality there were (and are) very wide disparities between costs and prices. For many years, for instance, coal and timber prices were far below cost. By contrast, many kinds of machinery and a wide variety of other goods yielded very high profit margins. The fact that prices were changed infrequently, while costs altered, led to wide disparities in profit margins, even in those instances in which they had been similar to begin with. Sometimes prices were deliberately manipulated to encourage (or discourage) utilization of a resource for policy reasons: the case of Moscow-basin coal has already been mentioned. Higher prices for key products of heavy industry were resisted because it was alleged that this might discourage growth or technical progress.

Some critics also seized upon the fact that turnover tax was charged mainly on consumers' goods, so that they were sold 'above their values', and this distorted the money measurement of proportions of the national economy. The influence of these critics was directed towards a more systematic and uniform cost-plus.

Cost plus what? Should it be cost plus a percentage of costs? Cost plus a percentage of the wages bill? Cost plus a percentage of the value of capital? After prolonged debate, which it seems unnecessary even to summarize here, the majority view settled ultimately upon cost plus a percentage on capital, claiming that this accorded with Marx's 'production price' of Volume III of *Das Kapital* (see Chapter 12 for more on this doctrine). This found its reflection in the price recalculations of 1967, though, as we shall see, the principle was not consistently applied.

However, *any* cost-plus prices suffer from an important deficiency, if one considers their use at any level for purposes of resource allocation, or indeed of any choice between alternative outputs or methods of production. The point is easy to grasp. Such prices reflect *neither* utility *nor* scarcity. Let us take utility first. Let us suppose that two goods, or baskets of goods, exist which share the common property of costing exactly the same amount to produce, with exactly the same amount of capital. They would only have the same *use-value* by the purest coincidence, unless, of course, there is a means through which demand (or value-in-use) can affect price. It therefore follows that prices of this type cannot serve as any sort of guide as to the needs of society or of the customer, i.e. as to social utility howsoever defined.

Nor do such prices reflect scarcities. No doubt in equilibrium this would not matter, since unequal degrees of scarcity are by definition inconsistent with equilibrium, but the real world is not one of equilibrium. If prices are to have an active role as indicators, whether to management or planners, they ought to indicate scarcity, by making it more advantageous (profitable) to produce the item in heavy demand, and by discouraging unnecessary uses of particularly scarce inputs. If prices do neither of these things, then a number of consequences follow. Firstly, scarce inputs would then have to be 'rationed' by the planners between alternative uses (i.e. an administrative allocation system is required). Secondly, responses to shortages, in the sense of the taking of remedial action, would also require the conscious decision of the planning organs, based upon a *quantitative* analysis (since price and money indicators will not provide any automatic signal of shortage). Thirdly, if the planners do not take the necessary actions, and prices remain below the level at which supply and demand balance, one can (does) have such phenomena as shortage, *tolkachi*, grey or black markets, and/or access to scarce items regulated by rank or privilege.

As discussions on reform progressed, and became linked with the price debate, it soon became apparent that cost-plus prices were not enough – unless, of course, one opposed any reform. The logic of this will be gone into at length in Chapter 11. The essential point is simple: no solution which stresses profitability *(rentabel 'nost')* as a criterion for decision making, and especially as the substitute for the criterion of the fulfilment of plan-instructions, can possibly work unless prices serve as signals. It has been said before, and will be said again, that price information is by no means the only information required for action, in any economy. None the less, such information is plainly vital. It follows that those reformer-economists who argued for market-type decentralization had to develop a price theory appropriate to a market-type economy. Those who, like Liberman, and also (on a higher theoretical level) Novozhilov, took the view that 'What is

needed by society should be profitable (advantageous) for the enterprise' advocated the species of prices which made desirable actions
profitable, and this, needless to say, does *not* mean cost-plus prices. In
fact Liberman did not develop any coherent price theory, but Novozhilov did. In his view, prices should be such as to inform the enterprise
what should be produced, of what quality and what, in his words, was
the 'socially necessary limit *(predel)* of production costs'. (Novozhilov,
EkMM, 1966, No. 3, p.328.)

On similar lines, Petrakov advocated supply-and-demand-balancing
prices, arguing that no equilibrium price makes sense in a disequilibrium situation: if disproportions develop, and prices and profits rise,
'thereby are created the conditions for the liquidation of the shortage
and the restoration of proportionality'. (Petrakov, 1966, p.48.) Or
again: 'If an enterprise or a citizen has a sum of money and wishes to
obtain a product, then this product should be available in wholesale
or retail stores. This should be an axiom of economic life.' (Petrakov,
1971, p.49.)

Nemchinov, who did much to advance the cause of mathematical
economics, developed the concept of fixed prices being confined to
basic materials and fuels, with many or most of the state's needs put
out to competitive tenders; this plainly envisaged many prices being
settled by negotiation or bargaining. (Nemchinov, *Kom*, 1964, No. 5.)

Nemchinov, Novozhilov and Petrakov were involved in the development of the mathematical school, and their attitude to the micro-
economic function of prices reflected their realization that central
control could only relate to aggregated magnitudes, especially in the
context of a longer-term plan. An optimal plan would contain – would
indeed use for its elaboration – plan-prices. For the long-term plan,
these would be the shadow prices appropriate to the scarcity relationships, to the resource availability and constraints, implied by the plan
that is adopted. The plan that is adopted, in turn, would be formed in
the knowledge of the scarcity relationships implied by alternative
drafts and variants of the plan. These prices would accord with what
Kantorovich called *obyektivno obuslovleniye otsenki* ('objectively
determined valuations', or o.o.o.). They are the dual of the adopted
programme. If land, minerals or any other resource is particularly
scarce in relation to the plan, it must be given the appropriate valuation. It was (reasonably) argued that if land were regarded as a free
good, because it is a gift of nature (or because landlords used to derive
an exploitation income from it), it follows that its scarcity will not be
assessed when alternative projects are considered. Thus, let us take
an example: a hydroelectric scheme involving a dam and the loss of
10,000 hectares of good farmland under an artificial lake. If land were
'free', then one would not include this land as a cost in the computation of the costs of the project, in comparison with an alternative

scheme (e.g. two thermal power stations which do not require any artificial lake). The same point is made in respect of the valuation assigned to capital: if it is free, or charged much less than the sum represented by opportunity-cost (i.e. alternative uses forgone), then the programme will be out of balance, and cannot be efficient.

So these would be *efficiency prices*, determined in the process of endeavouring to arrive at the desired plan in the most expeditious manner. The objectives of the planners, the desired end-result, create the relative scarcities, which, of course, the planned investment programme is designed, as far as possible within the time-scale of the plan, to overcome. Be it noted that this version of the mathematical school's price theory is concerned primarily with longer-term planning and is fully consistent (in theory at least) with the objectives of policy being determined by the political leadership and the central planning organs.

But, as we have already seen in Chapter 2, optimization is far easier to define in abstract theory than in the real world. We have also seen that *current* planning involves a great multitude of variants, literally millions of products, which cannot be effectively planned in disaggregated detail. Nor can their prices be controlled in any rational way, for reasons to be explained in a moment.

Much confusion is sometimes engendered by a failure to realize the consequences and complexities of disaggregation. No central computerized programme can be so detailed that actual operational prices of specific products can be derived from it. There are over eight hundred kinds of ball-bearings alone. There are many thousands of variants of farm machinery. There is no such thing as 'the price' of ball-bearings or of farm machinery, save in the form of some weighted index of a multitude of 'micro-prices' of specific items.

If these (and millions of others) are none the less priced by the planning organs, under the aegis of the State Committee on Prices, then the following must be the consequences:

First, the task of price fixing is immensely costly in time and human resources. The 1967 price revision, for instance, was preceded by many years' hard work 'continuously since the end of 1960 by thousands of specialists of the most diverse kinds'. (Petrakov, 1971, p.46.) Partial revisions (especially of machinery prices) have occurred since, but all price reviews are extremely time-consuming. This in itself is a reason for the relative infrequency of price revisions. It is simply impossible to expect all-inclusive price control to function flexibly, to reflect changes in costs, demand, scarcities. The task is too big.

Second, to carry out the task one needs information, including information about costs. This information is supplied by the productive enterprises. But they are interested in inflating costs, because they are judged on the value of sales *(realizatsiya)* and, since 1965, are interested also in profitability. Furthermore, it 'pays' managers to be able to show that they have reduced costs, and so it is advantageous to start with a high figure. At the stage at which prices are being determined, management tries to write into the plan the dearest possible inputs, for they serve to justify a higher price and this is helpful in terms of plan-fulfilment. Hence the paradox already noted earlier: it is sometimes the case that a higher price for an input can stimulate demand for it on the part of management.

As we have already seen, some members of the mathematical school take the view – a view I share – that *micro*-economic rationality requires supply-and-demand-balancing prices, and this in turn requires that many prices (not necessarily all) be freed from administrative control, that they be determined by negotiation between customer and supplier, or by wholesaling or retailing organs. This has been the line taken by the Hungarians in implementing their reform of 1968: while key industrial materials and consumer necessities are price-controlled, the less important items (covering, numerically, the greatest number of prices, though a much smaller part of the value of turnover) are more or less free. Much more will be said about the Hungarian reform experience in Chapter 11.

However, some of the 'mathematicians' are attracted by the possibility of computerized central control, or market simulation, and it is sometimes asserted that this is reconcilable with the preservation of the centralized planning system. This helps to explain the political backing received in recent years by the Mathematical-Economics Institute and its director, Academician Fedorenko. I have already expressed some scepticism as to the feasibility of this approach, both in Chapter 2 above, when discussing optimal planning, and earlier in this chapter when stressing the importance of the disaggregation problem.

The 'mathematicians' are by no means unanimous. A powerful group, which includes the influential S. S. Shatalin, has argued for the 'coexistence' of two pricing or valuation principles: one based on an optimizing programme and used for drawing up central plans, and another for the unavoidably decentralized micro-economic decision making, in which market-type relations would rule, (See *EkMM*, No. 6, 1974, Nos 1 and 2 1975, and more detailed discussion of the theoretical implications in Chapter 12, below.)

One is inevitably driven back to the same fundamental issue: who is best able to decide, in micro-economic detail, what needs doing and how best to do it? Given that the centre has imperfect and necessarily aggregated information, given the necessity of devolution of decision making, what signals should prices be making, and to whom, at what levels of the decision-making hierarchy?

The 'market mathematicians' argue that the centre requires the information which a market gives to take those decisions which do fall to the centre. In a discussion in Moscow in 1967, the point was made to me as follows: unless the purchaser is able to purchase, unless he faces supply-and-demand-balancing prices, micro-demand cannot be known to the planner. A record of actual purchases will not serve as a guide to demand, will not reveal preferences, because in many cases the purchaser (be he a citizen or a manager) may be making do with sub-stitutes. One cannot get far with mere collection of information about wants (what has been called 'registration of clamour') because wants usually exceed availabilities, this being the very definition of scarcity, and the centre will not know about the intensity of wants and require-ments, which receive (though admittedly imperfect) recognition in the willingness to pay a price. Hence it is vital to be able 'to vote with the rouble'. In aggregating these 'votes', the centre will discover the need to create new capacity, to shift existing capacity to new lines, to import, etc. etc.

Such reasoning as this underlay the conception of the Hungarian reform of 1968, and the price logic of this reform required the decontrol of many prices, for reasons already explained. Such decontrol had to be preceded by the elimination of excess demand, which would otherwise force up prices in the uncontrolled sector. In the presence of inflationary pressure, there is clear danger that, if price control is confined to 'essentials', it will be relatively more profitable to produce and distribute the uncontrolled non-essentials, which can lead to very unfortunate results. But more about inflationary pressures in Chapter 9.

Official Soviet thinking has rejected, so far, the whole logic of the above position. The use of prices as one way of influencing managerial behaviour is not denied, but it is best to quote the words of Sitnin, the head of the Prices Committee: 'Market prices are, in our view, alien to our economy and contradict the task of centralized planning. It is . . . incorrect to imagine that prices should balance supply and demand. The balance between demand and supply . . . is the task of the planning organs.' (Sitnin, EkG, 1968, No. 6, pp.10–11.) Quite logically, the same author opposes 'the abandonment of compulsory quantitative indicators' in planning, and opposes competition between suppliers. He also, in the same article, regards an increase in profits arising from a shift by the enterprise to a cheaper material as somehow improper, as something 'which they are clearly not entitled to keep'.

Fully in line with the above principles is the view, still predominant, that any increase in profits arising from a change in the product mix is illegitimate, requiring a modification downwards in the payments into the incentive funds (see Chapter 4). The basic conception is that the *centre* issues orders on the product mix, and that consequently a change which might lead to a rise in profits is not the enterprise's responsibility. Alternatively, if the enterprise has altered the product mix of its own volition to obtain a higher profit, this is likely to be irrational or undesirable, a view which rests on the belief (often a correct belief) that there is indeed no rational link between prices and profits and the needs of society. This emerges at once from even the most superficial study of rates of profitability. In the 1967 price-review losses (e.g. in the coal industry) were eliminated and differences in profit rates between sectors reduced. But differences persist, as Table 7 shows.

Table 7   *Profitability as per cent of basic and working capital*

	1965	1972	1978
All industry	13·0	19·3	13·5
of which:			
Electricity	4·6	10·2	6·4
Oil	10·4	24·2	11·0
Coal	− 17·0	6·3	− 3·2
Ferrous metallurgy	8·6	16·0	10·7
Chemicals and petrochemicals	16·4	19·8	18·4
Machinery and metalworking	16·7	20·2	15·2
Timber and paper	6·9	17·7	7·9
Building materials	5·4	17·7	6·4
Light industry	29·9	36·9	25·3
Food industry	24·4	24·5	20·7

(*Source*: *NKh*, 1972, p.700, and *NKh*, 1978, p.518.)

The very high figure for light industry seems to be due, at least in part, to its relative undercapitalization. Profit margins used to be expressed as a percentage of costs, and the margin for light industry would look lower. This point was made in an authoritative textbook as follows: 'Profitability is measured as the relationship of total profits to the value of capital funds. But profit is also the excess of price over cost of production. . . . But in respect of the structure and turnover of capital various sectors greatly differ.' Thus output (at cost) per rouble of basic capital is 0·27 roubles in electricity generation, but 2·92 roubles in light industry. Therefore if the average level of profitability, say 15 per cent of the value of capital, were applied in electricity, there would be a profit margin over costs of 75 per cent, whereas in light industry the margin would be only 6 per cent. If 6 per cent of the value of capital were deducted from profits as a capital charge, the relative figures would be 45 per cent and 3 per cent. This, argues the author, would be wrong; for instance, where would the incentive funds for light industry come from, and why should electricity be made so much dearer? (Mayzenberg, 1973, p.168–9.)

Even abstracting from this, there is still considerable variation. The general magnitude of profit margins was deliberately raised, since, in the Soviet method of computation, the capital charge (introduced in the 1967 price reform) is paid out of profits and is not included in costs (on the formal 'Marxist' grounds that it is part of the surplus product). Yet the new prices for coal were such that the 'normal' capital charge of 6 per cent could not be levied.

Much greater variation occurs *within* each industrial group, nowhere more so than in the machinery sector. Evidence of a wide variation within the 'machine-building' group may be found in several Soviet sources. Thus in 1972 profitability for 'instruments' *(priborostroyeniye)* was twice as high as for agricultural machinery, whether this is computed as a percentage of capital or as percentage of costs. (Yakovets, 1974, p.95.) This particular variation may have a quasi-'political' cause, in the sense of being deliberate: no increase in prices of farm machinery was permitted in 1967, as part of the effort to improve the situation in agriculture; it appears that in some cases wholesale prices *were* increased, but sales to farms continued at the old prices, the difference being made up by subsidy. (Skvortsov, 1972, p.95.)

A sizable critical literature draws attention to the high profits which arise when 'temporary prices' for new products (based upon inflated cost estimates, or the genuinely high cost in the first period of production) are left unchanged for several years. There are also wide variations in the profitability of sub-items within the same product group: different kinds or models of farm machinery, salami-type or frankfurter-type sausages, and so on almost *ad infinitum*. Thus although we have seen that consumers'-goods production is, as a whole, profitable, there remain some 'unprofitable' prices, though much fewer than before the price reform introduced in 1966 and 1967, as Table 8 shows.

Table 8   *Number of loss-making commodities*
(light and food industries examples):

	At the old prices	At the new prices
Perfumes, cosmetics, toilet soap	75	11
Synthetic scents	15	0
Confectionery: RSFSR	37	5
Ukraine	104	17
Latvia	75	7

(*Source*: Skvortsov, 1972, p.154.)
(The reference here to republics is explained by the fact that prices for many of the more minor items are fixed by republican organs, subject to central guidelines.)

As already argued, infrequent price reviews covering literally millions of prices *must* produce (or generate through time) a great many price anomalies. They are 'irrational' in the most elementary sense of the word: the differences in sub-product profitability are not (with a few exceptions) deliberately intended, they are not price-reflections of policy objectives, they are the consequence of the functioning of a vast and unwieldy price-determining apparatus (why, after all, subsidize any species of confectionery or perfumes?).

As well as differences in average profitability between groups and sub-groups of products, there are very wide differences between profitabilities as between different enterprises producing the same thing. In part this is inevitable in any dynamic economy: some factories will be better equipped, better managed, better designed than others. In the Soviet case, the situation is exacerbated by two other factors. The first is that marginal cost pricing is rejected in principle, the official view being that prices should be based on *average* cost plus a profit margin; therefore some enterprises must be expected to make a loss. Secondly, and more important, the cost differences are generally very wide in the Soviet Union, because of the practice of fully utilizing any available productive capacity, even if its costs are high where, in most 'capitalist' countries, it would have been scrapped long ago.

Given that these profitability differences are (with rare exceptions) neither linked with planners' nor with consumers' micro-preferences, it logically follows that such prices are inherently inconsistent with any reform designed to enhance the role of profits as a basis for decentralized decision making. There is as yet no sign that any other species of prices are likely to be adopted in the near future.

There has been some debate in the USSR on the issue of marginal cost pricing. Some of it was conducted on formal-ideological lines: Marx did write of *average* socially necessary costs. On the other hand, such economists as Novozhilov, as we have seen, argued for what he called a 'socially-necessary limit' to production costs, meaning by this that prices should cover the costs of any producing unit whose output is socially desirable. Other formulations of the same point speak of a price which should cover the costs of the highest-cost *group* of enterprises producing this particular commodity. These are all variants of the principle that prices should be such as to cover marginal costs. The supporters of this view do not assert that prices should cover the costs of the highest-cost enterprise now producing, since they are aware of the existence of extreme variations in costs at the present time; they would urge that such enterprises be phased out, or transferred to other work, at the earliest date. In fact something approaching a consensus is developing. Even Sitnin, who denied the need for supply-and-demand-balancing prices, also argued for the elimination of the bulk of subsidies, and therefore for prices which cover costs most of the time. Perhaps the present unsatisfactory situation is due not so much to a rejection of marginal cost as the basis of price-fixing as the pressure to keep inefficient and high-cost units in production, exercised by planners themselves under pressure to fulfil overambitious plans, and who carry no responsibility for the financial outcome of their instructions. There is also the clumsy slowness of the price-fixing process itself.

Let us return to the authoritative textbook already cited, in which the author of the chapter on prices is the official economist Mayzenberg. He makes the following case. Loss-making enterprises are now few, only 3 per cent of the total, since the 1967 price-reform, which raised wholesale prices, in some instances by very high percentages (coal by 78 per cent, gas by 50 per cent, iron ore by 127 per cent). A wide variety of profitabilities unfortunately continues to exist. Some economists 'propose basing industrial wholesale prices on the highest costs in enterprises included in the national-economic plan' (for the production of the given commodity). Mayzenberg rejects this, on the grounds that prices would then lose their role as 'an objective criterion of costs and results in production'. By this he doubtless means that prices should play a role in evaluating performance, by reference to the costs incurred by the bulk of the enterprises producing the given commodity. He objects to fixing prices by reference to the least efficient, highest-cost enterprise; prices would then automatically cover the highest costs actually incurred, even when this is due to extremes of inefficiency, which would indeed be unreasonable. Steps should be taken, by reorganization or re-equipment, to reduce costs in such cases. In some instances, the planners may be compelled to order the production of needed items in enterprises where this causes a loss, but then they should compensate the enterprise by subsidy. (Mayzenberg, 1973, p.175.) The same point was made by another author: there are indeed enterprises in bad (high-cost) economic conditions, 'but this is a problem of production and not of prices. Of course by raising prices one could eliminate loss, but this would cover up the inefficiencies, instead of facilitating their elimination'. (Gusarov, 1971, pp.419–420.)

Economists like Petrakov put up a well-argued case – with interpretations of Marx to back it – for marginal cost as a basis for price, and they do not fail to point out that there may be conditions of increasing or decreasing marginal cost as output increases. Petrakov also, as did Novozhilov, seeks to link pricing with supply-and-demand balance, so that 'the amount the consumer is prepared to pay for obtaining a unit of the given commodity coincides with expenditures on production'. (Petrakov, 1971, pp.113–121.) He has no difficulty in demonstrating that, at the level of abstraction of Marx's *Das Kapital*, marginal and average costs would be equal. However, one cannot imagine Petrakov favouring fixing a price at the level of costs in the most inefficiently conducted production unit.

On the face of it, then, the practical implications of the views of Petrakov and of officials like Mayzenberg or Bunich may not seem to differ greatly. However, they do disagree in a vital respect: underlying them is a quite different concept of planning and of the role of the market, and therefore a different view both of the role of prices and of how they should be determined. The point can be briefly illustrated by another quotation from Petrakov's book: 'Thus the (desirable) pattern of functioning of a socialist enterprise in the system of social production appears to us as follows. The enterprises, seeking to maximize net profits, make contracts with suppliers and customers. The contracts become the basis of the economic plan of the enterprise. The enterprise informs its superior organ about the plan, and if necessary puts forward proposals for additional financing.' The superior organ can decide whether to provide this, and indeed in this proposal can cancel contracts already made and insist on producing some items it considers vital, but must bear the economic consequences. In the main, the centre would act through 'a tough system of payment for the use of social resources, credits, penalties for breach of contract . . . and a profits tax at progressive rates'. (Petrakov, 1971, pp.43,44.) The implied price system would indeed be different to one where it is assumed that enterprises will generally obey orders as to what they should produce. For Petrakov most of the price-signals are intended to guide managers in their commercial activities. The official view does not deny that prices should be one way of encouraging managers to act economically, but the product mix is seen as a matter of central decision, and choice of inputs one of central allocation.

RETAIL PRICES, TURNOVER TAX, CONSUMERS' DEMAND

One of the most serious defects of Soviet pricing is the virtual non-existence of any direct influence of the customer, or of consumer demand in general, on price. Therefore it follows that it is normally impossible for a user (whether he be a manager of an enterprise seeking inputs or the totality of consuming citizens) to make it economically worth the producer's while to satisfy his requirements. We have seen how this adversely affects the production and supply of machinery from the standpoint of the user-enterprise; in fact there is a formal possibility of adjusting the price by arrangement, but it seems that it is rarely used. (Mayzenberg, 1973, pp.180–182.) The same is true of consumers' goods.

According to an oversimplified but not totally inaccurate version of the Soviet pricing system, while wholesale (factory) prices are based on cost-plus, retail prices are calculated separately with particular reference to the demand situation ('to clear the market'). There must be a large difference between the cost of production of consumers' goods and services on the one hand and the total income of the population on the other. The difference arises from the fact that citizens are paid for undertaking many activities other than the provision of purchasable goods and services (investment, free social services, defence, administration, etc.). Since direct taxes are few, the costs of all these activities are met out of a mark-up on the costs of goods. The bulk of this mark-up, as we shall see in Chapter 9, consists of profits and turnover tax. As we shall also see, most (not all) of turnover tax is levied on consumers' goods. It is distributed among different consumers' goods at different rates, to help clear the market. Imagine a simple example, in which two goods cost the same to produce, but one of them is more popular with the consumers. One might have a situation like that shown in Table 9 (assuming the same profit margin on the same value of capital).

Table 9

	Good A	Good B
	(prices in roubles)	
Costs	100	100
Profit margin	20	20
Factory wholesale price	120	120
Retail price	140	180
Less handling costs	10	10
TURNOVER TAX	10	50

In this imaginary example, there is no extra inducement to produce B, insofar as profit and sales are (for the manager) the same as if he produced A. Thus turnover tax serves as a species of barrier between the supply-and-demand price and the factory wholesale price: in this model the intensity of demand *does* affect price, but only the retail price, without serving as a signal to the management of any productive enterprise. We shall see in Chapter 9 that turnover tax is in many cases levied in the form of a 'tax by difference', i.e. the varying margins between producers' prices and retail prices (after allowance for handling costs) determine the rate of tax, rather than the rates of tax determining the margins.

Assuming that it is not the management but the planners that decide what is to be produced, there can be said to be some logic in this. One could imagine the *planners* basing their decisions upon the size of these margins: suppose, to re-use the previous example, in the case of good B the tax yield per unit works out at 50, and of good A at

10 roubles. This could lead to planning organs deciding to produce more of good B. However, there is no sign that this actually happens. Probably the reason for this is the production planners at that level have no motive to act in this way, and the Ministry of Finance is interested only in the revenue aspect. However, there have certainly been instances in which a large planned expansion in the output of some previously highly scarce good – as has happened for a number of consumer durables – leads as a consequence to a reduction in the retail price ('to clear the market'), which is in fact achieved by reducing the rate of turnover tax levied on this item.

It is sometimes argued that the fact that prices of consumers' goods bear the main burden of turnover tax introduces a major distortion into pricing, since consumers' goods are sold 'above their values'. True enough, the use of such prices can be held to distort the proportions of the national economy, inflating the relative share of consumption as against investment, for instance. This could be corrected, if desired, by eliminating turnover tax (and subsidies) from the calculations. It must be borne in mind that many countries confine indirect taxes wholly or largely to consumers' goods, however. Thus British purchase tax and US local sales taxes were or are so confined. A domestic refrigerator bears tax, a refrigerator used in industry does not. Nor has the introduction of value-added tax changed matters: the industrial user gets his tax payment returned to him, and the ultimate consumer has to pay it. So if these practices are in some sense irrational, most countries are guilty, regardless of system. (For discussion of the nature of tax burdens on the citizens, see Chapter 9).

Much more serious is the fact that, as we have seen when discussing profitability, many opportunities have been forgone in the consumers'-goods industries as a result of two generations of priority for producers' goods. Stalin in his last work made this point clearly enough: in a situation in which resources could be much more profitably devoted to light industry than to heavy industry, resources none the less go to the latter. (Stalin, 1952, p.49.) Note that Stalin did not say that this was due to some errors in pricing. Politically determined plan-priorities were at issue. While the relative importance of citizens' needs has become greater since the despot's death, the fact remains that most consumers' goods yield *both* a much higher rate of return on capital in terms of factory wholesale prices *and* bear turnover tax in addition.

In the preceding section we have been discussing the logic of a model based upon market-clearing retail prices. In practice Soviet retail prices pursue several inconsistent objectives and have become considerably 'politicized'. In a few instances this can be said to be due to social policies which are common to many countries: thus vodka is heavily taxed, vitamins for nursing mothers can be subsidized. But in other instances the logic is less clear.

Anyone who knows the Soviet Union is unlikely to deny that shortages of various consumers' goods and services are commonly encountered. This is less visible in the largest cities because they are higher on the priority list for distribution. Thus, to take but one instance, oranges have in many years been on sale only in Moscow, Leningrad and Kiev. Some foodstuffs or manufactures could be in short supply anywhere at almost any time. This can give rise to under-the-counter sales, black or 'grey' markets and also conditional sales (e.g. in a case reported in *Krokodil* purchasers of chairs were compelled also to buy some rather elderly herrings). The price of meat is very far below cost, i.e. far below the price paid to the farms plus processing and handling costs. A huge budgetary subsidy covers the resultant losses (see below). Yet at this low retail price meat is frequently unavailable in state shops.

At the same time some goods, especially textiles and clothing of less attractive designs, remain unsold, and excess stocks of some items in retail trade coexist with shortages of others.

This could be blamed in some measure on clumsy planning, i.e. the right goods are not made, or the price controllers work slowly and bureaucratically. But this cannot explain the persistent maintenance of certain prices – not only for meat but also a number of manufactures – at prices at which it is well known that supply cannot possibly match demand. Thus Soviet calculations have shown that elasticity of demand for meat is 1·49, for furniture 1·50, for woollens even as high as 2·29. (Korovkin, 1973, p.405.) (The demand for cars seems almost to equal infinity!) As incomes and living standards rise, shortages are bound to develop if prices do not alter, in those instances in which output cannot be increased sufficiently rapidly. In the case of meat, for instance, the bottleneck is supply of fodder, and it is easy to demonstrate that there is no hope of supplying enough meat at the present low subsidized prices for many years.

There seem to be two species of explanation which can be advanced, though neither can be directly documented from official statements. The first is a general policy of stable retail prices. The leadership plainly attaches great political importance to this. In addition, prices of basic foodstuffs (including meat) are regarded as particularly sensitive. It was widely rumoured that the last increase in the price of meat (in 1962) was followed by some riot and commotion – which, given the nature of the Soviet press, remained unreported. Admittedly, the fact that a rumour has not been reported in *Izvestiya* or any local paper does not prove that the rumour is well founded! But there seem really to have been riots in Novocherkassk, at least. It is well known (and well reported) that in Poland in December 1970 a sharp rise in prices of meat, though accompanied by some cuts in prices of manufactures, did cause riots big enough to topple the party first secretary, Gomulka, from his position. There was trouble on the same issue in Poland in 1976. If the state fixes all prices, and takes full responsibility for economic life, all price rises have potentially dangerous political consequences. This severely limits the willingness of the leaders to authorize economically justifiable price adjustments.

A second reason has occasionally been advanced in conversation. It is that shortages are in some way preferable to a higher price, on grounds either of social fairness (the goods go to those who stand in line, or have prior information as to availability, rather than to those with more money), or because one creates an illusion as to what one can afford to buy with the given level of income (one could afford it, if only one could find it). There is even a species of ideological predisposition not to 'ration by price', a predisposition which affected many Labour Party members in the first difficult postwar years in Great Britain. There are, however, two disadvantages in this kind of pricing. The first is that it has a disincentive effect: what is the point of earning more if the goods one wishes to buy are not available? Second, the really rich and powerful can obtain scarce goods at the official low prices without standing in line: the goods are to be found in 'closed distribution centres' or are delivered to their homes under special arrangements. Administered privilege becomes more significant whenever the unprivileged citizen cannot freely purchase goods and services; there is no advantage in having 'privileged' access to furniture at the official prices, say, if any citizen can purchase furniture by just going to a furniture shop.

PRICES AND THE STIMULATION OF NEW TECHNIQUE

A considerable literature has appeared in the USSR on the relationship between pricing and technical progress. As was already mentioned in Chapter 6, there exists a dilemma: if prices in the early period of production of new machinery are high enough to be profitable for the producing enterprise, then they are so high as to discourage its use by the customer enterprise that instals the machine. If, on the other hand, they are not high, the producing enterprise suffers financial loss and the production of new machines is thereby discouraged. The use of high 'temporary prices' for new machines meant that they remained unchanged for too long, because, in the machinery and engineering field, the number of new products, and therefore temporary prices, became so great that the price-control organs could not cope with the task of revising them. Therefore in 1966 the number of 'temporary prices' was reduced, with tighter control over the relationship between price and cost. (Komin, 1971, pp.150–1.) There was to be greater reliance on the 'fund for new technique' (which began its life in 1961).

This fund was based on a levy on the costs of production of machinery. This is supposed to compensate producing enterprises for initial losses arising from the production of new machinery and equipment, 'before the period of their mass production', and also for costs incurred in improving quality. This fund is administered by the ministries, and applications have to be made to the appropriate ministry by the enterprise management. (Komin, 1971, pp.151–2.)

This does not seem to have been effective. The use of the fund has been insignificant. Not only is the fund itself too small, but it has been underspent. Ministries are reluctant to finance what *might* be wasteful expenditures which are outside their control. 'The system of financing out of the fund for new technique is extremely complex and excessively centralized', writes a Soviet critic, who advocates an allocation of funds to management, especially of the *obyedineniya,* to give them the possibility of autonomous financial manoeuvre in this field. (Mayzenberg, 1973, p.165.) Meanwhile it is repeatedly asserted that the production of new and better machines at existing prices is often unprofitable, compared with producing old machines. Some economists advocate 'sliding prices', which diminish gradually as the machine in production ages. This has the merit of gradually making the production of obsolete equipment less profitable. Also, since the downward sliding scale of prices would be fixed in advance, it provides important information for producer and user alike. (Komin, 1971, p.155.)

These and other proposals may help to overcome that part of the negative incentives in this field which depend on price and profitability. However, as we have seen in earlier chapters, this is only part of the problem: other success indicators are more important. Nor has any effective step been taken to facilitate direct inducements (through prices) on the part of the users to persuade producers to introduce improvements. What has been introduced is a series of rules allowing higher prices for products of definably higher quality. This has been applied, for instance, to tyres of greater durability and to certain metal goods. (Komin, 1971, pp.125–6.) Efforts have been made to define minimum standards, and to introduce a 'state certificate of quality'. Indeed, as we saw in the appendix to Chapter 4, a minimum percentage of top-quality goods can be specified as an obligatory plan-indicator. Yet in many instances the concept 'quality' is elusive: it depends on the customer's evaluation, and/or on value-in-use, not by any means easy to define for pricing or bonus-earning purposes. Notoriously, quality control (the so-called OTK, *Otdel tekhnicheskogo kontrolya*) is under heavy pressure to certify inferior goods as of first quality: 'The managers of the factory see the OTK as an obstacle in the way of plan-fulfilment', and the party bureau in the factory is shown as joining in an effective attack on the quality controllers. (*Pravda,* 19 August 1975.) As we have also had occasion to observe, the all-pervasive sellers' market weakens the influence of the customer: the familiar slogan is *beri chto dayut*, 'take what you are given'. A recent article in the party's leading periodical asserts: 'The actual user needs not *the value* of all the supplying enterprise's output but a *value-in-use* in its precise material form.' (Lobachev and Yefimov, *Kom*, 1975, No. 16, p.24.) The authors deplore (yet again) the fulfilment of global value or tonnage targets, to the detriment of user demand.

Mention could be made of one other form of price: the price of technical information. Patents exist, and of course research and project-making institutes are paid for the work they do, either out of the budget or on contract. But it is a feature of the Soviet system, seen by some to be its advantage, that commercial secrecy is excluded. Inventions are freely available for use throughout industry. Inventors are paid, but the state has the right to compulsory purchase. An industrial enterprise (as distinct from a research institute) which has devised some new method cannot charge a price for informing others about it. This is contrasted with Western practice, to the West's detriment.

However, as was pointed out in a Hungarian paper (Havas, *Public Finance*, 1971, No. 2.) this procedure can have a negative effect. To make a new technique widely known takes trouble: documentation, blueprints, secretarial time and stamps cost money. If all this is free, and cannot be charged for, it is also not worth bothering with. In Hungarian practice, therefore, it has been found expedient to allow a charge to be made, i.e. to make the circulation of technical information profitable. It is then more likely to circulate.

AGRICULTURAL PRICES

Prices paid to *kolkhozy* and to peasants have had a quite special history and special function. Unlike those paid to state enterprises (including state agricultural enterprises, *sovkhozy*), the level of prices determined to a considerable degree the incomes of the farms and of the peasants. During the period from 1930 until at least 1958, these prices contained an element of barely disguised taxation: farms and peasant houscholds were compelled to deliver a quota of produce at prices which, in the case of staple foodstuffs at least, were extremely low, even confiscatory. The comparative examples in Table 10 illustrate this.

As prices have been increased several times since 1956, this gives one some idea of the extremely low prices of 1952. Indeed Khrushchev stated that the procurement price for potatoes was in fact negative, since it was less than the cost of transporting them to the delivery point, this cost having to be borne by the *kolkhozy*. Higher prices were paid for most industrial crops, notably cotton, and also for deliveries

Table 10   *Average procurement prices (per ton in* new *roubles)*
(Weighted average of quota and over-quota prices)

	1952	1956
Wheat	9·70	62·72
Potatoes	5·31	43·25
Beef	50	254
Milk	28	94

(*Source*: S. Stolyarov, 1969, p. 96)

to the state over and above the (often arbitrarily varied) delivery quota. For example, in 1956 the quota price for grain averaged 24·30 roubles, the over-quota price 81·94 roubles. (Stolyarov, 1969, p.96.) A large part of the grain procured by the state was not 'bought' at all, but was delivered by *kolkhozy* as payment in kind for the services of the state's Machine Tractor Stations. Finally, very much higher prices could be obtained in the legal free market.

The state obtained a significant part of its turnover-tax revenue by reselling the procured farm products for processing (e.g. to its flour mills and sausage factories) or to and through its retail stores. This was the financial expression of the exploitation of agriculture for the benefit of the urban sector. The burden of compulsory deliveries at low prices reduced farm revenues and helped to impoverish the peasantry, though some were able to find compensation in free-market sales (much depended on accessibility of urban markets).

Compulsory procurement prices remained very low until 1953. After Stalin's death they were repeatedly raised. An important change occurred in 1958. In that year the MTS were abolished, and their equipment was sold – compulsorily and at high prices – to the *kolkhozy*. It followed that the large quantities of grain (over half the total of state procurements) formerly paid for the services of the MTS had now to be bought (while the expenses of operating and replacing MTS machinery now fell on the farms). New prices were devised, and these were applied to all state procurements: that is to say, the distinction between quota and over-quota prices was abolished. This was justified on grounds of economic rationality. Under the system that existed until the 1958 reform, over-quota deliveries commanded a much higher price, as we have seen. This had three consequences. Firstly it produced the paradoxical result that the higher the harvest, the higher the average price paid, since more would be available for sale over the quota. Secondly, the unsuccessful farms were artificially depressed, since they would have nothing left to sell at the higher price. Thirdly, the existence of multiple prices made economic calculation exceedingly difficult: at what prices could costs be related to results? In the same year, compulsory deliveries from peasant households were abolished.

Prices were differentiated by zone, in rough proportion to estimated costs (more on the question of zonal prices later in this chapter). But this did not mean that the new prices were fixed to cover costs of different products. Insofar as .these could be calculated, they were far above the prices of many livestock products in particular, as the figures in Table 11 show:

Table 11   1964 *Profitability* (as per cent of costs)

	kolkhozy	*sovkhozy*
Crops	+69	+18
Livestock products	−17	−20
TOTAL	+20	−7

(*Source*:   Skvortsov, 1972, p. 114.)

Thus at the very time when Khrushchev was urging Soviet peasants 'to overtake America in the production of meat and milk', any expansion of output of such items added to losses, which, given the 'residuary' nature of *kolkhoz* members' income, fell primarily on the peasants. For this reason, and also because of the general level of farm and input prices fixed in 1958, the average level of *kolkhoz* members' pay fell in the period 1958–61.

Prices for livestock products had been increased in 1962. In 1965, following Khrushchev's fall, there was a general price review in an upward direction, and the principle was reintroduced of paying a higher price for over-quota deliveries: a 50 per cent bonus was to be paid to farms selling to the state in excess of the delivery plan. This bonus price applied at first to the principal grains, but was then extended to many other products, including meat. Prices paid to farms were further increased in 1970. Retail prices of staple foodstuffs remained unaltered, and this had consequences for revenues and for subsidies to be examined in a moment. The bonus price is open to the same objections as were made against multiple prices before they were abolished in 1958. Thus again the average price in a bad weather year (1975, for instance) must be considerably lower than in the record year 1973, contrary to common sense.

Prices paid to *sovkhozy* lagged behind; *sovkhozy* did not have to meet investment and social-security expenditures out of revenue, and were supplied with inputs at lower prices. They were also much better equipped and had lower costs. Many produced at a loss all the same, and had to be subsidized; in 1964 there was an overall loss, as we have seen. By stages the prices paid came into line (with some exceptions) with those paid to and by *kolkhozy,* and increasingly the *sovkhozy* were also instructed to finance their own investments. With the conversion of many *kolkhozy* into *sovkhozy*, and the evening out of input costs, differences in costs between the two categories of producers diminished. In fact already in 1967 costs were higher in *sovkhozy* than *kolkhozy* by 15 per cent for grain, 24 per cent for potatoes, 8 per cent for milk, but 10 per cent lower for cotton, 9 per cent lower for pork, and so on. (Skvortsov, 1972, p.98.) Therefore 'differences in purchase prices (from *kolkhozy*) and delivery prices (for *sovkhozy*) now apply to only an insignificant portion of farm produce', though wheat and rye in most European territories is a not insignificant exception. (Skvortsov, 1972, p.99).

Though profitability has risen considerably as a result of the price increases, there are still very wide differences as between different products. Despite repeated increases, the high labour costs and poor mechanization in the livestock sector still causes profits to be well below average there. This doubtless contributes to the need to maintain *compulsory* procurements.

It has been argued that until recent years agriculture had been 'exploited' for the benefit of industry, and this was achieved largely through prices. One more example will suffice. A ton of rye was sold in 1948 to the state millers at 338 (new) roubles. (Suchkov, 1949.) The *kolkhoz* received at most 8 roubles, about the same as they did in 1928. A kilogram of bread at that date cost *thirty times* more than in 1928, and of course prices of goods bought by farms and peasants were also many times higher. The large turnover tax levied on rye, and which accounted for the bulk of the difference between 8 and 338 roubles in the above example, can be seen *both* as a tax on the peasants and on the urban consumers, in conceptually uncertain proportions.

Gradually the gap between prices paid to farms and the procurement agencies' wholesale prices diminished. In the case of livestock products, the state began to operate at a large loss: by 1966 for every hundred roubles of beef at retail prices the state spent 155·20 roubles (Stolyarov, 1969, p.168), and the disparity increased greatly after further price increases in 1970 and subsequently. State investments in agriculture and in its needs also increased by large percentages. As already suggested, in the last analysis the presence or absence of 'exploitation through prices' must find expression in the incomes of the producers. These incomes have increased rapidly, and certainly more rapidly than those of the urban sector. State farm workers were much better paid than were the *kolkhoz* peasants in the 'bad old days', but they too were underpaid compared with workers in industry.

The relative gain of *sovkhoz* workers is plain. Since they incur fewer expenses and have extra incomes from the household plot, the pay now compares reasonably with industrial workers, having risen much faster since 1960.

Table 12   *Wages, roubles per month*

	1960	1965	1973	1978
Workers in industry	89·9	101·7	145·6	176·1
State-farm workers	51·9	72·4	117·3	141·9

(*Source*: NKh, 1973, p.586)

Pay per worked day (not work-day unit, but a day's work) in *kolkhozy* increased as shown in Table 13, including payments in kind:

Table 13

1960	1965	1973	1978
1·40	2·68	4·38	5·22

(*Source*: NKh, 1973, p.456.)

Kolkhoz members do not get paid for days in which they do not work for the collective, but they obtain higher incomes from (usually) larger plots than do state-employed persons. It should be borne in mind that these figures cover collective incomes only; incomes in cash and kind from the household plot have risen little in this period. For 1976 the average wage for all workers and employees was planned at 150 roubles per month (+2·7 per cent over 1974), for *kolkhoz* peasants (collective work only) 98 roubles per month (+5 per cent over 1974). (Baybakov, *Pravda*, 3 December 1975.) It should be borne in mind also that *kolkhoz* members include a large proportion of unskilled middle-aged women. When all allowances are made, the relationship between the urban and rural sector incomes does not appear to sustain any accusation of 'exploiting' agriculture, or certainly not more than any other sector of the economy. When one considers the subsidy, the huge investment expenditures and the increasing share of the state in covering such items as drainage, irrigation and other soil improvements, and also (since 1966) in social insurance for peasants, it might be argued that agriculture is now less a milch cow than a millstone for the rest of the economy.

The subsidy mentioned above is paid to cover the gap between the retail price of livestock products, mostly meat, and the expenses incurred in purchasing, transporting, processing and retailing it. In 1971 it was reported as 9·3 milliards (*Finansy SSSR*, 1971, No. 5, p.65.) Changes in prices and volume of procurements led to further increases, which led to Western estimates of upwards of 16 milliard roubles (Constance Kruger, 1974). According to *Pravda*, 8 February 1977, the subsidy is now almost 19 milliard roubles. These are huge figures, unheard of in the world's history of agricultural subsidies. It must be borne in mind, however, that the state budget continues to benefit (to an unknown extent) from revenues arising out of the resale of grain, sugar beet and some other crops.

ZONAL PRICES AND LAND RENT

To return to prices. For some crops there are sizable zonal differences. Grains provide the most striking example in Table 14.

Table 14 *Wheat (roubles per ton of standard quality)*

	Kolkhozy	Sovkhozy
RSFSR (black-earth)	86	59
RSFSR (non-black-earth)	130	130
Ukraine (except Polesye) and Moldavia	76	45
Kazakhstan	80	65
C. Asia and Transcaucasia	90	90

For livestock the upper zonal limit is 156 per cent of the lowest zonal category in the case of sheep, less than this for pigs and cattle. There are also variations for all products based on type, quality and (in some cases) date of delivery (e.g. early potatoes command a higher price). (Skvortsov, 1972, pp.100–3.)

The variations are in fact greater than those shown above, as the authorities within the zones can vary the price paid by sub-zones, provided the average prices are those laid down centrally. The 50 per cent bonus price for over-quota deliveries is added where applicable.

A prolonged discussion has ranged with regard to land rent, and this is relevant to an assessment of the logic of the above price system. Wheat costs more to grow in (for instance) Smolensk *oblast'* than in the black-earth regions of the Ukraine or the North Caucasus. Does this justify paying farms in Smolensk 50 per cent or even 100 per cent more? This difference can be treated as a land rent in disguise. In the Stalin years there were also wide regional differences in compulsory delivery quotas at the then low prices, and also in payment in kind for given quantities of work by the MTS, and these also could be treated as a form of land rent (or tax). (There are still differences in delivery quotas, but the much better prices now paid have altered the nature of compulsory deliveries.) All this reflects the knowledge that some areas are much more favourably situated than others, and that since rent has been abolished by the revolution, and is alleged to be contrary to Marxian principles, one corrects for this in other ways, e.g. by paying farms in the Kuban' (on the best grain-growing land) much less than those in Smolensk. This can be said to be a variant of accounting prices which existed in the oil industry, where high-cost oilfields are paid more, but the customers (in the case of grain the millers, for instance) pay the same price regardless of where the product comes from.

Voices have been raised that this is wrong, that land rent is not

any more 'un-Marxist' than any other monetary payment. We have
seen that the 'mathematicians' have urged that natural resources
should be valued and charged for. Reforms in prices of minerals have
introduced the concept of rent or 'fixed payments'. It has been argued
that land clearly is a resource that should be charged for, with differential rent according to the all-round economic quality of the land.
Strumilin (*VEk*, 1967, No. 8) sought to reconcile this with the labour
theory of value by pointing out that land is not really a free good:
labour is devoted to improving it and making it productive. Others
agree with his objective but disagree with his explanations. In practice it is often the inferior land that requires more labour, but its
productivity is lower.

Many Soviet economists have urged a systematic valuation of land
(kadastr), and the need has been recognized, though only completed
in a few places. One obstacle to valuation is the problem of distinguishing natural or geographic advantages from those arising from hard
work or superior husbandry. In theory, of course, the distinction is
clear, but in practice less so: thus it would be improper to deduce the
quality of land from variations in actual output per hectare, since
this would reflect all these factors in unknown proportions. (For a
discussion of this see *VEk*, 1968, No. 8 and Krasovsky, 1970, pp.10–20.)
Presumably, if a *kadastr* were available, it would be possible to pay
similar prices in all areas and 'correct' for natural advantages by a
differential rental charge or graduated tax. This is in fact done in
several East European countries (in Hungary and Czechoslovakia they
still use the *kadastr* of the old pre-1914 Empire, expressed in gold
crowns).

It would be possible to envisage the procurement organizations using
the existing prices so as to minimize costs. Thus obviously it would
'pay' them to purchase wheat from the Ukraine or North Caucasus at
lower prices, rather than from central Russia at higher prices. This
could be a basis for specialization. This is not how it works out in
practice. As we have seen, the procurement organs tend to sub-allocate
between farms in their area whatever they have been ordered to procure, and any losses fall upon the state budget. However, it is the case
that *central* planners can so amend the regional procurement plans as
to avoid the highest-cost areas for particular products, save in those
instances when shortages render necessary the procurement of any
available supplies. We have seen that some areas have in fact been
exempted from contributing to all-union needs for products (e.g. the
Baltic states in respect of grain in most years), but local needs may
still have to be the subject of compulsory procurement quotas at what,
in that locality, could be very high prices, made all the higher if the
sales are in excess of the delivery quotas and therefore attract the
50 per cent bonus.

No one can say that farm prices are logical or rational. But it is only fair to add that very few countries in the world, East or West, have logical or rational farm prices. Anyone from Western Europe in particular should be restrained in criticizing Soviet pricing in agriculture!

PRICES: CONCLUSION

Market-type reform is plainly impossible so long as the price system is in its present shape. Alternatively, the price system is in its present shape because market-type reform has been rejected. One can also assert that the central planners themselves are at times misled by the prices which they use in their calculations, and also that departures from market-clearing retail prices inhibit consumer choice and adversely affect the flow of information about consumer demand. One must also repeat that the inflexibility of these prices makes the effects of errors and shortages, however caused, more visible, and therefore the economy as a whole seems less 'efficient' than would otherwise be the case.

This last point may not be obvious, so let me enlarge it with two examples (one of which has been used earlier). If in the West the output of any agricultural product falls (either because of the 'cobweb effect' of an earlier price reduction, or because of drought), and demand remains constant or rises, the price will rise. The shops will still have plenty, but let us say it costs 25 cents instead of 15 cents a pound. This will balance supply and demand and also signal to the wholesalers and farmers (and importers) that more will be needed. In the Soviet case the product disappears from the state shops and the free-market or black-market price rises disproportionately, giving the impression of physical shortage which, in the Western case, is concealed. The same is true if one considers the consequence of an incorrect investment decision, which in this example can be an act of omission: the desirable investment was not made. In the West the error (assuming it was an error) will scarcely be visible in most cases: the profitability of the other domestic producers rises, and/or more is imported. In the Soviet Union frustrated housewives or enterprise managers will seek in vain, since, once again, the immobile price will fail to reflect supply-and-demand balance. Which system, then, is more inefficient? In the examples given, the production pattern could be identical, and so could the errors. The difference, the shortage, will be induced largely by prices.

It is, finally, necessary to restate two points. The first, as already stressed in Chapter 6, is that prices are never and nowhere a fully reliable guide to the future, and that consequently no one can rely on price signals alone, even though their significance is evidently great. Second, price distortions of various kinds, arising out of mono-poly or government intervention, exist in varying degrees in all economies. One must not compare real Soviet irrationalities, serious though they are, with a theoretical free-market model.

This said, one can scarcely doubt that no change of substance in the planning system can occur without a major alteration in the principles underlying price determination, and in the prices themselves.

A price revision has begun, and new wholesale prices are likely to be decreed in 1982. It would seem that no new principles are involved, though efforts will be made to take quality more into account, and also to discourage the production of obsolete machinery by enforcing price reductions.

The subsidy that covers losses on livestock products rose in 1979 *at least* 23 milliard roubles annually. The evidence is as follows: Finance Minister Garbuzov has stated that it will be 100 milliards in the five years 1976–80, i.e. an average of 20 milliards a year. Since then, increases in procurement prices of livestock products were decreed, which 'cost' another 3·2 milliards (*Planovoye Khozyaistvo*, No. 10, 1978). Note the *fall* in profitability in the past five years (see Table 7).

CHAPTER 8

LABOUR, WAGES,
TRADE UNIONS

A LABOUR MARKET?

Labour should not be a commodity, indeed, in Soviet official theory, labour *is* not a commodity: It is not exploited, since there is no private capital and the Soviet state is not strictly speaking an 'employer'. Khrushchev favoured the words 'state of the whole people', in which case the people who own collectively the means of production, employ themselves. This form of words has gone out of use, but the idea remains. The Soviet society is not regarded as classless. There are two 'friendly' classes, the workers and the (collectivized) peasantry, with a 'stratum' *(prosloyka)* of intelligentsia. Who, then, can exploit whom? Under socialism, so the official theory runs, one has 'from each according to his ability' and 'to each according to his work'. The state, acting on behalf of the working masses as 'their' state, assigns to groups and to individuals the incomes which represent a fair equivalent to their contribution to society and its material and non-material needs. For example, a Soviet textbook puts the point as follows: 'labour under socialism is not the utilization of labour-power by society, but its application by the owner, i.e. the direct participation of a member of society in total labour. Thus the wage represents a measure of the extent of this participation, and its magnitude depends both on the size of the whole social product and on the results of the individual's work.' (Chukhno *et al*, 1968, p.268.)

Since effort is affected not only by moral but also material incentives, and since labour is not subject to systematic direction, it follows that the state, in determining relative incomes, will take into account the qualifications, skills, responsibility and also the heavy or disagreeable nature of the work, and also its geographical location, so that labour is distributed in a manner appropriate to the planned tasks which require to be carried out. Some incomes, it is true, may be related more or less directly to the market for goods or services. Thus, as we have seen, *kolkhoz* peasants' income from 'their' farms can rise and fall in accordance to how much produce is marketed and at what prices, and the peasants themselves derive income from sales of vegetables, milk etc. Writers can earn large sums from royalties if citizens buy their books (if a state publishing house can be persuaded to publish them). But in the main, so it appears, incomes of individuals and groups are determined by the state. The labour market seems to have no part in this model.

We leave aside for the moment the issue of what income differentials actually are, or should be, and the extent and forms of privilege and inequality. At this stage, let us confine ourselves to identifying the relative importance in income determination of the state and of what must, in my view, be called market forces.

It may be said: the Soviet government can decide on the price of ball-bearings or shirts. Why, then, not simply say that it decides also the rewards of labour, describe the institutions whose task it is to take these decisions, list a few anomalies which must inevitably arise when incomes of a hundred million human beings are determined, and then get on to the next subject?

This, however, would not do at all. Human beings, unlike ball-bearings and shirts, have a will, two legs and can travel. Unlike ball-bearings and shirts, they are not (with a few exceptions) subject to administrative allocation. There is no 'reserve army of unemployed'. The passport system inhibits free movement into some big cities and makes it difficult to leave rural areas. The provision of passports to rural residents, now in progress, may make their movement to town easier, but they will still need a registration permit, *(propiska)*. There are, however, ample statistics showing that millions of people change their jobs annually of their own volition, as they have the formal right to do, and migrate from area to area in total disregard of the planners' intentions. Labour mobility is far from perfect (where *is* it perfect?), but enough mobility exists to ensure that very serious problems would arise if the wage rate in an industry, profession or region were such that the necessary labour force could not be attracted and retained.

True, the government can affect supply by training schemes and by the gearing of higher and secondary technical education to the expected needs of the economy. But in the short run the supply of labour to particular jobs and skills is to a considerable extent under the control of the labourer. In the period from 1940 to 1956 the right to leave one's job was abrogated, but even before its repeal the law became increasingly unenforceable, (or it was increasingly not enforced).

Then we must appreciate that the state is not a monolith employer. Again the concept of 'centralized pluralism' comes to our aid. Ministries and enterprises in practice compete for labour, and have to be restrained from overpayments (not always very effectively restrained).

In this situation, market forces, i.e. supply of and demand for different kinds of labour, affect relative incomes in two ways. Firstly, *they affect the decisions of government.* Thus if at a given wage-rate there are not enough instrument mechanics, carpenters, miners, computer operators or anyone willing to work north of the Arctic Circle, then the official income-scales can be (and often are) altered to ensure a supply response. Secondly, since official scales are altered seldom and may not fit the local situation, managers try to find ways of *evading the official wage-scales.* As we shall see, there are limits to evasion, and there is no doubt that the government agencies do have a range of arbitrary choices as to incomes. None the less, as will be demonstrated, forces of supply and demand are an important influence on actual earnings, and on the regulations also.

Wage- and salary-scales are laid down by decrees issued on the authority of the Council of Ministers, on the advice of the State Committee on Labour and Wages. Basic policy decisions on differentials, and on such topics as minimum wages, doubtless belong to the Politbureau. Between the abolition of the People's Commissariat (Ministry of Labour) in 1933 and the setting up of the State Committee in 1955, there was, astonishingly, no central state body responsible for labour and wages. There was also, during this period, no general review of wages and salaries, and no one to undertake it. Of course, this did not mean that wages remained unchanged. There were several across-the-board increases in the thirties, and a so-called 'bread supplement' *(khlebnaya nadbavka)* was introduced in 1946 in connection with derationing and the sharp rise in the prices of necessities which accompanied it. There were also *ad hoc* amendments to wage-scales within particular ministries, but no one sat down to consider wage relativities or to work out a national grading scheme. (Mayer, *Voprosy istorii KPSS*, 1975, No. 7.) Not very surprisingly, numerous anomalies developed. Similar work was paid at different rates, according to the ministerial subordination of the enterprises concerned. Different ministries adopted different zonal differentials. Wage drift took the form of an ever-widening gap between basic rates and take-home pay, the latter inflated by easy-to-fulfil piece-rate norms and bonus schemes. (See, for instance, Bulganin's speech to the July 1955 plenum of the central committee.)

It took many years for the State Committee on Labour and Wages to bring order into what had been close to chaos. There is now one basic tariff-qualifications manual, i.e. national grading scheme, applicable to all types of work which occur in many industries, which in practice is the large majority (thus lorry-drivers, fitters, carpenters, etc., are to be found in every branch of the economy). There are also separate tariff-qualification manuals for trades specific to particular industries. Analogous grading schemes, with definitions of the qualifications, skills and responsibilities for each category of job, are issued for engineer-technical and administrative-clerical staffs (known respectively as *inzhinero-tekhnicheskiye rabotniki,* or ITR, and *sluzhashchiye*).

The magnitude of the task can be judged from the fact that, when the process started, there were no less than 1900 different wage-scales *(tarifnyye setki)* for workers, with 'several thousand' different wage rates for the lowest grade of skill. The number of scales was reduced by the mid-sixties to 10, and, although the numbers then grew a little, it is the intention to reduce it to 3. The number of wage-rates for the lowest grade of skill (of which more in a moment) was reduced first to 50, then to 40, and is now to be further reduced to 17. (Sukharevsky, 1974, p.241.) The ITR and administrative-clerical staffs have their incomes determined, within given limits, in terms of the rank they hold and (for directing staffs in particular) the size as well as the relative import- ance of the enterprise or office which they administer. The number of different staff salaries *(dolzhnostnyye oklady)* was reduced from 700 to 150. (Kapustin, 1974, p.264.) To this day the scales laid down for heavy industry, and also construction and transport, are higher than the 'non-priority' industries and services (Kapustin 1974, p.250), which helps to ensure that the best managers, engineers and workers gravitate to the branches deemed most important by the state and party – i.e. those which are not providing the needs of the citizens (though, to be fair, the differentials have diminished).

According to an authoritative source, 'the link between the tariff rates for workers and the ITR (engineer-technicians) is ensured by determining the pay of the foreman *(master)* in a given relationship to workers' tariffs. On the basis of the *master*'s salary there is deter- mined the scales for salaries of all other engineer-technical staffs.' (Kapustin, 1974, p.264.) However, as we shall see, major and partly unintended changes have greatly affected this relationship, with the pay of many engineers now below that of skilled workers.

It is, of course, logical that the state, as the *de facto* 'employer', should decide upon national grading schemes, a process in which the all-union trade union councils play a vague and undefined role (the signature of the trade union sometimes appears on various decrees and circulars, but sometimes not). It is equally essential for the state to determine the rate of pay applicable to each grade.

In the case of workers, the various categories of skill are arranged into a series of grades, from I (unskilled) to V or in some cases VI or VII (most skilled), with ratios determined between each grade. The number and the 'spread' of the grades has tended to diminish with the introduction and repeated increase in the minimum wage, of which more will be said when we discuss income differentials.

EVASION: ITS CAUSES AND CONSEQUENCES

In view of the importance of actual or proposed forms of wage con- trol in Western countries, it is clearly important to analyse the effec- tiveness of such controls in the Soviet setting. Given the passivity of

Soviet trade unions, and the apparent all-pervasiveness of state control over the economy and in particular over monetary flows (including the 'wages fund'), the circumstances seem to be highly favourable for effective centralized wage determination. If, therefore, there is wide-spread evasion even in the Soviet Union, there is a moral to be drawn regarding the likely effectiveness of wage controls in less propitious settings.

The first point to make is that the task of determining relative earnings of millions of workers and other employees, scattered over a vast area and operating under a great variety of technical and economic circumstances, is a task of great complexity. While the neglect of the whole problem in the period 1933–55, and the resulting major anomalies, must be treated as an odd aberration rather than anything inherent in the model, almost a decade of hard work by the new State Committee was required to bring some sort of order into the wages system. In the nature of the problem it cannot be satis-factorily resolved by a set of centrally imposed rules.

Let us see why this is so, utilizing the following examples. Suppose it is decided, for good reason, to pay a bonus to compensate those work-ing in the harsh northern climate. Clearly, this requires a line to be drawn, and those north of it qualify for higher wages; but this creates an area just south of the line where it becomes very hard to recruit labour at the rates applicable there. (For one example, see Gukov, *EKO*, 1975, No. 1.)

Or, to take a different instance, men (or women) come to see the management and say that unless their wages are increased they will go to work elsewhere. Or similarly, labour cannot be recruited to carry out planned tasks in that locality or industry at the official wage rate.

True, one can appeal to patriotism or to party loyalty. Campaigns through the Komsomol, for instance, have provided recruits for great new developments such as the virgin lands campaign and the con-struction of the Baikal-Amur railway. But – and this is recognized – these can only be very partial substitutes for an incomes policy which makes it worth the individual's while to go where his work is needed and to stay there. Of course, not only wage-rates are involved, but also housing, amenities, a regular supply of consumers' goods, and so on.

The essential point is that no wages system imposed by the centre, no matter how skilfully prepared, can cover all local eventualities, i.e. can ensure that the right number of all the necessary kinds of labour are attracted to a shipyard in Murmansk or the 'October revo-lution' factory at Krasnodar.

The resultant stresses and strains give rise, as already indicated, to pressure to alter wage relativities. But in many instances, as is inevit-able, the adjustments have to be made on the spot, and as a result the official relativities are amended and/or evaded.

The most common ways of achieving this are by easy piece-rates or bonus schemes, and by regrading. Both these methods were seen in their most vivid form in the Stalin period, because, as we have noted, there were no systematic wage-review procedures at all, and therefore the contrast between the supply-and-demand (or labour market) situation and the official tariff-scales was particularly great. It was also a time at which piece-rates were most prevalent: 'In 1936 76·1 per cent of all industrial workers were on (individual) piece-rate payments. . . . Collective piece-rates were severely criticized . . . In economic literature the view was expressed that time-rate payments should be abolished.' The maximum percentage was 77·5 per cent, reached in 1956. (Shkuro, 1974, pp.275–6.) It was, finally, also a period of extremely wide tariff wage differentials, ranging (for workers only) from 1 : 3·8 or even in some cases 1 : 4·4 (Kapustin, 1974, p.261) with 'take-home-pay' differentials much wider, as discussed below.

Unskilled labour, under these scales, was very poorly paid. So poorly that very few individuals indeed were graded as unskilled.

What occurred was the almost total 'statistical' elimination of unskilled labour, because the rate for the job was too low. Everyone was regraded as at least semi-skilled, and so there was a spontaneous unofficial 'correction' of the official wage relatives.

The wage, as we have seen, is a function of the skill classification, and of the piece-rate or bonus schemes in the particular factory. The centrally determined tariff-rate could only specify the amount which should be paid for 100 per cent fulfilment of the norm by a worker in a given grade; it could not specify what the norm should be. The official line was that the norms should be frequently revised upwards, and be based on work-study methods and not on past performance. In practice, in periods at which basic rates remained unaltered for many years, wage drift took the form of a gradual increase in the extent of overfulfilment of norms. In fact the basic tariff-rates ceased for most piece-workers (and therefore for most workers) to have any recognizable relationship with actual earnings. Thus *on average* the overfulfilment of norms was 39 per cent in 1950, 55 per cent in 1956 (96 per cent in the electrotechnical industry, 81 per cent in the automobile industry). (Kapustin, *PKh*, 1957, No.7, pp.29–30.) Since during this period in some industries there were so-called 'progressive piece-work' schemes in operation, under which extra was paid per piece above a given level (sometimes, as in coal, after only 80 per cent of the norm), actual payments differed widely in their relationship to the basic rate in different industries, and indeed in different factories and mines.

Though various bonus schemes also affected earnings of time-workers and white-collar staffs, their take-home pay could not so easily be 'inflated', and as a result a considerable income redistribution in favour of piece-rate workers took place, due in large part to uncontrolled and unintended adjustments.

Unfortunately there is little printed evidence about the relationship of actual earnings and tariff wages in particular factories. In one instance I was able to obtain figures for a power station, which showed on average a difference of roughly 40 per cent (i.e. that earnings were 40 per cent higher), but in the case of one occupation the difference was 120 per cent. On inquiring the reason, I was told that this required shovelling coal, an unskilled but unpleasant job. So, of course, the norm was adjusted not to the tariff-rate but to the expected and desired level of earnings. While the purist might call such evidence 'anecdotal', it is entirely consistent with the realities of the situation.

The wage revisions begun in 1956 led to a sharp rise in both tariff rates and norms, designed to bring the basic rates much nearer to actual earnings. The share of the tariff or basic rate in earnings of piece-workers increased from 45–55 per cent to 70–75 per cent. (Kapustin, 1964, p.66.) No doubt, given the large number of anomalies, some workers lost money, but the average rose steadily. The proportion of workers on piece-rates fell to 57·6 per cent by 1965 (Shkuro, 1974, p.277), and much more use was made of group bonuses. The average percentage of overfulfilment of norms fell sharply. A further upward revision of norms brought the average percentage of fulfilment to 118 per cent with 10·6 per cent of workers *not* fulfilling their norms (S. Novozhilov, *EkG*, 1975, No. 44.) However, despite these reforms, there remain considerable variations in norm overfulfilments and bonus schemes, and evasion through regrading too. I was told by a Soviet professor that the reason why there appear to be so few typists in the USSR is that, as their pay-scales are too low, they have to be reclassified as being in some other better-paid occupation. A cartoon recently published had the following caption: 'she is an excellent secretary, and so I appointed her as a turner of the 5th grade'. (*Krokodil*, January 1976, p.1.)

The moral of all this might appear to be that economic forces play a major role in the determination of relative incomes, and that government regulations can be swept aside. This, however, would be going too far.

The evidence certainly shows that anyone who is paid by results cannot have his income determined by the government, since it must depend on results, and these, in turn, must be related to a norm decided on the spot. This, plus local initiative in regrading and promoting, does strongly suggest that income controls cannot be effective, or rather that they are bound to create grave distortions and unfairness by being effective for some groups (time-workers and any-one on a fixed salary) at the expense of others (especially piece-workers). The effective control in the USSR is of a quite different type: it is the planned wages fund.

In other words, the centre cannot in practice determine earnings differentials in factory, shop or mine. But it can set a maximum to the *total* expended on wages and salaries, and enforce this limit through the banking system.

This sets a limit to overpayment by managers anxious to recruit or retain labour. The wages fund can only be exceeded after an elaborate procedure involving higher ministerial organs. In some cases, over-payments are made none the less and 'disguised' elsewhere in the accounts, but there is no means of showing that such practices are widespread.

In the period from the end of 1946, after the 'bread supplement', until 1956, i.e. for ten years, there were no appreciable increases in official wages and salaries. Average earnings in fact rose by about 35 per cent, i.e. there was a wage drift of almost 3 per cent per year. The percentage overfulfilment of norms gradually rose, and so did the wages fund, which was and is based not on tariff rates but on past performance. If productivity is rising and norms are not revised up-wards proportionately, there is bound to be upward pressure on wages, the more so as output norms for workers are not calculated as a function of the output plan of the factory. In other words, usually it was necessary to overfulfil work norms by an increasing margin in order to fulfil the output plan, and the wages-fund plans reflected this by moving upwards every year, while tariffs remained unaltered.

In more recent years the plans have included a percentage rise in average wages. In 1966–70 this was exceeded (plan +20 per cent, actual +26 per cent) but in 1971–5, in connection with a shortfall in output of consumers' goods, the announced plan for the quinquen-nium (an increase in average wages of 22·4 per cent) was not realized (the actual increase being 20 per cent). This shows, especially by con-trast with Western countries, the comparative efficacy of income controls in the USSR if these are seen in terms of global income. It is otherwise, as already demonstrated, with *relative* incomes of groups and individuals. The effect of this on wage relativities and income inequalities will be further discussed in a moment.

One consequence of the wages-fund limits is to create inflexibility where the problem is one of the *general level* of wages. The most relevant example relates to zonal wage coefficients. Thus the wage-and salary-rates applicable to south Siberia were 10–20 per cent higher than in the centre of European Russia in industry, but *no* higher in other spheres of activity. (Kapustin, 1974, pp.265–6.) This caused (or contributed to) a labour shortage. The remedy could not be one of rearranging relativities, which would serve if the problem was one of shortage of a given category of labourer. It proved necessary to increase the zonal differential, and with it the wages fund, of enter-prises located in Siberia.

There appear to be several conclusions one can draw from Soviet experience in this field. One is that it is extremely difficult, if not impossible, to arrive at logical and generally acceptable criteria on the basis of which relative incomes can be determined. The second is that, howsoever they are determined, the forces of the market (or of supply and demand) will find some ways of influencing or modifying the income relativities which the state organs lay down. The third is that evasions occur in certain predictable ways, and that the only effective wages 'stop', under conditions in which labour is often short, and management can afford to be generous with the state's money, is the 'wages fund' planned limit. We have seen, however, that this control method has a cost: management is unable to take on extra labour without time-wasting applications for permission to amend the wages-fund limit.

INCOME RELATIVITIES AND MINIMUM WAGES

An examination of wage relativities and of government policy at different periods can shed some light both on what incomes policy was being followed and on its relative effectiveness. It is well known that Stalin intervened personally in 1931, to demand wider income differentials, denouncing 'petty-bourgeois egalitarianism' (uravnilovka). As a result, differentials were indeed increased, as we have seen, to 1 : 3·8 (or even in some cases 1 : 4·4) for workers, while at the same time engineers, technicians, directors, also gained. There were also big differences in pay between priority and non-priority industries. Various categories of 'shock workers' and 'shock brigades', later also so-called Stakhanovite record-breakers, were rewarded by very large wage increases. The gap between the auxiliaries (cleaners, janitors, messengers, who are paid less than 'workers') and the upper categories rose to 12 : 1 and more. We have seen that this policy had been modified by elemental economic forces by the mid-thirties, with the regrading of most unskilled workers as semi-skilled, but as the evidence will show, the differentials were extremely high. One asks oneself the question: was this because of government action? In one sense, the answer must be 'Yes'. But why the action? Why did Stalin make his statement? Surely because, in the period of the first two five-year plans, there was a desperate need for skilled workers and technicians, and the large number of unskilled ex-peasants migrating from the villages produced little and needed to be encouraged to learn a trade and settle down. To put it another way, the supply-and-demand situation pointed strongly in the direction of widening differentials, e.g. between a skilled man with factory experience and the newly arrived villager, in the context of rapid industrialization, and the trend would have been in this direction even if the government had issued no edicts.

In the postwar years, when incomes policy was given so little attention, we have noted how workers on piece-rates gained from wage drift. Major distortions emerged, because time-rates and most salaries remained unaltered. Particularly severe relative losses were suffered by white-collar staffs, clerks, teachers, medical personnel, and also the unskilled auxiliaries. In 1956, the first of a number of measures was taken to establish (and later increase) a minimum wage. This immediately benefited the underpaid auxiliaries. In the process of revising workers' wages (i.e. in the period 1957–65) those of the teachers and doctors were also raised, though, as we shall see, this did not restore their relative position of the thirties. Higher-level incomes rose slowly or not at all in this period, which also saw the diminution of individual piece-work, the elimination of the more extreme kinds of 'progressive' piece-rates, and also the modification downwards of managerial bonus schemes.

As minimum wages rose from 30 roubles (1956) by stages to 70 roubles (1976) per month, the payments for skill differentials diminished even too far, requiring some upward adjustment in the pay of skilled workers and engineer-technicians. But even after this adjustment, the differentials among workers now range only from 1 : 1·86 (in mining) to 1 : 1·58 (in the light and food industries), while even the new rates for a foreman *(master)*, 120–55 roubles per month (Kapustin, 1974, p.268), approximate to the *average* wage of workers, i.e. are below the income of skilled workers.

The relative position of different categories has changed dramatically in the last three decades as shown in Table 15.

Table 15   *Pay in industry*

	1940	1965	1973	1978
Workers	32·4	101·7	145·6	176·1
Engineer-technicians	69·9	148·4	184·9	208·4
'Employees'*	36·0	85·8	118·5	142·7

*i.e. white-collar staffs, clerks, etc.
(*Source*: NKh, 1973, p.586.)

These figures show how the category 'workers' has gained, relatively. But the categories are very broad, and conceal even bigger changes. For example, it would appear that such white-collar occupations as book-keeping are at or very close to the present minimum, i.e. 70 roubles per month, i.e. half the *average* wage of a worker, while in the mid-thirties their pay approximated to this average. The starting pay of a graduate research assistant *(mladshy nauchny sotrudnik)*, as seen on advertisements in Moscow University and confirmed in private conversations, is 105 roubles per month, and this appears not to have altered since the war, i.e. instead of earning almost double the workers' average they now earn nearly 30 per cent less. Despite two increases since 1956, both teachers and doctor-general-practitioners are on pay rates which are below the workers' average; a Moscow bus driver's reported earnings (220 roubles) may well be 70–80 per cent above theirs, though precision on this point is impossible because of the existence of various extras (e.g. a teacher's pay can be affected by the number of class essays she corrects, her academic qualifications, etc.). The feminine gender is here used advisedly: the poorly paid teaching and medical professions are overwhelmingly female.

We have also seen that junior engineers are poorly paid in comparison with skilled workers. Despite the high status of engineering, this must surely have begun to affect recruitment; what is the point of higher technical education if it yields so little material reward? The category 'employees' has lost ground particularly severely, the extent of this loss being partially concealed by the inclusion in this category of well-paid 'employees', such as directors of enterprises. Indeed the trend towards equalization seems to have gone too far. A good Soviet source anticipates that in the period 1969–78 the average wage will rise by 37–9 per cent, while minimum wages will go up by 17 per cent (Mayer, 1976, p.33.)

Until recently there was little evidence upon which to base any precise analysis of actual earnings. Handbooks citing tariff-rates and salary-scales are useful but inadequate, in that there is often a sizable difference between tariff-rates and take-home pay, and we are usually not told how many individuals are in various pay brackets. However, some data appeared in 1972, from which calculations could be made. It is to the credit of Peter Wiles and Janet Chapman that they independently noticed this and made the calculations. Subject to an insignificant margin of error, the data make it possible to determine figures by deciles. The evidence point to a ratio between the top 10 per cent and the bottom 10 per cent of more than 7 : 1 in 1946, falling to 3 : 1 by 1970. Comparing the top 5 per cent with the bottom 10 per cent, the ratios were respectively just under 10 : 1 and 3·5 : 1. (Chapman in Abouchar, with grateful thanks to the author and editor for an advance copy.) Janet Chapman points to certain doubts and inconsistencies, such as the possible effect of part-timers on the figures in the lowest decile, but there seems no reason to expect the distortion (if any) to be greater in any one year.

The 1946 figures show extraordinarily high differentials, and relate to a date prior to the 'bread supplement', which was confined to those earning less than 90 roubles per month (900 old roubles) and had the immediate effect of diminishing differentials. No doubt the repeated increase in minimum wages was the main cause of a continued steady decline in the ratio after 1956. Of course, it must be stressed that we are not here comparing the highest with the lowest, but the top 5 or

10 per cent (i.e. groups containing 5 or 10 million persons) with the bottom 10 per cent. Needless to say, comparisons with the top 1 per cent would yield much higher ratios, but these too must have declined.

The proper measure of real income differentials is complicated in the USSR (and nearer home too) by various extras and 'perks': for instance the use of a car, a better apartment, lavish travel expenses, sometimes the so-called 'envelopes' containing extra banknotes. In addition there is the value of privileged access to goods and services unobtainable by lesser mortals: imported liquors, scarce foodstuffs, good furniture, hotel rooms, the chance to travel abroad. It is hard to know how to take these things into account. For example, if citizen A earns 400 roubles a month and B earns 150 roubles, the fact that A is a senior official and is able to buy caviar, whisky, good furniture and best sausage, while B cannot, certainly increases A's welfare, but by what percentage?

If one makes comparisons with the West, the existence of 'perks' is common to both systems, but the value of privileged access to goods and services in short supply depends on their being in short supply. In most circumstances, the Western business executive or high official is able to buy the things which are available to anyone who has the money. In the USSR shortages are very much more common, and so special allowance – unquantifiable, unfortunately – must be made for this.

But to return to our analysis of the relative effects of government policies and market forces on income relativities. The much-increased supply of literate citizens qualified for office work, and of engineers, doctors and other specialists, and the substantial dimunition of the inflow of unskilled ex-peasants to the towns, are the fundamental explanation of the changes we have been noting. Clearly, the difference between skilled and unskilled workers is much smaller than it was in the thirties. Clearly also, the scarcity value of engineers, accountants, teachers, relative to factory workers, has substantially diminished. It is also possible to point to Western experience: in a completely different institutional setting, the relative advance of workers in general, the less-skilled categories in particular, in comparison with white-collar occupations is a notable feature of the last thirty to forty years.

All this must be seen as an important part of the explanation of recent trends in the Soviet Union. None the less, one must repeat that the regulations, though influenced by market forces, can and do have an autonomous effect. Thus it is hardly to be doubted that the increase to 70 roubles of the minimum wage has had a positive effect on the pay of the lowest categories, an effect which cannot be wholly attributed to supply and demand. Also it is worth noting that the fixing of a low wage or salary for a particular occupation can have a long-term effect in lowering the status and the quality of recruits, rather than setting up forces which cause the disparity of pay to be corrected. To mention two examples, medical doctors and retail trade staffs have been poorly paid for a generation. This has turned both these occupations into largely female preserves, and may well have lowered the general quality of the services rendered by them. (*Not*, let me hasten to add, because women cannot be efficient doctors or retailers! More will be said about women's earnings in a moment.) The systematic preference, in terms of salary-scales, for heavy industry as against the rest of the economy has had, and was intended to have, the result of shifting a large proportion of able and ambitious personnel towards these priority sectors, and plainly this is an example of deliberate government policy, and not market forces, determining sectoral differentials.

One cannot conclude this discussion of differentials without raising the question of whether they were or are excessive. What is the appropriate criterion? There have been controversies on this among socialists, not least in China and Cuba. The issue can be presented as a contrast between material and moral incentives. In practice both exist, in all these countries, but the degree of the Soviet emphasis on material incentives has been criticized by Mao, among others. This is not the place to enter into a debate on this point. It may be enough to note that one can believe that good work and responsibility should be rewarded, and still hold that differentials and privileges are 'excessive'. Thus any socialists, in and out of the USSR, would probably be unanimous in regarding the 1946 differentials cited on p.209 above as grossly excessive. Whether the more modest ratios of the seventies are excessive must be a matter of opinion. Some hold that certain differentials – e.g. between workers and engineers – have become too small or even negative, with unfortunate economic results. Attention is sometimes concentrated on the very small group of high officials, who, together with a few successful writers, ballerinas, musicians and top academicians, constitute the upper stratum of Soviet society in material terms. It is widely believed in the USSR that the highest officials live in great luxury, and that most of it is provided for them not as salary but as fruits of office, so to speak (villas, servants, cars, etc.). The secrecy surrounding this, and silence concerning the special shops open to only those of appropriate rank, feeds rumours of a land of milk and honey behind seven fences and seven locks, to cite a dissident song. (Hedrick Smith, 1976, devoted a chapter to this.) We should admit that we do not know its full extent, while deploring the secrecy.

PEASANT INCOMES AND RURAL LABOUR PROBLEMS

Until 1966, *kolkhoz* peasant incomes depended wholly upon the amount which the farm in question had available for distribution, in money and in kind. As already explained in Chapter 5, the *trudoden'* (work-day unit) was used as a measure of work performed, and the payment for each *trudoden'* was determined finally only when the *kolkhoz* made up its accounts at the end of the year, though most farms gave their members some 'advances' during the year. The number of *trudodni* assigned for tasks of a given duration were varied according to the skill and effort deemed to be required, the ratio in the fifties being usually of the order of 5 : 1, or even more if 'mechanizers' (tractor drivers, combine-harvester operators) were included. It is important to stress that, under this system, there were very great differences between farms in the actual value of each *trudoden'*. There have been documented instances when semi-bankrupt *kolkhozy* distributed to their members no money at all. While this was exceptional, and some *kolkhozy* (especially in cotton-growing areas, and on the Black Sea coast) were able to provide their members with a good income, the average was very low indeed. For example, in 1952 the cash paid out per *trudoden'* in the USSR as a whole was, in terms of new roubles, only 0·14. (Osad'ko, *VEk*, 1959, No. 2, p.83.) Some guide to regional variations is provided by the fact that in 1954–6 average payments for a day's work in Kazakhstan, West Siberia and Uzbekistan were more than double that of the 'central non-black-earth region', i.e. Central Russia. (Teryayeva, *VEk*, 1959, No. 1, p.110.) In the same *kolkhoz* there would be immense variations: thus the *Strana sovetov kolkhoz* in North Kazakhstan distributed 2·17 roubles per day in 1956, when it rained, and 0·37 roubles in 1957, when it did not. (Lisichkin, *VEk*, 1960, No. 7, p.62.)

The Soviet sociologist-demographer Perevedentsev noted that despite increases in the second half of the fifties, in 1963–4 a *trudoden'* was worth a mere 0·30 roubles and 1½ kilograms of grain, and was little more than half of the pay in *sovkhozy* for the same work. At this time, *sovkhozy* pay was only about 58 per cent of that of industry. In addition, one must take into account the much greater accessibility and entitlements to social services in state employment. (Perevedentsev, 1975, pp.134, 135–7.)

These indefensibly wide variations, as well as the low average level, were the consequence of the residual nature of payments to *kolkhoz* members, as well as of the low prices paid by the state for farm produce. Prices were raised by stages to much more reasonable levels, as we have seen. In 1966 it was finally decided to base *kolkhoz* members' pay on *sovkhoz* wage-scales. This has also meant the reduction of inter-*kolkhoz* differentials, with the raising of the minimum wage. It also reduced, without eliminating, differences between *kolkhozy*. The evidence shows that the *kolkhoz* average rate of remuneration is still below that of workers. Thus the plan for 1976 specifies an overall average wage of 150 roubles per month and average *kolkhoz* incomes of 98 roubles. (Baybakov, *Pravda*, 3 December 1975.) The *sovkhoz* average can be estimated as 130 roubles by extrapolation from 1973' data. However, it must be borne in mind that a greater proportion of *kolkhoz* members consist of ageing women, and also that their income from private plots (and the size of these plots) is greater, so the difference is not large, though it should be recalled that *kolkhoz* members are not paid for days in which there is no work for them to do. In the late Stalin period, by contrast, most peasants were in a state of acute poverty, and it is therefore worth recalling that they were not included in the 10 : 1 ratio for 1946, quoted on p.209 above. If they were, the differentials would have been even wider.

It is necessary to stress that some peasant families benefited greatly from proximity to the urban free markets, or from being able to grow and sell items at very high prices (thus citrus fruits from the Caucasus could be flown to Moscow by their owners at a big profit). Also members of peasant families sometimes worked in nearby state factories, and some peasants left the village annually for seasonal work. All this is significant still, but was of much greater importance when collective pay was so dismally low. For reasons of geography, peasant families differed and still differ widely in their opportunities to earn extra: thus lack of roads and means of transport can inhibit access to the market and/or to places of employment outside agriculture. In smaller and more densely populated countries, such as Hungary and Czechoslovakia, the mixed worker-peasant family is much more common, making it possible for members of families to shift from industry to agriculture (and back again) without changing their place of residence.

In Chapter 5 we have already discussed some key problems in devising a wage-incentive scheme for agriculture within the giant farms, whether these are *kolkhozy* or *sovkhozy*. This is partly due to the (missing) link between piece-rates applicable to specific tasks and the final product (see p.139, above). There is also the lack of interest of many peasants in earning more, now that incomes are at a much higher level than in the past. Cultural levels are low, rural shops are poorly supplied, and so the attractiveness of additional sums of money does not, in many cases, compensate for extra work effort. No doubt this will be overcome in time.

A major problem, as in many other countries, is migration to towns. This is only partly a question of earnings. Several authors have drawn attention to the high proportion of physical unmechanized labour in agriculture. As traditionally the 'mechanizers' are overwhelmingly male ('the percentage of women among tractor and combine drivers . . . does not exceed 0·5–0·6 per cent') (Fedorova, *VEk*, 1975, No. 12, p.57), it follows that the overwhelming majority of women perform burdensome physical labour: 'in some republics the proportion of women engaged in hand labour reaches 90–98 per cent'. In consequence, by contrast with the past, young women leave the village faster than do young men. (Fedorova, *VEk*, 1975, No. 12, p.57.) Many machines create an intolerable amount of noise, vibration and pollution, and are also badly designed from the standpoint of maintenance, which adds to the disutility of rural labour in general, for women in particular. (Fedorova, *VEk*, 1975, No. 12, pp.58–9.)

While a larger proportion of women in the livestock sector work with machines, even there it is a minority, owing to inadequate mechanization. The tendency persists to work the milkmaids and others who tend livestock at very inconvenient hours, with little free time. Evidence of a very long 'spreadover' for milkmaids, for instance, was presented in one of my very first articles, (Nove, 1951). In 1967 a Soviet critic again deplored the fact that shift-work was rare, and that most milkmaids began work at 3.45 a.m. and ended at 9.45 p.m. – with rest periods in between, of course, but such a schedule is disruptive of normal life. (Shinkarev and Bogomolov, *EkG*, 1967, No. 15, p.32.) Yet despite repeated criticisms, 'two-shift working . . . has not yet become widespread' (this in 1975), and the working day, with breaks, spreads over thirteen to sixteen hours. Livestock workers are unable to take days off: indeed milkmaids worked an average of 314 days a year in 1974, which, far from giving them a five-day week, meant that they were unable to rely on even one day's rest a week! (It may be some slight consolation to know that in 1965 they worked 333 days a year, which meant roughly one day free every two weeks.) The Soviet critic rightly points out that recruitment of young labour to work under such conditions is bound to be difficult. (Fedorova, *VEk*, 1975, No. 12, p.62.) One wonders why they have been tolerated for so long.

Rural labour is more regularly employed in the livestock sector, where work is required the year round, than in field work, for obvious reasons. However, somewhat surprisingly, Perevedentsev cites evidence which shows that total hours of work (*including* private plots) is higher, leisure hours notably fewer, among *kolkhoz* members (women especially) than among industrial workers. Indeed, in the busy summer months *kolkhoz* women had a mere 7·8 hours of free time a week. (Perevedentsev, 1975, pp.143–5.) Taking also into account mud, poor communications, lack of amenities, inadequacies of schooling (and thus of opportunities for upward mobility), it is hardly surprising to learn that even in *kolkhozy* where pay-rates had been very substantially raised, the net effect was even to speed up migration to towns. One milkmaid reportedly said, as she sent her four daughters to town to study: 'Now I can maintain you. You at least need not bother with cows' tails.' Urban living, even in cramped surroundings, is much more highly esteemed than rural occupations. (Perevedentsev, 1975, pp. 150–1.)

Rural labour is very unequally distributed. While Soviet official statements deny the existence of unemployment, one form of this is the under-use of (especially) female labour: thus the same source speaks of 'large reserves of underutilized labour (Moldavia, Central Asia)', (Perevedentsev, 1975, p.57.) though as we have seen this can coexist with large-scale 'import' of labour from the cities to cope with the harvest peak. Areas of especially severe shortage of labour include Siberia, where labour is short also in cities and so it is relatively easy for the peasant to move. Meanwhile labour-saving equipment lies unused for lack of skilled operatives and maintenance personnel. 'As at January 1974, 19,000 milking machines were not in use', for instance. (Perevedentsev, 1975, p.61.)

All this is evidence that the problems of agricultural labour are only partly to do with rates of pay and the weak link between material incentives and efficient production, though no one would deny that these are important too. Much attention will have to be paid to the 'culture' of the work process, the need for leisure, for a marked improvement in general living and cultural standards, and for better supplies of consumers' goods and services. The planners know all this, naturally, and there has been much discussion about the urgent need to improve rural amenities of life, to provide much more 'infrastructure'. Some effort is being made to build modern rural settlements, with three- and four-storey housing, running water, central heating, moving the peasants in from scattered hamlets. This reminds one of the 'agro-city' (agrogorod) scheme which Khrushchev first expounded in 1950, and which was quite premature: in the poverty-stricken Russian villages, in a country still recovering from the disasters of war, with urban housing in a deplorable state, trying to shift peasants into new 'rural townships' was out of the question. But a move in this direction is in progress; a few such townships exist and others are projected. (I visited one in 1970 in Belorussia.) Some peasants prefer separate houses or cottages to flats, especially bearing in mind the need to 'house' private livestock ('you cannot keep a pig on the third floor', to cite a Belorussian official, off the record).

In 1976–80 it is intended that 170,000 families shall be moved from small hamlets; the number of 'settlements with a future' (perspektivnykh posyolkov) will be 29,000, and these are to be 'fully reconstructed and extended'. (Gladyshev and Gokhberg, PKh, 1974, No. 12, p.55.) Judging from some scattered evidence, the peasants sometimes prefer to remain where they are, and elementary services are sometimes denied to settlements deemed to be 'without a future' *(neper-spektivnyye)*.

This may be yet another instance of a good idea bureaucratically deformed. Better housing and amenities are essential, and peasants from scattered hamlets could be provided with better facilities if they moved to a large central settlement – if, of course, better roads will be built, and also that the peasants' opinions about moving, and their views as to the kind of house they wish to live in, are taken into account. Past experience suggests that this may be an imposed 'campaign', which may go too far too quickly, but further evidence is needed as to the scale and pace of 'rural urbanization'.

WOMEN'S PAY AND EMPLOYMENT

The USSR relies greatly on women's work, and participation rates are high. One reads occasionally of pockets of underemployment in heavy-industrial areas such as the Kuzbas, and there are some 'voluntary' housewives, but in 1973 51 per cent of all persons employed in the national economy were women (ranging from 24 per cent in 'transport' to 85 per cent in 'health, physical culture and social security'). Over 52 per cent of all graduates employed were women. The frequently proclaimed official doctrine is that there is equal pay for equal work. Women scientists and engineers are numerous by Western standards, women predominate in teaching, medicine, banking, insurance, and they constitute over 60 per cent of those engaged in the 'apparatus of the organs of state and economic administration, and of co-operative and social organizations'. (*Nk*, 1973, p.583 and p.591.) Women constitute just 50 per cent of all students in higher educational institutions, 61 per cent of the students specializing in economics and law. All this might appear to be evidence of a very satisfactory situation. True, the proportion of women in the upper reaches of the party hierarchy is extremely small, but this (so it might be held) is another matter.

In practice things are not so satisfactory. Two modifying factors must be mentioned. The first is that women tend to occupy the lower end of every category of employment. The second is that those occupations in which women predominate tend to be the lowest paid.

Several examples can illustrate the above propositions. One was mentioned already: in agriculture, the better-paid 'mechanizers' are nearly all men, the unskilled field-workers mostly women. Among 'scientific workers' (i.e. staffs in higher education and research institutes), the proportion of women diminishes sharply with each category as shown in Table 16.

Table 16   *Proportion of women to total, 1973*

		Per cent
All 'scientific workers'		40
of which:	Junior researchers and assistants	49
	Senior researchers	24·3
	'Docents'	22
	Academicians*, professors	10·2

*including corresponding-members.
(*Source*:   NKh, 1973, pp.175, 176.)

Similarly, while women constitute 80 per cent of the classroom teachers, they provide 27 per cent of the heads of secondary schools. (*NKh*, 1973, p.706.)

Finally, all the predominantly female occupational groups have below-average incomes: posts, education, medicine, banking, trade, administration. In industry the clerical and accounting work is generally female, and is the lowest-paid. There is also ample sociological evidence about the burden of shopping and housework, which falls disproportionately on working women.

While all this is so, we must refrain from drawing excessively sweeping conclusions. It is doubtful whether the low pay of 'female' occupations was the result of a deliberate policy. The priority of heavy industry, for example, was not of sexist origin, but the typical heavy industry has a largely male labour force. Miners and steel-workers are better paid than book-keepers and textile workers. It is not clear whether medicine and teaching have become low-paid because female, or became female because low-paid (i.e. the extent to which medical salaries fell behind average earnings attracted potential male recruits to other occupations, at a time when scientific-technical manpower was scarce and pay in industry was higher). Nor can the figures on scientific workers be used to prove that women suffer from discrimination. For reasons familiar in all countries, men usually predominate in higher posts in nearly all walks of life. In other words, if 49 per cent of junior academic and research staff were female, it is not really surprising, even if all discrimination were absent, to find that only 10 per cent of the professors were. This is, of course, not to deny that the attitude of men to women, or of women to themselves, are not strong 'discouraging' factors in the USSR, as elsewhere. Family burdens unequally borne are a serious handicap. The inadequacies of retail distribution also bear heavily on women, who often have to stand in line in overcrowded shops after a day's work. All this has a depressing effect on the birth-rate, despite the extensive network of crèches and kindergartens.

There is no doubt that women's earnings are well below those of men. Exactly how far below we do not know: no statistics on average wages by sex are published. This is the effect of the predominance of women in low-paid occupations, and is consistent with the observance of the principle of equal pay for equal work in any given occupation.

THE PLANNING OF EMPLOYMENT

Since, as has been pointed out, unplanned labour mobility exists, as workers are free to resign and try to obtain a job elsewhere, the planners must proceed by inducement and persuasion, and/or adapt the labour-utilization plans to availability. They can affect supply also by their control over education and technical training, but this too can operate only by persuasion: if more electrical engineers are thought to be needed, more places can be provided in appropriate technological institutes, but no individuals are compelled to occupy these places, if they happen to prefer philosophy or physics. This, therefore, is a field in which planning could be described as 'indicative', rather than of the 'directive' type. Inevitably this gives rise to problems.

The system might appear to possess solid advantages as against the West. The plans for various sectors are drawn up in the knowledge of available labour resources, in various areas and of requisite qualifications. The long-term plan includes a segment concerned with labour needs. The provision of specialist training courses at all levels can be geared into the projected requirements in a manner impossible under capitalism. There is a duty to provide employment, there is explicit recognition of the right to work, and also of a *duty* to work, so that one could be accused of the offence of being a parasite. Labour productivity plans take into account both the possible savings of labour in various industries through technical progress, and the alternative uses of such labour in the provision of other goods and services; a notable shift of labour to the previously neglected services sectors has been a feature of the last two decades, and is likely to continue. A weakness which was corrected was the absence of labour exchanges. After 1933, when the Commissariat of Labour was abolished, they were abolished too. There were, it is true, various bodies charged with recruiting labour for specific purposes, and a worker could turn to his trade union, to the Komsomol or to his local soviet for help or information. But these were inadequate substitutes, widely criticized as such. Enterprises seeking labour devised various methods of communication: local radio advertising, public notice boards, even notices pinned on telegraph poles. (I once saw one such in the town of Gomel', notifying citizens that workers were needed to fell trees in West Siberia.) In 1967, there were set up in each republic state committees for the utilization of labour resources, and these have offices in cities. While this system is not yet all-union, this represents a notable improvement over the past.

However, while recognizing the potential advantages of the Soviet system of labour planning, there is plenty of evidence that it runs into many difficulties. Let us begin with the controversial subject of unemployment. The official position is that it does not exist. This causes perplexity to Western observers, since even in an ideally organized society there must be a gap of varying length between leaving one job, and starting another. Such unemployment naturally exists in the Soviet Union, though we do not know its extent. But there is frequent recognition in specialized articles of two other kinds of more persistent unemployment. The first relates to employment opportunities for women where mining and metallurgy predominate. The second arises because of lack of employment opportunities in the smaller towns: 'While the share of those engaged in domestic and individual auxiliary activity [mainly household plots] in the country as a whole is 13 per cent of the total labour resources, in small and medium-sized towns the figure is much higher and in some instances rises up to 30–40 per cent'. (Zagorodneva, 1968, p.435 and Manevich, VEk, 1965, No. 6, pp.26–7.) Evidently this means that some who would normally be expected to work in state enterprises cannot do so for lack of opportunity. We do not know what proportion of this consists of married women, and possibly nor do the planners, since 'up till now the balances of the labour force are not drawn up by sex, as the existing statistical returns do not provide for this'. (Zagorodneva, 1968, p.454.) One must add that an unknown number of married women (and not only in Russia) might prefer to be housewives, especially when children are young, but are compelled to go out to work to supplement the family income.

Many of these problems are discussed in an article by Pervukhin (formerly a party leader, now a Gosplan official). He complained about the habit of ministries of siting new factories in large cities in European territories, where labour is scarce. He noted the rapid population increase in Central Asia and Azerbaydzhan, and the need for more investments there. As an example of sex imbalance he pointed to the situation in the oblast' of Ivanovo, where 70 per cent of all employment is in light industry and mainly female. In 1970 there were 132 women to every 100 men in Ivanovo, 'which causes certain difficulties in arranging a family'. (Pervukhin, PKh, 1974, No. 7, p.156.)

It is only fair to point out, however, that unemployment is a much more severe problem in the West. In the USSR there is a high level of job security, and this, together with freedom (within limits) to move, is bound to cause locational problems, especially in new industrial areas. One such difficulty, to which reference has already been made, concerns the unwillingness of citizens to work in Siberia, at the existing level of income, housing and amenities. While the plan envisaged migration eastwards, in fact large numbers of people migrated out of Siberia towards what are described as 'labour surplus areas, which is in plain contradiction with the tasks of economic development'. (Zagorodneva, 1968, p.434.) The reasons have been frankly analysed: conditions of life, availability of vegetables, fruit, sunshine, are not good in Siberia, are much better in the Caucasus, Central Asia, Moldavia. It also turns out that the native Central Asians tend to stay in their villages for national-cultural reasons, since a move to town brings them into an alien (and Russian-speaking) environment (Perevedentsev, 1966), while migrants from other areas are attracted by industrial investment in Central Asia and Azerbaydzhan. (Kostakov, *PKh*, 1974, No. 7, p.77.) Again, all this is consistent with underemployment or misemployment, if not unemployment. Yet it is accompanied by acute shortages of labour of other types in other places.

Another familiar complaint concerns the difficulty that enterprises face in shedding surplus labour. Unless alternative employment can be found locally, pressure is exercised to retain labour (Arutyunov, *EkG*, 1967, No. 4, p.13) and this is another explanation of the existence of pockets of under-utilized labour along with shortages of workers elsewhere. So is the tendency of some managers to hoard labour, for the same reason as they hoard materials: planners may suddenly demand that they produce more of something. The so-called Shchekino experiment, a much-publicized method of stimulating labour productivity, constitutes only a partial exception to this rule. In the chemicals complex of Shchekino, the management was authorized to use for additional wage payments a large previously fixed proportion of the sum saved by shedding redundant labour. This is, without doubt a promising experiment. However, the *total* employment at Shchekino changed little; there were projects in hand to expand the enterprise, and the redundant personnel were absorbed in these. One can compare the Shchekino case with a scheme introduced ten years earlier in the Urals electricity undertakings and explained verbally to me at one of the power stations: orders were given to redeploy the labour force so as to staff several new power stations in the area without taking on any additional personnel. This too aimed at raising labour productivity and taking up the labour slack without net redundancies. The Shchekino model has the advantage that the workers secure an immediate material benefit from this sort of redeployment. (This, however, raises a point of principle, familiar also in the West: to what extent should an increase in productivity in one plant benefit those directly employed in the plant? It is a hard question to answer.)

More difficult still has been to ensure consistency between supply and demand of different types of workers and specialists. Of course, in any conceivable economy rapid and sometimes unpredictable technological change can lead to shortages of some category of technologist; this is the necessary consequence of imperfect foresight in an imperfect world. But Soviet critics have found a very considerable 'inconsistency between the technical qualifications of trained workers and the needs of the national economy'. According to one author, there is a particularly severe shortage of persons who have completed a secondary education and then attended technical colleges for three to four years: 'by our calculations, the need for [such workers] was covered in industry in 1973 only to the extent of 40–42 per cent'. Thus 'in the Kharkov "Malyshev" transport machinery and aviation factories, the number of [machine] operatives is insufficient for even one normal shift of the work of machine-tools, and one operative services 6–15 machine-tools when the norm is 4–5. Particularly severe is the lack of specialists to service electronic equipment.' Courses run at enterprises have to make up for training deficiencies, but labour productivity and quality of output suffer. Investment completions are delayed. Thus a sample survey covering seventeen large new enterprises in light industry in the RSFSR showed that none had reached full production, because they had been provided with qualified workers to only 58 per cent of need. (Moskovich, *VEk*, 1975, No. 12, pp.46–7.) In the chemical industry, the delays in start-up *(osvoyeniye)* ('instead of one year, six to seven years') were also 'to some extent due to lack of qualified personnel'. (Moskovich, 1975, No. 12, p.48.) The author of the above also points to disequilibrium of a more general kind: thus unskilled or unqualified workers exceed requirements for such workers by 15–33 per cent, while qualified workers were scarce overall, though some were in excess supply. (Moskovich, *VEk*, 1975, No. 12, p.50.)

Various causes are cited to explain the unsatisfactory state of affairs. The flow of information about future needs for skilled workers is defective. The level of pay and status attained by those who attend technical training centres is insufficiently attractive. Many technical training institutes are poorly equipped, have grossly inadequate premises and unqualified teaching staffs. (Moskovich, *VEk*, 1975, No. 12, p.53.) No doubt also there is the difficulty which must arise when young people complete 'ten classes' (i.e. full secondary education): they may by then have aspirations other than those of becoming skilled workers. Also, the tendency to very narrow specialization, in many types of technological education, impedes adaptation to new needs.

There is much talk in the USSR about 'NOT' (*nauchnaya organizatsiya truda*, scientific organization of work). The situation is improving, including also the quality and quantity of technical training. The general level of skill is much higher than it was, as can be seen by figures as to the output of training schools. In 1973 29·7 per cent of industrial workers had 'completed secondary education' or better, against 2·4 per cent in 1952, and for the under-thirties the 1973 figure was 50 per cent (*NKh*, 1973, p.589.) The deficiencies listed above are not particularly surprising. It is very difficult indeed to ensure that human beings who are free to choose in fact choose the occupations which the economy and society needs. This would be hard enough even if the planners were fully cognizant of what was actually needed. It is worth recalling that some Bolsheviks argued for universal direction of labour under quasi-military discipline as can be seen in the writings of Trotsky and Bukharin in 1920 analysed by Szamuely (1975). This idea was dropped, though under Stalin (as we have seen) criminal penalties were for a time introduced for leaving one's work without permission. Free choice inevitably complicates labour planning. In a rapidly changing environment, with imperfect information, inertia and other deficiencies which are by no means peculiar to the USSR, disequilibrium between supply of and demand for various kinds of labour must arise, and particularly so if there is little overt unemployment to provide the necessary flexibility. The low birth-rate in the USSR (except in formerly Muslim areas) will ensure a slowdown in the rate of growth of the labour force. It therefore becomes all the more important to plan the intake of new labour, and its training, with somewhat greater efficiency.

CONDITIONS OF WORK, SOCIAL SERVICES

The length of the working day in the USSR has substantially diminished, and the five-day week has become widespread. It is stated that the average length of the normal working week was 40·7 hours in 1973 (it was 47·8 hours in 1955), and that, allowing also for extra free days (over and above normal rest-days and the annual vacation) actual hours worked in industry were 40 hours. (*NKh*, 1973, p.590.) There seems to be little overtime. Yet this seems improbable. Various reports, some printed in the USSR and some based on conversations, repeatedly assert that overtime is very common, especially in the last ten days of any month, or quarter, or year, This is the phenomenon known as *shturmovshchina*, 'storming', the great rush to fulfil the plan. It is partly caused by the common tendency for materials to arrive late, which is caused by *shturmovshchina* in the supplying enterprise which is caused by *its* materials arriving late, and so on. It is, therefore, frankly incredible that so little overtime is worked.

The most likely explanation, which in the nature of things cannot be documented, is that overtime is worked without being reported or paid as such. The rules specify extra payment at overtime rates, but this would lead to the overspending of the wages fund. Yet the plan must be fulfilled, and the trade union (whose consent is required by the rules if overtime is to be worked) is unlikely to obstruct the carrying out of superior orders. More will be said about Soviet trade unions in a moment. It seems that we do not know how much overtime is worked, and that the actual working week is very probably longer than 40 hours, but that this cannot be conclusively proved.

The effect of *shturmovshchina* on work effort was vividly illustrated by a leading economist, Ya. Kvasha. He pointed out that in the last nine days of each month there is produced far more than in the first fourteen days: 2·6 times more machine-tools, 1·9 times more spindles and rail wagons, 1·8 times more tractors and combines. He cited figures to show that workers are frequently underemployed in the first part of each month, largely through lack of materials. (Kvasha, *EKO*, 1975, No. 6, p.104.)

Again, it is hard to evaluate some scattered evidence, mostly from conversations, about work morale. The official picture is highly favourable as can be seen from smiling, keen workers' faces which decorate the first page of *Pravda* almost every day of the week. But one hears of work-avoidance, absenteeism, drunkenness, petty and not-so-petty pilfering, bribery, and other negative phenomena. One must mention such reports, which are very familiar to readers of the satirical *Krokodil*, without being able to evaluate them. There may in any case be wide variations in these as in so many other respects.

We do not know the extent of illegal or unreported economic activities, but it would be wrong to ignore them altogether in our assessment of incomes and labour inputs. Bribery and on-the-side payments alter the distribution of income, without in themselves causing any extra output. However, in the USSR (and in Britain too) there is work 'on the side' – for instance by decorators and plumbers – which constitutes unreported production. One reads of criminal cases in which large-scale diversions of materials take place, these being used to produce many kinds of consumers' goods in secret. In Georgia in 1975, with considerable publicity, a trial was held in which such practices were exposed. On a less 'criminal' plane, but still extra-legally, one reads of freelance groups of construction workers hiring themselves out; these are known as *shabashniki*. It is sometimes claimed (by émigrés, or in private conversation) that a great many individuals earn extra in a wide variety of unreported ways. Thus lorry drivers are said to charge for lifts and sell 'official' petrol coupons, tyres are sold on the side (*na levo*, 'on the left', in Russian), and so on. This suggests *under*-reporting of both income and output, and our picture of income relativities also requires correction. There is, however, no means of quantifying any of this.

Turning to social services and benefits, one can only briefly indicate their importance, since they do not as such raise problems worth long discussion in the present context. Paid vacations cover fifteen working days as a minimum, many heavy and unhealthy occupations qualify for four weeks. (note that *kolkhoz* peasants do not have an entitlement to *paid* vacations, as they are paid for the work they do only when they do it). One must also take into account paid maternity leave, disability benefit, sick pay, old-age pensions and children's allowances, with now a supplement for those whose *per capita* family income falls below 50 roubles a month. Pensions were very low for most workers until the method of calculation was altered in 1956. There is now an effective minimum, for those duly qualified, of about 35 roubles per month, and a maximum of 120, save to specially favoured individuals. *Kolkhoz* peasants receive smaller sums, and this only since 1965. There is, as is known, a health service, and (except in 1940–56) no charge for tuition in secondary schools or in higher education. Allowance must be made for all these things, and for subsidized housing, in any assessment of overall living standards. But merely to list the various entitlements, analyse the figures and assess the quality of various services could easily occupy a book. It will not be this book.

TRADE UNIONS

Soviet trade unions are organized on an 'industrial' basis, covering all grades, including managers, in the given branch of the economy. The structure of the unions is nominally democratic, with elections of officials and the all-union central council (AUCCTU) elected at national conferences. However, the Communist Party is in full control at all levels, and indeed there was only one national conference to elect the AUCCTU between 1932 and 1954. This central body must be regarded as a quasi-governmental labour agency, which is charged with administering the social insurance fund, and with taking such action as will mobilize the workers in the struggle to fulfil output plans and other policies of the party and the government. At local level, trade union officials are supposed to reconcile these essentially official functions with the task of protecting workers from abuses on the part of the management. Collective agreements between the management and the union branch were revived in 1954 after a prolonged period of disuse. They generally specify a number of measures concerned with welfare and amenities, as well as including undertakings on behalf of the workers to work harder and better, but they do not determine wage-rates. With the object of stimulating output, the unions endeavour to organize various forms of 'socialist competition' between workshops, groups and individuals. Subject to the overriding general aim of increasing production and fulfilling the plan, union officials on the spot are concerned with planned piece-rates and thereby have a hand in deciding how much is in fact earned by the workers, even though they have no power to negotiate about basic rates. The local branch plays an important role in the settlement of disputes between individual workers and the management (e.g. over grading, demotion, bonus entitlements, allegedly illegal dismissals, etc.), participating on equal terms in the 'conflicts commissions' which, in enterprises, settle such disputes. If the trade union and the management fail to agree in the conflicts commission, the matter is referred to the *trade union* for final decision according to a Supreme Soviet decree of 31 January 1957. (Dvornikov and Nikitinsky, 1957.) If worker or management still considers the decisions to be contrary to the law, they can appeal to the courts. (McAuley, 1969.)

During the Stalin era, the task of mobilizing the workers was heavily emphasized at all levels, and the representational and protective tasks of trade unions took very much a second place. This was justified by arguments such as there being no need to protect the workers against the workers' state. The highly unpopular decrees of 1940, which forbade change of employment without permission and introduced severe penalties for lateness and absenteeism, were stated in the preamble to have been promulgated at the request of the AUCCTU. The trade union branch was directly concerned with the unpopular task of compelling everyone to subscribe to the virtually compulsory but nominally voluntary state bonds. Eventually, things reached a stage which proved intolerable to the government itself. There were too many instances of failure on the part of local trade unions to defend their members against local abuses, breaches of protective legislation were all too common, the so-called 'socialist competitions' organized by the unions frequently remained on paper; the unions, in other words, were failing to mobilize because, *inter alia*, they were not protecting the members and were not felt by their members to represent them. A sizable crop of articles, expressing dissatisfaction with the trade unions, appeared in the years following Stalin's death, and these culminated in the decisions of the December 1957 plenum of the central committee, which sought to stimulate the local unions to take their protective tasks more seriously, while re-emphasizing their role as 'mobilizers' of the workers and increasing their functions within enterprises, both directly and through the 'permanent production councils' in which they play a major role.

The argument that Soviet trade unions are not trade unions at all is often heard in discussions in the West. It is clear enough that they are not independent of state or party, and that their purpose is to organize the workers for the carrying out of state and party policy. Against this, it is sometimes argued that, under Soviet conditions, it is unreasonable to expect conflicts between the managers and the labour force, because the managers are also employees of the state (and, indeed, members of the same union), and/or that the unions do in fact have powers to protect members against arbitrary acts of neglect on the part of the management. Indeed, the powers are there and are impressive. The difficulty, however, is that the unions' task as a 'transmission belt' of party economic policies is often hard to reconcile with their 'protective' duties *vis-à-vis* their members, and, owing to the strong element of party control, in any conflict of loyalties the officials respond first and foremost to those above them, who in fact appoint them or arrange their 'elections', rather than to the membership. Thus if compulsory overtime or rest-day working is resorted to as a means of hastening plan-fulfilment, it is in the highest degree unlikely that the union branch would fail to back the management, whatever the feelings of the members. In other words, in assessing the economic forces at work in the Soviet Union, it would be misleading to view the unions as any kind of independent pressure group, even though action is commonly taken by the local branch to ensure that, for example, an expectant mother receives the paid vacation to which the laws entitle her, or a grade IV carpenter is not unjustifiably demoted, though even here the union often neglects its duties. Often such failures of the unions are corrected by the courts, especially in cases of unjustified dismissal in which the union branch supported the management. (For two of many examples, see *Byulleten Verkhovnovo Suda SSSR*, 1960, No. 2, pp.1, 3.) In one area, roughly half of all cases of appeal against dismissal were upheld by the courts (see *Sovetskaya Yustitiya*, 1964, No. 5.)

The trade unions administer the social insurance funds, and benefits to members much higher than to non-members, which helps to explain why the vast majority of those eligible are members of their unions.

In view of our own experiences in the field of wages and labour relations in this inflationary age, one would have to be a bold critic simply to contrast Soviet party-controlled trade unions with free collective bargaining in the West and leave it at that. What *ought* to be the functions of unions, how far should they pursue with vigour (and with disregard of the more general interest even of the working class) the sectional interests of their members? It is, of course, also important to consider the context: what does the government or dominant party stand for, whom does it represent, what is or should be the distribution of income and of property? This is not the place to go further into such matters, except perhaps to reiterate that *any* income differentials are bound to cause some dissatisfaction: dockers, doctors, train drivers, miners, garage mechanics, and saxophone players are unlikely to be unanimous about their respective shares of the social product, and nor are unions which represent their views and interests. In a modern, industrial, highly interdependent society, the attempt by any group to impose their interests by force can wreck the economy.

So while recognizing the Soviet trade unions for what they are, the serious reader should ponder the very complex question of what they ought to be. There is no easy answer.

WORKER'S PARTICIPATION

There has been much dispute among socialists about this issue dating back at least to the time of the revolution itself. Lenin, once power had been achieved, was sceptical: he did not believe in 'railways for the railwaymen and tanneries for the tanners'. He found himself under attack from the so-called workers' opposition, on the issue of managerial powers. As has been shown, the formal position in the USSR is that the director is in command, that his subordinates must obey him. True, there are checks and balances, his powers over labour, welfare funds and the like are limited by the trade union. But his primary responsibility is clearly to his superiors, not to the workers.

This constrasts with the Yugoslav model (of which more in Chapter 11), where the management is responsible to the workers and employees of the enterprise. It contrasts, too, with the formal – if not the actual – position in a *kolkhoz* in the USSR itself.

There is, in state enterprises, provision for consultative committees, known as 'production councils' *(proizvodstvennyye soveshchaniya)*, in which elected representatives of the labour force take part. However, judging from the lack of any reports of their activities, it would seem that they are of little importance.

As was shown at the beginning of this chapter, the Soviet official view is that the Soviet working masses *(trudyashchiyesya*, literally 'toilers'), jointly own the means of production and thus employ themselves. Few indeed would accept that this represents the feelings of the 'toilers'. Inevitably, when decisions taken within a complex planning machine are converted by 'their' director into *orders (prikazy)*, the executant of the orders is not likely to feel himself a co-owner.

This can lead to feelings of alienation and indifference, and also in some cases to pilfering and work-avoidance. The Soviet authorities are, of course, aware of the need to instil a sense of participation and of 'belonging', and official propaganda urges directors to rely on the *aktiv*, while the party and trade union organizations seeks not only to mobilize but also to call meetings to discuss how best to carry out the plans and how to overcome various difficulties.

A foreign observer is not in a good position to assess the sparse evidence about what actually happens, but the indications are that the sense of participation is notably lacking. Many of the means used to encourage it, such as 'socialist emulation' and discussion of undertakings within collective agreements, become distorted by a species of formal bureaucratization, remain on paper. Party meetings at factories and farms can approximate to that described by Alexander Yashin (1956) in his short story *Rychagi* ('Levers'), in which the participants mouthed party-line platitudes, even though before the meeting opened they were informally exchanging sharp critical comments.

An important aspect of the problem is the extent to which decision making actually occurs at the level of the enterprise. If the director himself is seen primarily as executant of orders from above, then the interest of workers in participating in consultative (or even, on paper, decision making) organs at that level is naturally rather small. This is why some reformers argue that micro-economic decentralization to enterprises is a precondition for any effective participation. (See for instance Brus, 1973, p.14.)

Needless to say, there are difficulties in the way of any solution. In a modern, interconnected industrial economy it is by no means easy to overcome the feeling of many 'toilers' that they are minor cogs in a vast impersonal machine which they do not influence or control. The mere fact of social or state ownership does not make a fundamental difference to such attitudes, either in Russia or anywhere else. Conversely, if one splits up a modern interconnected economy into self-governing fragments, the advantages of planning could disappear, external diseconomies would not be identified, inequality, waste through duplication of effort and other negative phenomena might prevail. We will return to these themes in subsequent chapters.

The State Committee on Labour and Wages is now renamed the State Committee on Labour and Social Problems, and its activities extended.

The expectation that the wage differentials would increase seems not to have been realized.

There has been increasing evidence of official concern about work discipline: absenteeism, lateness, poor workmanship, drunkenness, pilfering, failure to enforce the rules, these things are all too common. A decree (*Pravda*, 12 January 1980) 'on greater strengthening of work discipline and reduction of labour turnover' instructs management to enforce disciplinary rules, and also provides additional incentives for long service. Here and elsewhere there is emphasis on the work *brigade*, as a unit for organizing work and as a basis for incentive payments.

Brezhnev and others have deplored the hoarding of labour, at a time when labour is short. In his speech of 28 November 1979, he gave as the reason the frequent mobilization of workers for bringing in the harvest and other campaigns, which impels managers to keep a reserve, just in case. Efforts will clearly continue to be made to discourage hoarding, of both labour and materials.

CHAPTER 9

PUBLIC FINANCE,
MONEY AND INFLATION

THE NATURE OF THE SOVIET BUDGET

The role of the budget is (in all countries) to transfer resources, in accordance with government decision, from one part of the national economy to another. The USSR is no different in this respect. However, the relative importance of the budget is very great there, because of the direct responsibility of the state for the bulk of economic life. Thus in 1973 the national income (in its Soviet definition) amounted to 337·2 milliard roubles, while the revenues of central plus republican and local governments came to 187·8 milliards, or well over half. (*NKh*, 1973, pp.603, 778.)

However, Soviet finance has an essential feature which distinguishes it from the West: its intimate inter-relationship with the process of economic planning and management. Expenditures on investment and on other aspects of the economy are the financial reflection of decisions about economic growth and priorities. Revenues predominantly originate in the operation of the state sector of the economy, and, as we shall see, a large portion of expenditure also derives from the economic plan itself. Similarly, financial institutions operate with a copy of the plan before them. Their resources, and their allocation of moneys for credits and other purposes, are intimately related to the output and investment plan and are intended also to serve as a check on observance of regulations issued by higher authority in the course of organizing plan-fulfilment. Thus financial plans and economic plans are elaborated simultaneously, and it has become the practice to submit the annual economic plan and the budget to the same session of the Supreme Soviet.

One feature of the state budget is that it includes the expenditure of all republics, and local authorities. Thus the expenditure of, say, the Omsk town soviet in repairing the drains will appear under the appropriate head in the budget voted by the all-union Supreme Soviet. This does not mean, of course, that the repair of the Omsk drains is specifically authorized by the Supreme Soviet. Republics and local authorities have their own budgets, and only the principal headings of expenditure require approval of the centre, though some detailed items are the consequences of plans decided at the centre, which also decides how much of the total revenue is made available to the republics (more of this in a moment).

Let us look at a recent Soviet budget statement (Table 17) for illustrative purposes.

Table 17

			(milliards of new roubles)	
	1940	1965	1973	1978
TOTAL REVENUE	18·0	102·3	187·8	265·8
of which: Turnover tax	10·6	38·7	59·1	84·1
Payments out of profits	2·2	30·9	60·0	78·6
Taxes on co-operatives*	0·3	1·5	1·5	1·6
Mass bond sales	0·9	0·2	0·4	0·6
Direct taxes	0·9	7·7	15·8	22·1
Social insurance contrib.	0·9	5·6	9·3	13·1
(Total from the economy)**	(16·0)	(93·9)	(170·9)	(242·3)

(*Source*: NKh, 1973, p.778, and NKh, 1978, p.533.)
*Including *kolkhozy* and 'enterprises of social organizations'.
**'From state and co-operative enterprises and organizations.

The bulk of revenue came, and comes, from the operations of the economy. It may be useful to envisage the great corporation, USSR Ltd, financing its overheads by a mark-up on the prices of the goods and services which it sells. If the USSR were regarded as a firm, then investments, defence, police, training labour and management, health, etc. etc., could be legitimately seen as overheads. A historical parallel is the East India Company before the Mutiny, which did *(inter alia)* maintain an army and an administration. (It is, of course, not suggested that the USSR *is* a firm!). Income tax and other personal taxes are of minor importance. As already pointed out in Chapter 7, since incomes are received from a variety of activities, including many that do not produce consumable items (defence, education, administration, investment, etc., plus various social benefits), the prices of the goods and services available for purchase must be raised far above the costs of production. The difference, expressed as a mark-up over costs, must vary with the monetary costs of the defence, investment, education, etc. (of course taking into account any reduction in disposable incomes by direct taxation). Thus the total tax burden may best be seen as equal to the total difference between cost of production and final sales prices of all goods and services, plus direct taxes less subsidies. Of course, a part of the 'burden' returns to the citizen in the form of transfer payments (pensions, etc.) and other social services.

The 'tax burden' so defined includes revenues which never reach the budget at all. The reasons for this may be illustrated with the following examples. In the first, industry A finances its entire investments out of retained profits. In the second example, the enterprises of which it is composed transfer their profits to the state budget, and the investments are financed by budgetary grants. Imagine that in the two examples the investments are identical. Then, obviously, so is the burden. The only circumstance which alters is the method of financing, which in *both* instances may be deemed to originate in the mark-up on the price of the goods produced by industry A.

In practice the distinctions are not so sharp, but undoubtedly part of the expenditures of the Soviet budget *could* be financed out of retained profits, and the proportion of investment expenditures so financed has risen, as we have seen.

In assessing the *types* of revenues, we must again note that to some extent their proportions can be altered without making much difference to the citizen. Let us again illustrate (Table 18), taking an imaginary commodity and two different structures of the same final price.

Table 18

	A	B
Costs	40	40
Profit margin	20	5
(of which: to budget)	(16)	(4)
Turnover tax	10	25
Trade margin	3	3
Retail price	73	73

The final price is the same, but the share of turnover tax and of profits has greatly altered (in the examples, the budget revenue is somewhat smaller in A than in B, since the larger retained profit would be used for more self-financing, e.g. of investments). Reference to Table 17 shows that a tendency towards relying more on profits as a source of revenue certainly exists, especially in comparison with before the war. It seems that a past preference for taking revenue from enterprises and later returning it out of the budget was explicable in terms of strengthening central control. The 'locals' cannot misappropriate money they do not have. In more recent years, however, either managers are more trusted or the local control mechanisms are more efficient. Another way of looking at this trend is to see a greater tendency towards redistribution of profit and loss within ministries, since this too would 'bypass' the budget. One example is the case of 'accounting prices' in the oil industry, already referred to in Chapter 7. In this instance the high-cost Baku oilfields do not receive a budgetary subsidy, since the costs are covered by the prices paid by the

Ministry of Oil Industry, payments which are much higher than those made to low-cost oilfields. When 'accounting prices' (and rental payments) did not exist, one could and did have a budgetary subsidy to loss-making enterprises in a given industry, while the budget derived revenue from profitable low-cost enterprises in the same industry.

So the budget totals and the level of subsidies are to some degree dependent on accounting practice and organizational boundary-lines.

It follows that, to compare the Soviet 'tax burden' with that borne by citizens in a capitalist country, one must include in the latter not just budget revenues but also the profit margins of firms. This was in fact done by Holzman (1955). Let us not forget that the purchaser of a pair of trousers in the West pays not only the rate of indirect tax applicable to trousers but also a price which provides the firm with a profit margin, which could be used (inter alia) for investment. The trousers-buying individual is thus making a contribution, through the price he pays, to savings and investment, a contribution no more voluntary than the Soviet citizen's when he purchases trousers.

TURNOVER TAX

For some reason, the nature of this tax has puzzled students. It is equal to the gap between the industry's wholesale price and the final selling price, less handling margins. This gap, or 'difference', is in many instances the rate of tax. In other words, instead of deciding that the tax on that pair of trousers shall be (say) 25 per cent, one calculates the difference and then works out the percentage (if one wants to know it). This 'tax by difference' technique is useful in those instances (analysed in Chapter 7), in which multiple variations exist of the same product, and where it is convenient to relate the retail price to some estimated market-clearing level. In other instances, where the commodity is more homogeneous, the tax closely resembles an excise duty: salt and vodka are two examples. Finally, there is the revenue obtained from state agricultural procurement and processing organs, representing the difference between the prices at which farm produce is purchased and re-sold. As we have seen, in the case of livestock products this difference has been negative in recent years.

Unfortunately, the actual rates of tax charged, with occasional exceptions, are kept secret. The official line is that turnover tax is not a tax, that it is a part of the 'surplus product' created in industry and to some extent also in agriculture. (Zverev, 1970, p.171.) As we have seen, it is in fact difficult to distinguish turnover tax from other forms of price mark-up. This, however, does not justify Soviet propagandists claiming that taxes are much higher in the West, ignoring turnover tax ('not a tax'), while treating all Western indirect taxes as a burden on the working masses.

Some Western analysts wrongly assume that the entire turnover-tax revenue originates in consumers'-goods industries (including food), and that therefore it can be expressed as a percentage of total retail turnover. However, though the bulk of producers' goods industries do not pay this tax, it is levied on most kinds of fuel (except coal), and there was recently under discussion a proposal to levy turnover tax on 'highly profitable machinery and other branches of production of heavy industry'. (Garbuzov, *PKh*, 1974, No. 8, p.18.) At present, about 40 per cent of all turnover-tax payments are made by wholesaling organs of the Ministry of (internal) Trade, and the rest by industrial enterprises and disposal organs under industrial ministries, and also (agricultural) procurement organs. (Zverev, 1970, p.172.) Despite which, in any Soviet statistical table showing the sector of origin of the national income, the whole of turnover-tax revenue is 'credited' to industry.

An interesting observation made by a Soviet critic is that turnover tax is paid when the goods are produced or reach the wholesalers, and before their sale to the ultimate customer. If in fact no one buys them, the payment is made all the same, but this means that in the end it is paid by the financial system to itself. (Stolyarov, 1969, p.189.)

PAYMENTS OUT OF PROFITS

Until 1965 this item was wholly covered by the phrase 'deduction from profits'. It consisted of the profits of state enterprises, less the amount they were permitted to retain for specified purposes. It was thus not a 'profit tax' or corporation tax, which suggests a payment at some fixed rate. It too was, in a sense, a tax by difference, but whereas turnover tax was related to the volume of goods produced, the state's revenue from profits depended in some measure on the actual level of profits.

After 1965 there was introduced the charge on capital and also rental (fixed) payments, both already discussed in Chapter 7. Enterprises which were subject to the reform of that year had to pay into the budget the 'free remainder', i.e. the residual profits over and above what they were allowed to retain. Other enterprises were unaffected, paying 'deduction from profits', old-style. The breakdown of this whole item of revenue was as shown in Table 19.

TAXES ON CO-OPERATIVES AND KOLKHOZY

These are levied on the profits of retail co-operatives and their subordinate enterprises, and on the net income of *kolkhozy*. The latter were at one time taxed on their gross income, but, as can be observed from the figures, this burden is now small (see Table 17).

Table 19

	(milliards of roubles)		
	1970	1973	1978
Total payments out of profits	54·2	60·0	78·6
of which:			
Capital charges	13·7	17·7	26·6
Fixed (rental) charges	2·5	2·6	1·1
Free remainder of profit	24·8	27·1	38·0
Deduction from profit, and other	13·2	12·6	12·9

(*Source*: *NKh*, 1973. p.778. and *NKh*, 1978, p.533.)

BOND SALES

The compulsory sale of low-interest-bearing bonds was a feature of the Stalin era. Officially it was voluntary, but, to put it mildly, it was made difficult for anyone not to volunteer. The sums were deducted from wage-packets. This continued until 1958, when a moratorium was declared on repayments and on prizes (most bonds had become lottery or premium bonds), and compulsory sales were simultaneously abandoned. Probably most Soviet citizens imagined that they would never see their money. However, regular drawings are now made to repay these old bonds, and a sum of 600 million roubles is provided for this purpose in the 1976 budget.

Bond sales since 1958 seem to be genuinely voluntary.

It must be added that the increment in *savings bank deposits* used also to be included in budget revenue. This formed part of the residual in Table 17. However, since 1963 these sums are retained by the State Bank, which uses them as one of several sources of expanding short-term credits. (Massarygin, 1974, p.83.)

DIRECT TAXES

The tax on income from employment in any state institution (i.e. the bulk of incomes) is on a modest scale. The tax on 100 roubles per month is 5·92 roubles, and the top rate charged on income in excess of this sum is 13 per cent. The top rate for those engaged in literature and art is also 13 per cent, though the progression differs in detail to that of the state-employed person. (Burmistrov, 1968, pp.25, 34.) However, Soviet authors are charged at very much higher rates, ranging from 30 to 75 per cent, in respect of royalties from publication abroad, under a new decree adopted in 1973. (*Vedomosti verkhovnogo soveta SSSR*, 12 September, 1973.)

The argument is sometimes made that these very low rates, accompanied as they are by high profit-and-turnover-tax margins on goods, are 'regressive', in comparison with the high progressive taxation of incomes in Western countries. However, since the state determines income relativities, there seems no very cogent reason to make major corrections to these relativities by taxes. If, say, it is considered that a professor or manager is overpaid in relation to a junior lecturer or unskilled worker, surely the necessary corrective action can be taken by the state, simply by altering the pay-rates for these categories. Indeed, Khrushchev undertook to abolish income tax. This has not been done, but the level of exemptions has been raised.

The above argument does not apply to income from private activities, and to these a very different scale of tax applies. Thus income from private medical practice, private teaching, rent from lettings and the work of craftsmen, seamstresses, etc., is taxed at a much higher scale. An income of 1200 roubles a year (100 roubles a month) is liable to a tax of 221·40 roubles (note that from the same income from state sources the tax is 70 roubles a year). For income over 7000 roubles a year the marginal tax rate is 81·0 per cent (Burmistrov, 1968, pp.36–7.)

Other taxes include the bachelor-and-small-families tax, introduced during the war, but which now applies only to men (20–50) and married women (20–45 years old); also exempted are military personnel, full-time students and a few other categories, including dwarfs. Tax is no longer paid if there are any children (before 1958 there was a tax if there were two children or fewer). The present maximum rate is 6 per cent. (Burmistrov, 1968, p.50.)

The 'agricultural tax' has a very special history. In the later Stalin years the tax was not only very high, but it was levied on crops planted and animals owned. Thus a hundredth of a hectare of potatoes or fruit trees, or a cow, or pig, was deemed to yield an income upon which tax was levied at rates which eventually rose to 48 per cent. (For source see Nove, 1953.) Since at this period (i.e. up to 1953) the peasants were also compelled to deliver produce to the state at very low prices, the effect was very severe, production was discouraged, fruit trees were chopped down to save tax (as Krushchev himself told us).

In 1953 the tax basis was altered. Since then, the payment has been calculated in relation to area cultivated; livestock is disregarded (excepting working stock), unless the numbers exceed the norm laid down for that republic. A typical tax rate is 0·85 roubles per hundredth-of-a-hectare, but the rate is much higher on irrigated land (for instance 2·20 roubles in Tadzhikistan) and lower on lands of low fertility (0·30 roubles is the lowest rate in the RSFSR, and 0·20 roubles in the Western territories of Belorussia and the Ukraine). There also seems to be continued favourable treatment for the former Polish territories that were collectivized after 1948 as the rates in the 'old' territories of these two republics are at least twice as high. It is noteworthy that the tax liability rises by 50 per cent for those *kolkhoz* members who do not work the prescribed number of days for the *kolkhoz*. There are complex variations and exemptions not worth recounting here, applicable to workers and employees in rural areas and also to urban citizens whose holdings are below 0·15 hectares. (Burmistrov, 1968, p.55ff.)

OTHER REVENUES

These are quite numerous, but the figures in respect of them are hardly ever published. Thus there is what would be called *stamp duty (gosudarstvennaya poshlina)* paid on legal documents, including divorce, registration of birth and deaths, passports, hunting permits and the like. This item of budget revenue also includes payments by enterprises, e.g. to arbitration courts. Under this head also is the nearest Soviet equivalent of an inheritance tax: the public notary charges a maximum of 10 per cent (on sums exceeding 1000 roubles) for 'proof of the right to inherit'. (Burmistrov, 1968, p.82.) By Western standards this is a remarkably low tax.

There are also *local taxes*. These include a species of property tax *(nalog so stroyenii i zemel'naya renta)* charged to co-operatives and individuals, taxes on cars (2·50 roubles per horse-power in big cities less outside them), boats, horses, other livestock (unless the owner pays agricultural tax), tax levied in the *kolkhoz* market in towns, and the so-called self-levy *(samo-oblozheniye)* in rural areas. The latter is subject to a maximum of 2 roubles per family for ordinary *kolkhoz* members and *sovkhoz* employees, but 15 roubles for priests (Burmistrov, 1968, p.103.) Another item which cannot be quantified consists of the payments into the budget by those foreign-trade corporations which make a book-keeping 'profit' out of the conversion of *valuta* into roubles at the official rate of exchange (see Chapter 11). These are not included under the heading 'payments out of profits'. They are listed (without a definite figure) as 'revenues from foreign trade' in a list of miscellaneous revenues by V. Garbuzov in presenting his budget for 1975.

Stated proportions (sometimes 100 per cent) of various revenues are retained by republics and local soviets. The share retained by republics varies, being highest in Central Asia.

Referring back to Table 17 it is worth remarking that miscellaneous items of revenue add up to a high total. Taking the 1973 figures as an example, the total of the itemized revenues is 41·7 milliard roubles short of the total. It would appear from the table that almost all of this gap consists of payments from the economy and not from individuals. The magnitude of this remainder is something of a mystery. Could it possibly include some form of advance from the banking system?

However, the uncertainties about the meaning of budget revenue are insignificant compared with the problems of interpreting expenditures. to which we will now turn.

EXPENDITURE PATTERN

The basic data are as in Table 20.

Table 20

		1940	1965	1973	1978
TOTAL		17·4	101·6	184·0	260·2
of which:	National economy	5·8	44·9	91·3	141·3
	Social-cultural	4·1	38·2	67·3	89·1
	Defence	5·7	12·8	17·9	17·2
	Administration	0·7	1·3	1·9	2·3
	Other	1·1	4·4	5·6	10·3

(*Source*: *NKh* 1973. p.780. and *NKh*, 1978. p.533.)

In the analysis that follows, I intend only to inquire into items either peculiarly Soviet or just peculiar – or unusual. For this reason there will be very little discussion of *social-cultural expenditures*. Important though these are, they are largely self-explanatory. Therefore the very extensive evidence about the exact sums spent on primary education, universities, physical culture, maternity benefit and so on will not be presented here. The only item which causes some problems is 'Science' *(nauka)*, which reached 7·5 milliard roubles in 1973, and which covers the budget of the Academy of Science and many other research institutes financed out of central and republican funds. (If non-budgetary financing is included, the total was 15·7 milliards *NKh*, 1973, p.780.) Many Western analysts believe that some sizeable portion of this budgetary item is of military significance, but it also includes many things of unmistakably civilian character, from higher mathematics to archaeology. A new 'social' item for 1975 is the income supplement to families with a low *per-capita* income, mentioned in Chapter 8; the total provided in 1975 was 1·8 milliard roubles. (Garbuzov, 1974, p.21.)

ALLOCATION TO THE NATIONAL ECONOMY

This, the biggest item in the budget is also the one which causes the biggest headaches to students of Soviet finance. The reason is the lack of information and of definitions. In principle one can divide the total in two ways: by *sector* (e.g. agriculture, transport, etc.) or by *type of expenditure* (e.g. investment, increase in working capital). Either method leaves one with numerous question-marks. Take as an example the following statement: 'for the financing of industry in

1975 there will be provided 110·7 milliard roubles, from the budget, own resources and bank credit'. (Garbuzov, 1974, p.9.) How much from the budget? We do not know. But even when there was a breakdown of *budgetary* grants by sector, there was always a sizeable unexplained residual.

The same is true of expenditure by type. The data in Table 21 were provided by a Soviet source:

Table 21

	Per cent of total allocations*
Investment	34·19
Construction services	0·13
Increase in working capital	3·40
Capital repairs	2·05
Subsidies and losses	0·88
Operational expenditures	9·34
Other expenditures	50·30
Bonuses and loans	0·25

(*Source*: Yevdokimov, 1974, p.141, with acknowledgments to W. Lee of G.E.C., Washington, for the reference. Figures probably relate to 1973.)

*Figures relate to *khozraschet* activities, and omit some minor grants to so-called 'budgetary institutions', i.e. those maintained fully out of public funds. The figures in the original add up to a little more than 100, presumably owing to rounding.

The major part of 'subsidies', as we shall see, are within 'other expenditures'. 'Capital repairs' presumably is the budgetary contribution to an item which ought to be financed out of enterprise depreciation funds, and also looks like a *de facto* subsidy. 'Operational expenditures' are defined by the source as covering such items as land melioration, fabrication of prototypes and costs of icebreakers. It may also include what are sometimes called *puskovyye raskhody*, starting-up expenses, incurred between the formal completion of an investment project and the bringing of the plant into full operation.

But obviously one is struck by the size of the item 'other expenditures'. These certainly include the following, listed by the above source:

> State material reserves
> Foreign trade
> Wage adjustments *(upordyadocheniye)*
> Agricultural procurement price subsidies
> 'Frozen' construction sites.

The last item is self-explanatory. The agricultural subsidies (to cover losses on livestock products) might be roughly estimated at 18 milliard roubles in 1973, or over a third of 'other expenditures' (see Chapter

7 for evidence on this subsidy). 'Wage adjustments' may not occur in every year: these are a wage subsidy paid to enterprises to cover extra expenditures on wages if a decree increasing them is issued during an annual plan period. The foreign trade item is presumably the obverse of the one already noted under revenue: this must be the book-keeping loss of foreign trade enterprises arising out of the conversion of their deals into roubles at the official rate. Other expenses on trade *may* be involved. Finally, 'state material reserves' would clearly cover acquisition by the centre of reserve stocks, for instance of grain or copper.

In 1973, applying the above percentages, 'other expenditures' amounted to just under 46 milliard roubles. Subtracting estimated agricultural subsidies still leaves 28 milliards. Presumably the biggest component of this must be 'state material reserves', and this still leaves one perplexed: it is simply too big. One has only to compare the entire defence budget, 17·9 milliards. Such reasoning has led those who regard the declared level of Soviet military expenditure with scepticism to put forward the hypothesis that some military hardware is paid for out of 'allocations to the national economy', under 'state material reserves'. This may well not be so. But if so little information is provided as to the breakdown of allocations to the national economy (or of military expenditure), such suspicions are inevitably generated.

DEFENCE

A full account of the many controversies on this theme would take us too far afield. The fact seems to be that Soviet procurement of modern weapons has been accelerating, and accelerating far more rapidly than the size of the defence budget. Or, to put it another way, if the Soviets have achieved parity with the United States, they have done so with incredibly little expenditure: compare the Soviet military budget of 17 or so milliard roubles with the US expenditure of six times as many dollars. Even allowing for the much higher rates of pay of US servicemen, it seems odd. Various ideas have been mooted:

(a) The Soviet defence industries, enjoying high priority, are superbly efficient and low-cost; hence the low rouble total.
(b) These industries sell their products at artificially low, subsidized prices, with the object of concealing the real level of expenditure, so that the rouble total understates the real burden of defence.
(c) There is massive expenditure hidden elsewhere in the budget (including science and allocations to the national economy, particularly the latter, plus internal security troops financed out of the Ministry of the Interior vote).
(d) It's all lies anyway (on this interpretation, a nuclear submarine could be in the budget under the heading of aid to lonely mothers).

Apart from rejecting (d), it seems proper to refrain from comment, in the absence of hard data as to just what is covered by the budget vote. But this implies that we remain very uncertain about the real burden of military expenditure to the Soviet economy.

ADMINISTRATION AND POLICE

The small total in Table 21 for administration also includes justice. It covers government offices at all levels, including, of course, *local* government. It does not include economic management, below the level of a ministerial division *(glavk)*. Neither does it include the *Ministry of the Interior* or the *KGB,* which seem to have been financed separately, and must now be the largest item in the residual 'other expenditures' of the budget. The only evidence is for rather remote years when, in his budget speech in 1948, the Finance Minister gave the Interior and Security vote (MVD and MGB) as well as administration expenditures. It was then twice as large as administration. In more recent years there has been silence.

THE BUDGET SURPLUS

All peacetime budgets in living memory have shown a surplus. It is explained that this is devoted to increasing the resources of the banking system, which are used for credits. But it does not follow that the increase in the total volume of credits is equal to the budget surpluses, as was at one time thought. Thus the volume of short-term credits increased by almost 14 billion roubles, of long-term credits by a further 4·8 billion roubles, in the year 1973, when the budget surplus was only 3·8 milliards. (*NKh*, 1973, pp.778, 782.) It must, however, be recalled that the increment in savings bank deposits is also used as a basis for short-term credit, and that this increment was almost 7·9 milliard roubles in 1973.

REPUBLICAN AND LOCAL BUDGETS

The respective shares of the all-union and republican budgets change over time. The figures show that in 1940 75·8 per cent of all expenditure was all-union; the figure was 41·2 per cent in 1960, and 52·2 per cent in 1973. In practice the chief cause of the differences is to be found in the item allocation to the national economy; when many industrial ministries were union-republican, and even more when (as in 1960) most enterprises were subordinate to *sovnarkhozy* which formally came under republics, the republican percentage rose, but it has now fallen. This to some extent reflects the degree of centralization, though it must be borne in mind that union-republican ministries sometimes are merely the conduit for central orders. Most social service expenditures are financed by republican budgets. All defence expenditure is central. Republican budgets include the local-authority budgets in their area.

THE FINANCING OF CAPITAL INVESTMENTS

The details that follow are designed to assist the reader of a typical Soviet budget speech or similar document. Evidence is often incomplete, and definitions can be confusing. Here as elsewhere the figures often relate to estimates or plans, less often to the actual outcome. Another source of doubt relates to prices: thus a plan may be expressed in one set of prices, the fulfilment data perhaps in another, and this is not made clear. For example, the five-year plan for the period 1971–5 specified a total value of investments in the five years of 501 milliard roubles. Suppose the sum of reported expenditures were 501 milliards. It may have been affected in some unknown way by changes in prices of machinery and construction, which occurred in 1973. Sometimes the figures are in *smetnyye tseny* (cost-estimate prices), whereas expenditures have to be adjusted to take into account any differences between these and actual prices. One therefore needs care in comparing figures given by different sources.

There are three kinds of figures quoted. It may be convenient to give them for 1975, because all three are available for that plan year (Table 22).

Table 22

	(milliard roubles)
Total investments	113·0
State investments	98·6
Centralized investments	85·4
(of which: budget-financed: 'over 40·0')	

(*Source*: Garbuzov, 1974b, p.15.)

Total investments include those by *kolkhozy* (out of their own resources and financed by bank credit) and also individual investments in housing. These are excluded from *state* investments. *Centralized* investments are only those state investments included in the central investment plan. Therefore there were 13·2 milliard roubles of decentralized state investments. Over 40 milliard roubles of budgetary funds were devoted to centralized investments, but some smaller sum (not given) was added to finance decentralized investments, though the bulk of these were financed out of the enterprises' own resources.

Non-budgetary financing in the state sector predominantly comes from two sources: retained profits and the amortization (depreciation) fund. Note that the major part of *centralized* investments were financed from these sources, which means that enterprises were allowed to retain funds which were earmarked for projects included in the central plan. Therefore an increase in the scale of self-financing does not necessarily indicate that management has any greater power in deciding what to invest in. Part of both the profit and the amortization fund may be redistributed by the ministry (or an *obyedineniye*) to other enterprises without it passing through the state budget.

Decentralized investments are financed in a variety of ways, one of the most important being that part of retained profits which is allocated to the investment ('development of production') fund and to the welfare fund in the manner described in Chapter 4. These funds amounted respectively to 3·9 and 1·7 milliard roubles in 1973 (*NKh*, 1973, p.776). The latter is used in large part for investment in housing. Bank credits may also be used, and this could increase somewhat as a result of a decree published in *Pravda* on 6 January 1977, in which *obyedineniya* and enterprises are permitted to make additional investments for expanding production of consumers' goods, this to be financed by bank credit for up to six years. The credits are to be repaid out of the investment fund, reinforced when necessary by sums out of profits and/or by 50 per cent of the turnover tax yielded by additional production.

There are other less important sources of investment finance: the proceeds of sales of surplus equipment, of additional production of consumers' goods out of by-products, and so on.

In the 1965 reform speeches it was stated that bank credits would play a major role in investment finance. The argument was that investment money is free of charge to its recipients, non-returnable, and that this led to over-application for such funds. As we have seen, a capital charge was introduced, so one cannot say that investment funds are free any more. However, grants, or 'own resources' still provide the bulk of investment finance. The role of credit is still quite small. Thus in 1973 the total volume of long-term credits to the entire state sector of the economy increased by 2·8 milliard roubles (*NKh*, 1973, p.782.) Nearly 3·0 milliards of long-term credits were granted to *kolkhozy*, however (*ibid*, p.784). The banking system is in any case much more adjusted to its dual role of paying agent and 'financial policeman' than as an authority able to decide between applications for long-term investment credits. In Hungary, for instance, the role of interest-bearing credits in investment finance is vastly greater, but this goes with a greater autonomy (*vis-à-vis* the central planners) both of interprise management and (though within strict limits) of the investment bank.

Interest on these credits is very low. According to the authoritative economist P. Bunich, they are still a mere 0·5 per cent calculated on the amount not yet repaid, which Bunich (*Kom*, 1972, No. 15, p.104) properly describes as 'insignificant'. He contrasts it with the 6 per cent capital charge payable by enterprises, which he considers in its turn far too low. Another author, Massarygin (1974, p.24), considers that the 'average social effectiveness of (capital) expenditures is represented by a rate of return of 14 per cent', though he argues that one should reduce this to a capital (and credits) charge of 8 per cent, so as to leave a '*khozraschet* stimulus' to enterprises, i.e. presumably some additional retained profit.

As we can see, the role of *private* savings in financing investments is very small. Apart from savings bank deposits and purchases of premium bonds, the main contribution is in the field of private and cooperative housing.

THE BANKS, SHORT-TERM CREDITS, MONEY SUPPLY

We have already noted in Chapter 3 the role of the State Bank as a financial control agency. All but the smallest payments have to be made by cheque through the Bank, which has the duty of monitoring these payments and to stop those which are in breach of rules (e.g. excess payments to labour, prices higher than official ones, use of earmarked funds for unauthorized purposes, etc.). The bulk of investment funds are concentrated in *Stroybank* (literally 'Construction bank'), and are doled out as needed to cover investment expenditures.

The State Bank is also the bank of issue, but there is no information about the amount of money in circulation. Presumably the printing presses respond to demand for paper money and coins, which arises in the main from the requirement to pay workers and employees in cash. The one possible unexpected cause for a rise in demand for cash would be a run on the savings banks. This could be serious: the total amount of these deposits in 1973 was 68,660 million roubles (plus a small amount, 156 millions, in the State Bank) (*NKh*, 1973, p.634). Since 1963 the savings banks are operated under the control of the State Bank (Gerashchenko, 1970, p.204).

A vital function of the State Bank is to provide short-term credits for enterprises so as to help to finance the inevitable gap between incurring expenditure and receiving payment, and also stocks. Part of this gap is covered by the enterprises' own resources, and credits in fact cover a little less than half of the total needs for working capital. (Titarev, *PKh*, 1974, No. 1, p.134.) Outstanding credits at the end of 1973 were 134·7 milliard roubles, compared with 68·0 milliard roubles in 1965. (*NKh*, 1973, p.783. This also shows a breakdown by type. Note that the total sums issued as credits during the year very greatly exceed the above sums, but most are repaid in the course of the year and then re-issued.) These credits are formally granted against the security of material assets or on the basis of payments due, and their volume and purpose are planned ·to correspond to the planned flows of goods and to the financial counterpart of centralized control over management, an important element of *kontrol' rublyom*, by the rouble.

The chief criticism levied against short-term credits relates to their 'automatism'. That is to say, they cover any expenditures which seem legitimate and do not conflict with the plan, even if the logic of 'control by the rouble' is thereby violated (e.g. Massarygin, 1974, p.72.) The most commonly cited example relates to the production of unwanted goods, Suppose that a factory has produced a poor-quality and therefore unsaleable cloth. It is part of a plan in square metres, and so any credits necessary to pay its workers and suppliers will be obtained. True, the wholesalers may refuse to accept the cloth, whereupon there will be a problem: how to repay the credit. But, for reasons amply discussed earlier (sellers' market, etc.), the wholesaler may well receive and pay for the cloth. The customer may refuse to buy. But the unsaleable cloth can then act as the collateral for a credit to the trading organs, which can be carried over indefinitely. The planning organs are aware of this weakness, and it must be stressed that, if unsaleable goods are produced on a sufficient scale, the resulting effect on the volume of short-term credits outstanding can give rise to inquiry, and to orders to desist from producing the items in question (see also Chapter 10).

Interest rates on short-term credits vary somewhat according to who borrows and for what purpose. They are always very low. A critic has pointed out that, while interest rates on many forms of credit were raised from 1·7 per cent to 2·2 per cent in recent years (and charged to profits instead of against costs), it is always cheaper for the enterprise to borrow than to use its own resources, because own working capital usually pays a 6 per cent capital charge, while no charge is payable on borrowed working capital until the credit is repaid. (Massarygin, 1974, pp.23, 24.) Other rates charged for short-term credits cited by this source include 2 per cent on credits to trading organs (4 per cent if repayment is delayed), 3 per cent (5 per cent) to *sovkhozy* and 1 per cent (3 per cent) to *kolkhozy;* the Bank now makes advances against future deliveries to *kolkhozy* in the form of a credit; these advances were made before 1966 by the procurement organs. (Massarygin, 1974, pp.115, 117.)

The authorities are conscious of the need to restrict credit, as a means of holding back demand from enterprises for material resources. This reinforces the materials allocation scheme, which 'rations' these resources administratively. However, one cannot expect credit restriction to achieve the desired result if the plan itself is overambitious, i.e. if it gives rise to greater demand for inputs than can in fact be provided. The experience of Poland showed that, if bank credits are denied when the plan targets in fact require them, an equivalent increase occurs in involuntary credits by suppliers; payments are delayed (see Podolski, 1972.) No doubt the same can happen in the USSR also. This is a point worth recalling, since the official rules (since the credit reform of 1931) do nót allow credits to be given by one enterprise to another; the Bank alone can do so. Yet by delaying payment one is in fact receiving, without appearing to do so, a short-term credit from one's supplier. (Garvy, 1966, pp.67–86.)

The problems with *Stroybank* are principally of three kinds. One is linked with the issue, already discussed, of payments for uncompleted work; financial disciplinary measures are insufficiently stringent to compel the construction industry to hand over completed buildings on schedule; yet pressure to hand over too often results in the claim that incomplete work is in fact completed, a recurrent theme in critical and satirical literature. Secondly, cost estimates are very often below actual cost (Garbuzov, 1974, p.17), and this can create disequilibrium between the financial resources available and the amounts actually needed. Thirdly, the process of doling out investment money is frequently inconsistent with, and causes delay in, building and installation work. Complaints are common that the sums available each year are such that the process is slowed down – to which the minister's reply is to blame the constant rise in unfinished construction on the tendency to scatter investment resources over too many projects, starting too many new ones before old ones can be completed. (Garbuzov, 1974, p.16 and also see Chapter 6.)

One can see in this a clumsy attempt to cope with excess investment demand by a species of monetary control. Thus it would seem that the total resources tend to be overstretched: to finish all that has been started requires more building materials and labour than are in fact available. The total of investment in money terms is supposed to be balanced by the investment goods available, and, insofar as it is the case, the result is that lack of money holds back the volume of investment, brings it into line with the possible. This may seem to be a desirable and effective form of monetary control. In practice, however, there must inevitably be numerous cases of what might be called micro-mismatch. Thus, to give an example, a project half-finished, in an area where the needed materials and labour *do* happen to be available, is held up because of lack of funds. In other words, the process of rationing investment cash and the process of allocating investment resources are very difficult to keep in conformity with one another, when one considers not macro-magnitudes but operational micro-detail.

This may well be part of the cost of overcentralization. It is just one more aspect of the very great difficulty of detailed, micro-balancing *(uvyazka)* of production, allocation, labour and finance, applied in this instance particularly to the investment process, a process which of its nature has to deal with the future and is affected by choice of and change in technique. No doubt existing procedures can be improved, but these problems are likely to persist.

INFLATIONARY PRESSURES

Is the USSR inflation-proof? How does one measure the degree of inflation, if any?

One could argue that the Soviet system facilitates the prevention of inflation, or even that, if it functioned properly, inflation would be impossible. We have seen that incomes are under tight control, especially effective being the 'wages fund' limitation on overpayment by enterprises and institutions. Prices are fixed by state organs. The availability of consumers' goods and services is planned, and (except in the case of harvest variations) reasonably predictable. Therefore the planning organs can consciously link the total income of the population with the volume of goods and services at prices which they determine. The institutional means of ensuring balance plainly exist. It may also be argued that, while there were large price rises in the thirties and in the first postwar years, retail prices were cut repeatedly in the period 1948–54, and have remained stable. The official price index for the period 1962–75 shows an increase of precisely zero per cent, the increases in certain prices (liquor, cars, jewellery, for instance) being balanced by reduction of others.

Turning now to producers' goods, it is clear that demand is planned demand, that it is the task of the planning organs to ensure that output plans are in conformity with input availabilities. The mere possession of liquid bank balances by enterprises does not entitle them to obtain inputs: in most instances, as we have seen, this requires an allocation certificate. Prices are fixed by the state. Again, it follows that a balanced plan excludes inflation. If, it may be argued, imbalances none the less occur (and no Soviet economist would deny that they do), this can only be due to errors in planning. It would presumably be argued that if a manager requires dyestuffs or screws and cannot get them, this is a regrettable example of malfunctioning of the supply system, but inflation it is not.

There has been a tendency for (wholesale) prices to rise in recent years, due partly to rising costs (especially labour costs) and partly to the decision to increase profit margins. This has affected different products very unequally. Thus in 1967 coal prices were increased by 80 per cent. However, the overall index of wholesale prices is fairly stable, by Western standards very stable: an increase by 9 per cent on average in the year 1967, using indices excluding turnover tax, has been followed by a fractional fall in 1973. (*NKh*, 1973, p.250.) The overall rise in the twenty years 1955–75, if the official index is to be believed, is less than 12 per cent.

It must be added that the USSR can be insulated from imported inflation, because, as we shall see in Chapter 10, there is no automatic link between internal and foreign-trade prices. If the price of imported wheat goes up by 100 per cent, or of exported oil by 300 per cent, this need make no difference at all to domestic prices of the items in question; the necessary book-keeping adjustments will be taken care of in the settlements with the foreign trade corporations, and it will all be absorbed by the state budget.

The Soviet Union is better able to cope with imported inflation than her smaller partners in Comecon. A country such as Hungary or Poland is far more dependent on foreign trade, and therefore there is much greater interest in maintaining some coherent relationship between domestic and foreign-trade prices. But we will leave this problem aside for the moment.

What, then, is the evidence which points to the existence of inflationary pressures?

Let us examine the consumers' goods and retail trade sectors first. There are shortages, a sellers' market. That is to say, demand tends often to exceed supply, though this excess is very unequally distributed between areas and commodities. Indeed there are excess stocks of some items.

A way of measuring excess demand is to observe free market prices. These apply only to foodstuffs, and one must allow, in interpreting them, for two other factors. One is that *kolkhoz* market produce is often of better quality (vegetables especially). The other is that peasants tend to bring to market those items for which the free-market price is particularly high, a fact which naturally affects the product weighting. None the less, the disparity is both large and increasing. Of late it has had to be roughly calculated from indirect evidence. In Table 23 the official data are shown in the first two lines, the third line is derived from them:

Table 23   *Share of free market in total trade in food*, per cent*

	1950	1965	1970	1973	1978
In actual prices of sale	28·7	10·0	8·5	7·9	8·8
At official retail prices	27·6	7·3	5·5	4·8	4·4
Free market prices (official prices=100)	104·0	137·0	154·5	164·5	200·0

*Comparable items (i.e. presumably excluding bread, for instance).
(*Source*: NKh, 1973, p.652, and NKh, 1978. p.433.)

This unmistakably shows that the disparity between official and free prices has been rising, an indication of concealed inflation, or excess demand. The very substantial rise in savings bank deposits, larger than planned or expected, may be used as further evidence of frustrated purchasing power.

One must also express some scepticism about the official index of retail prices. This scepticism is based upon the fact, well known in all countries where price control exists, that one can evade it by introducing new models at higher prices. To take a British example, suppose there were a price freeze imposed on women's dresses, or restaurant meals. A new dress, or a new dish, is then introduced at a price, respectively, of £15 and £2. Let us further imagine that dresses at £12 and a dish at £1.50 are no longer provided. The new and higher-priced items *may* be genuinely better-quality, *may* accord better with consumer demand. If they are, and do, then we would not consider that prices have risen. If, however, demand for the lower-priced variant is frustrated, if the object is to increase prices while pretending not to have done so, then naturally an official index which claims that prices are unaltered is misleading.

It may be objected that new products, often at higher prices, are being introduced in all countries, and that the distortion, insofar as it exists, is universal. There is indeed no perfect way, anywhere, to measure the change over time in price and volume of a rapidly changing product mix, and we will return to this theme in Chapter 12. The point, however, is that the typical Western firm in normal circumstances has no interest in tampering with price indices or evading (usually non-existent) price controls. It is interested in profits. The effect of this on the calculation by official statisticians of a price index is random. Whereas not only are Soviet managers bound by officially imposed prices, but they are also interested in increasing the gross value of their sales. There is also a sellers' market. So the opportunity to shift to a higher-priced variant exists, and the motivation too. Unfortunately, it is, in the nature of things, quite impossible to measure the resultant upward price drift.

There are also some officially encouraged and sanctioned disguised price increases. The best-known example is the replacement of cheaper brands of vodka by a 'new' brand which costs a rouble more, in 1974.

All this implies that the retail price index must have risen since 1962 by more than the officially claimed zero per cent, but we do not know by how much.

Turning now to producers' goods and investment, we have already noted repeatedly the tendency for demand for industrial and construction materials and components to exceed supply, with delays in completions the inevitable result. The Minister of Finance annually deplores the increase in 'uncompleted construction'. The use of *tolkachi*, the emergence of black or grey markets and of informal barter, are evidence of supply difficulties. Here again the official price index is incredible. The index for 'machinery and metal-working' shows a downward tendency, and yet over and over again Soviet critics point out that new machines are dearer, sometimes very much dearer, than the ones they replace. This, as will be argued in Chapter 12, affects the volume index as well as the price index. One has frankly to say that the official index for machinery, which shows a price fall of 36 per cent from 1955 to 1973, is just not credible (especially in the face of considerable increases in prices of metals and fuel, and in labour costs).

The evidence implies that prices *have* moved upwards, and that many phenomena of suppressed inflation would seem to be present. One is left with the important question: why?

The following reasons suggest themselves.

Taking the consumers' goods sector first, there is strong evidence both of a tendency for wages to rise a little faster than planned and for output of consumers' goods to rise slower than planned. For example, the five-year plan for the period 1966–70 envisaged a rise of 20 per cent in average wages. The 'actual' was 26 per cent. It is true that, as we have seen, the 1971–5 wages plan was slightly under-fulfilled. However, the consumers' goods output plan was underful-filled by more than this. Average wages increased by 20 per cent against a plan of 22·4 per cent. Consumers' goods output was planned to rise by 48·6 per cent, the 'actual' was 37 per cent, and agriculture was also below plan (see plan documents, and *Pravda,* 1 February 1976). The aim of ensuring a closer balance between supply and demand, by increasing the former faster than the latter, proved unreal-isable. But prices were kept nominally stable, by political decision.

Then, apart from the question of macro-balance between demand for and supply of consumers' goods and services, there are the very marked imbalances affecting particular goods. Sometimes these are due to planning errors, unresponsiveness of production to demand. Sometimes price-inflexibility may be 'blamed'. The obvious example of the latter is the case of the heavily subsidized retail price of meat, already referred to in Chapter 7. If income-elasticity for a product is high, and incomes rise, then, unless supply response is equal to rising demand, there is bound to be serious shortage if price relativities are unaltered. Matters are exacerbated in some cases by the fact that disguised price increases occur primarily in items with a complex and multiple product mix. Thus prices for clothing and crockery can drift upwards, price increases of milk or pork chops are harder to disguise (though some dilution of quality can occur). The effect, naturally, is shortage, with all the ancillary phenomena: under-the-counter sales, bribery, high free-market prices and so on.

One has to add a general observation: even if the planning system were more efficient than it is today, micro-balance and centralized decision making cannot be expected to coexist. The reason is contained in the analysis in earlier chapters. The centre can only issue orders in aggregated terms. Unless micro-balance can be assured by some sort of market mechanism (i.e. by the direct or indirect influence of demand on supply, bypassing in micro-questions the central planning mechanism), imbalances are bound to occur. The supply of red blouses in Tashkent or a small size of women's brown shoes in Novosibirsk cannot be ensured by *central* orders. But, with resources fully stretched and with no spare capacity, adjustments to identified changes in demand (or to the discovery that it does not correspond to expectations) are difficult to make.

Consequently, even if total demand and total supply were in equilibrium, micro-imbalances would be inevitable. Let me illustrate this with an example. Suppose that, in London or in New York, the total supply of restaurant places at dinner-time exactly equalled the average daily demand for them. We may be sure that there would be long lines of customers in some places, empty tables in others. Common sense would tell one that a precondition of the customers' freedom of choice of meals is that there be spare capacity.

This argument has been well and strongly put by the Hungarian economist Janos Kornai. He argues that it should always be difficult to sell. Otherwise the familiar defects of a sellers' market will show themselves (Kornai, 1971b.)

The same point can be made with regard to producers' goods. If total demand equalled total supply, some shortages would still be highly probable. Thus for instance even if total output of spare parts equalled total demand for them (which it does not), there could still be a shortage of carburettors, and it would be no consolation to the individual who needed them to know that there is overabundant supply of radiator-caps and piston-rings.

But there is strong evidence, already presented in Chapter 6, that, apart from micro-imbalances, the whole investment plan exceeds the limits of the feasible. The reasons relate to the 'centralized pluralist' model: there are many pressure groups making demands, many local and ministerial chiefs ordering a start to be made on new construction, in the hope of getting more money and materials in order to complete the project in due course. It is abundantly clear, firstly, that the steps taken to discourage over-investment by economic means have been ineffective. As we have seen, capital charges are low and are incorporated into the price structure. Secondly, the task of the central planning organs to cut down the applications for investment resources to match the material resources available is not carried out sufficiently ruthlessly. Cuts are made, of course, but the final plan is still too strained. In some years it may be that unexpected increases in military procurements complicate matters: this would be partly the consequence of external factors, such as technical achievements in weaponry in the United States, and partly to pressure from the military. Demands arise from many quarters: agriculture, retail trade, various industries, regions, republics. There is here some parallel with 'excess demand' which, in the West, causes or compels the state to increase public expenditure and to print some of the money needed to cover them. And finally, taut plans are consciously preferred. (See percipient article by Keren, in *Soviet Studies,* July 1976.)

This said, it must be admitted that the Soviet-type system does have stronger weapons than we have to restrain inflationary pressures. These weapons are, however, rather costly in terms of micro-efficiency, for they include price and wage controls, and quantitative allocations, which generate many of the bureaucratic deformations which we have been discussing in earlier chapters. Inflation also causes serious deformations, as Western experience abundantly shows. There is a species of trade-off between economically inefficient controls and economically destructive inflation. Soviet experience also shows us that some of these controls are only partially effective as an anti-inflationary device, and also that to prevent the organized emergence of sectional interests requires the political monopoly of the party, within which, none the less, sectional interests can still find some expression.

Again, there are no simple solutions.

Inflationary pressures have increased. By 1978 free-market prices rose to *double* the official prices of goods, a reliable indicator of greater food shortage. Shortages of many manufactures became more common. Brezhnev in his speech (28 November 1979) mentioned needles, thread, the simplest medicines, babies' diapers, toothbrushes, toothpaste. There have been official admissions of macro as well as micro imbalances between supply and demand: 'savings bank deposits have almost trebled in eight years, and the incomes of the population increase much faster than the supply of goods and services' (*Pravda* editorial, 27 July 1979).

Recent developments in public finance include a reduction in rental ('fixed') payments out of profits, and an unexplained increase in 1979 in the expenditure residual.

CHAPTER 10

TRADE

This chapter divides itself into two parts: internal and external trade. Under the first of these headings it seems proper and convenient also to consider consumer demand and living standards generally.

INTERNAL TRADE: WHOLESALE AND RETAIL ORGANS

In the present chapter, we shall be concerned almost wholly with consumers' goods. As we have seen, most producers' goods are subject to allocation, and the role of wholesale trade in this field is still small.

Wholesale (*optovaya*) as well as retail (*roznichnaya*) trade is, in principle, under the Ministry of (internal) Trade. Before 1953 wholesalers' functions were carried out by the disposals (*sbyt*) organs of the producing ministries, which operated about 2,000 wholesaling centres (*bazy*). In subsequent years there was some decentralization to republican ministries, also to city soviets. In fact, going too far, it was decided in 1958 to abolish the all-union Ministry of Trade, transferring the remaining central functions to the chief department of inter-republican deliveries (*Soyuzglavtorg*) within *Gosplan*. After further organizational changes, the all-union Ministry was revived in 1965, though in this field the republican and local authorities remain important. (Lazarev, 1967, pp.61–77.) However, as we shall see, wholesale trade is still in some organizational confusion.

Retail trade is divided into *state trade* (urban) and *co-operative trade* (rural). Both are guided by the ministary and (mainly) supplied by the state's wholesaling organs, and both are subject to state planning. From most practical standpoints co-operative trade is equivalent to state trade, and its employees are counted as state-employed persons. However, the co-operatives are still formally subject to committees elected by members or 'shareholders' (*payshchiki*), and it has its own central organ, *Tsentrosoyuz*, with republican organs, some of which exercise some wholesaling functions. as will be shown in a moment.

A part of what is called state trade is not under the operational control of the Ministry of Trade. Thus some shops and stores are run by the Ministries of Transport, Timber, Oil, Coal, Non-ferrous Metals, Defence, Health, etc. In some instances this is due to geographical location (e.g. the need to supply workers in remote areas where regular state and co-operative trade is undeveloped), in others to the specialized nature of the trade (e.g. the chemists' shops are under the Ministry of Health, and bookshops and newspaper kiosks under the State Committee on the Press.) In addition there are the so-called ORS *(Otdely Rabochego Snabzheniya*, workers' supply departments), which are subdivisions of productive enterprises which run canteens and also sell a variety of goods to those employed in these enterprises; sometimes these goods are foodstuffs grown on a factory's auxiliary farm. The ORS have a somewhat anomalous status, being subject to orders from the workers' supply 'directorate' *(Glavurs)* of the appropriate ministry, rather than to the director of the enterprise of which it is a part. Turnover plans for ORS are laid down by *oblasti,* or by republican organs in the smaller republics. (Lazarev, 1967, pp.22–3.)

While in large cities the predominance of the Ministry of Trade's network brings coherence to the system, there is criticism of the adverse effect of 'parallelism and duplication' in some small towns. For instance 'in the town of Volkhov, with 50,000 inhabitants, trade is carried on by the ORS of the "October" railway and the local trade organization *(torg)*. Both are of about equal size in the volume of trade turnover and number of outlets. But the existence of two trade organs in the same locality complicates planning, distribution, analysis of demand . . . stands in the way of specialization, causes irrational use of transport. . . .' (Kokushkin, 1969, p.12.) (Apparently no advantages accrue from competition, possibly because both find it easy to sell whatever they have to offer.)

The Ministries of Trade at all-union and republican levels exercise some measure of control over the various ORS, even though they are not within their formal jurisdiction: thus the *Glavurs* of the Ministry of Non-ferrous Metals was told to 'eliminate shortcomings', and there was also an order concerning the 'minimum assortment' of dishes in industrial canteens. (Lazarev, 1967, pp.84–5.)

The 'normal' trade network functions under the direct guidance of the all-union and republican Ministries of Trade. There is a wide variety of organizational forms. State shops, in urban areas, are generally grouped in so-called *torgi,* mostly on *khozraschet* lines; in large cities these specialize in types of goods (e.g. *Tekstilshveytorgi* will run textile and clothing shops) while large *univermagi* (general stores) have a separate *khozraschet* existence. In small towns all the shops could be subject to one *torg*. Catering establishments are combined into *tresty*. There are also a variety of relationships with the republican ministries; mostly these are through local soviets, whose trade departments are under dual subordination, i.e. they owe 'allegiance' both to the local soviet and to their ministry, but some *univermagi* and large *torgi* are directly subordinated to the Ministry. These distinctions, however, need not detain us.

The rural retail co-operatives have upwards of 50 million 'share-holders', and, as already noted, are grouped territorially, with the *Tsentrosoyuz* at their head. While subject to guidance from the appropriate trade ministry and planning organs, the co-operatives are not under the local soviets, which are instructed not to interfere with the co-operatives' autonomy and only to issue 'recommendations' (Lazarev, 1967, pp.31–2.) The 'shareholders' elect local committees, and their representatives elect the next level in the pyramid, all the way up to the *Tsentrosoyuz*. Binding instructions are passed down this pyramid.

Both the Ministry of Trade and the *Tsentrosoyuz* participate in the process of planning the output of consumers' goods and services, together with *Gosplan* and the producing ministries. They collect and pass on the requests *(zayavki)* from the shops, and distribute centrally allocated commodities *(fondy)*. Other functions include the study of consumer requirements, and also 'making proposals to the Ministry of Foreign Trade to import goods which are in demand'. (Lazarev, 1967, p.86.)

A CLOSER LOOK AT WHOLESALE TRADE

But to return to wholesale trade. The Ministry of Trade's role is still challenged or incomplete. The producing ministries exert pressure to reconstitute their disposals *(sbyt)* organs. For example, this was requested by the Ministry of Meat and Dairy Produce (without success) and by the footwear *glavk* of the Ministry of Light Industry of the RSFSR (for a time successfully). The comments of a Soviet critic bring to light the important principle involved. He contrasted the behaviour of the footwear *baza* before and after its transfer back to the producing ministry: 'before, these *bazy* partially checked on the quality of the footwear . . . returned some for alteration, levied fines, etc. Now these *bazy* are a species of storage-places for the factories, with the duty of receiving the products, and not to insist on the production of high-quality footwear.' (Orlov and Shimansky, 1970, p.95.)

Evidently the point at issue is that wholesaling organs integrally linked with *trade* are more likely to reflect the requirements of the final purchaser, more often reject sub-standard or unwanted goods, than would wholesalers controlled by the producing ministry, even though, as the author does not fail to point out, 'so far this barrier to defective goods is not very reliable: low-quality goods still reach the shelves'. (Orlov and Shimansky, 1970, p.95.)

Wholesaling is even more subject to duplication and parallelism than is retail trade. There is, firstly, the division between all-union and republican lines of responsibility. Under conditions in which production is very unevenly distributed between republics, 'some wholesaling organs have become obstacles to the normal circulation of goods between republics. They often show 'commodity-fear', refuse goods that are in demand, take up 'localist' positions on a number of questions, hold up deliveries of goods to other republics or send them a poor assortment.' (Orlov and Shimansky, 1970, p.96.) ('Commodity-fear' *(tovaroboyazn')* is a term which means either aversion to risk or not wanting to take the trouble to handle goods in very heavy demand.) Here we see the familiar problem of regional powers: any regional (republican) authority knows best the needs of its own territory, shows insufficient responsibility for those outside its own borders. Yet the concentration of control over trade at all-union levels has its own disadvantages (remoteness, excessive aggregation, etc.).

Secondly, the wholesaling organs tend to see their function as 'distributional' rather than 'commercial', to cite the same Soviet critic. (Orlov and Shimansky, 1970, p.96.) Too often they fail to study or reflect demand, or to exercise pressure on producers. Examples cited included soap and margarine. In both instances the trade organs over-ordered, and industry over-supplied, in relation to demand, failing to learn from experience. The wholesaling organs of the Ministry of Trade bear no responsibility, since their requests *(zayavki)* to industry do not constitute contractual documents. (Tyukov, 1969, p.12.) We shall see that there are other and perhaps weightier reasons why trade organs in general fail to exercise their functions in the desired manner.

Thirdly, despite efforts to rationalize the system of wholesaling, there are a number of mutually unconnected organs involved. Thus *Tsentrosoyuz* and its RSFSR and Ukrainian organs supply consumer durables and some other items to co-operative shops, with their wholesaling *bazy* located in towns in which the republican Ministry of Trade has *bazy* for identical products. Some of the producing ministries have also retained, despite everything, their own wholesaling functions, covering such items as bread, vodka, milk, wine, mineral waters and vegetable oil. (Orlov and Shimansky, 1970, p.98.) In addition, those ministries which operate extensive chains of retail stores (e.g. Transport) maintain their own wholesale *bazy*.

Fourthly, there is 'extreme shortage' of storage space and of modern equipment, and lack of facilities and materials for packaging. The result of all this is that the major part of stocks are held not in wholesale but in retail trade, though this too suffers from the same shortages, and has to devote many thousands of man and woman-years to sorting and packaging, almost all by hand. (Orlov and Shimansky, 1970, pp.97 and 99.)

One also has the impression that all trade activities are affected by the long neglect of this sector, i.e. by the priority of 'production' as against distribution. By affecting status, esteem, salaries, career prospects, this has discouraged able individuals from entering this sector of the economy. This, plus lack of the spur of competition, and the chronic sellers' market, may have at least as much to answer for as merely organizational deficiencies. A further analysis of these problems will follow later in this chapter.

THE PROBLEMS OF RETAIL TRADE

Retail trade suffers from low priority also. Much has been said and written in recent years about the importance of the services sectors, and trade in particular, and the need to raise the status of the employees has been recognized. The number of trade and catering establishments, and of those engaged in them, has greatly increased, as a glance at any statistical annual will show. So has the value and volume of sales.

Table 24   *State and co-operative trade, including catering*

	1950	1960	1970	1978
Number of shops (000)*	298·4	413·0	500·0	695·9
Number of catering establishments (000)	95·4	147·2	237·3	292·1
Numbers employed (000)**	1,967	3,295	5,746	7,091
Value of turnover (millions of roubles)	35,958	78,555	155,208	241,300

(*Source*: *NKh,* 1973, pp.653, 680, and *NKh,* 1978, pp.438, 442, 450–1.)
    *In addition there were and are temporary stalls (*palatki*).
    **In trade *and* catering.

However, average wages remain among the lowest in the USSR, which, in a full-employment economy, must affect the quality of the recruits.

Table 25   *Average wages and salaries*

	(roubles per month)		
	1965	1973	1978
Average wages and salaries, industry	104·2	147·3	176·1
Average wages and salaries, trade, supply, catering	75·2	101·8	124·1

(*Source*: *NKh,* 1973, pp.586–7, *NKh,* 1978, pp.372–3.)

Only Health, Social Security and Art *(isskustvo)* are below trade, and then only just, in the wages 'league table'.

Very numerous reports speak of widespread dishonesty among the underpaid employees, or of a widespread belief that this is so. A curse said to be common among trade employees: 'May you live on your salary'. The location of shops in inconvenient and badly equipped premises is another frequent complaint. The slow spread of self-service supermarkets appears to be due partly to problems of packaging (lack of mechanization and of materials), and partly to the pervasive fear of pilfering by customers. Anyone shopping in the USSR must be struck by the difficulties often experienced in gaining access to goods, and a number of Soviet sources have complained that customers in supermarkets have their purchases rechecked after paying for them, at the exit. The indifference or rudeness of staff is proverbial. There is much criticism also of the standards of service in catering establishments.

Thus far we have stressed such factors as the low quality of personnel and the shortage of space, equipment and other physical 'lacks'. In assessing the performance of Soviet trade, these must, of course, never be overlooked. Thus no amount of incentives or reorganization will provide fresh milk if there is nowhere to keep it cool, and there will be a line of customers waiting even for goods in ample supply if there are not enough shops, and many authors do point out that turnover has increased faster than the number of shops and salesmen. For one of many 'local' analyses, see *Pravda*, 7 July 1975, on the shops shortage of the city of Tomsk. However there are some more strictly economic problems to which we must turn.

The first relates to the very nature of trade. In Marxist tradition, it is an activity both unproductive and in a sense demeaning, which will be replaced under communism by direct distribution of some kind. While Soviet statisticians treat trade as part of national income (see Chapter 12), they do so on the grounds that the bulk of the activity consists of physical handling, sorting and packing of goods, a view challenged by some critics, who point out that most of those engaged in trade do in fact engage in *selling (realizatsiya)*. Furthermore, if the job of selling is under-rated, this can lead to 'neglect of the time spent by the population in obtaining goods, the underestimation of the cost of consumption'. It leads also to inadequate emphasis on the study of the consumer market. (Orlov and Shimansky, 1970, pp.14, 18, 19.)

The second point concerns the nature of *khozraschet* in trade. The revenue of the shops is based upon fixed trade margins (*torgovyye skidki* or *nakidki*, depending on whether they are subtracted from the retail price or added to the wholesale price). As a Soviet critic pointed out, it makes no difference whatever to the retailers whether they are handling goods in heavy demand or not. (Tyukov, 1969, p.65.) Admittedly, goods in heavy demand might seem to be easier to sell, but, under chronic conditions of sellers' market, customers have become accustomed to buying whatever is available. Price controls prevent the (legal) sale of scarce goods at higher prices. Furthermore, because of pressure to reduce costs and margins, revenue is often inadequate to cover costs, especially of perishables. 'Harsh economy in this sector of the economy is in some respects holding back the development of social production, causes considerable losses, increases the costs of consumption. The weakness of its material-technical base causes losses for trade itself'. (Trifonov, 1969, p.26.) Hence the repeated stories about the unwillingness of the trade network to handle fresh vegetables and fruit. 'The sale of some goods is profitable and of others not, often to the detriment of the interests of the purchasers (Sapee'nikov, 1969, p.109.) According to Orlov and Shimansky (1970, p.134), the trade margin for potatoes and vegetables in 1968 was 9 per cent, while actual costs were 11·8 per cent. This situation does not seem to have altered.

The question of profit margins in trade is linked with that of the role of prices and profits in industry. Indeed, one of the proposals made by a critic is that trade could find it worth its while to *reduce* margins on those goods which sell particularly rapidly, to the benefit of the producing enterprises, and conversely to demand higher margins for goods that remain long on the shelves. (Tyukov, 1969, pp. 65–6.) Many problems arise from the reluctance of industry to produce items in heavy demand, either because prices (profits) are too low, or because they do not 'fit' the plan targets. Price flexibility is rare at retail level. One needs permission from the ministry to organize a sale of goods which cannot find purchasers at established prices. The Soviet source quotes with approval the apparently unusual example of Latvia, where, at a time of surplus milk supply, 'instead of returning sour milk for processing, and writing reports, they sell the milk in the shops at half price'. (Tyukov, 1969, p.66.)

The next point concerns plan-indicators. Retail shops and catering establishments receive from above obligatory plans for turnover in roubles, sometimes subdivided into main categories (in the case of catering, usually indicating the value of 'own production', meaning by this meals served, as distinct from sales of bottles of vodka, for instance). As in industry, plans tend to be based on past performance, and bear little relationship to the real possibilities. Pay of personnel is linked with the fulfilment of the turnover plan which fails to interest the individual salesman, 'either in increasing turnover or in the quality of service'. (Kozlov, 1969, p.113.) As rewards are paid for plan-fulfilment and not for increases in turnover, management is interested in low plan-targets. What is 'profitable' from the standpoint of plan-fulfilment statistics may or may not accord with the needs of the customer. In catering, turnover and wages are too closely linked with the cost of dishes served. As it takes equally long to serve a cup of tea or steak and two vegetables, waiters can be impolite if tea is ordered, and they (and their managers, with a monetary plan to fulfil) prefer vodka to beer. *Krokodil* had a cartoon showing a bottle of vodka, with a human face, addressing a teapot (in a catering establishment): 'May I introduce myself; I am in charge here'.

But even if we were to assume that the problems of motivation of salesmen and trade officials did not exist, the fact remains that they can sell only the goods they can obtain, and many problems arise because goods conscientiously ordered by the trade organs do not arrive, either in total or in the desired assortment. One major obstacle is administrative allocation *(fondirovaniye)*, based still on rough percentage increases over past performance. Says the critic:

'Today . . . people buy quality goods and refuse poor ones (let us note that both are often sold at the same price). The producer of dear and poor-quality goods still lives well: he is protected from the difficulties of selling. by allocation, by plans of distribution. . . . Practice shows that he can still safely ignore the demands of the market: the purchasers of his output [i.e. the trade outlets] are designated in advance. Strictly speaking, they cannot even be called purchasers, since one should call by that name those who are free to choose whether to buy. . . . About 60–70 per cent of the staffs of the Ministries of Trade of the USSR, the republics, plus the trading departments of *kray*, *oblasti* and cities, are occupied with documents relating in various ways to allocation *(fondirovaniye)*. . . . The *fondy* . . . depend not on effective demand or its structure, but on the 'baseline' of the previous period, the share of the region in total sales, plus the average increase in the plan period in cases of goods in deficit.' (Orlov and Shimansky, 1970, pp.72–3.)

The critic advocates moving much more boldly towards free trade, direct links, etc.

Despite much renewed emphasis on the role of contracts, especially after a new decree on deliveries issued in 1969, there are still difficulties if contracts conflict with allocation decisions or output plans. However, one deficiency has apparently been corrected, at least in part: before 1969, in many cases the trade organs received goods allocated to them *(po naryadam)* which they did not order and did not want, and they had not even formal redress. The power to refuse to accept goods not ordered, or of the wrong type, has been enhanced. Unfortunately, there are instances still of the trading organs feeling unable to use this power, lest they get nothing (one of the consequences of a sellers' market).

Furthermore, they are under pressure from officials. A Soviet critic pointed out that the fulfilment of the plan of *sales* (as distinct from gross output) does indeed compel the producing enterprise to find customers. However, 'this also concerns many other organs, regional, city, *oblast'*, because their own success indicators depend on the fulfilment of the sales plans. As a result, *trade organs are often subject to very strong pressure* . . . when the question of accepting unwanted or poor-quality goods arises. Therefore at times the process of "sales" becomes a purely formal operation, when goods move from the enterprise's warehouse store-room to the shop's warehouse, and money from one account to another.' (Tkachenko, *EkG*, 1976, No. 1, p.10.)

(Emphasis mine.) This means that the state and party authorities, far from supporting the trade organs, tend to prevent them from refusing unwanted goods, because they – the authorities – are desirous of claiming that productive enterprises in their area have fulfilled their plans.

It is worth recalling that, in principle, consumers' goods in ample supply need not be administratively allocated, and that industrial output plans are supposed to be based on contracts, which 'will go ahead of the plan and determine its content'. (Orlov and Shimansky, 1970, p.84.) These things happen slowly in practice, but it is worth watching developments in this direction. Especially important would be the elimination of global targets imposed from above, in tons, roubles, etc., which still seem to be the rule and which contradict 'production for the customer'.

There exists an 'interdepartmental council for the study of consumer demand' attached to the Ministry of Trade of the USSR, and it began (in 1973) to publish a journal, *Kommerchesky vestnik*. (*Pravda*, 4 May 1975.) But its editor complains of the lack of interest in market research and in advertising, and of the adverse effect of this on production of and demand for new items.

There are, in the system of state and co-operative trade, bodies which analyse the market and demand, and 'such units have now appeared in a number of industrial ministries. Thus the flow of information is considerable, but unfortunately in many organizations market reports collect dust on shelves and decisions are taken by rough intuition', in the words of another Soviet critic. One requires the combined efforts of trade and industry to order and to produce good-quality consumers' goods, and to reflect and to influence consumer demand. 'Both industrial and trade officials often complain about the capriciousness of customers. Yes, the purchasers have become more demanding, and we should rejoice at this.' (Kanevsky, *Pravda*, 18 June 1975.)

The trade organs themselves react clumsily to actual or anticipated consumer demand. For example, the ministries of trade of the Turkmen and Tadzhik republics placed orders for electric light bulbs which varied, over a period of five years, from 1·1 to 10·5 million bulbs per year, which could hardly be justified by variations in demand. Grossly excessive requests were made for recording tape. (Kanevsky, *Pravda*, 18 June 1975.) Large numbers of examples can readily be assembled, either of trade organs failing to place orders sensibly, or of industry failing to respond with the desired assortment. Thus between them they provided far too many obsolete and undesired washing machines (Kanevsky, *Pravda*, 18 June 1975) and output was sharply cut in and after 1975. To cite just one more example, the trade organs of Tomsk, in Siberia, cannot obtain the goods which they need to fulfil their turnover plan, and have to appeal through party and state channels to find something to sell. A delivery of cars enabled the plan to be fulfilled in total, but the author lists many items which the inhabitants of Tomsk were unable to buy. (Petrov, *Pravda*, 7 July 1975.)

These are not simply isolated anecdotes. The system seems not to be geared to respond to consumer demand, indeed it can be argued that it was not created for any such purpose. Central planning of the Soviet type, of its very nature, is unable to handle micro-economic detail, must delegate it to relatively junior officials. The political leadership doubtless desires the provision of better-quality products which accord with demand, and frequently say so. Their problem is, within the centralized system, to convert their desires into effective instructions. For many officials, at all levels, the consumer is low-priority, a residuary legatee, and this further complicates matters. This is not a hostile judgement by an unfriendly observer. We have Brezhnev's own words. He spoke of this, critically at the 24th party Congress in 1971. He repeated his strictures at the 25th Congress in February 1976: 'Many ministries and planners regard consumers' goods as secondary . . .'. He drew attention to the inadequacy of 'the quality of (official) work and attention to the consumer and his requirements in trade, catering and services.' (*Pravda*, 25 February 1976.)

A useful example of how the system obstructs a well-meant and sensible innovation is the fate of the 'trade-fairs' *(yarmarki)*, which were organized in order to establish closer links between trade and industry. They are held, indeed, and contracts are made. The *yarmarki* are of some help in disposing of goods hard to sell, but a key element is missing: there is no link between the *yarmarki* (and the contracts signed there) and the determination by superior organs of the output plans of industrial enterprises and *obyedineniya*. '*Yarmarki* should be places where commercial deals are made, not a kind of office for disposing of surpluses of allocated commodities *(otovarivaniye fondov)*.' (Orlov and Shimansky, 1970, p.77.) Furthermore, these trade-fairs take place in November–December, when the output plans of enterprises are already drafted. (Tyukov, 1969, p.64.) In any event, an enterprise anxious to produce that which the customers need may be unable to secure the necessary materials, which originate in other enterprises which are subject to the usual plan-instructions from *their* ministry. Again and again one finds that the entire system of allocations and production-instructions is (inevitably) aggregated, and that precise specifications cannot be defined in the central plan, and therefore they need to be negotiated, between trade and industry and between input-providing and input-utilizing industries, with familiar difficulties arising. Blame for the resulting malfunctioning can never be clearly identifiable.

To recapitulate: trade suffers from low priority, low pay, low morale, under-equipment, under-financing, shortage of suitable premises and storage space, and a system which fails to provide either an adequate motive or adequate means to satisfy demand. Without means *and* motive, information is not enough. Thus a trade official, even if fully 'motivated', is hamstrung by the allocation system and/or can only try to place orders (either by utilizing limited 'direct links' where the goods are not 'funded', or by passing his requests up the trade hierarchy). The conscientious industrial manager may be unable to obtain inputs of the requisite specification or quality, or may find that the assortment asked for contradicts global output and sales targets, or profitability, or all of these.

Information, it must be stressed, comes from official reports (e.g. on low or high stocks, or shortages, or complaints of dissatisfied citizens), and not from any specifically economic *mechanism*. One can contrast the free or *kolkhoz* market, in which shortage or abundance have an immediate effect on prices, and so on the willingness of peasants to bring produce to market. But, of course, one can have perfectly clear information and still choose not to act. Thus the lack of restaurants and cafes in Moscow has been notorious for decades, but supply still lags far behind known demand.

Some critics underline the unresponsiveness of the *political* system, treating this as a major explanatory factor. It is undeniable that this is a relevant factor in the low priority of the needs of citizens, of which Brezhnev himself complained at the 25th Congress. (High officials can usually obtain scarce items 'by the back door', and value this privilege.) There might well be a different approach to resource-allocation priorities if there were wider possibilities of public protest and pressure. This could result in a sharp corrective to the 'allocational', take-what-you're-given approach to trade.

Yet the entire logic of the system, its inherent complexity and clumsiness, its deliberate playing down of the role of the market, has much to answer for. A 'vote with the rouble' can simultaneously inform and provide some incentive for action (provided, of course, that the purchaser can exercise choice: if there are shortages, his or her real preference cannot be revealed, since he or she purchases substitutes). A vote, however freely expressed, on a ballot can hardly have the same practical micro-economic impact. The reason should be clear. Fifty citizens buying pullovers or refusing to buy obsolete washing-machines exert an influence to which, evidently, the system *ought* to respond; why, after all, should it not meet consumer preferences if these are not harmful (like vodka or the poems of a dissident)? These citizens can scarcely form a pullover or anti-obsolete-washing-machine party and go to the polls. They can, it is true, raise their voices. Why, argued one radical economist, not have a 'registration of clamour' as the basis of estimating consumer demand? (Bose, 1975.) Why is 'voting with the rouble' better? Is one not idealizing the (usually imperfect) market?

Undeniably protest and the vocal expression of demand are useful and legitimate correctives. Among the few Western economists who have recognized it as a fact of economic life (in all countries) is Hirschman (1970). However, while this can help to correct malfunctions, 'clamour', like voting, cannot be a micro-economic functional normality. Two essential reasons for this are:

(a) Clamour can scarcely be measured meaningfully. Willingness to pay tells us something significant about individual or social demand, at a given distribution of income. Clamour tells us of willingness to shout. It is unrelated to price. The total amount 'demanded', in *this* sense of the word 'demand', is certain to be far greater than the available supply.

(b) As repeatedly pointed out in earlier chapters, the problem, in a modern industrial society, is that production requires the co-operation of many industrial organs scattered over a wide area. To ensure production one needs either a market-type economy, with purchased inputs and with the suppliers and *their* suppliers reacting to market-indicated opportunity, or a complex planning-and-allocation system. In a market economy, clamour *could* lead a local authority to run a bus service, without there being a need for other *administrative* organs to ensure that buses and fuel are provided. It could just *buy* a bus in the market. In the Soviet model, the *plans* of several ministries must include the production and allocation of buses (and tyres, engines, metal, ball-bearings, etc. etc.) and of fuel. (This is one reason why the local-authority budgets are incorporated in the state budget.)

In other words, in a non-market economy we have to assume the existence of a large production-and-allocation bureaucracy, divided between many authorities, without which the democratic procedures and 'clamour' cannot be converted into action. In the example of Tomsk, which has already been used, the local soviet *did* apparently try to respond to its citizens' needs, but was frustrated because it could not purchase the goods and equipment required. Those who failed to supply them were not (or need not have been) obstructive and unfeeling bureaucrats, any more than this is the case with a British educational official who does not authorize the re-building of an obsolete schoolhouse. They are constrained by shortage of resources. Within such a setting, clamour is effective only in the general sense that national pressure-groups affect macro-allocation of resources, or bring to light particularly scandalous shortages, errors or omissions.

There is one other important point, perhaps *the* most important point, which must be made. If a critical reader of this chapter is acquainted with Western practice, he may well have said to himself many pages ago: 'But in the West a great many shops are 'administered' branches of great supermarket chains, with a complex supply-and-allocation system of their own, operating in many instances on fixed trade margins. Prices of many consumers' goods are administered too, and do not in fact fluctuate much (or at all) in response to changes in demand or in stocks. There is indeed a visible difference in quality between the two systems, so far as trade is concerned, and the reasons given above explain some of it. But a key element of the explanation is surely missing.'

This key element is unquestionably the chronic sellers' market. In the West, 'excess demand' pushes up prices, but almost all goods are available almost all of the time at the prevailing prices, there is unused productive capacity, it is usually difficult to sell. Consequently, even if a Western 'capitalist' faces (or fixes) prices of goods A, B and C which are out of line with relative scarcities, he will not overproduce A as against B and C because his self-interest will compel him to adjust to demand. According to the textbook model, overproduction of A would cause its price to fall and profits to decline; with administered prices this need not happen, but the necessity of finding customers would still compel the necessary adjustment, allowing for exceptions like the Common Market agricultural policy, in which the surpluses are bought and stored (hence the butter, beef, milk and other 'mountains'). The usual process is doubtless imperfect, but it works, more or less, though only on one condition: that sellers are seeking buyers, that it is difficult to sell.

A *sellers'* market changes everything. True, even in the USSR one can and does have excess stocks of unsaleable, poor-quality or obsolete goods. But over a wide range, as we have repeatedly noted, the buyer is anxiously seeking a seller willing and able to supply him (or her). Under these conditions, when purchasers know that they have to make do with substitutes, when the alternative to acquiring what is offered is to get nothing at all, the system of plan-indicators and related incentives is bound to cause serious distortions. Those of us who remember wartime and postwar shortages will certainly recall their effect on the behaviour of shop assistants and other suppliers. Instead of a valued customer one became a species of petitioner. We have seen in earlier chapters that this applies to managers as purchasers of inputs as well as to citizens in the shops. Both suffer from what the Russians call *prinuditel'ny assortiment,* 'compulsory assortment', insisted on by the seller. Under these conditions, a mixture of exhortation plus emphasis on the need to observe conditions in delivery contracts is not enough. The customer seldom dares to enforce his rights. The supplier can be fined, but this is ineffective. (See e.g., Praude, *Pravda,* 5 February 1976.)

Internal trade is a weak spot in the Soviet economic system. Lenin in 1921 launched the slogan, 'uchites' torgovat' ', 'learn to trade.'. For all the above reasons, there is yet much to learn.

THE FREE MARKET

This is often called a 'kolkhoz market, though the sellers are not only kolkhoz peasants and kolkhozy, but also state-employed persons who have allotments or livestock. Also found in a typical urban market are stalls operated by co-operatives selling produce on commission, and small state shops selling goods mainly to visiting peasants. Some peasants also sell produce in villages, and at railway stations. Statistics on market turnover generally relate to urban markets only. They probably omit many deals in second-hand goods and products of individual craftsmen, which take place in or just outside many markets (the so-called tolkuchki). This is apart from illegal deals of a black-market character, of which we have only fragmentary knowledge but which certainly occur. (Katsenellenboigen, 1977.)

We have seen in Chapter 9 that prices in the free market are as a rule much higher than in state shops. Prices are uncontrolled, or at least this is the official position, but occasional reports speak of attempts to set maxima. A Soviet writer puts it as follows: 'However, despite the law, in practice we still encounter attempts by executives of local soviets to introduce maximum prices in the kolkhoz market and even to post obligatory price-lists.' (Lazarev, 1967, p.38.) The author deplores the practice. From personal observation at many markets, it would seem to be exceptional.

An important problem facing both peasants and kolkhozy is transport of goods and their sellers to markets. Owing to poor communications, this can be costly and time-wasting. On any one day, a grossly excessive number of peasants are selling small quantities of produce, often far away from their farms. The opportunity-cost must be huge. This is not an efficient method of distribution. Matters are not helped by the fact that, legally, one can only sell one's own produce, not one's neighbour's (though no doubt this rule is often ignored in practice).

One could put the point as follows. The absence of professional traders (whose activities are illegal in the USSR), and the inadequacies of co-operative commission trade, daily compel hundreds of thousands of peasants to take their onions, cheese, beef, potatoes, etc., to often distant markets at great expense in time. Given the conditions of Soviet agriculture and the supply situation in towns, any administrative interference with the free market is bound to be both unpopular and harmful. But one must suppose that, with higher rural incomes and improved official trade in foodstuffs, the peasant market will diminish not only relatively but absolutely.

The purchasers in the free market are private individuals. State institutions are forbidden to buy in them with the exception of fresh vegetables. (Lazarev, 1967, p.39.) This helps to explain the absence from the menus of restaurants of items obtainable (in that locality) only in the market.

Some restrictions are sometimes imposed on movements of goods to market. Thus the Georgian authorities have stopped the lucrative journeys by peasants to Moscow and other distant cities to sell citrus fruits, and decrees are sometimes issued allowing the sales of certain products only after all delivery obligations to the state have been met. Lazarev (1967, p.39) quotes such a rule as applying to melons and pumpkins and some other products.

A NOTE ON LIVING STANDARDS

There is considerable interest in the problem of comparing living standards in the USSR with those in other countries, communist or capitalist. This is not the place to attempt the complex task of actually making the comparisons, involving as it must the collection and analysis of output and price statistics and the usual perplexities caused by the index number problem. All that can be done here is to draw attention to some problems which arise out of certain features of the Soviet economic system.

On the positive side, one must take social services into account, and low house-rents, subsidized vacation *putyovki* (package-tours), low-priced factory canteens and cafeterias. Most basic foods are cheap, so is tobacco and (for some odd reason) petrol. So are telephones, urban transportation, heat and light. There are no social insurance contributions by the worker. Taxes are low also. Consequently, if one takes the earnings of a semi-skilled worker – say 100 roubles a month – his expenditure on 'basics' is very modest by Western standards.

However, some items are expensive (i.e. cost more than in the West at any reasonable exchange rate). These include some foods (butter, sugar, chocolates), almost all clothing, many consumer durables. A quarter of all urban housing and the vast bulk of rural housing is private, and there is also a growing number of so-called co-operative housing schemes, in which individuals have to make large down-payments. The cost of all these houses, and especially their maintenance and repair, is far higher than is the case when housing is rented from local soviets and other state institutions. (Much greater differentiation in rents for state-owned houses, with high rents for space in excess of a minimum norm, is advocated by S. Shatalin, in *EkMM*, 1976, No. 3, but this runs counter to established practice.)

Private houses are often discriminated against. To quote from a letter of complaint: 'In neighbouring local authority housing there is water supply and daily collection of rubbish, and the residents do not have to worry about capital and current repairs, while we are deprived of all this.' They even had to put up poles themselves to get electricity to their houses and complained of being referred to as 'privateers'. (*Pravda*, 7 March 1975.)

This brings one to the very important factors of quality and availability. 'Official' housing is cheap, but often unobtainable and of very variable quality. Though far fewer now live in communal apartments, the space available in the new blocks of flats is very small. The satirical *Krokodil* devotes much space to stories and cartoons about poor finish, burst pipes, buckled floors, lack of local shopping facilities and the like. Soviet clothing has improved, but is certainly far below Western (or Eastern) standards. While the output of refrigerators, washing machines and other durables has shown an impressive upward trend, the models produced are of very modest quality. (Quality is said to depend partly on the date at which the goods are made: if in the last few days of the month, everyone will be engaged in *shturmovshchina* and quality will be low). Spare parts are notoriously difficult to obtain.

In fact many items are difficult to obtain, though there is much variation in time and place. Poor service, delays, standing in line, must all be taken into account also. In these respects, the USSR compares unfavourably with Hungary, Czechoslovakia and East Germany, let alone France or the United States, and so we cannot be sure what proportion of the defects are explicable by 'the system'. Some of the deficiencies may be 'Russian', as is also suggested by the fact that, within the USSR, distribution is better organized in the Baltic states. Some arise from the consequence of the sellers' market, itself partly the consequence of price policies previously discussed. There is also the effect of the lack of competition and of various forms of bureaucracy. Also we must note that non-availability of desired goods acts as a disincentive: why earn more if one cannot buy what one wants?

Therefore any calculations of purchasing-power, based on appropriately weighted price comparisons, must be modified to take into account the usually inferior quality of manufactures, and the very widespread non-availability of many commodities. But, while certainly relevant to any international comparisons, these factors are, of their nature, hard to quantify. One can derive a rouble–dollar ratio from the information that a kilogram of pork chops costs 4 dollars in Detroit and 3 roubles in Kharkov, but how does one allow for the fact (if it is a fact) that pork chops cannot be found in Kharkov for most of the year?

FOREIGN TRADE: THE MONOPOLY OF THE MINISTRY

The state monopoly of foreign trade is as old as the Soviet Union. Even in the NEP period, private enterprise was firmly kept out. However, as some Soviet critics have been arguing, this principle should not necessarily imply the monopoly of the *Ministry* of Foreign Trade and of its foreign-trade corporations. The latter, under the control of the ministry, actually do the buying and/or selling. (The designation of the corporation can be misleading. Thus *Eksportkhleb* can and does import bread-grains.) The corporations are represented in the trade delegations attached to embassies abroad, in countries of import-ance in the relevant sphere.

This means that, with minor exceptions to be noted, Soviet indus-trial ministries and republican authorities cannot engage in foreign trade, though in some cases they can be involved in negotiations and in the carrying out of trade deals alongside officials of the Ministry of Foreign Trade.

The exceptions concern barter deals involving frontier areas (Leningrad-Finland, the Afghan border, the Far East). Some of these have given rise to administrative frictions, as when the Far Eastern coastal trade organ *Dalintorg*, with headquarters in Nakhodka near Vladivostok and the formal status of an 'all-union trading office', developed trade with Japan to an extent deemed excessive by the central organs. (Davis, 1976.) There is also some barter trade under-taken by the consumer co-operatives (Tsentrosoyuz). Finally the State Committee on Foreign Economic Relations concerns itself with deliveries under economic and technical aid.

Let us look first at the 'traditional 'pattern and its functional logic. The object of the state monopoly of foreign trade has always been to isolate the Soviet Union from the influence of capitalist countries and corporations, and from the effect of changes in world-market prices. In the context of the centrally planned economy of the Soviet type, foreign trade must be 'fitted' into the process of operational control. One can analyse the process in a number of ways.

First, the long-term plan must include provision for the level of exports that will pay for the desired imports. *Gosplan* must play a key role in making the necessary calculations, drawing upon information from the Ministry of Foreign Trade concerning foreign markets and from industrial ministries about needs and availabilities. Policy con-siderations naturally play their part: on Comecon integration, for instance, or the possibility or desirability of large-scale exchanges with the United States. But more of the politics of trade later. At this stage it is necessary simply to note that the long-term plan would include investments designed to expand exports, or provide for reliance on foreign sources for materials, foodstuffs, machines of various types (or, alternatively, for import-saving investments to lessen dependence on foreign suppliers). Thus the tenth five-year plan provides for an export surplus of oil, and imports of a wide range of capital goods.

In current planning decisions matters are, as usual, more complicated. One needs to disaggregate and address instructions to specific executants, and negotiate with foreign officials and businessmen about specific transactions. Clearly, in the Soviet model the task cannot belong to the management of enterprises or *obyedineniya*. They are told what to produce, and for whom, they are told what inputs to obtain and from whom. In other words, their customers and suppliers are designated by the central planners even when they are all within the Soviet Union. *A fortiori*, autonomous transactions with abroad are out of the question. If a manager in Omsk cannot freely decide to buy from Minsk, then, evidently, he cannot decide to buy from Prague or Düsseldorf. Nor can he decide whether the resources of his enterprise should be devoted to supplying the domestic or the foreign market. Nor, finally, can he ensure that the inputs necessary to enable him to produce will be available to him, unless these are allocated by the planners, who are (or claim to be) in a position to decide which of their alternative uses (and destinations) is best from the standpoint of economic efficiency or policy.

Given the structure of the system, this is quite logical. As we have had occasion to note repeatedly, neither the price system nor other information flows can provide management with a guide as to what is actually most needed. Material inputs are 'rationed' between alternative uses by the planning agencies whether these are of foreign or domestic origin. Foreign currency is also scarce, and, as we shall see, some currencies are more scarce than others, matters being further complicated by the logic of bilateral balances and bilateral trade agreements, not to mention political considerations. Of all this the manager in Omsk can have no cognizance.

Enterprises, *obyedineniya*, industrial ministries, can and do make proposals involving imports and exports. But the task of actual buying and selling is the effective monopoly (with the few exceptions already noted) of the Ministry of Foreign Trade and of the trading corporations which are under its control. This must take place in close collaboration with *Gosplan,* this being the nerve-centre of the resource allocation system.

There is an evident disadvantage in such a system. The producing enterprises are remote from foreign markets, the managers seldom travel abroad, and this affects their abilities to design a product suitable for the foreign market. But more of this and similar matters later.

FOREIGN TRADE CRITERIA AND PRICES

Given the material balance system which *Gosplan* operates, it follows that most foreign-trade decisions are taken in quantitative terms: if there is a shortage of chemical machinery and fodder grain, then import. If there is a surplus over requirements of timber and oil, export. Since domestic prices do not reflect either scarcity or abundance, they will not and cannot act as meaningful signals. At any given exchange rate, good A can seem profitable to sell abroad, and good B can be profitably imported, but in fact the opposite may happen: good A may be in short supply, while there are ample availabilities of good B.

Of course, in real life one must introduce complications. Thus the identification of a shortage need not lead to imports: much depends on alternative uses of the given currency and the degree of priority of the item being considered. The shortage may be tolerated, the internal users cut or compelled to seek alternatives. It is also possible to reduce domestic use of (say) timber in order to make more available for export, if this is judged to be urgently necessary. And, of course, in the longer run export capacity and import needs are affected by the investment programme. Non-convertibility and bilateralism introduces further complications, to be considered in a moment.

First, however, one must examine prices. The Soviet domestic price system is effectively isolated from world-market prices. Thus, for instance, the huge rise in world prices of oil and many other materials in 1973–4 was not accompanied by any significant revision of Soviet internal prices for these items. While Soviet imports and exports appear in the official statistics at rouble values, these are 'foreign-trade' or 'valuta' roubles, which have absolutely nothing to do with internal rouble prices. Transactions with Western and most developing countries are undertaken in Western currencies, which are then converted into roubles at the official rate. Thus if the USSR sells oil to the United States for $133 million, this would appear as 100 million roubles. Trade within Comecon is conducted at prices based loosely on world prices of the recent past, ostensibly cleansed of speculative fluctuations. These prices in turn are converted into valuta roubles at the official rate. However, prices for the same items can differ quite widely as between Comecon and the world market, especially when drastic changes in prices have occurred, as with oil in 1973–4.

Some trade within Comecon is conducted under special arrangements, involving barter deals, and these can be at a wide variety of price ratios. Thus according to Csikos-Nagy (1975, p.316), the Hungarians are 'paid' for components supplied for the Soviet Zhiguli car in completed cars, at ratios derived from the Fiat Italian catalogue! The same components supplied to other Comecon countries, or to the USSR for other purposes, would have a different price. With the increase in joint projects and specialization agreements, and also 'non-trade' transactions such as tourism, a bewildering array of special prices and rates have emerged. In some Comecon countries, Poland for instance, multiple exchange rates exist further to complicate matters. Some scarce commodities are supplied to Comecon partners at one price up to a given quantity, but must be paid for in dollars at the world price for additional quantities. In 1976 this provision is being applied to oil and several other commodities, according to verbal information.

The foreign trade corporations pay the Soviet suppliers, and charge the Soviet purchasers, the appropriate domestic wholesale price. Very wide disparities are common between these prices and those in *valuta* roubles. Thus an export of some item at $133 results in revenue of 100 roubles to the trade corporation. If the price of this item in internal roubles is 60, then there is a sizeable profit. If, as well it might be, the internal price is 150 roubles, there is a loss. As we saw in Chapter 9, the necessary adjustments are made via the state budget. The foreign trade corporation is quite unaffected by this. Its job is to buy and sell in accordance with needs and availabilities as these are communicated to it. This too is logical, given the system, since the disparities between internal and external prices, and indeed the official exchange rate, have no connection with the desirability of the given transaction.

A not inapt parallel is trade in agricultural products under the Common Market's agricultural policy. With artificial support prices, a decision to sell may arise because a surplus exists over requirements, and the price at which a surplus is disposed of bears little relation to (is usually a good deal lower than) the price paid to the domestic producers.

This does not mean that prices and costs do not enter into calculations as to the desirability of foreign trade. One solution consists of relating domestic costs to net earnings of foreign currency. Thus, to give an example, if commodity A costs 100 roubles to produce and sells at $200, then, other things being equal, it should be preferred to one which earns $200 but costs 175 roubles to produce. (Note that the *valuta* import content of these commodities would need to be deducted.) While this may not affect short-run decisions, guided as they are by shortages and availabilities, it does affect investment. In view of the nature of domestic prices, errors and omissions are highly possible. However, we should not forget how irrational are many trade restrictions (and prices) which operate in the real Western world, not least within EEC.

There exists a so-called 'provisional methodology for determining the economic effectiveness of foreign trade', issued in 1968 by *Gosplan*, and 'provisional methodological instructions for calculating the effectiveness of specialization . . . within Comecon', the latter confirmed by the State Committee on prices, *Gosplan* and the Academy of Sciences of the USSR in 1973.* The former is based upon comparing

Vremennaya metodika opredeleniya ekonomicheskoi effektivnosti vneshnei torgovli (Gosplan, 1968), and *Vremennye metodologicheskiye ukazaniya dlya raschyota effektivnosti spetsializatsii. . . . so stranami – chlenami SEV* (May 1973).

valuta earnings with rouble expenditure (and, in the case of imports, *valuta* expenditure with domestic selling prices); the use of the official (or any other) exchange rate then gives one comparative coefficients of effectiveness. The inadequacy of internal prices as a criterion, or as a measure of real domestic costs, is widely recognized, and so the 1973 'methodological instructions' are more sophisticated, with two recommended calculations: one in actual Soviet wholesale prices, the other 'converted' *(privedennyye)* by corrective coefficients, to take into account full cost (e.g. of direct and indirect investments, which are 'valued' in terms of a normed recoupment period), and also those instances in which domestic wholesale prices have a redistributive function (i.e. are below cost, or yield a high rate of profit, on social grounds). (Rybakov, *PKh*, 1974, No. 12, p.22.) There exists also a computerized system of calculations for foreign trade (abbreviated *ASOP-vneshtorg*) within *Gosplan* the structure of which is described by Zakharov and Sulyagin (*PKh*, 1974, No. 12, pp.40ff.)

The increased importance of foreign trade in general, of Comecon trade and integration in particular, has stimulated the appearance of numerous works in a subject previously somewhat neglected, and a bibliography of books and articles on foreign-trade criteria published in the last five years in the USSR and Eastern Europe would cover many pages. Some interesting problems arose in attempting to calculate the effectiveness of imports. Thus if one compares the cost of imports with the cost which *would* have been incurred had the goods in question been produced in the USSR, then bananas would look very 'effective', because the cost of growing them in glasshouses in Russia would be very high indeed. Alternatives discussed include the cost of goods which are exported to pay for the imports, or the use (where they exist) of the costs or prices of analagous goods made in the USSR. The factor time is taken into account in some of these calculations, and is linked with the interest rate paid on credits, which enable machinery or other goods to be obtained earlier than would otherwise be the case (see Rybakov *PKh*, 1974, No. 12, and Rybakov, 1975.)

However, all these methods have notable limitations, of which their authors frequently show themselves aware. Thus how does one identify *which* of a vast range of exported goods, with widely different profitabilities in forms of *valuta,* makes possible any one particular import? There is also the wide gap between domestic prices, foreign-rate prices and scarcity prices. Exchange takes place 'at world-market prices, which have no relation to the internal economic transactions of the country'. In the end, it is admitted that 'the practical application of the (above-mentioned) recommendations is so far not large'. (Rybakov, *PKh*, 1974, No. 12, p.18.) Or, to cite another author, 'in planning decisions at present, calculations of effectiveness are not obligatory, and in fact value indicators generally play a minor role'. (Grinev, *PKh*, 1976, No. 1, p.149.)

All the above discussion concerns criteria for decisions at the centre, the sort of calculations which can be made in planning offices, not by managers. For the latter there is no advantage in terms of prices as between selling to the home and a foreign market: the normal wholesale price applies. True, certain export orders are regarded as vital and attract high priority and the necessary inputs. But this, from the manager's standpoint, is by no means unusual. He receives specific instructions also on high-priority internal requirements. Not surprisingly, there have been proposals to provide special export incentives. In some countries this takes the form of allowing the retention of a percentage of the *valuta* earned. In fact this seems to have been a potent influence in encouraging Far East coastal trade: *Dalintorg* is able to acquire scarce Japanese consumers' goods for part of its export earnings. Such proposals remain almost wholly on paper, however, and a leading Soviet analyst draws attention to the conflicts which can arise between 'converted' profitability calculations made by planners and 'the *Khozraschet* interests of enterprises, ministries'. (Rybakov, *PKh*, 1974, No. 12, p.22.)

It has been reported verbally that some manufacturing enterprises and *obyedineniya* have been allowed to keep 10 per cent of their hard-currency earnings, under a decision taken in May 1976, and that they are allowed to spend the money on purchasing foreign equipment and also on maintaining contact with foreign firms and markets. This could contribute significantly to the diffusion of Western technology, as well as achieving the obvious objective of encouraging production for export.

The use of foreign currency as a managerial incentive is impeded by the shortage of *valuta*, especially convertible Western currency. The list of potential imports, originating in numerous enterprises and institutions as well as in the planning agencies, always very considerably exceeds the possibility of paying for them. Many requests have to be cut back, whence the dislike by planners of schemes which threaten to divert scarce *valuta* to possibly low-priority purposes. Because of currency shortage, Soviet planners sometimes authorize purchases of certain items only on condition that the necessary *valuta* is earned by additional exports. Western firms know this when their Soviet partners (the appropriate trade corporation) try to persuade them to purchase or market Soviet goods as a condition to the deal. In such a case one must surmise that the Soviet would-be importer is told: 'Yes, but only if you can arrange for the foreign-exchange costs to be covered.' This can be a major nuisance to the Western firm concerned, which may have neither the oragnization nor the desire to market the Soviet goods in question.

Another way of paying for needed imports, especially of capital goods, is through so-called 'compensation-agreements' or credit-barter. One example among many was a deal with Japanese firms to supply timber-cutting and processing equipment in Eastern Siberia, the credit to be repaid in timber over a period of years. Large-scale discussions have been undertaken with American interests involving developments in Siberian oil and gas fields, to be repaid in oil and gas. These are sometimes known as self-liquidating credits: they are used to produce the means of their own repayment.

Needless to say, many imports are paid for quite straightforwardly out of foreign currency earnings (and gold exports). It depends on circumstances, the nature and priority of the transaction, currency availability and the demands of the Western partner.

The balance of payments as such is never published: it is a state secret in all the Comecon countries. Trade statistics appear, and these show (for instance) that, after a favourable shift in 1973 and 1974, Soviet trade with the West moved into a very large deficit in 1975, because of the combined effect of big grain purchases, large orders for Western technology, increases in import prices and a drop in sales to the West due to the impact of the recession. Consequently, as these lines are written, there is a particularly tight situation *vis-à-vis* the West, with very considerable indebtedness incurred in the last few years. Poland is in a particularly difficult position, because of very large credits obtained to purchase capital goods for her overambitious investment programme.

One curious consequence of the price system must be mentioned. It is quite possible that there could be a trade surplus if the goods entering trade are valued at Soviet internal prices, and a deficit at world or *valuta*-rouble prices, or vice versa. In fact an adjustment is made in the Soviet national accounts, though not specified in detail.

BILATERALISM AND NON-CONVERTIBILITY

Soviet trade deals are most often bilateral, and particularly within Comecon. To understand why, it is necessary to return to the *modus operandi* of foreign-trade planners and their role within the planning system as a whole. By these same means one can explain why the rouble is not convertible.

The USSR is an economy whose resources are fully utilized, indeed there are many shortages. Items for export, and the means of producing or mining them, are earmarked in the process of drawing up the instructions and allocations of which the current operational plan consists. It is therefore important that the requirements of the foreign customer be, as far as possible, known in advance. But this is rendered more difficult in multilateral trade. Let me illustrate: suppose that the USSR negotiates an agreement with Ruritania for an exchange of goods worth (at world prices) $100 million. The agreement will contain lists of goods. Before it is signed, Gosplan and other planning agencies will have incorporated the imports and exports into material-balance, allocation and production plans, and the ministries and enterprises concerned will have their plans and instructions appropriately adjusted. But now suppose that Ruritania acquires a convertible rouble surplus of (say) $50 million. It uses it to cover its deficit with the imaginary country of Paphlagonia. In due course either Paphlagonia or one of *its* trading partners will present to the USSR a request to buy $50 million-worth of goods, the product mix being unknown and un-negotiated up to this moment.

It is not being asserted that all Soviet trade is conducted on the basis of prior bilateral agreements, but it is clear that it is very convenient that most of it should be, that unpredictable demands on resources be minimized, because, given the taut nature of plans, there will be so little spare capacity with which to adjust to the unexpected. This is one reason why the Soviet official view of convertibility is negative. Another is an almost instinctive dislike of making the rouble subject to currency deals and to the effect this might have on exchange rates (see below, page 277, for a note on the black-market rate and its significance).

The USSR's trading partners, those in Comecon especially, are also aware that a claim on Soviet resources can only be turned into actual goods if these goods are provided in the plan. This is sometimes known as the 'problem of convertibility of goods', and is another way of looking at the cause and logic of bilateralism. Let us suppose that Czechoslovakia (to take a real country this time) acquires roubles and wishes to purchase goods in the Soviet Union with them. Unless these are already entered in a list during bilateral negotiations, they may simply not be available. In fact the typical intra-Comecon bilateral negotiations are a prolonged bargaining session, in which it is assumed by both sides that the values expressed in *valuta* roubles do *not* reflect the importance, priority or relative scarcity of the items entering into trade. This is a consequence of the price 'system' already described, and to quantitative 'priority' planning. To this must be added the fact that internal prices in different Comecon countries are not aligned to each other in any logically definable way, so that the ratios between internal prices and foreign-trade prices, and between both and relative scarcities, vary greatly. It therefore follows that an exchange of goods worth $100 million (or its *valuta*-rouble equivalent) between the USSR and Czechoslovakia is by no means regarded by the planners of either side as representing an exchange of goods of equal value (value meaning value to the planners or the economy). Goods are divided notionally into 'hard goods' and 'soft goods', the former being particularly scarce within Comecon and therefore undervalued at the 'world' prices used, the latter being readily available and of relatively low priority.

In general, raw materials and fuels tend to be 'hard', obsolete machines and many consumers' goods 'soft'. The logic of such negotiations, and their connection with the nature of centralized planning and the price system, has been well analyzed in a Hungarian publication. (Ausch, 1971, pp.75ff.) So in practice the process of bilateral bargaining between Comecon countries extends beyond bilateral balancing overall into bilateral balancing of product categories by degree of 'hardness'.

Convertibility would mean making a reality of the so-called transferable rouble, now little more than a unit of account. But this, in turn, would require a substantial move towards a market economy in the *internal* arrangements of Comecon countries in general, the USSR in particular. Of this there is no sign. So, according to the same Hungarian commentator, for the present 'the USSR will, relying on her immense economic resources and gold reserves, most probably prefer centrally directed bilateralism. For this form ensures her the greatest freedom of manoeuvre in the political and economic field, exposes her least to the effects of changes in the monetary position of other countries, and does not require co-ordination of her monetary policies with the latter'. (Ausch, 1971, p.91.) Therefore convertibility, and therefore also multilateralism, are unlikely to make headway. But this inevitably means annual bilateral bargaining about quotas of 'hard' and 'soft' goods, and also the frustration of those countries which, like Hungary and (to a more limited extent) Poland, have attempted to introduce greater market-type flexibility into their economic systems.

Similar negotiations took place between pairs of Western countries in the first postwar years, when many currencies were non-convertible and many prices failed to reflect scarcities and demand. (I recall that in 1948 the Belgians were only prepared to sell the then very scarce steel on condition that Britain also took some 'soft' goods, which included azaleas.)

Obviously, this kind of problem reinforces the practice of bilateral negotiation. One must re-emphasize the close connection between this and the internal planning-allocation system. In a very real sense the rouble is not convertible *within* the USSR: the manager at Omsk cannot turn his money into needed inputs without an allocation certificate issued by *Gosplan* or *Gossnab*. A precondition for convertibility and multilateralism would be an internal reform of a 'liberalizing' kind, which eliminated all or most of the material allocation system.

A further cause of bilateralism is the situation or demands of the trading partner. Thus some Western countries insist on a given level of Soviet purchases as a *quid pro quo* for giving the Soviet Union access to their markets (more of this in a moment), and this constrains the Soviet foreign-trade corporations, which might otherwise simply buy in the cheapest market, using surpluses of convertible currency with one Western country to obtain imports from another. Then there is also the position of many developing countries; they have weak currencies and can only pay for Soviet deliveries (or repay Soviet credits) with their own goods.

One cause of difficulty is the evident preference of all Comecon countries for convertible 'hard' currency, as against each others'. This can be seen in the often higher quality of their exports to the West, and in the existence of special shops (*Beryozka* in the USSR) which sell scarce goods for hard currency only. One effect of this attitude is that each Comecon country tends to spend or keep any Western currency it earns, which hardly facilitates multilateralization.

THE EXCHANGE RATE

At the time of writing the rouble is officially worth about $1·33 (100 dollars for 75·80 roubles). It has appreciated, more or less in line with the Deutsche Mark: the rate originally fixed when the new rouble was introduced in 1961 was $1·11 to the rouble (100 dollars = 90 roubles). What significance, other than accounting significance, should be attached to the official rate?

The evidence suggests that the official rate is not far off purchasing-power parity, in terms at least of wholesale prices. Prices have risen quite rapidly in the West, much less rapidly in the USSR. It is true that, at this exchange rate, some items seem very dear in the USSR (the price paid to farms for pork, say, or most kinds of clothing and footwear), but others are cheap (many kinds of machinery and equipment). Consumers' goods and services raise other problems, as already pointed out above (availability, quality etc.), but there too there are very inexpensive items (bread, tobacco, rents, telephone, public transport, for instance) to take into account. Purchasing-power parities and exchange rates are seldom in line for any group of countries, East or West. There seems no very strong evidence to regard the official rate as grossly out of line, but one should never forget that, even if this is so overall, there are very big disparities by sector and by product.

Sometimes a critic of the above view points to the free-market rate for the rouble as evidence that it is greatly overvalued at the official rate. However, this is not a sound argument. There are several reasons for the low valuation of the rouble in the black market, in and out of the USSR. Firstly, certain goods and services are *only* obtainable for foreign currency, and/or are very cheap in such currency. Imagine that one could freely buy duty-free whisky in Scotland for dollars at $2·50 per bottle, whereas the price in the shops for ordinary citizens was £4. In such conditions there would develop a kind of whisky dollar-sterling ratio, at the rate of $0·65 per £1, which would have no connection with the relative price levels of the two countries. It would be a product of high taxes plus opportunities in a narrow area. Secondly, Soviet citizens are severely rationed for foreign currency if they go abroad, and there are certain items (for instance electronic calculators, or jeans, or woollen sweaters, or certain books) which are worth buying abroad even if the purchaser pays four times the official rate to a black-market dealer. It would be wrong to value Soviet output or consumption at exchange rates based on black-market rates.

COMECON AND 'EAST-EAST' TRADE

The Council of Mutual Economic Assistance (CMEA, or Comecon) was founded in 1949. Its members were the USSR, Czechoslovakia, Hungary, Poland, East Germany, Roumania, Bulgaria, plus Albania (which withdrew), Mongolia and Cuba (as from 1972). Yugoslavia is an associate member. For its first fifteen years it led a somewhat shadowy existence. While providing an institutional link and a discussion centre, the fact was that almost all trade took place on a bilateral basis, bilaterally negotiated. There was very little co-ordination of plans. Therefore references to Comecon in a textbook on the Soviet economy could have been very brief indeed.

Times have changed. There are now more frequent high-level meetings, more co-ordination of plans, more joint projects. There are a number of international industrial-sectoral corporations: *Intermetall* (metals), *Interkhim* (chemicals) and others, involving the joint planning and utilization of production in these sectors. There have been numerous international specialization agreements: thus the Permanent Commission on Machinery, set up in 1966, endeavoured to avoid needless duplication in the production of machinery and equipment; though it was an uphill struggle, a series of recommendations were gradually adopted (Faddeyev, 1974, pp.217–19.) Specialization agreements also covered ball- and roller-bearings, components for motor vehicles, lorries, radio-electronics, rolling-mill equipment, and so on. Standardization of computers brought to an end a situation in which there were 'twenty-seven different kinds of computers, incompatible in mathematical, technological and construction characteristics'. (Faddeyev, 1974, p.225.) A growing number of major investment projects combine the capital, technology and (sometimes) labour of several countries, which then share in the output (or, in the case of pipelines, throughput) when the project is completed. Thus in East Germany a large nitrogenous fertilizer plant is jointly the work of Soviet, Polish, Czech, Hungarian and Yugoslav technicians, using Soviet natural gas in the production process. (Faddeyev, 1974, p.231.) Other examples are the Ust'-Ilim woodpulp complex, the Kiyembayev asbestos works, the Biisk ore enrichment plant, a gas-condensate work in Orenburg, and the gas pipeline Orenburg-Western frontier of the USSR, all being built on Soviet territory with credits, equipment and in some cases labour of several other countries. (Kapranov, *EkG*, 1975, No. 52, p.18.) All this is apart from the still very large number of bilateral trade agreements, which include, of course, agreements on specialization: thus the USSR is buying much of the output of Hungarian buses, East German cranes and locomotives, Polish ships. Some large Soviet projects now assemble parts made in several countries: thus the Zhiguli (Soviet Fiat) car includes Bulgar and Yugoslav accumulators, Bulgar starters and generators, Czech headlights, Polish shock-absorbers, Hungarian radios and instrument panels. (Isupov, *PKh*, 1974, No. 12, p.33.)

One cannot, therefore, ignore Comecon. However, the above list of activities, though incomplete, may give a mistaken impression of its scope and importance.

Each country has its own plan, the responsibility of its own political and planning authorities. Despite considerable effort, the process of planning is not, except at the edges, joint. Of course, the five-year and annual plans do incorporate the input-output consequences of major trade agreements. But, as we have seen, annual operational plans (and their quarterly and monthly subdivisions) are full of amendments, as unexpected shortages develop and new needs are indentified. These amendments can disrupt the fulfilment of contractual obligations, across borders as well as within them. In other words, sectoral international planning, e.g. by *Intermetall* and *Interkhim,* and the work of the equivalents of *Gosplan* and of priority-determining organs in each country, can easily conflict. It is not easy to see, in the context of centrally planned economies, how this can be remedied without super-planners armed with supra-national authority. But this is only possible, as things now are, if the party chiefs of all the member states meet together and agree. This level can only consider major policy issues. Operational detail falls to more junior officials, who cannot commit their respective countries without constant reference back.

One consequence is that the annual trade agreements, and the quotas within them, negotiated at inter-governmental level (and still usually bilaterally) become highly inflexible. It is said to be easier to sell and buy as needed from the West, and in fact there are Western businessmen who have grown rich by acting as intermediaries between pairs of Comecon countries anxious to make deals outside of the annual bilateral agreement.

We have already discussed the causes of bilateralism and non-convertibility. Yet this is plainly a cause of economic loss. After all, money was invented some millenia ago precisely to ease multilateral trade, to get away from the inconvenience of bilateral barter. This practice stands in the way of a major extension of integration within Comecon. In the words of Csikos-Nagy (1971, p.105) 'commodity trade between the CMEA [i.e. Comecon] countries is organized on a bilateral basis. . . . The advantages of a united socialist world market cannot assert themselves. The system of bilateral relations puts a brake on the efficiency of foreign trade. And the principle of identical commodity patterns simply contradicts the requirements of efficiency.' By 'identical commodity patterns' the author means exchanges of 'equally hard commodities', and also of machinery for machinery, i.e. the balancing by categories already referred to earlier in this chapter (see also Csikos-Nagy, 1975.)

Closely connected with these difficulties, in part causing them, is the price system, or rather lack of system. To repeat, neither the prices at which trade is conducted nor the domestic prices of each country reflect scarcity, utility, need. So long as price and exchange-rate relationships between Comecon countries are neither logical nor co-ordinated, it is inevitable that 'international agreements on the exchange of commodities between CMEA countries are based on international co-ordination of national plans and are regarded as central state affairs. Accordingly *prices play hardly any role in shaping the volume and pattern of foreign trade.*' (Csikos-Nagy, 1971, p.103 – my emphasis.) One can also agree with the view that 'so long as the internal and the external mechanism by necessity brings about a foreign-trade price system of this character, it will not be possible to establish any type of multilateral trade and convertible currency'. (Ausch, 1971, p.73.)

Furthermore, the planners of each country resist the elimination of any productive unit which is already operational. At an earlier stage, the East European communist regimes had aimed at a species of industrial autarchy: such countries as Czechoslovakia suffered by producing (in small quantities) virtually every kind of machine. But, this situation once established, it is hard to alter. Despite all brave talk on specialization, the author of a glossy and (on the whole) rosy-coloured account of the growth of Comecon had to admit that 'specialization and co-operation in the production of the basic kinds of machinery are still weak. . . . Universalism, the existence of parallel lines of production in different countries leads to lower effectiveness. . . . For example in the GDR there is produced today over 80 per cent of the world's assortment of machine-tools. The situation in Czechoslovakia is similar. This is to a great extent small-scale production.' (Faddeyev, 1974, p.251.) He goes on to refer to 'objective difficulties'. Among them are the absence of generally accepted criteria for specialization. Some countries (Roumania and Bulgaria, for instance) regard themselves as developing and therefore claim that new industrial activities ought to be started there, especially as they have a labour surplus, even if this appears not to be justified on comparative-cost or economy-of-scale grounds. There are indeed 'unequal degrees of interest among members of Comecon in questions of specialization'. Then there is (again) the problem of prices: thus 'world prices, on the basis of which prices are formed for specialized production, often are at a level at which it is more advantageous to produce for oneself than to purchase' (these items). (Faddeyev, 1974, p.257.)

So there is still much to do. A very ambitious scheme for 'complex integration' was adopted in 1973, but one must not take these schemes for joint international integrated planning as representing reality. In the view of some East European officials, progress towards integration and multilateralization will proceed through the deepening of *sectoral* international activities, under such bodies as *Interkhim*, and of joint investment projects with repayment of credits with the goods produced. Also one must note the growing role of the Comecon Bank, including its role as a source of credits and, increasingly, in operations in convertible currencies. Its further development is worth watching.

The theory of foreign trade has been poorly developed so far. Marx had little to say about it, also his theories are used in a manner unhelpful to trade. For example 'some economists, citing Marx, claim that the less developed countries lose in specialization and co-operation on the world's markets' (this in the context of Comecon). (Faddeyev, 1974, p.252.) The neo-Marxist economist Arghiri Emmanuel has developed a theory of unequal exchange (1969), according to which equal exchange (the product of one hour's labour for a product of one hour's labour) becomes in practice impossible between countries with differing productivities and living standards. Thus there would seem to be no 'equal' exchange possible, at any prices, between the United States (say) and Brazil or Bulgaria. There is talk in general terms of socialist world-market prices, but no one quite knows how to decide what they should be. (It is twenty years ago that I heard a Czech delegate at Geneva say, over a cup of coffee: 'When the world revolution comes we shall have to preserve one capitalist country. Otherwise we will not know at what prices to trade'.)

All this helps to explain the obstacles that stand in the way of integration, or indeed of a rational use of the principle of comparative costs as a guide to specialization. Criticisms are made in the specialized press, the critics urging the greater use of economic criteria in foreign-trade planning, a closer link between the foreign-trade transactions (especially, but of course not exclusively, within Comecon) and the *khozraschet* interests of enterprises. One example of lack of such a link relates to credits, granted by some Comecon countries to others in an effort to break out of the practice of annual bilateral balancing: 'The "interest" to be paid on credits in international trade is, as a matter of fact, at least as much isolated from the earnings and profits of economic units as the prices abroad of the export and import goods are indifferent to them. It is only to the finance ministries that interest means an additional income or additional liability,' but even this is not really money, as the credit will be repaid by 'future commodity deliveries . . . which are decided upon by other organs of state administration.' (Ausch, 1971, p.75.)

It must also be recalled that each country faces its own internal problems, and has at times sharply altered domestic economic priorities for political reasons, and this inevitably complicates the international co-ordination of plans. Thus after the riots of December 1970, Poland increased imports of consumers' goods and also very greatly increased the volume of investment, which involved her in heavy indebtedness, especially to the West, and clearly the consequences of this and of the renewed troubles of June 1976, are bound to affect the allocation of resources and of currency, and so also Poland's role within Comecon as an importer and an exporter. The Soviet Union had to respond to the poor harvest of 1975, and has also taken decisions to enlarge her imports not only of food but also of consumers' goods and the means of making them. This again is an aspect of the role of politically determined priorities, as against calculations of rates of return or profitability. The Soviet government decided to buy the Fiat car plant, or Pepsi-cola, or oranges, not because it discovered that the coefficient of effectiveness would be high (it was doubtless very high also ten or twenty years previously), but because of a policy decision. But if each Comecon country not only controls resource allocation but also makes different policy decisions (as, in micro-economic matters at least, they can do), plan-co-ordination based upon some agreed economic calculus becomes very difficult.

The essential issue may be formulated as follows. In the West, a customs union or Common Market enables the countries composing it to 'integrate' their economic activities through the market, through multilateral deals between business firms. Finished goods, components, materials, fuels, cross borders without paying customs duty. By contrast, as we have seen, a Soviet-type economy operates on the basis of central instructions. Each country has, in the words of a Soviet author, 'a totally unlimited competence to take national planning decisions. The planned organization of the world socialist market . . . is precisely carried on through national state organs in Comecon.' (Zotova, 1969, p.25.) But this logically calls for supra-national planning organs, whose will can be enforced, as against 'localism', by a supreme political organ. Thus under capitalism an effective customs union presupposes the minimization of official obstacles to trade, whereas in Soviet-type economies the same result can only be achieved if the central planners themselves are integrated. But this is not politically feasible. Each country has its own central plan, its own central committee and Politbureau, its own internal prices and varying degrees of shortages which these prices fail to reflect. Acute problems arise both in making calculations (e.g. of comparative cost), in reconciling often conflicting interests, and in devising operationally effective ways of 'joining' the central plans of many countries, (I abstract for the moment from market-type reforms within certain countries; see Chapter 11 for these) and also of involving and interesting management in the process of foreign trade in general, Comecon in particular. New organizational forms are being devised, to ensure that joint projects and their input-output consequences are written into the operational plans of the countries concerned, with appropriate priority, calling for the development of 'an agreed five-year plan of multilateral integrated activities'. (O. Rybakov and N. Khmelevsky, *PKh*, 1976, No. 2, p.41.) We may see some important changes, even though past experience leads one to expect a great deal of frustration and delay. It is, however, only right to note that there is now some progress in the direction of integration, and also that Western countries and their currencies are in very considerable disarray.

ISSUES IN EAST-WEST TRADE

There are a number of problems which arise in trade between Soviet-type economies and those of Western countries. Some are essentially of a political nature. Both sides have been nervous of excessive dependence on each other, fearing the disruptive effect of possible embargoes. Thus, for example, controls over 'strategic' exports to the USSR were imposed, and, though now of much lesser importance, could be reimposed, or supply of commodities urgently needed by the USSR might be made conditional upon political concessions (this is advocated by those who consider that 'America should use the grain weapon' in years when the Soviet Union has a bad harvest). A powerful school of thought in the West is arguing that the West ought not to be supplying high technology, stressing also the vulnerability of the West to future and unpredictable changes in Soviet policy. Often the holders of these views believe that anything that strengthens the USSR is to be deplored, that trade strengthens the USSR and that, therefore, East-West trade is inherently. suspect. To the objection that trade usually benefis both parties to a freely negotiated deal, they reply that the USSR gains more, either because of the advantages of the state monopoly in dealing with competitive Western traders, or because technology confers a special advantage on its purchaser (e.g. Wiles, 1976.)

My own view is somewhat different, but this is not the place to debate the *politics* of East-West trade. The point of the preceding paragraph was only to stress that one obstacle to its growth is political. Despite this, the volume of East-West exchanges has in fact grown substantially, as a glance at any volume of trade statistics will demonstrate. It is the *economic* problems of trade between systems that will be our concern for the rest of this chapter.

One issue concerns most-favoured-nation treatment (MFN), and the linked issues of discrimination and reciprocity. Soviet officials complain of discriminatory tariffs or quantitative restrictions, which a number of Western countries impose on their goods, and also about the insistence of some countries on bilateral balancing. It may seem in Moscow that these are manifestations of politically motivated prejudice. There are, however, economic grounds for discrimination, which we must now examine.

In the first place, a Western country offering MFN provides access to its markets. What can the USSR offer in return? What does MFN mean in Soviet-type economy? There is no 'access', except to the state monopoly of foreign trade and its agents. Customs duties are insignificant. It may well be that, as they claim, the Soviet trade corporations use strictly commercial criteria when deciding what and from whom to purchase, but there is no way of telling whether this is so, or whether preference for a particular supplier is laid down in an unpublished inter-office memorandum. What, then, is meaningful reciprocity, what can be gained by a Western country if it grants MFN?

Secondly, it is held that Soviet dumping represents a danger. Only crude propagandists believe that this dumping is deliberate, in the sense that they sell cheap in order to disrupt. They sell cheap only when they cannot sell dear. The point is simply that, as we have seen, the foreign-trade corporation is instructed to sell (at the best price it can) and is automatically compensated through a budgetary subsidy for any loss which it incurs. It is uninterested in domestic costs. Therefore – so it is argued – there must be restrictions which it is unnecessary to apply to normal Western firms, which cannot disregard costs. (In those cases where Western dumping is commonly encountered, as with many agricultural products, restrictions exist in most Western countries against imports from non-communist countries also.)

Thirdly, Western governments are subject to pressures from their industries to secure access to 'Eastern' markets for their products. This can be done by attaching conditions to the entry of Soviet goods, either particular items (e.g. 'We will grant a quota for canned salmon if you purchase x tons of herring') or in general ('We will allow entry to your goods if you spend the *valuta* so earned in our country'). The Western country concerned may in this way be gaining a competitive edge over other Western countries, in negotiating for special advantages for its exporters in the 'Eastern' market. In these circumstances, a Western country which does not impose restrictions and does not demand a *quid pro quo* may find itself at a disadvantage. Thus, since the Soviet planners would like to increase their earnings of convertible currency, they may well instruct their traders to buy less from any country which does not insist on bilateral balancing, so as to acquire a convertible surplus. Similarly, if (say) the French insist on the Soviets buying French hats while the British do not, British hat exporters would strongly complain that they are denied access to the Soviet market. All this is, of course, quite inconsistent with MFN.

The Soviet view is very different. They would argue that it is unfair to compare the right to *try* to sell in the West, which is all the West can offer, with an insistence that the Soviet side undertake to purchase specified quantities of goods. That, they would maintain, is not reciprocity. They also understandably dislike being compelled to spend their earnings in any particular country, preferring to buy the cheapest and best wherever it is available. It must seem odd to them to hear us lecture about the virtues of multilateral trade and then insist on bilateral balancing, as several Western countries do. There is also the cogent argument that the Soviet planners, being in urgent need of many kinds of Western goods, spend up to the limit of currency availability (plus the proceeds of credits and gold sales), and that restriction on their ability to sell reduces their ability to buy from the West as a whole. Total Soviet exports represent only a small percentage of total Western imports from all sources. Soviet and East European exporters are in any case restricted by availability. If all frontiers were open, if MFN were universal, no spectacular increase in 'Eastern' exports is likely, and fears of dumping and disruption are vastly exaggerated (or are the consequence of the restrictions; obviously, if all markets but one are closed, there could be unintended disruption in the one market that is open). Several East European countries (notably Poland and Hungary) have grounds for complaint about the impact of the EEC's Common Agricultural Policy upon their exports of farm produce.

In 1976 there was – at long last – a formal approach from Comecon to EEC in Brussels, though the content of this approach has not so far been substantial: exchange of information, mutual representation and the like. A complication is being introduced into the hitherto customary bilateralism, as EEC restricts such separate bilateral deals. Both politically and economically it would not be attractive for the USSR if each Comecon country made its own deal with EEC as a whole, and we must anticipate some proposals designed to facilitate a more general all-European set of trade rules.

According to some Western businessmen there are other obstacles to trade. Thus market research and contact with potential customers in the USSR are impeded by the system of controls, Soviet orders and supplies can vary very widely and unpredictably over time, there are disconcerting occasions when sales are made conditional upon the firm concerned disposing of Soviet goods of an equivalent value. The institutional environment is unfamiliar.

However, a major obstacle (in my view) is the effect of the planning system itself on production for export. It is necessary to distinguish between raw materials and fuels on the one hand and manufactures on the other. Soviet exports to the West consist overwhelmingly of the former. The USSR has had long experience in selling such items as oil and timber, and the basic problem is not one of marketing techniques but simply of the quantitative limitations on export surpluses: more could be sold if more were available to sell.

It is quite another matter with manufactures. There are considerations of quality, of adapting the produce to the needs of specific foreign markets, of the knowledge and material interests of managers. '. . . Countries are reluctant to invest in export purposes', because of 'a permanent scarcity of resources available for investment', according to a source already quoted. (Ausch, 1971, p.85.) This point relates to the priority of investment for export under conditions of shortage. Closer links with foreign markets are impeded by the state monopoly exercised by the Ministry of Foreign Trade, that (as we have seen) jealously guards its powers. In some East European countries, in which foreign trade plays a much bigger role, this monopoly has been broken or modified. There is scope for reform in this direction in the Soviet Union also. In his report to the 25th party Congress, Kosygin noted the weakness in exports of manufactures and suggested the creation of enterprises specializing in export. (*Pravda*, 2 March 1976.)

New forms of East-West economic co-operation are developing, which should help to overcome bureaucratic and other barriers. Factories have been erected in the Soviet Union by Western firms and consortia. 'Compensation agreements' are negotiated involving long-term Western credits to be repaid by part of the output which these credits are used to expand. The smaller countries of Eastern Europe have concluded a variety of agreements with Western firms, ranging from the production of components to joint projects to which Western firms contribute capital (e.g. such hotels as the Intercontinental in Budapest and the Forum in Warsaw). Rumania has adopted laws making possible direct investment by Western firms.

The Soviet system, by contrast, has changed very slowly, in this as in most other respects. It is sometimes described as 'autarchic', but this term requires to be qualified. It is true that Soviet planners have tended to cover their requirements from internal sources whenever possible, and from within Comecon if domestic supplies are inadequate.

On the other hand, as already pointed out, they buy in the West to the limit of resources available for the purpose. As for the smaller countries, their ambitious industrialization programmes have led to much greater dependence on foreign trade, because of the need to import materials and fuels for the new industries. In recent years one could ascribe trade limitations to the failure to expand sufficiently rapidly production of items saleable in Western markets, rather than to conscious pursuit of autarchic aims (save where these are motivated by national security considerations).

Much having been said in this chapter on irrationalities of Soviet trade and pricing procedures, it seems only right to end by referring again to the trading and currency problems of the Western world. It is also interesting and perhaps paradoxical to note that the Soviet system benefits from *our* dumping. A recent example is the purchase at prices far below cost of part of the EEC's butter mountain. When Soviet planners desire to import, the cheaper the better. It is we who, when offered goods cheaply, insist on stopping them by anti-dumping restrictions. At least in this respect they may be more sane than we are!

It is also only right to stress that the trade of all Comecon countries, both with each other and with the West, has rapidly increased. Also that much more attention is now being paid, by theorists and planners alike, to the problems of foreign-trade criteria, and to specialization agreements and joint projects. So in this area there have been some significant advances in the past decade.

The present (February 1980) exchange rate is 0·62 roubles to the US dollar. It did not, as stated earlier, change in line with the West German mark, but has reflected the steady devaluation of the dollar against most other currencies.

The American embargoes which followed the Soviet 'intervention' in Afghanistan will doubtless have adverse effects on the general levels of East–West trade.

CHAPTER 11

ALTERNATIVE MODELS

The Soviet system suffers from overcentralization. We have had repeated occasion to note that it cannot function effectively because of the sheer volume of interconnected decision making which the model requires. Also it is clear that centralization is functionally inescapable, given the absence of criteria for decentralized decision making. If the model is based upon the proposition that 'society' determines what is needed and how best it should be provided, then in a modern industrial economy, only the centre can determine need and can allocate resources so as to provide what society requires. It has also been clear that the great practical problem is one of handling operational detail, the micro-economics of the system. 'Strategic' decisions on large-scale investments, e.g. developing West Siberia or the setting up of new industries, plainly not only belong to the centre but are well within its capacity to handle.

Reformers, therefore, have tended to concentrate upon devising means of freeing the centre of detailed control over the functioning of existing enterprises. The product mix should be determined by the needs of the customers, directly or (via trade) indirectly, because the centre cannot know precisely what these needs are. It has been stressed that 'customers' are not only citizens but also other managers. This has already been touched upon in Chapter 4, above. In Chapter 6 we have also seen that investment decisions also suffer from the consequences of overcentralization, as for example when considering the production and installation of new equipment, devising and adopting new technique, and so on.

It is natural that some reformers should discover or rediscover the virtues of a market solution. If a factory needs an efficient lathe, a farm a milking machine, a hundred women are seeking shoes of a given size and colour, it is desirable that these be provided. If they are not, this is not evidence of a clash between user preferences and planners' preferences, but much more probably a consequence of the malfunctioning of the system, owing to aggregation, bureaucratic inertia, non-transmission of information or inter-departmental confusion. Consequently, it seems obvious that the correct way forward is to cause producers to respond to demand without involving the unavoidably bureaucratic and hierarchical pyramid of planning, supply and production agencies. This, clearly, is a market-type solution to the problem. Management (or management *and* workers) would find that it 'pays' them to produce what is needed. They would respond to signals which are essentially commercial rather than administrative.

On the appropriate balance between central plan and decentralized market there is a wide range of opinion. One should also note that most reformers would accept the proposition that the centre is not only entitled but bound to influence the market, e.g. by price controls, subsidies, taxes, and that, acting for society, it should affect production and resource allocation, but that its methods should be economic and not administrative, i.e. that it should operate by affecting the calculations made by management rather than by instructing management what it should do and how it should do it.

An early model of market socialism is that of Oskar Lange (1938). In it socialist managers behave as capitalists should do in a competitive market, equating marginal revenue with marginal cost, and the planners exercise their control by so adjusting prices as to bring supply and demand into balance, increasing prices if stocks fall, reducing them if they increase. This (as its author later admitted) is altogether too simple. There is no growth in his model. The sheer number of prices which require to be flexibly controlled is, in the real world, impossibly large. Motivation is not discussed: thus why should managers and planners behave in the way prescribed? External economies and diseconomies, complementarities, indivisibilities, are assumed out of the way. One is also reminded of Kornai's very sensible dictum (1971a) that no one in reality takes decisions based on price-information alone. It is worth recalling that Lange devised his model not for a functioning socialist economy but as an answer to the argument, advanced by Mises and Robbins, that a socialist economy could not cope with the multitude of simultaneous equations which the central planners would need to solve. His reply was on a level of abstraction similar to that on which Mises, Robbins and other economists analysed a competitive market economy. They too abstracted from growth, externalities, etc. But, of course, *we* cannot, in the present context.

Therefore we must explore ways in which plan and market can be combined in a coherent whole. By 'coherent' one cannot mean in a smooth and frictionless way. Such a happy outcome can exist only in books (one is tempted to say 'in fairy tales'). In *any* division of any process between centre and management, or between any organs or departments, there are bound to be problems of demarcation of responsibility and differences of perception and interest. To imagine anything else is quite unreal. All that can be hoped for in an imperfect world is that the systems function, and that the advantages of the chosen method or system outweigh the disadvantages.

With these considerations in mind, we can turn to the experience of one country which has experimented with a 'new economic mechanism', Hungary.

THE HUNGARIAN REFORM MODEL

What has actually happened in Hungary has differed somewhat from the original intentions of the reformers. It is useful first to set out what these intentions were, and then, by identifying problems, try to distinguish those which were, so to speak, inherent in the chosen reform model from those which could be described as external or incidental to it. Among the latter, for example, was the very sharp worsening of Hungary's terms of trade in 1973-6, for reasons which had no connection whatever with either Hungary or reform, but which affected both.

In the period 1950-5, Hungary, like other countries within the Soviet bloc, had adopted a carbon copy of the Soviet planning system, with unfortunate results. The shock of the 1956 uprising led to a modification of agricultural policy (extensive decollectivization was followed by recollectivization on a more flexible basis, with much more consideration of peasant interest), and also to an attempt to revise the industrial planning system. Gradually, after much discussion among academics, managers and party leaders, the 'new economic mechanism' was elaborated, its introduction (on 1 January 1968) carefully prepared.

The original document introducing the reform contains a number of principles very different from those which underlie Soviet planning of the traditional type. Enterprises are to be free to decide 'what and how much they want to produce and market' and 'from what enterprises and in what quantities they wish to purchase for their own money the inputs they require'. There is to be 'greater scope for competition between enterprises' to stimulate efficiency and 'to satisfy the demands of the consumer more fully'. In the field of consumers' goods and services 'state enterprises will compete with each other and with co-operatives', and also with the limited but still significant private sector (especially in services). Large enterprises in a semi-monopoly position would be subjected to competition from imports, or otherwise prevented from exploiting their position.

Most important, prices are seen as having an active role: they should 'balance supply and demand', they should reflect 'value judgements emerging from the market' as well as economic policy. 'Differentiation of profits should influence the shaping of the pattern of production and supply . . . and help in bringing about the equilibrium of the market.' Profitability is to be the principal criterion of enterprise activity, with retained profits used in a 'profit-sharing fund' (for incentives to management and labour) and an investment fund.

Foreign trade could not be overlooked in drafting reform proposals in a country so heavily dependent on the outside world. 'The new economic mechanism will have to establish an organic connection between the domestic market and foreign markets. It will have to heighten the impact of external market impulses on domestic production, marketing and consumption.' There must therefore be 'an organic relationship between internal prices and foreign trade prices', with appropriate adjustment of exchange rates.*

This could be described as a market-socialist manifesto. Its essential features were, above all, the abandonment of obligatory production-plan indicators for enterprises, and of its corollary, administrative supply allocation (no more *Gossnab*, in other words), with prices, profitability and commercial contract determining what is produced and who buys it. Managers of state enterprises remained responsible to their economic ministries, and could be dismissed by them. Major investments remained the responsibility of the centre, but enterprises could invest in expanding or adapting their output, obtaining funds from the state banking system and/or using their own investment funds. This is, of course, essential: there is no point in using profits as a 'stimulant' if the profit-making enterprise cannot obtain the funds necessary to ensure that it produces in accordance with market requirements.

Taxes on enterprises, related to their net income, wages bill and capital asets as well as to their profits, largely replaced turnover tax as the major source of revenue, as Table 26 shows, comparing percentage revenues in a pre-reform and post-reform year:

Table 26

	1956	1968
Charge on assets (capital charge)	—	21
Wage-bill tax and social insurance	10	16
Taxes on profits and revenues of enterprises	19	33
Production tax and rents	—	2
Centralized amortization	6	5
Turnover tax	53	7
Customs duties and import taxes	—	4
Other revenues	12	12

(*Source*: B. Csikos-Nagy, 1969, p.148.)

Enterprises were free to hire additional labour, and no limit was set to the wages fund. However, to avoid excessive wage payments, increases in *average* wages exceeding a given norm (at first set at 3 per cent per annum) led to a sharp rise in the tax liability of the enter-

*All quotations are from the Resolution of the Hungarian socialist workers' party, circulated in English by the information service of the Hungarian chamber of commerce (undated, but presumably written at the end of 1967).

prise, and was thus 'discouraged'. Enterprises with liquid assets were encouraged to put them into the State Bank where they would earn interest.

Agriculture, though collectivized, was also run very flexibly, on market lines. Compulsory deliveries were abandoned even before the reform was promulgated. Farm management was thus left free to decide what to produce and what to sell. There was real life breathed into the formally co-operative structure; farms were left free to make their own internal arrangements with many expedients designed to provide effective incentives, some on the lines of the *beznaryadnoye zveno* (autonomous work group) described in Chapter 5 above. Limitations on private ownership of livestock were largely lifted. No restrictions were placed in the way of selling in the free markets in the cities, in which prices differed little from those in state shops. Farms were also allowed to undertake non-agricultural activities, and many made substantial profits out of running construction contract work, car repairs, small-scale manufactures, restaurants in Budapest and much else besides. There were also, as already mentioned, urban co-operative artisans and a limited private sector of craftsmen, shops, hairdressers, etc.

All this required a new role and a new basis for prices. They were divided into four categories: fixed, maximum, 'limit' (maxima and minima) and free. Essential consumers' goods and basic materials and fuel were in the first of these categories. However, the majority of intermediate goods (semi-manufacturers and the like) were decontrolled (thus 78 per cent of all prices charged by 'processing industries' were free of control, according to information given to me in 1974), and, most important, so were hundreds of thousands of relatively minor items, which, though a small percentage of total turnover, would have created impossible log-jams in the price-control mechanism. As was pointed out in Chapter 7, flexible control of all prices is a physical impossibility. Hungarian experience confirms that a precondition for effective control of what requires to be regulated is that minor items be not controlled. By 'effective' is meant here the ability to manoeuvre in the light of supply, demand and profitability, so as to ensure a flow of desired output without having to issue administrative orders that it be provided. (A Polish economist once said to me, in informal conversation: 'if such items as baby powder are on the list of centrally determined prices, rational pricing is out of the question'. He had in mind not only the volume of price-fixing required, but also the fact that then all prices, including even baby-powder, become political issues.)

Hungarian prices, then, were designed to elicit the desired product mix. They had, therefore, to reflect market conditions in some degree, whether or not they were centrally fixed. For example, state purchase prices for grain were and are on the list of fixed prices, but, since farms are compelled neither to grow nor to deliver any crop, the range of arbitrariness is much restricted, unlike the situation in the USSR, where compulsory delivery quotas are still the rule.

It is worth dwelling for a moment on the words 'desired product mix' in the previous paragraph. Desired by whom? This point was picked up by a Soviet commentator, evidently friendly to the Hungarian reform. In a published *reportage* he had a puzzled Soviet official exclaim to his Hungarian colleague: 'But suppose an enterprise stops making cups and increases the output of plates, although the state needs cups?' To which the Hungarian official replies: 'The state actually *needs* neither cups nor plates. The people need crockery. They buy it in shops. . . . The shops can buy plates or cups from several enterprises, or import them from abroad. . . . The market must be a real market, not a pseudo one. Otherwise we will have to return to administrative methods of control. And a real market requires competition.' (Volin, 1969, pp.159–64.) This probably imaginary conversation is meant, among other things, to underline the point that the state has in fact usually no interest in ensuring a product mix other than that indicated by demand in a genuinely functioning market.

One other point must be stressed. A reform of this type could not possibly work in the presence of excess demand. The consequences would be highly disruptive. 'Limit' prices would all rise to the maximum, free prices would rise sharply, and this would make profitability inversely proportional to the importance of the product, given that a multitude of the less significant items were left free. Demand for industrial materials would exceed supply, causing disruption of production and an urgent call for the reimposition of administrative allocation. Similarly, liberalization of imports, under conditions of immense put-up demand, would have led to the speedy exhaustion of currency reserves.

Therefore the reformers proceeded carefully, cutting back on excess demand (by appropriate credit and wage policies and price changes) before the reform was introduced. The foreign exchange coefficients were such (i.e. the forint was effectively so devalued) as to reduce demand for imports, but this had to be reinforced by a system of quantitative limitations and licensing, though this was intended to be temporary. Firms were, however, given greater access to foreign markets, as buyers or as sellers, in some cases directly, in more cases through specialist intermediaries.

How did the reform work out? Fortunately two most useful books exist, published in Budapest in English, of which the first describes the reform in detail and the second assesses its effect after three years. (Friss, 1969 and Gadó, 1972: see also B. Balassa, 1973 and D. Granick

1976.) The analysis that follows is inevitably brief and incomplete. Interested readers are urged to follow up the references, and, better still, go to Hungary and ask questions.

There were, of course, many difficulties, some inherent in the reform, some due to external causes.

One difficulty, much discussed during visits to Budapest, could be described as reluctance to accept the discipline of the market. Competition (except the so-called perfect competition of the textbook) is a battle with casualties. Competition hurts. No one likes to be hurt. Therefore, while accepting it in principle as applying to others, neither management nor workers welcomed it if it affected them adversely. They would claim that an exceptional situation existed, seek subsidies and restrictions, and in doing so behave in a manner familiar to us in Britain, where the same pressures exist. But, whereas it is true that rescue operations for semi-bankrupt companies are mounted here in some instances, bankruptcies none the less occur, and the discipline of the market does operate much of the time, however imperfectly. In Hungary, there are no bankruptcies. The pressures exercised through the ministries and party officials are such that the unsuccessful are sustained, subsidized, or, at most, reorganized.

Competition is also restricted by the existence or creation of monopolistic units, due in some cases to the small size of the country (only one producer), but in others to mergers, or to the continued use of monopolistic wholesaling organs created in the earlier period. Since state monopolies, if judged by profit-making criteria, could try to increase prices or reduce quality and service, this justified retention of controls which, if competition existed, would have been unnecessary. It should be stressed that a 'market' reform without competition is very likely to be a cure worse than the disease. 'Yet the domestic market cannot operate without competition,' to cite a Hungarian comment. (Gadó, 1972, p.21.)

Subsidies grew not only because of the pressure to 'protect' existing enterprises, but also because of the need to prevent price rises. This related particularly to consumers' goods and was part of the struggle to contain inflation and control wages, to which further reference will be made in a moment. It was also a consequence of the effort to prevent or mitigate imported inflation. By the mid-seventies the total level of subsidies grew formidable and their scale became inconsistent with the logic of the reform.

Next on the list are issues connected with income distribution and labour relations. It is in the nature of any market-type reform that it lays stress on income differentials, linking these with commercial results. Also, since the Hungarian reform has not altered the dominant role of managers vis-à-vis their subordinates, it followed that they would have to be the principal beneficiaries in the event of commer-

cial success, as this would depend so greatly on their decisions, judgement, willingness to take risks. Reflecting this, the original reform
measure laid down the following limits to the profit-related bonuses
paid out of the 'sharing fund' (Retained profits were divided between
the 'sharing fund', used for bonuses and wage supplements, the investment fund and reserves), 80 per cent of monthly salary for managers,
50 per cent for other senior executives, 15 per cent for workers.
Unsuccessful managers could have their salaries reduced to 80 per cent
of the basic rate, while workers were guaranteed 100 per cent of *their*
rate even if the enterprise made a loss. None the less, this looked anti-
egalitarian. It is true that, under Stalin especially, the Soviet system
was even less egalitarian, with very large bonuses payable for fulfilling
plans. It might therefore be argued that it was good to pay bonuses
for commercial success, insofar as this meant satisfying the customer,
rather than for obeying orders, with all the familiar distortions to
which this gave rise. However, Hungary, in common with most other
East European countries, never went as far as the Soviet Union in the
direction of material inequality.

Nor was it easy to link profit with efficient performance, under
conditions of a very imperfect market, so there were understandable
grumbles that managers and workers alike were rewarded, or deprived
of rewards, for reasons quite outside their control. A further cause
of friction was the growth of earnings in the relatively uncontrolled
co-operative and private sectors, including the collective farms. While
a 3 per cent limit was applied, by the use of tax sanctions, in state
enterprises, earnings of those not employed by the state rose by much
bigger percentages, as figures in Table 27 show.

Table 27   *Average wages per month (forints)*

	State industry	Agricultural co-operatives		Construction state workers	Construction building co-operatives*
1965	1767	1002	1966	1845	1581
1970	2115	1680	1969	2096	2407
1972	2297	2032	1972	2392	2973

*Operated by co-operative (collective) farms.
Source: (Hungarian Central Statistical Office, 1974, pp.107, 193, 239).

This was a consequence not only of imperfect markets, but also of
the greater freedom of co-operatives and collectives to diversify. They
could move into profitable productive activity, in situations in which
the state enterprise would be unable to follow them, since the latter
was and is prevented from switching to a totally new line of production (as distinct from adapting or modifying their product, which they
are, of course, free to do). Some were also concerned with the numeric-

ally small but conspicuous entrepreneurs on private account (a Hungarian colleague called them 'Nepmen') who operate on the fringes of the system. Add to this the normal desire of normal workers for higher wages, and pressures build up. These pressures were utilized at two opposite ends of the political spectrum. An intellectual 'left' opposition emerged, which drew attention to the comforts and privileges of the managerial-technological stratum. Also the old party bureaucrats disliked the entire reform (and also disliked the intellectual 'left opposition'), and sought to influence the workers against it. The old-style party bureaucrats are inclined to believe that privileges should be reserved for themselves, or handed out by them to those who do their bidding. These attitudes and discontents weakened the reform by affecting adversely its support base among the population. The critics also seized upon price increases which occurred, blaming them on the reform, and we know from our own experience that most people want higher incomes and strictly controlled prices *and* supply to equal demand in the shops, and cannot easily be persuaded that these objectives are incompatible.

A key difficulty, also related to labour, was described by one Hungarian economist as an attitude of 'one-sided flexibility'. The Soviet-type system, whatever its defects, did provide job security (unless, of course, one was arrested). Now, workers claim the right to move whenever they wish, while protesting against being moved or declared redundant. It is plainly difficult to grow and to modernize if people retain their old jobs, under conditions of full employment. There is little point in installing labour-saving devices which do not save labour, or to build a new factory unless overmanning elsewhere is reduced. These are familiar problems also in the USSR and not unknown in Britain, but they present particular difficulties in the context of a Hungarian-type reform. The political commitment to full employment, and the growing influence of the trade unions (or of party officials holding senior trade union posts), do not make things any easier. In some form this must be a problem in any country, socialist or no, aiming at full employment: to move or be retained is often inconvenient, it is only human to wish to stay put, and compulsory labour-direction is not acceptable either. Granick (1976, p.247) calls this not only a 'full employment constraint' but 'protection of jobs from changing product demands, and from alterations in technology which affect the skill composition . . . of the labour force'. He regards this whole area, rightly, as crucial.

The particular form of wage control, via the *average* wage, led to unforeseen difficulties and had to be modified. The reason was that one could alter the average by changing the mix between high-paid and low-paid labour. It therefore became 'unprofitable' to reduce the number of unskilled labourers, or conversely to employ additional engineers without also taking on some unskilled labourers so as to keep the average increase down to permitted levels. A more sophisticated method of defining the upper limit had to be devised.

Also it was said that managerial interest in short-term profits (with or without subsidies) was not sufficiently balanced by longer-term considerations. 'Methods for creating long-term interests have not yet been evolved.' (Gadó, 1972, p.21.)

Another problem is a consequence of the retention of centralized planning (though in varying forms) by Hungary's Comecon partners. This is important for a country so heavily dependent on trade. Decisions involving either the purchase or the sale of products to or from the USSR, for instance, are the consequence of bilateral agreements negotiated at inter-government level. The enterprises concerned must then conform. Efforts are made to associate the enterprises with the negotiations, to ensure that the deal is profitable for them. None the less, as Hungarian observers admit, this does cause 'systemic' misfits, and contributes to the retention of some directive powers at the centre.

The sharp rise in world prices of fuel and of many other items hit Hungary hard in 1973-4, while exports of livestock products to EEC countries were severely restricted by Common Agricultural Policy. The resultant strains on the balance of payments, with the West and within Comecon, had an adverse effect on the reform by limiting import possibilities, and also by opening a wide gap between domestic and 'world' prices. It also had to lead to unpopular measures to hold down wages while adjusting prices upwards, a consequence of the sharply worsening terms of trade. This was all more in the nature of bad luck than anything directly or indirectly due to the reform, but it affected the reform adversely all the same.

The net effect in the last few years has been some shift in the balance towards centralization, both formally and informally ('Don't forget that the party secretary still has a telephone,' I was told, 'and managers who ignore their ministry's instructions can be sacked'). Reality, as is its wont, departs from the model in many ways. But, though administrative measures are taken, the basic element in the reform has survived: though with exceptions, it is still the case that managers are not given an obligatory current-output plan from above, that they can buy their own inputs, and that the exceptions are still exceptional. Prices and wages have been increased in the period 1975-6, largely as a result of external factors and their effects on prices and costs. In 1973-4 some restrictions were imposed on non-agricultural enterprises of collective farms. None the less, the reform has not led to inflation on the Western scale. The increase in retail prices in the period 1970-3 did not exceed 3·5 per cent in any year (*Hungarian Statistical Yearbook*, 1973, p.342), though the figure for 1976 is likely to reach 5 per cent.

Has the reform been a success? How does one measure success? Any casual visitor to Budapest is bound to be impressed by the quality of service, the range of choice in the shops, the absence of queues. The contrast with a typical Soviet city is evident. Yet before one jumps to any conclusion, it is as well to recall that efficiency and choice in trade are superior, compared with the USSR, in Prague and Leipzig too, and neither Czechoslovakia nor East Germany has adopted the Hungarian 'new economic mechanism'. The real comparison should be with the Hungary that would have been, without this reform. Some critics may think that the rate of growth should reflect the success of the reform, but this is highly doubtful. Growth is a most imperfect measure, sometimes easier to achieve by concentrating on what is most convenient to the producer, rather than on what is most wanted by the customer. One recalls the title of one of Peter Wiles's early articles, 'growth versus choice'. One must also recall the deficiencies of the Soviet-type system, seen in the light of its statistical consequences. Two baskets of goods can cost the same to produce, can carry the same price tag, but one may be 'worth' much more to the user than the other. In a market economy this, in principle, could not happen, because, if the preferred basket were available, the less satisfactory one would not be bought at that price. In the USSR this could certainly happen, for reasons explored at length in earlier chapters. Therefore, if the effect of reform is to produce a more satisfactory basket of goods, the extra pleasure in the users' eyes reflects added welfare which is *not* measured by aggregate output statistics.

In actual fact, Hungarian growth rates were little affected by the reform, underlining the difficulty of quantitatively measuring its success or failure. (See the discussion of this by Granick, 1976.) We can, however, learn from Hungary's experience about the problems which are likely to be encountered if this species of reform is adopted. No painless or problem-free remedy exists to any country's economic ills, but it is as well to be aware of where the shoe is likely to pinch.

The Hungarian model, be it noted, contains large elements of central control, exercised by the spasmodic use of reserve powers to issue instructions, and by the key role of the centre in investment policy, partly directly, partly through the Bank. This is apart from the government's use of *economic* levers, such as subsidies, exchange-rate coefficients, import restrictions, and so on. Some Hungarian critics take the view that the many difficulties have arisen because the reform has not been consistently carried through. We should see it as a mixture of central planning and quasi-market decentralization. For reasons to be set out later in this chapter, the elusive optimal organizational form, if ever it is found, will surely be a mixture, though not necessarily *this* mixture.

THE YUGOSLAV MODEL AND WORKERS' PARTICIPATION

This may be distinguished from the Hungarian in several important ways. Firstly, the role of market forces is much greater, the role of central planning less, with a considerable role reserved for national republics and local authorities (communes). Enterprises try to increase profits, or more precisely their net income (net, that is, of purchase of inputs, capital charges, taxes, etc.), upon which the material interests of management and workers depends. Secondly, the model is based on the principle of workers' self-management. Unlike the USSR or Hungary or any of their allies, those employed in Yugoslav state enterprises elect a management committee (workers' council) and, jointly with the commune, also the manager, who is responsible to the workers' council. Thirdly, the incomes of the workers depend more on the financial results of their enterprise than is the case in Hungary or elsewhere, though there is a minimum below which wages cannot fall. Fourthly, foreign trade is very largely liberalized, much more so than even in Hungary. Agriculture is overwhelmingly in the hands of peasant smallholders, who respond freely to market stimuli (though the state is the principal purchaser of farm produce).

Prices should be free, in accordance with the model. However, in the face of inflationary pressures there has been an increasing tendency to introduce price freezes or to limit rises. The bulk of investment funds of enterprises are borrowed from the bank, which judges the various projects partly by reference to their profitability and partly in relation to state economic policies and long-term plans. Some preference is given to the underdeveloped regions in the allocation of limited central funds.

The Yugoslav leadership has moved very far since the days of the Stalin-Tito quarrel in 1949, at which date the regime was following Stalinist policies with enthusiasm. Forced by the split to devise a model of their own, Tito and his comrades hit upon a combination of free market and workers' self-management, and the logic of their position drove them further and further along the road to free enterprise, so much so that Belgrade at one point joined Chicago as the place where belief in the virtues of the market mechanism was most fervently held. Genuine disbelief in bureaucratic controls was reinforced by the centrifugal tendencies in the national republics. The need for a capital market and for foreign capital led to further measures of 'liberalization' – it became easier for enterprises to invest in other enterprises, and direct foreign investment was facilitated.

These tendencies reached their high point in 1965–71. In the most recent years there was a move back towards central control, though the Yugoslav economy is still much more market-oriented than the Hungarian, let alone the Soviet.

Yugoslav experience suggests that the market-and-workers' self-management model suffers from certain built-in defects. It is a matter of opinion whether these are counterbalanced by its advantages.

The principal advantage, much stressed by the ideologists of the regime, is the sense of participation which it engenders. Of course in practice self-management is not unlimited, the party and state organs can influence the outcome, many workers are indifferent and apathetic. None the less, it can be held that the principle, and also the practice, of self-management is in line with an important element of the socialist tradition. Marx spoke of the workers, the direct producers, running their own affairs in free association. This, so it is held in Belgrade, is inconsistent with centralized planning, which of necessity becomes bureaucratic and remote, giving the workers no sense of participating. If this feeling is to be real, self-management at enterprise level is a necessity. This, in turn, calls for a market, because, unless the workers' collective responds to demand through the market, there would have to be a central planning mechanism to assess need and issue instructions, and we would be back to Soviet-style centralization, within which workers' self-management would have no meaning.

There are several objections which can be made to such a model in principle. The first relates to external economies and complementarities. Surely it is the case, and socialists in particular must know it, that micro-profitability is not always consistent with the common weal. At their worst, Yugoslav free-market fanatics even required that a research institute in the chemical industry be profitable (does the research division of Imperial Chemical Industries make a profit *as such*?), and greatly confused railway administration by the separate profit-oriented operation of each republic's rail network. The essential point will be made again when we come to an overall assessment of reform models: since there can be occasions when the general interest conflicts with the interest of a firm (whether labour-managed or not), it is a weakness of the Yugoslav model that this point is so largely neglected.

This point was put vividly as follows: 'The ability to grapple with factors external to the success of the individual enterprise and small region have disappeared. . . . The Yugoslav economy is run along Adam Smith lines to a degree which is quite unusual for Europe as a whole.' (Granick, 1976, p.468.) However, we must bear in mind that extremes of laissez-faire need not necessarily accompany workers' self-management, that there are specific Yugoslav reasons (nationalist as well as ideological) for these extremes.

Secondly, the principle of workers' self-management contains a flaw. If the income of the workers is not significantly affected by the net revenues of the enterprise, then they have little material interest in the outcome. If, on the other hand, the successful enterprise pays much more to its workers than a less successful one, the material interest is indeed present, but the differential is bound to be resented, as it offends a widely held sense of fairness. Why should a worker who does his job well receive much less than another of equal skill and application, but whose enterprise happens to be profitable? This may, almost certainly will, be due to circumstances over which any individual worker has no control, and in reality the role in management of a rank-and-file worker cannot be significant. Equal pay for equal work is a principle which extends not only to pay rates as between men and women. In practice, knowledge that other workers in successful enterprises earn more is a cause of pressure for higher distribution of income to the workers elsewhere, and this constitutes an important source of inflationary pressure. The evidence clearly shows that the Yugoslav system is more inflation-prone than the Hungarian, and the powers of worker-elected councils over the apportionment of enterprise net income is surely one reason for this. One should not, moreover, overstate the extent to which the rank-and-file worker 'participates', and overcomes his sense of alienation as the official ideology would have it. (On this point see a very fair summary of the evidence in Granick, 1976, ch. 12.)

Thirdly, perhaps paradoxically, there is also a tendency to over-investment. The problem here is ultimate responsibility. If an enterprise wishes to expand, by borrowing from the bank, it puts up a good case for future profitability. Suppose, however, there is a loss. Who is to suffer? The manager may by then have moved elsewhere. The workers' council collectively cannot be financially punished, though in extreme cases it can be dissolved and a temporary manager appointed from above, as a consequence of insolvency, the nearest approach to bankruptcy. The rate of interest charged and the obligation to repay the loan are insufficient restraints on demand for capital. Lack of central control can also easily lead to duplication of investments, with loss of potential economies of scale. All this is consistent with a high growth rate, which Yugoslavia has indeed achieved. But it is a further spur to inflation.

Fourthly, and perhaps in the Yugoslav case most important, labour-managed enterprises are interested in maximizing the net product per employee, and to this extent are not interested in taking on additional employees, or less so than would either a capitalist or a Soviet-type enterprise, under conditions in which unemployment is a major problem.

There is a sizeable Western literature on the Yugoslav or 'Illyrian' model, to which Ward (1967) and Vanek (1970) are important contributors. Some of it is on a very abstract level: short-run, perfect competition, fixed capital supply. Even at this level of unreality, it can be shown that the labour-managed economies will find it worth while to refrain from expanding output and employment, for instance if the price of their product rises (indeed, on certain assumptions they might even find it 'pays' to reduce output). If one introduces a greater dose of reality and considers investment choices, it becomes even clearer that the aim of maximizing net product per employee can be a cause of unemployment: the labour-saving, capital-intensive variant would be preferred.

In a free market the profit-making capitalist would be more likely than the labour-managed firm to expand employment. A Soviet-type firm has to be prevented from taking on extra labour by limitations on the wages fund, or in some cases can be ordered to retain labour it does not need by local soviet authorities who have responsibility to find jobs for the people. In Yugoslavia, the fact that there are many unemployed – and would be many more if there were not hundreds of thousands working in West Germany – in no way affects the parameters within which the workers' council takes decisions.

This is one example of external diseconomies, of very considerable social importance. A workers' council opting for a capital-intensive variant, designed to increase net output per worker, in a situation of high unemployment, is surely placing narrow self-interest before the general interest. In a conference of the International Economic Association in Moscow, a Soviet delegate asked, with reason: 'Could enterprises as systems really be reduced to the interests of their employees?' What about the interests of the state and of other groups? (Maiminas, 1976, p.168.) He might have added: is there not a duty to absorb more of the unemployed?

There is also a left-wing critique, expressed in Yugoslavia itself by Mihajlo Markovic (1974), and in France by Charles Bettelheim (of whom more in a moment). Both stress the undesirable spread of commercialism, consumerism, advertising, income differentials (workers are willing to pay good managers well; they are not so egalitarian as left-wing intellectuals!). Both are unhappy with the market as a basis for any sort of socialism. Bettelheim (1969) wrote, à propos Yugoslavia: 'the workers cannot really dominate the use of their means of production, because their use is in fact dominated by market relations'.

In this short sentence is contained (in my view) a fundamental weakness of the entire 'new-left' position. What, then, is to determine the activities of the producers? Production is, ultimately, for use. If the requirements of the segment of society that they supply are not to communicate themselves through market channels, how are they to be communicated? Anyone would suppose that the producers produce for themselves alone. To this Bettelheim would certainly answer that the producers are also the consumers, that the needs of society should be determined by the 'associated producers'. Yugoslav theorists would instantly reply: but this in practice means centralized planning, the equivalent of *Gosplan*, allocation, industrial ministries (under whatever name), and this is precisely what the Yugoslav model was supposed to replace by grass-roots economic democracy. We shall return to this discussion later in this chapter.

OTHER VARIANTS

The *Czechoslovak* reform measures, which in some respects resembled the Hungarian, were halted by the invasion of 1968. No new model has emerged, although a modified 'traditional' system has been operating smoothly. Ota Šik, who was an influential reformer, is now in Switzerland, where, following on from his writings when still in Prague (esp. Šik, 1967), he has devised and discussed market-socialist models. The Czechoslovak reforms are discussed more fully elsewhere (i.e. Kyn, 1975.)

The *East German* model is having considerable influence, not least in the USSR. It could briefly be described as the 'socialist cartel'. Industries have been grouped into so-called VVB (*Vereinigung Volkseigener Betriebe*, united people's-property enterprises) and under them into *Kombinaten*. These antedate the Soviet *obyedineniya*, which resemble them, in that they are industrial associations or cartels grouping together all or most of the enterprises making particular products. This is the very opposite of competition, it is a logically organized set of monopolistic associations. Whereas in the USSR, at least so far, power resides primarily in *Gosplan* and in industrial ministries, with *Gossnab* playing a vital role in the administration of supply, in East Germany the balance of power is different. More authority devolves on the VVB, which can decide (within limits) how to fulfil plans sent down to them in aggregated terms and there is more scope to negotiate contracts with one another. They also exercise more influence than the Soviet *obyedineniya* on their superiors, or so the evidence suggests.

The East Germans followed the Soviet lead in abolishing industrial ministries (in 1958) and this was when the VVB were created, on the basis of the former equivalent of ministerial *glavki*. VVB were divided into sub-product groups, *Kombinaten,* formed of a number of enterprises. When ministries were re-established in 1966, the VVB had already been functioning, under the authority of the central planners and the National Economic Council, for five years. This doubtless affected their subsequent relationship to their ministerial superiors.

The East German reform, as originally promulgated in 1963, was intended to go further towards using 'economic levers', as distinct from directives. However, from 1967 there was greater stress on quantitative planning in what were called 'structure-determining products', or key items of output. Target planning and centralized allocation were reinforced in respect of these products. When, as in 1970, the plan as a whole was too ambitious, shortages and strain in the less tightly controlled sectors led to a further shift towards central control. The effective power and influence of the VVB, over prices, production and allocation, and the role of profit in its calculations, still compares favourably with those of the *obyedineniya* in the USSR. The central planners have, however, increasingly returned to production-target setting for VVB, at least for important items. As a wise commentator observed: 'How can centralized supply function when enterprises are led by an incentive system to produce what is profitable to them rather than what they have been ordered to?' (See Keren, 1973, pp.150ff; Keren 1973b and Leptin, 1975.) There is also the need to guard against VVB monopoly. The reform has not been formally abandoned, but the use of purely economic levers was found to be inadequate, various disproportions and strains accumulated, and, since the logic of a market system was not accepted, a partial return to 'directive' forms of planning seemed inescapable. Perhaps the great reduction in the number of units centrally planned, caused by the merging of many smaller enterprises into *Kombinaten* and the VVB, makes the centre's task more manageable, and this helps to explain the smoother functioning of the East German economy. Another factor must be mentioned. In reviewing Zielinski (1973), Keren remarked: '[East German] experience shows that it is apparently not entirely true that "the system needs administrative pressure in order to perform". When there is slack and a relatively free supply system, some sort of market pressure may develop even in a bureaucratic economy.' (*Soviet Studies*, July 1976, p.442.)

Evidence collected by Granick (1976) points to the survival of considerable *de facto* decentralization, and to the emergence of competent and responsible management at *Kombinat* and VVB levels, with powers over supply and the product mix which varies in different branches of the economy.

East German industries can engage in foreign trade, directly in many cases, without having to go through the corporations of a specialized ministry. The special relationship with West Germany creates a situation unique in the eastern half of Europe, but this, and also the peculiarities of East German agriculture, must be left to one side here, with just the remark that it is a pity that this, the most successful economy in the communist world, is so little studied.

Poland played a major role in the discussions on reform, especially in 1956. However, many of the original ideas of Lange, Kalecki, Brus and many other distinguished economists came to nothing; the first two have died, the last-named is in England. Another talented exile, Zielinski, has described in detail (1973) the industrial planning system as it evolved up to the early seventies. The Polish political leadership was shocked (and changed) by the riots of December 1970, occasioned by increases in food prices. The new leadership, under Gierek, embarked upon an ambitious investment programme and on improving living standards. The effect was an impressive growth rate in both investment and wages, with a resultant sharp increase in foreign indebtedness (especially to the West) and inflationary pressure. Dissatisfaction with the 'traditional' centralized planning system led to a careful study of both Hungarian and East German experience, and then, by stages in 1974–5, to the emergence of a Polish industrial planning reform. This is based on the so-called WOG *(Wielkie Organizacje Gospodarcze)*, the Polish equivalent of the VVB or *obyedineniya*. It is too soon to tell how they will work, or what will be the division of authority between them and the ministries. The intention is to decentralize effectively. Price control remains mainly at the centre (and, given the essentially monopolistic nature of the VVB and the WOG, limits on price increases are essential).

The WOG reform contains an interesting attempt to control wages, by linking the permissible rate of wage increase to increases in *net* output, or value-added. Differentiated coefficients (the so-called 'R') are laid down for particular industries. Thus for example if the 'R' coefficient is 0·6, then the wages bill of the WOG could rise by 6 per cent if net output rose by 10 per cent. The coefficient is always less than one, because provision must be made for wages increases also in the so-called unproductive sectors. (Otherwise how could there ever be any increases for teachers and musicians and others who cannot increase productivity: one cannot play a string quartet with three players!) Evidently, the rise in average wages in the industrial firm would then depend on labour productivity: thus if a 10 per cent rise in net output were achieved without increasing the size of the labour force, the average wage in the above example would rise by 6 per cent. In this way it is hoped to combine incentive to higher output with a built-in bar to inflationary wage rises.

This apparently ingenious device has its weaknesses and has attracted some criticism in Poland. On the face of it, it avoids the defect of the plan-fulfilment success indicator, since rewards are based on increases over the previous period. It is therefore unnecessary to express the plan in terms of net output, which saves all concerned a lot of time. Yet the following defects are apparent. In the first place, unlike profit, net output measures the activities of the producers, whether or not these are economically rational. Let me give an example relating to New York. As is known, the musicians' union there compels theatre-owners to employ so-called 'walkers', musicians who do not play as there is no music for them to play. This reduces profit, but increases 'net output', or rather would do so if the extra costs led to an upward shift in prices. In other words, cases can arise when net output (value-added) increases while profits fall, and in these cases resources may be irrationally utilized.

The second point relates to the effect of the net product indicator on the product mix. It could well be that an item worth producing if judged by the criterion of profit will not yield as much value-added (i.e. will require less work by that enterprise) than some other item, which will then be preferred for that reason. This could well bring perverse results. Note that this is the opposite 'deviation' to that which arises if the success indicator were the gross value of output *(val)*, when management is interested in choosing a product mix containing high-value inputs. Finally, the WOG becomes too directly interested in increasing prices. True, it is not authorized to increase them of its own volition, but it can affect the decisions of the price-controller by the proposals and evidence which it submits, and it can also introduce new products at as high a price as possible.

Another Polish critic has pointed out that the 'standard of evaluation of investment variants' (profit) is not consistent with the criterion by which the investing enterprise operates (maximization of value added) (Rychlewski, 1976).

Experience will show how far these objections are valid. According to a number of Polish sources, the original intention was to be flexible and experimental, the degree of autonomy of the WOG depending on the branch of industry and the degree of scarcity of its products. They were in many cases to have almost complete freedom to determine their product mix by negotiation with customers, and also, as in Hungary, the right of direct participation in foreign trade deals (Machowski, 1975.) The financing of investment and of technological innovation was also to be more decentralized. However, in 1975–6 these good intentions were at least temporarily set aside by the consequences of internal and external problems. The investment boom mentioned above led to overstrain and had to be halted, and this resulted in a sharp cutback in the rights of the WOG to make decentralized investment decisions. The foreign-trade deficit with the West compelled the introduction of stricter control over imported inputs. Finally, the very large price-fluctuations in world markets led to large variations in profitability and in net output, due to the reflection of foreign prices in the accounts of Polish firms, a situation which would have led (under the incentive rules adopted) to quite undeserved gains and losses to particular WOGi. The variations as between commodities, and also between 'world', intra-Comecon and domestic prices, became too large and disparate to be handled by the introduction of some over-all corrective exchange-coefficient. Limitations were therefore intro-duced to their powers over exports and imports, employment of additional labour and the disposal of profits. (I was assured, on a visit to Poland in April 1976, that these are unfortunate and provisional measures, quite inconsistent with what was and is intended, forced by circumstances. But, who knows, '*il n'y a que le provisoire qui dure*'.)

In June 1976 the Polish leadership attempted a major overhaul of the increasingly irrational price system. It was decided greatly to increase the retail prices of livestock products and sugar, which had been very heavily subsidized, while simultaneously increasing state purchase prices for a number of agricultural products and making an upward adjustment in the level of money wages. However, disorders broke out and the government beat a hasty retreat. At the moment of writing it is not clear how they propose to tackle the confusions of the price system. Changes are plainly necessary, and equally plainly dangerous. In August 1976 sugar rationing was introduced, with additional amounts available at a commercial price two-and-a-half times above the ration price.

Polish agriculture is very largely in the hands of peasant small-holders. For many years the government refused to sell tractors to the peasants, confining them to the few state and collective farms and to so-called 'agricultural circles', a species of co-operative hiring agency. Since 1968, however, peasants may buy tractors, though partly for traditional reasons and partly because of the small size of many holdings, they still mainly rely on horses. There are no longer any compulsory deliveries, but the sugar rationing scheme relates the ration for peasants to deliveries of farm produce to the state.

It would be most useful at this point to contrast Soviet and East European experience with that of the *Chinese* economy. However, this would necessitate a separate study, for which I am unqualified, apart from diffculties of securing reliable information. A Chinese visitor commented: 'We began by copying the Soviet model. Then we rejected it. We are still searching for a new way, still experimenting. Nothing is yet fully settled.'

Cuba, after a very radical phase, in which almost universal ration-ing was combined with an emphasis on exhortation ('moral incen-tives'), has, since 1974, been moving towards a system more on Soviet lines. This is apparently explicable by the failures of the previous policy, and the need for incentives, differentials, more careful economic calculation. It is only fair to add that both Sweezy and Bettelheim, who will be cited shortly as examples of ultra-left thinking, expressed the view that the Cubans went too far in their earlier radical phase.

SOVIET REFORMERS AND THEIR MODELS

It would be quite wrong to see Soviet would-be reformers as a homo-geneous group. Proposals range from minor improvements in the existing system all the way to a radical market-socialist overturn of all the existing arrangements. I leave out of account the type of dissident that would be happy to see capitalism restored. For the present we will concentrate on the 'schools' of reformers which have in common a desire to decrease the role of the centre while increasing that of 'commodity-money relations', i.e. of market forces, including those models in which the market is to be simulated by computers.

The debate developed during the Khrushchev period, and its most radical 'market' manifestations were probably seen in 1966, with the publication of a book with the title *Plan and market*. (Lisichkin, 1966). The author, a reforming economic journalist, quoted statements made by Lenin in the early days of the New Economic Policy (i.e. in 1921–2, when he was indeed in favour of economic and market as against administrative methods). Plan and market, he argued, must be intimately interlinked, and without a market valuation the planners cannot really test whether their plans are corréct. Prices, argued another market 'radical', should be determined by the market situation through competition; 'Socialist economics uses such things as prices, markets, credits, supply-and-demand, which ideological enemies regarded purely as prerogatives of capitalists'. (Rakitsky, *Komsomol'-skaya pravda*, 19 October 1966.) These and other 'marketeers' plainly had in mind some variant of the Hungarian reform. Without denying the necessity of planning, they desired to relieve the centre of its intolerable micro-economic burden.

A similar line was taken by some members of the Central Mathe-matical-Economics Institute. Petrakov, whom we have already quoted in Chapter 7, is an example of this. The reason why some mathemati-cians support market-type reform has already been indicated in Chapter 2, in discussing optimal planning models. The task of micro-economic planning is vastly too complex to be effectively centralized. It therefore follows, as one of these economists said to me in a discus-sion, that the users should be able to 'vote with the rouble', to provide irreplaceable micro-information for the planners. The role of prices must therefore be that of information-carriers, indicating what most needs to be produced and the most economical way of producing; prices should be such that scarce items, e.g. of machinery, should be used where they are most needed, most advantageous to use. (Novozhilov, *EkMM*, 1966 and 1967, No. 3, and Gofman and Petrakov, *VEk*, 1967, No. 5.) Fedorenko, the head of the above Institute, argued that 'every unit of the economy must have the possibility to take decisions, according to the principle that anything that is profitable for the economy as a whole must be profitable for each unit of socialist production'. (*VEk*, 1967, No. 5, pp.148–50.)

These last words remind one of the similar slogan of Liberman, set out five years earlier in a famous article in *Pravda*. (7 September 1962.) The essence of his plan was as follows. The basic criteria of success of enterprise operations were to be profits expressed as a percentage of the enterprise's capital. The management was to devise its own plans based upon orders negotiated with customers. Once approved or amended by the planning authorities, the output and delivery plan would be obligatory on the enterprise. (Liberman left rather vague what the relative functions of enterprise and planners would be in determining just what should be produced, and in the subsequent discussion he was variously interpreted by his critics.) Once this plan is approved, the enterprise's financial and labour plans would be left wholly to the management to decide, though they were to conform to the official wage-scales. It would no longer be the job of the planning authorities to decide the wages fund, the profits plan, costs plan and productivity plan for the enterprise. Liberman was very conscious of the harm done by the tendency, built-in to the traditional system, for management to conceal their production possibilities in order to obtain an easy plan. To encourage management to bid high, he proposed that the bonus rules be such that full bonuses should only be payable in respect of *planned* profits and output. Anything over-the-plan would be rewarded at half-rate. Under the Liberman rules, the amount of retained profits and of bonuses would depend on the relationship between the profit percentage and the value of the enterprise's capital, though in a later article he conceded that it might also be related to the wages fund. (*Pravda*, 20 September 1964.) He envisaged differential profit norms in different sectors and perhaps for different enterprises, to offset the 'unearned' advantages of modern equipment or location. This was his substitute for a capital (or rent) charge, intended to ensure that high profits due to the possession of lavish and modern capital equipment do not attract a disproportionate reward. Liberman never developed a price theory: prices were to be, in his words, 'fixed and flexible'.

While Liberman could be placed on the same side as the 'marketeers', he had no coherent model, and in his later work retired to occupy a moderate-reforming position, as can be seen in his book in English. (Liberman, 1971.) While some of his proposals could be discerned embedded in the modest (and largely ineffective) reform measures of 1965, his importance has tended to be over-rated by some Western commentators.

More influential, and thought to have pushed Liberman's ideas as well as his own, was the economist-statistician, V. Nemchinov, who also did much to encourage the mathematical school and shared the Lenin prize, shortly before his death in 1964, with Kantorovich and Novozhilov. Nemchinov argued for 'free trade in producers' goods' (*Pravda*, 21 September 1962), and later devised an original scheme, briefly referred to in Chapter 7, also, by which enterprises bid against each other in putting forward tenders: 'each enterprise will submit in advance to the planning organs its proposals as to the conditions upon which it is prepared to carry out this or that planned order for deliveries, with particulars of assortment, quality, delivery date and price. The economic and planning organs will then place their orders only with those enterprises whose proposals . . . are most advantageous for the national plan.' (Nemchinov, *Kom*, 1964, No. 5, p.77.) Note that in this proposal prices become a matter for negotiation. Nemchinov did not elaborate, and it remains unclear how such a model would function.

It was, in any case, not acted upon. No more effective was a plea by A. Birman (*MSn*, 1967, No. 11), boldly entitled '*Trade* in means of production', published of all places in the house-organ of *Gossnab*. Birman himself (1967) criticized what he called 'free-market dogmatists', but plainly belongs in the 'marketeer' camp.

Many of these reformers, especially the mathematicians, were well aware that the problem of devising an optimal decision-making structure is a complex task. To decide correctly one must have the relevant information, as well as the means to act. It should be intuitively obvious that the level at which decisions are taken should not be the same if the subject is West Siberian oil, or the supply of electricity to the Urals, as if the matter concerns the production of cabbages or a purchase of a new button-holing machine for a clothing factory. There is a growing literature in the USSR about efficient hierarchical multi-stage structures. It may well be that, in their realization of the importance of structure in the decision-making process, some Soviet economists have gone well ahead of the Western 'mainstream' theorists, among whom 'institutional economics' is regarded as unworthy of attention. Their Soviet colleagues, when considering practical proposals, cannot assume away a matter of such evident importance in the real world. Decisions are affected by the area of responsibility, and motivation, of the decision maker. Information is not only costly, but cannot be available in detail at all levels and branches of the hierarchy.

OPPOSITION TO REFORM AND ITS BASIS

It is important to stress these problems because the more naive reformers, including some Western critics, too readily assume that it is easy, through the use of the market mechanism, to reach a situation in which what is needed by society is made profitable for every enterprise. It is in fact very difficult, for reasons which, I hope, have been clearly indicated in earlier chapters. This attractive slogan is inapplicable within many large organizations, including most Western corporations. Indeed, this is one reason why they are large. The naive analyst has to be asked why Du Pont or ICI do not let the many dozens of sub-units of which they are composed simply maximize their separate profits, thereby economizing in central-office staff and stimulating local initiative. The logic of this would be that Du Pont and ICI as such had no *raison d'être*, as their constituent parts would be able to flourish as independent enterprises. One imagines that in reality the centre has vital information, especially non-price information: about the results of expensive research, the requirements and plans of the principal customers, developments by competitors at home and overseas, the consequences of the actions of sub-units on other sub-units, etc. There are organizational as well as technological economies of scale. I have dealt with this elsewhere under the title 'internal economies'. (1969b, p.847.) In the USSR, as already pointed out in Chapter 6, there is potential benefit from locating big investment decisions at the centre, where the expansion plans of various users are being elaborated, but many current allocation decisions can also benefit from being *administered*, and in East and West alike *are* administered. (Richardson, 1971.) An example already quoted is the oil project in West Siberia (and in Alaska). The essential point which is being repeated here is: if within Du Pont or Exxon its sub-units are subject to instructions from headquarters on many matters, why should it be otherwise with the enterprises in the Soviet Ministry of Chemical or Oil Industry?

Let me not be misunderstood. This is not an argument in favour of an (impossible) overall centralization of planning. There can be effective scope for competition and free initiative untrammelled by state or corporation bureaucracies, and there is a high cost to be borne if one prevents these things. Administered relationships need not necessarily take the form of hierarchical subordination: thus we have the widespread phenomenon of the sub-contractor. Textbooks tend to ignore sub-contractors, because they do not fit the analytical model; for it is the principal who decides what to do, by reference to *his* overall objective and profitability, and then makes it worth the sub-contractor's while to do his part. But evidently *some* inter-relationships are too close, some sequences too closely linked, for market structures to bear the burden.

This is not the place to develop at length more thoughts about organization theory. It is simply important to note that the opponents of market-type solutions can use these arguments, which fit their vested interests as ministerial, *Gosplan* or party officials who are engaged full-time in replacing the invisible hand by the visible hand – *their* hand. This combination of self-interest and objective circumstances is one of the more significant obstacles to reform of the 'Hungarian' type in the Soviet Union. This is reinforced by the fact that centralized planning has operated there for very much longer than in Hungary; no one now remembers any other system, and force of habit is combined with fear of the unknown.

Opposition is not only strong, but has clearly been reinforced since

1966. We have seen how even the timid reform of 1965 has very largely been frustrated. The logic of 'market' is strongly resisted. Already within weeks of the publication of Liberman's *Pravda* article the former Minister of Finance, Zverev, declared: 'Planning is one of the principal achievements of the October revolution; why abandon it?' (*EkG*, 1962, No. 42, p.6.) Bachurin, deputy-head of *Gosplan*, attacked competition, price-flexibility, free choice of customers and suppliers. (*EkG*, 1966, No. 45, pp.7–8.) These arguments have been repeated on numerous occasions since, and many have already been quoted in Chapters 4 and 7, above. Perhaps it would be sufficient to recall the following quotations: 'Market prices are, in our view, alien to our economy and contradict the tasks of centralized planning,' (Sitnin, *EkG*, 1968, No. 6), and 'Some argue that the customer should find his own supplier and supplier his customer. This must be rejected, or it implies the absolutization of the laws of supply and demand, the development of competition between suppliers and the underestimation of the role of the centre.' (*Pravda*, 26 September 1969.) For this type of official, it is evident that mathematical methods, computers, constitute a promising means of saving, indeed reinforcing, central planning, which is possibly why Fedorenko's Institute has had substantial support and encouragement.

Clearly, then, reforms are opposed. Let us look a little more closely at some reasons which have not yet been analysed.

To begin with, let us expand the point about vested interest. It is sometimes said that 'the party' is against reform. Put in this way the argument is too crude. There are fifteen million party members. Nearly all managers are members. In a country in which no other party has been tolerated for over fifty-five years, every interest group finds expression in the party, including those groups which would benefit from reform. However, the full-time party officials, especially in the localities but also central committee officials, exercise very considerable powers. They appoint, they dismiss, they allocate and reallocate, they interfere in current affairs, they adjudicate. (See Hough, 1969.) They clearly prefer this state of affairs to continue. Many an émigré economist has laid very great stress on this factor. Reform of the market type is inconsistent with the exercise of power by officials of the party at all levels, at least in the arbitrary form in which they are accustomed to exercise it. The same is true of many state planning and finance officials.

In defending their position, they can point not only to the organizational problems discussed earlier, but also to ideology. Ideology is a tricky and elusive concept. What is meant by it here is a set of principles which the party professes and, at least in some part, really does believe in. Marx said that under socialism there would be production for use, not production for exchange, that planning is superior to the anarchy of a capitalist market. Generations of socialists believed this. It underlies the 'new-left' critique which we will be discussing below. True, the 'new left' also criticizes the very same officials (calling them bureaucrats, state-capitalists or whatever) who invoke Marxian ideology against market-type reforms. But these officials naturally do not regard themselves as unreasonably privileged bureaucrats. They fulfil, in their own eyes, a necesary function, and to them the visible hand is certainly superior in principle to the invisible hand. Faced with problems about allocation, shortage, priorities and the like, *they* decide, not some impersonal mechanism which could produce unpredictable results. The recent disarray of Western market economies must reinforce their conservative caution: our inflationary instability is no advertisement for the virtues of markets.

The party-state bureaucracy does not wish to be replaced by computers and impersonal programming techniques, of this we may be sure. But, as we have seen, these techniques do have severe practical limitations. Indeed officials, because they are human beings, still have marked advantages over computers, as was well pointed out by Augustinovics (1975).

The party officials believe in discipline, obedience and hierarchy, since it plainly benefits them and their careers, as well as being (in their view) essential in the running of a vast country and its economy. Their major role in appointments ensures that the managerial strata feel responsible primarily to them. Ministerial, financial and planning officials may sometimes resent interference from full-time party officials, but share with them an interest in retaining powers *vis-à-vis* their subordinates in industry and agriculture. The state and party apparatus seems to prefer that not only appointments but also rewards be under its control, i.e. that bonuses depend on the fulfilment of plan-orders and not on impersonal market forces or on contracts with other managers. It is logical that so large a control apparatus, which has existed for so long, would resist change. Were it otherwise, selected quotations from holy writ could be presented to show why greater reliance on market forces is consistent with what Marx and Lenin said. Indeed, reformers in the USSR itself and in Hungary, Yugoslavia and elsewhere, have been doing this for years. We will look more closely at the role of Marxist economic ideas in Chapter 12.

Next on the list of obstacles to effective reform is what might be called the inevitability of gradualness, or the inevitable failure of gradualness. Piecemeal reform does not work, and one is driven back to the old system. The point is that the system has an inner logic which resists *partial* change. Thus if one frees an industry – say clothing – from central control, then what would happen to the industries which provide it with inputs? Unless they too responded to market stimuli (i.e. based their production on orders from the clothing industry), there would be acute problems in ensuring that they produce what is needed. The traditional system ensured – though imperfectly – that the central planners transmitted the input requirements in the form of production and delivery instructions, backed (most of the time) by the necessary inputs for the input-providing enterprises, and so on. A missing link in this chain disrupts the system. Consequently, the easiest way out of the resulting confusion would be to put the clothing industry back into the centralized system. This seems indeed to have happened to the experimental firms, *Bolshevichka* and *Mayak*, which were substantially freed of traditional controls in 1963, but only temporarily. Similarly, if one reduces the list of centrally planned commodities, some unfortunate consequences follow. If the commodities concerned are simply removed from the list, this, under conditions of taut planning, will be taken by everyone as a signal of low priority, and scarce materials will be diverted by the planning mechanism to other uses, so that acute shortages of the decontrolled items are highly probable. If the reduction takes the form of aggregating (say) salami-type and frankfurter-type sausage into one heading, sausage, then, given that neither profitability nor tonnage operate equally between them as success indicators, output of one will increase, the other decline, to the annoyance of customers. The simplest way out, again, will be to return to the *status quo*. (For Polish experiences, see Zielinski, 1973.)

This is why several efforts to reduce the list of centrally allocated products have been frustrated. The moral is that one must take a big step all at once, as the Hungarians did (after careful preparation), moving from a predominantly administered to a predominantly market-orientated form of current operational management. But, for many reasons already indicated, this the Soviet political-economic machine do not wish to do.

It is also worth mentioning that the centralized system is helpful to the priority industries, not least defence, and so one would expect the 'military-industrial complex', if such can be identified, to view reform with some misgiving.

Nor is it right to regard managers as a homogeneous pressure-group for reform. Apart from those managers in privileged sectors of industry who benefit from administered priorities, there are also those who welcome the status of subordinate, who fear responsibility. (After reading pro-reform articles by managers, I once argued about this with a Soviet economist. He replied: 'Those managers intelligent enough to write articles may be for reform, but what about the others?') Also, as already pointed out in discussing Hungarian experience, it is a mistake to suppose that all managers like competition and the disciplines of the market. Many prefer a situation in which their customers stand cap in hand anxious to win their favour, though admittedly they have sometimes to do the same to *their* suppliers. No doubt, as their published declarations show, many managers *do* desire major reforms from which they would gain in power and in responsibility, and which would free them from inefficient and unqualified interference and from endless worry about supplies. But they cannot be seen as a united pressure group.

Opinion among the masses, insofar as it can be discerned, is not pro-market. Naturally the citizens would like to see better goods in the shops, fewer queues, good service and so on. But they also resent higher prices, and generally fail to see the connection between market forces and the improvements which they desire. One encounters this among British trade unionists too: they often vote for resolutions to control prices, rents, imports, apparently unaware of the likely consequences. So one cannot say that pressure for freeing market forces exists among the masses.

Some may suppose that pressure for 'market' reforms would come from what the 'new left' designate as the new bourgeoisie or privileged elite. However, they benefit from the existing system by having privileged access (at low prices, too) to goods and services denied to ordinary citizens, a privilege not lightly given up and much valued by its beneficiaries.

This point is so important socio-psychologically that it is worth dwelling on for a moment. Suppose that hotel space is priced far below the level at which supply and demand balances, and you are an official with a priority right to obtain a hotel room. You derive from this two kinds of satisfaction. Firstly, your status entitles you to a privilege which is valued precisely because ordinary folk or more junior officials do not have it. Secondly, you save money, because the hotel room is cheap. However 'bourgeois' your mentality, what interest would you have to press for an increase in prices to 'rational' levels?

Therefore the lack of any powerful social group which favours reforms is one of the main obstacles to their introduction. Economists alone are not enough, especially as they are disunited. One may then ask: why has reform been in the air, why is it still worth discussing, as we have been doing?

The answer surely is this. The system is not working efficiently and cannot do so. The intentions of the party and state leadership are not being carried out. They desire an effectively functioning economy, producing more and better, no longer dependent on massive imports of grain or of the latest technology, with the producers responding to the requirements of other managers and of the consumers. Supplies should be arriving punctually and be of the right specifications. Plans should be balanced, materially and financially. All this the leaders repeat over and over again. L. Brezhnev's speech to the 25th party Congress, (*Pravda*, 25 February 1976), and those of Kosygin and others are only the latest examples. It is because the existing planning mechanism cannot, literally, deliver the goods desired by the leadership that they are compelled at least to consider the possibility of fundamental reform. Economic failures are bad for political careers. Successful espousal of remedies that work can help a second-rank leader to become a first-rank leader. At the topmost level the party officials should feel less threatened by loss of function than do local secretaries, as, under any conceivable reform, the centre would continue to carry very heavy responsibilities for economic strategy, major investments, and so on.

The party cannot simply seek to 'maximize its power', as some political scientists assert. It *also* desires results. In economic matters, at least. If the subject is, say, modern art, then control and power can take unquestioned precedence, since the leaders (and most of their followers) simply do not care for or about modern art. Industrial and agricultural production is quite another matter.

For the present, the 'market' route to reform is blocked, and we are in the midst of experiments in *obyedineniya*, cartels, mergers. But if troubles persist, the need for change will again appear on the agenda.

THE 'NEW-LEFT' CRITIQUE OF REFORM

This is a large subject. Interested readers may wish to dip more seriously into the literature, looking in particular at the articles and discussions by Sweezy (1971) and Bettelheim (1971, 1969) and also Lindbeck (1971), Nove (1972), Selucky (1974) and Ticktin (1974.) What follows is a bare summary of the argument.

For the 'new left', for example Sweezy and Bettelheim and their followers, the whole of the preceding few pages are highly suspect, anti-Marxist indeed. 'Beware of the market, it is capitalism's secret weapon.' The weight of the evidence strongly supports the view that, for Marx, socialism (at the end of a transition period of unknown length) meant the elimination of 'commodity production', in the sense of production for sale as distinct from use. 'Market socialism' is then a contradiction in terms. It cannot, by definition, be socialism at all.

The 'new-left' critics mentioned above do *not* say that the right course of action is to eliminate today, or even tomorrow, the categories of profit, money, wages, prices, purchase and sale. They admit their temporary necessity. They even admit, or some of them do, that Stalinist overcentralization could be combated by the *temporary* use of market categories. The following passage may be quoted as fairly typical of the views here analysed.

'When the bureaucratically-administered economy runs into difficulties, as it certainly must, there are two politically opposite ways in which a solution must be sought. One is to weaken the bureaucracy, politicize the masses and ensure increasing initiative and responsibility to the workers themselves. This is the road towards socialist relations of production. The other way is to put increasing reliance on the market, not as a temporary retreat (like Lenin's NEP) but as an ostensible step towards a more efficient 'socialist' economy . . . It is, I submit, the road back to class domination and ultimately the restoration of capitalism'. (Sweezy, 1970, p.21.)

Underlying this critique, there is a vision of a classless, stateless, moneyless socialist society, corresponding to what the Soviet theorists would call 'full communism'. Abundance, unselfishness, interchangeability of jobs, equality, peace, and all this worldwide, would characterize such a society. There would be no bureaucracy, no markets, there would be harmony. It can be shown, I think convincingly shown, that Marx had such an ultimate society in mind. But, it may be asked, what has this to do with contemporary reality? To this, if I understand them rightly, Bettelheim and Sweezy would reply: of course this cannot yet be. But there should be a transition towards it. They accept that the overcentralized control apparatus has many economically and socially negative consequences. They would accept as correct the picture of these consequences contained in the present book. Indeed they may well draw a blacker picture. But they regard some sort of revolutionary democratic process as the way forward, and not the market plus material incentives.

There is some logical parallel between the belief in a harmonious non-market, non-commodity economy planned by comradely 'associated producers' and the equally unreal concept of the withering away of the state. In practice, for as long as anyone can foresee, the state will, of course, exist. No serious political reform can be suggested, in the Soviet Union or anywhere else, that does not assume its existence. Its role can be modified, it can be democratized, the role of social organizations can be enhanced, but there will be a state. Marx, of course, defined the state as an organ of class oppression. In this sense, its disappearance in a classless society is a consequence of the chosen definition. However – and this has important economic implications too – it is simply not true that conflict within society is due solely to class divisions based on ownership. So long as there are more needs and aspirations than there are means to satisfy them, there must be opportunity-costs, gains and losses, achievement and (relative) deprivation. When there is not enough to go round, some get, others do not. This is the result of scarcity. It follows that some process of adjudication between competing claims is necessary, and it is pure evasion to assert that the resulting contradictions will be 'non-antagonistic'. All this is quite consistent with the view that class divisions exacerbate conflicts (over distribution of the product, or race, or whatever). 'Actual processes involve many participants whose interests inevitably conflict,' wrote Malinvaud, à propos planning. 'There are many conflicting objectives . . . such as is the case in all social systems,' wrote the Yugoslav, Stojanovic. (Khachaturov, 1976, pp.34, 152 – my emphasis.)

Let us take a different example. Suppose that there exist two socialist countries, and they are in dispute as to who should fish in an area of the sea, or mine iron ore in a frontier zone, or use scarce river water for irrigation. Sceptics like Nove have no difficulty in imagining a quite sharp conflict, analagous to a dispute between two capitalist countries. Presumably some of the 'new left' would argue that under a *real* socialism this could not happen, indeed they would so define real socialism. What is not clear about their model is whether they believe: (a) There could not be two socialist countries, since the world would be united, or (b) if there were, they would settle the argument in a comradely way, or (c) under socialism there would, again by definition, be ample fishing-grounds, iron ore and irrigation water, i.e. abundance, which would indeed be a precondition of (a) and (b). (My own view of Marx is that he imagined (c) to be the case.)

All this may appear to take us wide of the point, and yet it does not do so. It raises an important question: *by what criteria* do we judge practical and organizational questions in the real world? It seems to me no more sensible to attack Soviet or Hungarian reformers by citing Marx's vision of perfect socialism than it would be to attack them for not having established Walrasian general equilibrium and Pareto optimality. Or to criticize amendments to the Soviet criminal law because Marx's vision was a society without crime.

As already argued in earlier chapters, functional necessities *require* the creation of a highly complex and unavoidably bureaucratic apparatus, if plan-instructions and not market forces are the basis upon which the economic system rests. Democratic political reforms can alter the priorities of the regime. Opportunities to organize, to demand, to protest, can help in combating abuses. Privilege can be diminished, by publicity and by taxation. But, as was pointed out in Chapter 4, micro-economic operations simply cannot be handled through systematic 'democratic control' at the centre. The diminution of the power of the central bureaucratic apparatus is only possible if one diminishes its functions. It so happens that this is also the road towards greater micro-economic efficiency. But, as Yugoslav as well as some Polish writers have pointed out, this is also the way to enhance the sense of participation, which requires that major decision-making power should reside at the place of work, i.e. the enterprises where people are producing. Neither Bettelheim, nor Sweezy, nor any of their followers, have yet shown, even in outline, how these aims can be pursued if one reduces the role of market and commodity-money relations, while increasing the all-inclusiveness of the central plan. This is apart altogether from finding appropriate units in which to calculate costs and relating them to results and to need.

The 'new left' appear to be insignificant in the USSR, being more frequently encountered in the West and in developing countries. However, such a current of thought has surfaced in both Hungary and Yugoslavia. This suggests that the negative effects of markets, incentives, acquisitiveness, are most clearly seen where a market-type economy exists, and it is hard to deny that negative effects do manifest themselves, and that they are likely to seem particularly offensive to socialists. After all, they do aspire to a society in which human greed, money-making and profits, play a diminishing role. One appreciates these sentiments. One appreciates, too, the need they feel to combat excessive inequalities and the emergence of privileged groups. Indeed, it would be a sad world in which there is no such combat. However, one cannot escape from the fact that experience has taught us that the alternative, centralized 'directive' planning, brings with it many intractable problems, and leads to bureaucratic deformations which are also offensive to socialists; these have included very great inequalities and 'administered privilege'. Some critics may be satisfied by so *defining* socialism as to exclude both centralized bureaucracy *and* the market, rejecting all experience of all hitherto-existing countries as irrelevant: none of the problems described in earlier chapters would arise, because under a real socialism they *could* not arise, or else would be resolved by comradely discussion among 'associated producers'. Anyone who finds this an adequate answer has probably not studied seriously the issues raised in Chapters 1 to 10 of this book. Indeed, he or she has probably not read it.

One word should be added, on the subject of computers. The extremely rapid development of computer technology may well lead to greater technical possibilities of centralization than could yet be predicted. However, this should give a socialist (or, for that matter, a non-socialist) cause for concern. To receive instructions from a remote boss or bureaucrat can be very frustrating. One feels oneself a helpless cog in a machine one cannot control. One feels *alienated*. One would surely feel even more alienated if the instructions arrived from a computer. After all, it may be possible to argue with a human being. It is more difficult to argue with a print-out. (Those who still have not grasped *why* a non-market economy requires centralization are asked to re-read Chapters 2, 3 and 4.) Those who, like Bettelheim, insist that control by the 'direct producers' is vital to their picture of socialism must try to devise a model within which such control can be meaningfully exercised.

CONCLUSION: WHAT REFORM IS NEEDED?

There are two interlinked but distinct aspects of the problem. One is the *politics* of reform. The other is concerned with *economic efficiency*. They are linked because of the necessary question: 'efficiency for what?' and also because political objectives and economic performance can be in contradiction. This is so to some extent in every country. Thus an 'economically rational' price policy in France which infuriates southern vine-growers can (did!) lead to civil commotion and heavy expenditure on police reinforcements. Also it is quite legitimate to advocate political solutions which involve, and are known to involve, an economic cost.

This said, the following comments seem in order as a contribution to discussion (dogmatic certainty in this field is a sure sign of overconfidence or oversimplification).

Firstly, it seems that the 'new-left' type of critique bears little relation to the actual *economic* problems which beset the system, because there is no relevant remedy being proposed. (I accept, of course, that a political struggle against the 'elite' would have economic consequences, but if these critics came to power they would face the same problems, and could not deal with them by making speeches about 'revolutionizing the masses'; such phrases do not produce or allocate a ton of steel.)

Secondly, the resistance of the party and state machine to market-type reforms is very strong, especially in the USSR. Paradoxically, they can use the 'new-left' arguments against reform in defence of their essentially conservative position.

Thirdly, however, the pressure of necessity must compel the re-examination of the traditional system. Brezhnev, no radical, none the less spoke as follows at the 25th Congress: 'The revolution in science and technique *requires radical changes in the style and methods of economic activity*. This is a deeply party-political *(partiyny)* task.' (*Pravda*, 25 February 1976 – my emphasis.) It is not a question fundamentally of counterposing the preferences of the leadership to those of the consumers or of those indicated by the market. It is rather that the preferences of the leadership (except in a few, key priority sectors) are in fact not 'translatable' into action, so that what happens is too often desired by nobody. As was pointed out in Chapter 4, the production of an obsolete machine, or excessively heavy metal parts, is not wanted by the party leaders, the user-enterprises or even the manufacturers; these are unintended consequences of aggregated plan-fulfilment indicators. The central planners *must* shed some of their excessive work-load, if only to get done effectively the things they wish to get done.

Fourthly, for reasons already gone into, the optimal reformed structure, if it could be defined, would surely be a mixture of central, intermediate-level and grass-roots bodies. The level of decision-making will depend on economies of scale (technological, organizational, informational) found in the given industry, the importance of social and economic externalities, the nature of the decision, and so forth. Just as in the West one has firms the size of General Electric, but also tiny enterprises, and just as the degree of centralization varies in different Western corporations, so a wide variety of forms ought to be devised in the 'East'.

A key element in any market-type reform is competition. The Hungarian reformers understood this, though they have departed from it in practice. The East German reformers chose the cartel (or VVB) which deliberately creates or reinforces monopoly. The lesson to be learnt from East German experience seems to be that this does relieve the centre of some of its impossible burdens, by devolving a range of detailed decisions on the VVB-*obyedineniye* level, and this is doubtless why this is the solution chosen at present in the USSR also. However, this same experience teaches that a monopolist organ interested in profits and with influence over prices requires systematic supervision, and particularly so if the central plan is taut, i.e. there is a sellers' market, and that consequently the possibilities of devolution of power from the centre by this route are more limited than apparently was expected. Or to put the issue in another way: the only automatically functioning or self-policing species of micro-economic decentralization is a market, and a market *must* be competitive. Not 'perfectly' competitive, but one in which customers find it possible to go elsewhere, in which the suppliers cannot often say: 'take it or leave it'. To take a final illustrative example: it is no use 'decentralizing' to a restaurant trust, using profit-making as a criterion, in a situation in which the trust runs all the catering establishments in the town *and* the customers stand in line for vacant tables. No use, that is, if one is aiming at good cuisine; the *economic* motivation for taking trouble over quality would be lacking. Hence in the USSR there are imposed rules about minimum menu assortment, the weight of a schnitzel, and so forth, but these also create problems.

An observant reader might reply, using this same example: what about a committee of customers, what about a genuine co-operative, in which those who eat elect a committee and select a good cook, responsible to them? Here is a democratic solution which would ensure quality and participation at the same time. To this the answer is: yes, this is indeed a solution. The co-operative management would then go into the *market* and buy meat, vegetables, utensils, fuel. The line of responsibility of all concerned would be to the customers (including, of course, to the producers of meat, vegetables, utensils, fuels, in respect of *their* inputs). In other words, this is a decentralized solution of the market type. If the employees of the producing enterprises elect their management this could be a version of the Yugoslav model. Certainly this would be production for exchange and not for use. But the Yugoslav type model, as we have seen, is not without defects . . . Which is where we came in. But this should worry only a perfectionist. In the real world one must just hope to minimize inevitable deficiencies of the arrangements by which a complex, modern industrial economy can be run.

Another point to consider seriously is the pervasive sellers' market and its causes. Suppose there were less pressure, more slack, therefore fewer shortages, less striving after targets. No doubt this would have positive micro-economic effects. However, this overlooks several facts. Firstly, society's needs being far from satisfied, pressure arises out of the desire that they be satisfied sooner rather than later. Secondly, administrative pressure is a substitute for competition, part of the struggle against the dangers of slackness and inertia. Thirdly, tautness is an inevitable consequence of the endeavour to ensure full employment of productive factors, for reasons already explored. And finally, if the aim is abundance, the end of scarcity, there must surely be endeavours to bring this day nearer by high rates of growth and investment.

The Hungarian reform model has been under great pressure in recent years, due partly to the adverse terms of trade and their effects. Thus it has proved impossible to ensure any rise in living standards (real wages actually fell in 1979), and the large rise in world prices broke the link between them and domestic prices, with numerous levies, subsidies and other centrally administered 'exceptions'. This has weakened, without destroying, some of the basic elements of the reform introduced in 1968. Efforts are currently being made to modify internal prices.

The Polish economy also has been under very severe strain, with a particularly heavy burden of foreign debt. The reform based on the WOG has been greatly modified, if not abandoned.

Soviet reform discussions have not developed any new ideas. The changes in the plan indicator system summarized in the addendum to Chapter 4 is no more than a reorganization of the 'traditional' centralized system. Despite increased shortages, imbalances and slow growth (1979 the 'slowest' peacetime year in Soviet history), there is no sign that the leadership is yet willing to contemplate radical ideas of change.

The Chinese economy, after the convulsion of cultural revolution, is in process of adjustment, with far-reaching discussions in progress about decentralization, encouragement of local enterprise, flexibility, modernization. However, when the author visited China in 1979, it was explained that reform of an overcentralized planning system, while necessary, will take forms which are as yet undecided.

CHAPTER 12

CONCEPTS AND DEFINITIONS

It is now time to discuss concepts and theories. The fact that this is being done last is not intended to imply any opinion concerning the primacy of matter over mind, of material as against spiritual. It is simply that the concepts and ideas which Soviet economists use are hardly comprehensible unless the institutional framework and practical problems are discussed first. It is true, of course, that basic ideology of Marxism-Leninism exerts a powerful influence on structure and on policy decisions. However, a discussion on the philosophical basis of Soviet communism falls well outside the scope of the present work.

NATIONAL INCOME

The Soviet concept of national income is in line with the classical tradition, in distinguishing between 'productive' and 'unproductive' activities, only the former being considered as generating a real product. As in Adam Smith, civil servants, soldiers, teachers, doctors, 'opera singers and opera dancers', etc., are deemed to be unproductive. The national income therefore consists of the total value of the material product. In the USSR, this value is deemed to equal the sum of the final selling prices of material goods, net of all double counting and of amortization (depreciation) of fixed assets. Since final selling prices of many goods contain turnover tax, this means that such taxes are included in the national income, which becomes the equivalent of a species of 'net national material product at market prices'. (This definition is inexact, because there is only a very restricted sense in which prices reflect market relations, but the essential point is that factor costs are not used as a basis).

The adoption of a dividing line between 'productive' and 'unproductive' involves some awkward demarcational problems. In the Soviet Union, though not in all other Eastern countries, passenger transport and personal postal services are excluded from the national income, though several economists have protested that this is an illogical procedure, and some have urged that not only passenger transport but also 'commercial services' (e.g. baths, laundries) should be included in the national income, but so far in vain. The present concept involves, among other things, the idea that a railway signalman is productive when he lets a freight train past his signal-box, but unproductive when he performs an identical action on the approach of a passenger train. Similarly, a typist at a factory is productive, but the girl in *Gosplan* who may type the letter in reply is unproductive, because a line has to be drawn between 'administration' and productive enterprises, and the two typists find themselves on opposite sides of the line. However, before adopting a supercilious attitude, Western economists would do well to recall some of their own difficulties. Thus there is the old but true stroy that, in the Western concept, a man diminishes the national income by marrying his cook. Our definitions have also been challenged, by Western economists, among them Kuznets (1953, pp.192ff): some of our 'services' seem more properly to be treated as costs, rather than as an addition to wealth or welfare. The Soviet definition has, in fact, one quite impressive argument in its favour: that international (and to some extent also inter-temporal) comparisons of aggregates of material goods, however imperfect they may be, have a sounder basis than any aggregates of services. The latter are generally deemed in the West to equal the reward of the service provider – e.g. the value of a teacher or a soldier is equal to his pay. But suppose, as is the case, a US soldier's or teacher's pay is many times higher than that of a Russian soldier or teacher? One might well ask: what conceivable bearing have such figures as these on the comparative 'volume' of educational or military services? Whereas, at least notionally, steel can be compared with steel, and tractors with tractors, with no more than the usual index number and physical comparability problems (though, alas, these are bad enough). It is important to note that the difference in incomes derived from services are in fact a measure not of the quantity or quality of the services, but of the productivity of the productive sectors. A little thought will show that this is so. Suppose that the material product – or more strictly the consumable material product – per head of population is four times greater in the United States than in Italy. Then, other things being equal, it is quite probable that an Italian hairdresser or civil servant will earn about a quarter of the wages of an American hairdresser or civil servant. In this respect, and perhaps others too, the use of the Soviet concept is more practicable and even possibly more logical than the West's. However, for certain purposes, such as measuring resource allocation within a country, or the standard of living, the inclusion of services is often desirable, and Western national accounts have in fact been attracting the attention of Soviet scholars (e.g. Vaynshteyn, 1967).

In the application of the Soviet concept to the national accounts of the USSR, there are several points which could cause confusion in the minds of the unwary. The first is that some services, in themselves unproductive, do in fact form part of the national income, by being rendered to a productive enterprise. The latter's net product is calculated by subtracting from the total value of its output its 'material' expenditure, and also depreciation. But this means that certain services are not subtracted and so remain in the net product. This would apply, for example, to the services of lawyers and engineering consultants, or to journeys by passenger train of employees on behalf of the enterprise, and also to interest payments on credits from the bank. Consequently, these and similar services find their way into the national income – but not, as in the West, under heading of legal, technical, banking or transport services, but as part of the net product of the 'productive' branch of the economy to which they have been rendered. This affects the comparability of, for instance, the net product of industry under the Western and Eastern definitions, though, in the West too, the handling of such services by statisticians often lacks logic. The same services rendered to individuals, or to 'unproductive' sectors (for instance, education) would not appear in the national income in the USSR.

A somewhat odd situation arises with trade. It was common for Soviet economists to stress, in respect of capitalism, the wasteful and unproductive expenditures involved (e.g. advertising, 'speculation', etc.). However, the use of retail prices for national income purposes necessarily involves including the contribution of trade in the Soviet total. Some theorists consider that this is justified because the bulk of expenditures consist of genuine handling costs (e.g. packing, unpacking, sorting). As we have already seen in Chapter 10, at least one Soviet author is not happy with this. Quite plainly, only a minority of personnel engaged in Soviet trade enterprises is packing, sorting, etc.; most are *selling*.

Soviet national accounts for 1973 can be seen in Table 28.

Table 28

	(milliards of roubles)
Total national income produced	337·2
of which generated by:	
Industry	172·9
Agriculture	68·4
Transport (incl. pipelines) and posts*	19·8
Construction	36·1
Trade, procurements, supplies, etc.	40·0

*Services rendered to material producers only.
(*Source*: NKh, 1973, p.604.)

National income *utilized* came to 334·1, the difference being attributed to 'losses and the foreign-trade balance'. The latter requires the revaluation of imports and exports in domestic roubles (see Chapter 10, above). The table showing utilization incorporates the redistribution of the material product to non-productive sectors; thus consumption includes that of teachers, soldiers, pensioners, etc. One could envisage, say, the footwear industry generating a given value of national income, including a large profit margin and turnover tax, and part of these being redistributed through the budget, to maintain schools, hospitals, soldiers etc. The figures for utilization for 1973 are shown in Table 29.

Table 29 *National income, utilized*

		(milliards of roubles)
CONSUMPTION, all		237·3
of which:	Personal consumption	207·5
	Material consumption in institutions serving the population	20·7
	Material consumption in scientific institutes and administration	9·1
ACCUMULATION, etc.		96·8
of which:	Increase in basic funds	60·1
	(Productive)	(37·1)
	(Unproductive)	(23·0)
	Increase in inventories and reserves	36·7
TOTAL UTILIZED		334·1

(*Source: NKh*, 1973, p.605.)

It is interesting to speculate where defence expenditure appears. Pay and subsistence of military personnel is evidently in 'consumption'. But what about weapons, and current expenses such as fuel used in vehicles? The latter could be in 'material consumption in institutions serving the population', along with items which fit this sub-head better, such as the feeding of patients in hospitals, the use of school textbooks, etc. Perhaps the weapons (or the increase in weapons) most logically belong under 'increase in inventories and reserves'. There is another table in the statistical annual which separates out defence within the national income total, but on closer examination the figure is simply the budgetary defence vote, which does not help us in the present instance.

It will be observed that not only does the Soviet national income total include turnover tax, but also the whole of turnover tax is 'credited' to industry, even when the payment is made by trade, or if it is levied on unprocessed farm produce. This must be borne in mind in considering the relative weights of, for instance, industry and agriculture.

Note also that, to convert Soviet national income totals to a Western definition, it is incorrect simply to add 'unproductive' services. This is because the Western figures are usually at factor cost, i.e. exclude indirect taxation, which turnover tax resembles. Let us take a simple example. If (say) consumers' goods bear tax at 30 per cent, and the proceeds are used to finance education and health, in both a Western and an Eastern country: the former would exclude the tax and include the value of the educational and health services, while the latter would do the opposite. Of course in reality the totals would not be the same, particularly when direct taxes play an appreciable role, for then the expenditures of the state on services would not be financed through the prices of goods. The same would be true if a high proportion of services were not paid for by the state but, as in the United States, by individuals and corporations. The figures in the Western 'factor cost' definition would be affected by a change in the relative importance of direct and indirect taxation. Nevertheless the example does bring out the essential point.

GROSS INDUSTRIAL OUTPUT

'Industry' *(promyshlennost')* in the USSR includes all mining and manufactures, and excludes construction, which is regarded as a separate branch of the economy. It includes also the entire timber industry (except planting and looking after the trees), fisheries and all processing of agricultural products. The slaughter of livestock is regarded as an industrial, not an agricultural pursuit.

Figures on gross industrial output are the sum of the gross outputs of all industrial enterprises, whereas in the West the same designation relates to the output of industry with value-added weights. This affects not only the comparison of aggregate values – the use of the Soviet concept, which includes much double counting, will obviously give a much larger total – but, more important, it affects the index of industrial output.

There are two reasons for this. One is simply that the 'gross' weights used in the Soviet calculation give a disproportionate emphasis to highly fabricated products; in other words, relative to a net weight calculation, a machine or a pair of shoes is more 'important' in the index than the metal and the leather of which they are made, because the output values of machinery and footwear include the metal and the leather (and much else besides) entering into their manufacture. Clearly, this must have an influence on the index of growth. The second relevant factor is that the 'gross' total so calculated, and the index derived from it, is affected by the degree of vertical integration or disintegration. This follows from the practice of adding together the output of enterprises. If, for instance, the same enterprise makes both the tractor and all its components, then, in this respect, there is no double counting; only the value of the tractors appears in the gross output totals. But if it were decided to make these same components in a specialized enterprise which had a juridically separate existence, then they *and* the completed tractors would be counted, at their gross values, and consequently the total and the index would be increased, without there being any additional output in reality. Of course, the opposite could also happen, with opposite results (but, precisely because of these results, which would affect fulfilment of gross output plans, integration might be deliberately avoided). The prices used for the purpose of gross industrial output indices are described as 'wholesale prices of the enterprise (i.e. excluding turnover tax)'. (*NKh*, 1959, p.831.) However, this does not mean that turnover tax is excluded altogether, since only the taxes levied on the products of the enterprise in question are omitted, whereas taxes already paid on materials used by that enterprise are 'in'. The vexed question of price comparison over time is closely related to that of the reliability and credibility of the official growth indices, and will be considered in Chapter 13.

In calculating *net* industrial output, e.g. for national income purposes, double counting is eliminated, and with it the influence of turnover tax on weights *within* industry (turnover tax is added to the *total* net product of industry and thereby increases the weight of industry as a whole). No industrial index with net product-weights is available for the USSR, though some other 'eastern' countries publish it.

GROSS AGRICULTURAL OUTPUT

Agricultural statistics have a number of peculiarities and complications. These arise partly because of the existence of several prices for the same product and partly because a sizeable proportion of the output is consumed on the farm or by peasants without being sold at all. An authoritative Soviet textbook on agricultural statistics (Gozulov, 1967) asserts that in calculating 'gross agricultural output' the farms ought to exclude fodder crops fed to their own livestock, by analogy with the industrial enterprise utilizing components which it itself has made. However, his formulation (p.240) is in a vague, conditional tense, emphasizing the complexity of such a calculation and implying that it is not systematically made. Gozulov himself does not discuss seed, which should logically fall in the same category as fodder if, utilized on the same farm on which it is grown. It would seem, therefore, that the existing statistics of gross agricultural output contain fodder and seed whether or not they are 'consumed' on the same farm, and thus there is a great deal of double counting. The figures that we have, therefore, in no way measure the end product of agriculture.

It is interesting that in the Polish statistical annuals there are three figures given: *gross output,* being the value of every product added together, with no allowance for double counting, *final output,* which is net of agricultural inputs used in agriculture, and *net output,* which is net of inputs from outside agriculture. It should be noted that, with the very substantial growth of inputs bought from industry, the growth of net agricultural output must be substantially slower than that of gross output, but unfortunately the Soviet Union does not publish any figures for net output (except in current prices in the breakdown of national income, from which no volume index can be deduced). Interested readers may wish to refer to the calculations of Lazarczik (1974) as to the growth of gross and net output in a number of East European countries. I have myself calculated for Belorussia that, over a recent five-year period, the growth of inputs actually exceeded the growth of output, i.e. that growth of net output was negative. The calculations are not conclusive, but it is important to bear in mind that a number of statistical perplexities arise when one tries to evaluate agricultural performance on the basis of the available evidence.

It is recommended that prices used to value output sold should be the average prices of sale (i.e. average of the several state purchase prices and free-market prices). The output of *kolkhozy* and *sovkhozy* which is not sold as such (e.g. seed grain, or additional autumn ploughing) is valued at cost. Various problems then arise for Soviet statisticians, which can only be briefly indicated here, and which should be borne in mind in interpreting any published data. The first is that the average price of sale can differ quite widely between areas, farms and years, so that the overall average that may be used for all-union calculations may differ considerably from the average price actually obtained in any particular farm or district. Secondly, the price can differ by category of producer, either because the state buys from them at different prices or because they sell a larger or smaller proportion of their output at the high free-market prices. (This last point is particularly relevant in the case of peasant private plots.) Finally, there is the question of the valuation of consumption in kind by peasants, which presents statistical and conceptual problems in every peasant country. From the standpoint of valuing the total output of the USSR, presumably the output of the peasant private plot, whether consumed by the household or sold in the market, represents the same quantity and should be given the same valuation. In practice, the products *sold* by peasants are valued at the prices at which they are sold, those consumed by the peasants 'at average prices of sale' (*NKh*, 1974, p.810), though the source is not clear as to *which* average. However, if one is valuing peasant consumption, then one could well argue in favour of the use of retail prices, since these are used in valuing the consumption of the non-rural population. This is sometimes done, as we can deduce from the complaint by Perevedentsev (1975), who pointed out that this is illegitimate, because it notionally includes transport and trading services which are not rendered. A still further complication arises in a case (beef is one example) where the retail price is actually lower than the state purchase price, the difference being covered by subsidy. It is not being suggested here that all these ambiguities are deliberate and that the truth is being thereby concealed. Nearly all of them arise from the peculiarities of agriculture and of the price system. Perhaps the one exception is the doubtless deliberate suppression of a net output index.

According to Gozulov (1967, p.241) Soviet reporting agencies sometimes do not observe the rule under which processing is an industrial and not an agricultural activity. As we have already noted, the products of livestock slaughter, for instance, are industrial; agriculture produces not meat but live-weight animals. However, according to this source some meat and lard sometimes get into the reported value of agricultural output.

OTHER SECTORS

These present no especial conceptual problems, though, as in all countries, there are some difficulties in defining boundary lines. The gross 'output' of construction is the total value of building and installation work. It includes the value of building materials, excludes that of the actual installations. Material, fuel, etc., used up are excluded from the 'net' calculation. Similarly, the contribution of trade is the total trade margin (gross); these margins less the materials, fuel, etc., used by the trade network (packing materials, lighting, etc.) equal the net product. Transport and postal services are complicated by the somewhat artificial division between 'productive' and 'unproductive', mentioned above; some rough estimates are necessary in allocating common expenditures between these two categories; but otherwise the same principles hold.

'GROSS SOCIAL PRODUCT'

This concept represents the sum of the *gross* outputs of all the sectors, double counting and all. It is not to be confused with the national income. The purpose of such a total as this may appear far from obvious, but it exists, and a percentage breakdown by sectors has appeared in statistical compendia (e.g. *NKh*, 1973, p.57). Such a total is implied by the value figures of an input/output table à la Leontief.

PRODUCERS' GOODS AND CONSUMERS' GOODS

An essential feature of Marx's analysis is the division of material production into two main 'departments', or 'sub-divisions' *(podrazdel-
eniya)*, known as I and II. Department I is responsible for the production of all goods which are to be used in the process of production.
Department II produces goods for consumption. Both include industrial and agricultural products. These categories are used in analyses
concerning the basic 'proportions' of the economy, and as a means
of relating these with growth.

More familiar, and much argued about, is the division of *industrial*
production into group A (producers' goods) and group B (consumers'
goods). Group A in its turn is sub-divided into A1 (producers' goods
intended for making producers' goods, e.g. steel used in making
machinery), and A2 (producers' goods used for making consumers'
goods, e.g. industrial sewing machines, leather for shoes). Many careless commentators suppose A and B to be identical respectively with
'heavy industry' and 'light industry', but this is not the case. Thus the
entire machine building (engineering) industry is classed as 'heavy',
but passenger cars and domestic refrigerators made by this industry
are classed as B, along with such products of 'light' industry as clothing and shoes, while that part of the textile industry's output which
consists of cloth for the clothing industry is included with A. In fact
in 1973 as much as 26·7 per cent of consumers' goods were produced
by 'heavy industry'. (*NKh*, 1973, pp.207–8.) In principle, it is the *use*
of any unit of the given product which determines its category,
which means that many products are to be found in both groups. For
example, cloth sold direct to consumers, rather than to the clothing
industry, is in B. Electrical power is A, except when used for domestic
purposes, when it is B. In a number of instances, however, when the
end use is not precisely known, or one category of use is obviously
very much the largest, the product is included in A or B in accordance
to its 'predominant end use'.

It is noteworthy that Strumilin, in a contribution to a high-level
symposium, queried the convention of including military hardware in
the category of means of production, on the grounds, to put it crudely,
that they are not means of production. Nor are they consumers' goods,
as had been claimed by Kronrod. Strumilin (1964, pp.50–52) made fun
of such an interpretation: are they necessities consumed by workers
or luxuries for the capitalists? His own belief is that they should
belong to neither category and be treated as a separate item, perhaps
as 'means of annihilation' or inevitable social losses.

The respective shares of A and B in total industrial output altered
substantially, with that of 'A' reaching its peak in 1966 (74·4 per cent).

As we shall see, there has been a controversy about the relative rates of growth of the two sectors.

ACCUMULATION FUND AND CONSUMPTION FUND

Another means of dividing the national product is by reference to its use for consumption and for accumulation (investment). Clearly, this is an altogether different line of division to the ones discussed above: for instance, an increase in stocks of shirts, which are consumers' goods, is accumulation.

The accumulation fund covers, in practice, very much the same area as a Western capital account: increase in fixed capital, plus increase (minus decrease) in reserves, stocks, etc. The rest of the national income is deemed to consist of the consumption fund, part of which is distributed in the form of personal incomes of 'productively' and 'unproductively' engaged citizens, and part is consumed in institutions of various kinds.

Table 29, above, showed the statistical breakdown of this category in a recent year.

MARXIST ECONOMICS AND THE SOVIET ECONOMY

So far we have dealt only with statistical categories. These, it is true, bear some imprint of Marxian modes of thought, but, needless to say, they do not represent a body of theory. We should now see how, or whether, Marxian economics bears on Soviet reality. Before doing so, it is necessary to take a step backward in time, and to consider what could be called the 'liquidationist tradition', i.e. the view, at one time widespread, that economics and its laws relate only to economies based upon private property in the means of production.

Economics has been concerned with exchange relationships, with markets, with the unregulated activities of many men. What, then, is the economics of socialism? One possible answer, for which there is quite considerable warrant in the socialist tradition, is that the 'economics of socialism' is a contradiction in terms, and that the necessary administrative planning functions do not fall under the definition of economics at all. Engels (1936, pp.339, 340) showed himself affected by this kind of reasoning. For him, 'the only value known in economics is the value of commodities. What are commodities? Products made in a society of private producers . . . [which] enter into social use through exchange.' But from the moment when society enters into possession of the means of production, all these relationships change fundamentally. Social labour is no longer measured in money or value, but 'in its natural, adequate and absolute measure, *time*. . . . People will be able to manage things very simply, without the intervention of the famous "value".' It is clear from the context that Engels was not denying the existence of economic problems under socialism. However, he certainly thought that people would manage without 'commodities', i.e. without goods which acquire exchange value in relationship to one another, to which the analytical apparatus which Marx and he erected would have any significant application. Quantitative decisions by planners, which relate the desires of the citizens to the labour time necessary for satisfying these desires, would be sufficient, and this would be a 'simple' process, once private ownership of the means of production was eliminated.

Following him, Plekhanov made many observations in a similar spirit. One finds the most completely 'liquidationist' attitude to economics in Bukharin's famous *Economics of the transition period*, which appeared in 1920. Its title alone showed that he was not contemplating some far-off state of pure communism when he wrote the following:

'Political economy is a science . . . of the unorganized national economy. Only in a society where production has an anarchistic character, do laws of social life appear as 'natural', 'spontaneous' laws, independent of the will of individuals and groups, laws acting with the blind necessity of the law of gravity. Indeed, as soon as we deal with an organized national economy, all the basic 'problems' of political economy, such as price, value, profit, etc., simply disappear. Here the relations between men are no longer expressed as 'relations between things', for here the economy is regulated not by the blind forces of the market and competition, but the consciously carried out *plan*. . . . The end of capitalist and commodity society signifies the end of political economy'. (Lenin did not entirely agree.) (Bukharin, quoted in Kaufman, 1953, pp. 273ff.)

Illustrations about the imminent end of economics were largely shattered by the introduction of NEP in 1921. However, there was now no need to grapple with the awkward problem of the role of economic laws within the state sector, since the survival of money and value relationships could be attributed to the existence of a large private sector. The outstanding contribution to the economic thought of the period came from Preobrazhensky, but he concentrated most of all on the relationship between the private and state sectors, the pace at which the latter could grow at the expense of the former ('primitive socialist accumulation').

For Preobrazhensky too, economic theory as such is related to commodity production, i.e. is conditional upon the existence of private ownership. Under socialism, the 'science of collectively organized production' would replace 'the theory of political economy'. (Preobrazhensky, 1926, p.19.)

While both Bukharin and Preobrazhensky were themselves liquidated in the thirties, what we have called the 'liquidationist tradition' revived strongly under the first five-year plans. Economic laws seemed no longer to apply. Even the word 'statistics' was replaced by 'accounting', because 'statistics' suggested random and uncontrolled events.

This, however, was unsatisfactory, in that planners seemed to be constrained by no economic laws at all. We now know that a new textbook was in preparation in 1941. In the middle of the war, an unsigned article appeared, (written, according to verbal information, by L. Leontiev) which was regarded for ten years as authoritative. It attacked the view that 'since with the liquidation of capitalism the laws peculiar to it have been abolished, then economic laws in the socialist economic system do not and cannot exist. . . . To deny the existence of economic laws under socialism means sliding down to vulgar voluntarism, which consists in the substitution of arbitrariness, accident, chaos for the objectively determined (zakonomerny) process of the development of production.' It was wrong to abandon the teaching of economics, as had happened. A textbook was needed. One required 'a criterion for the correctness of this or that line, this or that policy'. The law of value exists, though 'in transformed form', also under socialism. (Pod znamenem marksizma, 1943, Nos. 7–8, pp.65–75.)

As we have seen, in Chapter 7, in the discussion of prices and 'values', Stalin revised this doctrine in his Economic problems of socialism, published in 1952. The 'law of value', relating to exchange and market forces, was confined to transactions in which ownership changes hands (i.e. consumers' goods and kolkhoz produce, in the main). It could not exist 'in transformed form'. Stalin returned to the older tradition of attributing the survival of the law of value to the existence of non-state property. He expressed the belief that the area of commodity-money relations should be gradually reduced.

Economic theory was at a very low ebb at this time. The economics textbook finally appeared after Stalin's death, but with his ideas incorporated in it. Its inadequacy was all too apparent. Even more apparent was the failure of the economic profession to advance new theoretical ideas. In 1955, a clarion call was sounded by the then director of the Institute of Economics, V. Dyachenko.

'Until recently, dogmatism and scholasticism (nachetnichestvo) showed itself quite openly in quotationism. Instead of independent and deep economic research, the authors of many works busied themselves with a selection of, and commentary on, quotations. Facts were selected and presented merely to illustrate and to confirm the assertions contained in the quotations. Matters went so far that the number of quotations was regarded as an indication of the author's erudition. An economist who found a quotation which had not been used many times in the works of other economists considered himself a creative researcher. After serious criticism of dogmatism and scholasticism in the party press, quotationism diminished, but only on the surface. In many instances matters went no further than the omission of quotation marks, editorial redrafting of the quotations, but in essence things remained unchanged'. (*VEk*, 1955, No. 10, pp.3–4.)

He went on: 'The elaboration of key problems of political economy is most backward. For many years not a single solid theoretical work in this field has been published.' And, even more significantly: 'Since the economic discussions of 1951, it has become customary in every work to refer to the objective character of economic laws of socialism, yet not a single work thoroughly examines in what the objective character of this or that law finds expression, how its requirement shows itself, in what respect and how breaches of these requirements can be identified.' (Dyachenko, *VEk*, 1955, No. 10, pp.6, 8.) Luckily, there has been a substantial improvement since their time.

The economics profession debated the scope and relevance of the 'law of value' in the Soviet economic system. A large majority came to assert that it operates throughout the economy, including transactions within the state sector, and that Stalin's contrary ideas were wrong. They also by a large majority took the view that the area of commodity-money relations should be increased, not diminished. In practical terms, this meant that they wished to stress the importance of rational economic calculation, a more active role for prices and profits, a lesser scope for arbitrariness, throughout the economy. In particular they sought objective criteria for pricing. The resultant discussions have already been referred to in Chapter 7.

In the present context, there is no need to go into them in detail. It is sufficient to identify the fundamental issues. Marx's value theory was designed for the analysis of capitalism, of a market economy. Let us leave aside the question of its adequacy for this purpose. What of socialism? The traditional view, as we have seen, is that the law of value, indeed any economic theories bearing on money, exchange, interest, etc., will fade away. There is a linguistic distinction in German and Russian which is lacking in English. They have *Okonomie* or *ekonomika*, and also *Wirtschaft* or *khozyaystvo*. The first pair concern economics proper, the second is the conduct of affairs, or business administration, allocation, etc. Of course under socialism or full communism there will be administration, problems of *khozyaystvo*, with an appropriate system of calculation (costs perhaps in hours, social utility of products in some units as yet undefined). But this would have nothing in common with the law of value.

One can see here the theoretical lineage of the 'new-left' critics of market-type economic reforms. They claim to be in the tradition of orthodox Marxism. They have a good case.

But, unlike the 'new left', Soviet leaders and economists have to deal with an actual society, and with a functioning economy. Stalin and his successors declared it to be socialist, with full communism a vision of a distant future. Most of the 'new left' would deny that it is socialist, giving it at best the appellation 'transitional'. There is no need for us to enter into this argument. The point remains: transitional or no, the economy must operate; how, by what criteria?

It would not be unfair to Marx to point out that very little of what he wrote actually relates to the economy of the Soviet type, or indeed to any economy which it could become, or could have become, in the present century at least. His theory of value cannot, and was not intended to be the basis of fixing prices in a real-world economy. As already argued in Chapter 7, this is not because of errors in the theory, but because it was designed to 'lay bare' the production relations of a capitalist society, and was not only abstract but also an equilibrium theory. Soviet economists in the second half of the fifties wasted much time and ink in discussing the causes of the survival of the law of value, and whether prices in the Soviet economy should conform to the model of Volume I of *Das Kapital* (proportionate to socially necessary labour) of Volume III of *Das Kapital* (transformed into 'prices of production'). The real problem was quite different. It was: what *role* should commodity-money relations, profits, exchange, play in the economy?

It may well be that a training in Marxian economics stood in the way of a clear view of the real problems, and this for the following reasons.

Firstly, while providing a basis for denying the validity of conventional economic efficiency criteria, it suggested no alternative, except perhaps the vague one of 'economizing social labour'.

Secondly, the basic Marxian idea, found at the very beginning of Volume I of *Das Kapital*, to the effect that commodities have in common *only* the fact that labour is expended in their production stood in the way of appreciating the inter-relationship of different wants, and delayed for decades the development of such concepts as income-elasticity of demand.

Thirdly, by concentrating on labour-cost the concept of *opportunity-cost* was largely bypassed, if not denied. It is extraordinary that Novozhilov had to devote many pages to justifying a concept which is understood by a first-year student in the West, and which has obvious application to the realities of the Soviet economy. (Novozhilov, 1959.)

Fourthly, both input-output techniques and linear programming, especially the latter, were resisted, because the explicit and implicit valuations were alleged to be inconsistent with Marxian value theory. One had to repel attacks of which the following, by Kronrod, is relatively enlightened: 'This is merely the resurrection in mathematical dress of the old concepts of the subjectivist school, the old marginalist pretentions. Their utter uselessness has long ago been proved by Marxist-Leninist political economy.' (Kronrod, *VEk*, 1960, No. 8, p.106.)

Fifthly, a possibly misunderstood Marxism obstructed the use in calculation of interest and rent. Long ago, Yurovsky wrote (1928, pp.115–19), *à propos* of the discussions on models of a marketless economy held in 1920, the following very sensible comment: 'Only the memory of the fact that interest on capital forms a class income in capitalist society can serve as a psychological basis for a refusal to make calculations of this type. No rational basis for such a refusal exists.' But such a refusal existed.

Sixthly, relative scarcity, and its relation to price, was ignored, or downgraded. This is not because Marx was unaware of its importance in real life, but rather a consequence of the equilibrium nature of his theory and his lack of interest in mere market fluctuations. But, of course, scarcity, like opportunity-cost, is constantly affecting exchange relationships and prices in any real-world situation in which exchange relationships and prices have any role to play. Marx surely took this for granted. He was analysing a market economy.

Then, despite claims to the contrary, Marxist economics is no more able than its Western counterpart to explain the level of either wages or profits, nor can it help determine the appropriate level of accumulation. Such phrases as 'to each according to his work' have no operational meaning, especially if accompanied by the claim that wages are not determined by market forces, that labour is not a commodity. (One *left*-wing critic of Hungarian reform told me, in Budapest, that he found this an important weakness in conventional Marxian theory. The criterion of a future equal and marketless society, he said, provides no criteria by which to criticize either excess inequality or market abuses, in a real world in which both inequality and market are bound to exist.)

Also Marx's neglect of marginalism, quite understandable in terms of his task, imposed barriers to the development of Soviet microeconomics. It must be admitted that Western theory is often guilty of what has been called by Paul Streeten 'misplaced marginalism'. One might call it 'inappropriate incrementalism'. Such decisions as the development of West Siberian oilfields are not incremental. External effects and increasing returns do not fit conventional marginal analysis. None the less, valuations of the marginal type do play an important practical role, particularly in programming techniques, as already mentioned. Progress was obstructed by the pejorative associations of the word *mardzhinalizm*.

Finally, there is the effect of a theory of value too exclusively based on costs. This is related to the earlier point about non-commensurability of use-values, and the linked rejection of *subjective* value theory. One need not deny either the vital importance of conditions of production, nor the fact that demand is a function of social circumstances (including the techniques of production), but it is still the case that, for all imaginable purposes, 'value' *must* involve user 'valuation. Marxists can reply that Marx did assert that, to have any value at all, commodities had to possess use-value. True, but this is an oversimple 'either-or'. Any two goods which are of *some* use and which take as much effort to produce are not, by this token, of the same value to the user, as was already pointed out in Chapter 7. Conversely, if two goods, both of some use, are unequally valued by the users, though they cost the same to produce, for every practical purpose in any type of economy their value is surely unequal. In fact, of course, this state of affairs could not subsist in a market economy. To a Western economist this is the merest common sense. Yet it required long (and to some extent still inconclusive) argument to establish the point in the USSR and to draw conclusions from it applicable to pricing. Probably in the end it will be found that demand reacts back on the degree of social necessity of the labour expended in meeting it.

Nemchinov, in his last year of life, came close to this. 'The socially necessary expenditure of labour must be determined by reference not only to the expenditure of labour but also to its results. Only those expenditures are socially necessary which correspond to the requirements of society in given objective conditions of production.' (Nemchinov, *VEk*, 1960, No. 12, pp.87ff.) Novozhilov (1959, pp.210–12) argued that it would be wrong to regard the costs incurred in producing one commodity in isolation as the basis for its value, as production processes of all goods, and the needs they fulfil, are inextricably intermingled. One must measure 'that increment of social expenditure associated with its production', including not only prime costs but also the 'feedback costs' (*zatraty obratnoy svyazi*, or opportunity-costs), which involves charges for the use of scarce capital and natural and other resources. Strumilin (1964, pp.53–5) spoke of something very like diminishing marginal utility. 'Any additional production (of goods) is valued not in accordance with its absolute significance, but relatively to those resources or goods which the given individual or collective already possesses.' He stressed the importance of taking into account 'the degree of saturation'. The younger and less eminent (but able) Petrakov wrote: 'to recognize the existence of value under socialism . . . while denying the law of supply and demand is the equivalent of denying the unity between value and use-value. Marx never called for the fixing . . . of prices corresponding to value.' (Petrakov, 1966, pp. 48–52.) (Of course, value is brought into 'unity' with use-value through the market; how else?)

Novozhilov brought the argument closer to the practical issues involved in the following passage: if 'prices do not inform producers of *what* needs to be produced, nor of what *quality,* nor the socially necessary limits on costs of production', then 'the missing information will have to be provided by plan-instructions. . . . If the information contained in prices often contradicts the plan-instructions, then the instructions must be strengthened by threats *(sanktsii).* But as the experience of centuries shows, fear is a less effective stimulus than economic or moral interest.' Socially necessary labour, as a concept, 'expresses that expenditure of labour rendered necessary by the conditions of *production,* and on the other hand the expenditure of labour which is considered necessary by Society for its *consumption'.* If the decisions influenced by prices are marginal, then the prices should be marginal too. But Novozhilov was well aware that not all information can be carried by prices, and there are many decisions to which marginal cost pricing is inappropriate: thus large investment decisions affect future scarcities, and technical progress affects costs. So the mathematically devised long-term development plans would require planning or shadow prices very different from those which could be used to elicit some marginal production or marginal economies in the short-run with given resources.*

Unfortunately, we have also seen how difficult it is to devise a long-term development programme with appropriate shadow prices in the real, complex, uncertain world.

Dogmatic interpretations of Marxian economics, interpreted furthermore by officials who were defending centralized planning against reform, were indeed obstacles to the development of relevant theory. It would be improper, however, to 'blame' the real Marx.

If we look again at the Soviet debate on the law of value, it went through several stages. In the twenties, it was understood to relate to the private sector and to its relationship with the state sector. Then, as we have seen, its applicability to the Soviet scene was denied or ignored in the thirties. Because this eliminated economic criteria and left the field wide open for arbitrariness, the official view swung to the formulation that the law of value applies 'in transformed form'. Since this had the authority of the Kremlin behind it (this being the status of an unsigned article in the then leading theoretical journal), no one

*See Novozhilov, *EkMM,* 1966, No. 3, especially pp.210–12. For a most useful summary, see A. Zauberman, 1960. It is interesting to note that G. D. H. Cole, in his introduction to Marx's *Capital* (1933), made much the same point about the concept of value in the last volume of *Capital* as does Novozhilov. For the continuation of the arguments of Kantorovich and Novozhilov, and discussions on progress achieved, see reports on conferences on mathematics in economics, *VEk,* 1963, No. 3 and especially 1964, No. 9, pp.63–110 and also V. Glushkov and N. Fedorenko in *VEk,* 1964, No. 7, pp.87–92. See also symposium *Ekonomisty i matematiki za kruglym stolom* (M. 1965).

dared ask what this meant. A rough translation of its meaning might be: 'value categories matter, but we e in control all the same'. Then, as we have seen, Stalin himself, in his very last work, revised *this* formulation, but his final version left pricing *within* the state sector without any coherent theoretical basis at all. The economists who argued in the 1955–60 period were sidetracked onto a multiplicity of largely irrelevant theoretical debates. *Did* the law of value apply? Did it apply because there was still a non-state sector, or is its existence within the state sector inherent in the state-owned economy at this 'socialist' stage? (All agreed that it could have no place under full communism.) Should pricing be based on Marxian values? Or values 'transformed' into prices of production? In the Marxian formula $c + v + m$, where c represents 'constant capital' (material inputs including depreciation of capital assets), v 'variable capital' (remuneration of the labour force) and m *(mehrwert)* is the surplus, how large should this surplus be, within the price of any given commodity? Proportional to v, proportional to $c + v$ (i.e. to costs), proportional to the value of capital assets? We have seen that the 1967 price reform was ostensibly based on the last of these, and also that real price relationships departed from this and indeed any other principle.

As pointed out in Chapter 7, this was a blind-alley. The real question related to the *role* of prices. Linked with it was the admittedly most complex task of discovering what prices could best be used as a basis for planners' calculations and to stimulate efficient behaviour on the part of managers, while also communicating information on demand, consumer preferences, relative scarcities, to all concerned. For these purposes, a formula such as $c + v + m$, or words such as 'socially necessary labour power', are just as unhelpful as would be formulae derived from a general equilibrium model of the Western type.

A fascinating debate, conducted with vigour on both sides, shows us the extent to which Marxist thought-categories appear to dominate the discussion, and yet at several points one wonders if they are not tangential to the real issues. A trio of authors, Grebennikov, Pchelintsev and Shatalin (*EkMM*, 1974, No. 6, and 1975, Nos 1 and 2) discuss 'value relations' (perhaps more strictly 'valuation relations', since they use the word *tsennostnye*, not *stoimostnye*) within the 'System of Optimal Functioning of the Economy', which is now commonly abbreviated as SOFE. They hold that 'the dialectical relationship between production and consumption' involves the category of 'social utility'. It is all wrong, in their opinion, to counterpose social utility to labour values. 'Labour value was based on labour only from the standpoint of its source, its substance, but not from the point of view of its social role.' Under capitalism, they argue, labour is alienated labour, and the law of value, or anarchic market forces, regulate its allocation between different lines of production, in pursuit of profit. Whereas under socialism it can be utilized consciously to produce use-values. The optimal plan would seek to maximize social utility, and to do this it is necessary to recognize the objective existence of social utility and the possibility of measuring it, or at least of getting utilities into rank order. All this doubtless presents practical difficulties, but is an essential feature of socialist planning, within which anarchic market forces do not determine the contours of the plan. But one cannot approach the problem, or reach the necessary plan prices and economic valuations, if one asserts that utilities are not commensurate, that the only common element in valuations is the quality of labour. This measures effort, not result. Furthermore, many decisions are incremental, requiring marginal valuations. Their view of the relationship between plan and market differs from that of many reformers, and is at first sight paradoxical. They cite the view that Marx and Engels 'did not have the historic evidence and so could not see that commodity-money relations will exist in a socialist economy. . . . ' But having said this, they also assert that 'planned relations and market relations exclude one another'. If anything is 'produced or allocated in a planned way, then it is "not a commodity".' So 'it is impossible to utilize in a planned way (planomerno) the law of value, since this means that it has ceased to function'. At the same time, this trio of experienced mathematical economists know well that an all-embracing plan is quite impossible, that the central plan must be aggregated, that it cannot cover micro-detail, that there are bound to be many 'horizontal' relationships, that many decisions will be taken autonomously, by autonomous units, in pursuit of sectional advantage, with an active role at micro level for commodity-money relations. So they believe in the necessity of the 'coexistence' of plan and commodity relations in a socialist economy but 'they are in no way elements one of another'.

The authors appear to be arguing that the law of value relates to capitalism, and to the unplanned or unplannable areas of a socialist system. In the planned sector the required valuations can only be based on conscious calculations of social utility, and cannot be based on labour values. From this follows, argue the authors, that an optimum can only be expressed in aggregated terms, and so the valuations related to this optimum will relate to aggregates also. The multitude of micro-agreements and inter-enterprise links, which decide on deliveries and specifications, should, in their conception, be at prices which will often be uncontrolled, and which will therefore be subject to the law of value and be different in their theoretical basis to the valuations of the optimal plan (and, insofar as they will respond to or utilize market forces, will presumably differ from Marxian labour-values or production-price, since these are of an equilibrium or static character).

These mathematical economists (of whom Shatalin is the senior) lay particular stress on conscious choice by society or its political and planning organs. Capitalists do not aim to produce use-values, they aim at profits, but the market mechanism establishes a link between utility and the allocation of labour and capital in the process of aiming at profits and accumulation. No such link exists where *planned* decisions are being taken. They must aim at conscious maximization of utility and welfare. Whatever the practical difficulties in establishing a utility scale, it is certainly essential (they argue) to attempt to do so, and this must plainly imply valuations which, in their origin, are not labour values.

The counter-attack was mounted by Kronrod. (*PKh*, 1975, No. 10.) SOFE is fundamentally erroneous. It is wrong to confine Marxian labour-value theory to capitalism. It is wrong to lay such stress on utility, it is quite inconsistent with Marxism. Utilities cannot be added together. The shift from direct measurement to rank order, i.e. from cardinal to ordinal utility, restates old bourgeois formulations. There is (he asserted) a direct line leading from the views of Wicksteed, through marginal utility to SOFE. At the same time Kronrod attacked the view that plan and market, allocation and commodity-money relations, are mutually exclusive.

The acrimony of the debate, and in particular the direct attack on SOFE, on which the authorities repose much hope, led to a reprimand from *Pravda*. The short summary given here does not do justice to the subtlety of the arguments, and anyone who reads Russian should, with advantage, read it all for themselves. (The journal *Ekonomika i matematicheskiye metody* contains much on a very high academic level.) What, perhaps inevitably, is missing is any frank examination of the political-institutional system (thus why should and how could an optimum based upon social utility emerge from the deliberations of the central committee apparatus?), and, with less excuse, there is little attempt to grapple with the issue of how any government or planning authority sets about identifying, measuring and choosing the desired optimum, a point already discussed at length in Chapter 2. There is also the problem, of which this group of economists is well aware, of how to ensure that the unplanned sectors act in a manner which does not disrupt the optimal aggregated plan, assuming that it be found.

'New-left' critics such as Bettelheim (1969) also argue that 'socially useful effect' (= social utility) and not market and profit should dominate. However, his analysis ignores the disaggregation problem. Denouncing the post-Stalin efforts to find objective criteria involving the use of monetary measures, his model (unlike the one quoted above) leaves no room for commodity-money relations, except as a transitional *pis-aller*. For him and those who think like him, the law of value represents the law of the market, of exploitation, with labour treated as a commodity, a state of affairs which reproduces (or will reproduce) capitalist relations of production. This can lead to an interesting discussion as to the nature of the Soviet economy and Soviet society. It cannot lead to the application of any economic theory to the problems of Soviet planning, pricing, investment criteria, mathematical techniques, or literally any other of the issues which have been debated – often at high intellectual levels – by Soviet economists in recent years.

It is as well to recall the weaknesses (indeed irrelevance) of so much Western mainstream theory, particularly in its dynamic aspects. It is also arguable that no general economic theory, in East or West, is applicable to the organization and operation of an actual economy. Theories of their nature abstract from many aspects of reality, and are right to do so. They purport to clarify our understanding of various relationships, causes, effects, trends, structures. Marxism in particular lays stress on 'relation of production' (classes, ownership, and also distribution, the surplus, and so on) and stresses the primacy of production. The theory of value is intended to bring into the open the sources of exploitation, of surplus value (profit, rent, etc.) in a capitalist society, and not to serve as a guideline as to the amount that should be invested in the USSR or anywhere else. If the attempt to deduce practically applicable economic laws from Marx's works proved unsatisfactory, this was not their purpose. Equally unsatisfactory would have been the use of any other body of theory for this purpose. A further reason for this is that most of economics, Western economics especially but also (when discussing capitalism) Marx's, is analysing the behaviour of large numbers of autonomous decision makers, largely spontaneous and uncontrolled phenomena, not the 'administration of things' by central planners.

The moral could be that we all need a new economics, which can help to provide criteria for deliberate action by planning authorities, more related to systems, hierarchies, complementarities, less abstract than either the Western-neo-classical or the Marxian systems. But this could be the subject of prolonged debate, for which this is not the place.

SOME ECONOMIC LAWS

From time to time, one encounters assertions that certain propositions constitute economic laws, though the word 'law' would appear to require inverted commas if the propositions in question are to have logical meaning. For example, there is said to be a basic *law of socialism*, defined by Stalin (1952, pp. 38 and 40) and frequently repeated since: 'The provision of maximum satisfaction of the constantly growing material and cultural needs of all society by means of a constant increase and perfection of socialist production on the basis of the highest technique.' Stalin also defined capitalism, though in somewhat less flattering terms (maximum profits, pauperization, exploitation, robbery, war, etc.). This is partly just propagandist generalization, but also, so far as socialism is concerned, involves a politically convenient but analytically disastrous assumption that whatever decisions are taken by the Soviet government at any given time (for instance, about the satisfaction of the people's wants) necessarily conform to the above-named law, and represent the objectively determined maximum at that stage of development.

The same is true of the often reasserted 'law of planned (proportionate) development of the economy', which always appeared in just this form, with the word 'proportionate' in brackets. As far as can be judged, this is little more than a statement to the effect that the economy is planned and that the planners, by reason of the social ownership of the means of production, can determine the correct 'proportions', e.g. between investment and consumption, industry and agriculture, and so forth. Occasionally it is pointed out that it does not follow that the correct proportions are in fact observed, only that it is possible, and indeed necessary for the proper functioning of the economy, that they should be. Stalin himself made this point (1952, p.8.) In this case, it is a 'law' in a quite special sense, and a different word should be used. From time to time one comes across this 'law' in the course of arguments against excessive reliance on 'automatic' economic forces; in this guise, it amounts to emphasizing the primacy of conscious control of the 'proportions' (i.e. primarily over investment). Unfortunately, it is seldom made clear by what objective criteria one is to judge whether the planners at any given moment are in breach of the 'law', save in those instances in which there are plain errors; for example, if the investment plan fails to provide the metal and energy required for the growth targets of the plan itself, clearly the 'proportions' are wrong. Similarly, the neglect of agriculture over many years could be regarded as leading to a breach of this 'law'. However, until the alleged disproportion is identified as such by the political leadership, it has hardly been possible to invoke the 'law' as a criterion.

The same 'law' used to be invoked to justify a necessarily superior rate of growth of department I as against department II, of producers' goods as against consumers' goods. This has caused much confusion, and is worth careful examination.

Marx's growth model ('extended reproduction') in Volume II of *Das Kapital* made no assertion concerning rates of growth of the two departments. In his two-sector model under 'simple' reproduction (no net investment, no growth) the output of department I is utilized in production by department II and for the replacement of worn-out capital assets in both departments. All this takes place in the course of a year. Marx imagined exchanges taking place between the two departments. Consumers' goods made in department II supplied the workers and capitalists engaged in department I, in exchange for producers' goods needed by department II. If, however, there is to be extended reproduction, *additional* producers' goods needed to be made, so that there are more machines and materials available in the next period, to make extended production possible. This is a useful way of looking at the process of production at a high level of abstraction.

It was Lenin who, in his early work *The development of capitalism in Russia*, deduced from these Marxian propositions that department I must grow faster than department II, under capitalism. He took into consideration two other factors. One was a rising 'organic composition of capital', i.e. a tendency for the capital–labour ratio to increase (more machines compared to living labour). This principle, developed by Marx, underlay his theory on the falling rate of profit. The other was his belief, also originating with Marx, that wages would remain low, which would hold back the output of department II. This, at least, seems to me how he would see it: a large increase in department II must contradict the law, in which he believed, of the immiseration of the masses under capitalism.*

Obviously, in its Soviet application this theory made no assertion about low levels of consumption. It rested on the theory of extended reproduction and the rising organic composition of capital. It must be stressed that it is obvious that any major *acceleration* of growth must indeed be accompanied by a relative rise in the size and output of department I. Thus if, as in 1929–32, the share of investment in the national product more than doubles, this has an immediate effect on the output of machinery, equipment, building materials, fuels, which evidently increases very much more rapidly than that of consumers' goods. But why should a steady rate of growth require *further* structural changes in favour of department I?

To answer this question one needs to look again at the 'organic composition of capital', and also at the nature of the statistics by which such assertions as these can be tested.

Firstly, the relationship between the *output* of departments I and II depends not only on the capital-*labour* ratio but also on the capital-*output* ratio. This, in turn, depends on the nature of technical progress. In some instances, surely, one has capital- and material-*saving* inventions. Output of final goods can then rise relatively faster. The relationship between the rise in consumption and that of investment

---

*Tugan-Baranovsky (1918) went so far as to assert that production could increase even if consumption declined. This was an extreme statement of the position, but in his argument he quoted Lenin in support of the proposition that capitalist growth creates its own market, cyclical fluctuations apart.

(or of the output of intermediate products) is not fixed for all time by any economic law, a point in due course taken up by Soviet critics, as we shall see.

Secondly, the statistics usually quoted are only partly relevant and are in an important respect distorted. They usually relate to *industrial* producers' goods (A) and consumers' goods (B). (See Table 30.)

Table 30

	(Percentage of total)	
	A	B
1928	39·5	60·5
1940	61·2	38·8
1965	74·1	25·9
1973	73·7	26·3

(*Source: NKh*, 1973, p.206.)

However, departments I and II cover the whole 'productive' economy, not just industry. Secondly, the percentages are greatly affected by the degree of vertical or horizontal integration, since they are made up of the gross total outputs of every enterprise. If a process formally carried on in one enterprise ended in the production of a consumers' good, its output is classed as 'B'. If, however, the *same* process is divided in two, this looks like a greater round-aboutness of production and the first stage of the process, if carried on in a separate enterprise, is now classed as A. Neither Marx nor Lenin, in their models, envisaged the effect of purely organizational changes on the measurement of the production process. Thirdly, the outcome is also affected by relative prices, and these change, so that the proportions would look different in prices of different years.

The price system also affects the meaning of the division of the national product between consumption and accumulation. This is not only due to the 'normal' index-number problem of prices and quantities changing over time, but also to the ways in which prices are used to redistribute the national product. Thus if profit margins are high in consumers'-goods industries, and turnover tax is levied primarily on such goods, evidently this would give a much higher percentage of 'consumption' in the national income (which, as we have noted, includes turnover tax) than would be the case if profits and taxes were more proportionately distributed among material production.

Until 1964, Soviet economists asserted dogmatically the validity of the alleged law of the more rapid growth of department I, and indeed of A over B. (E.g. Pashkov, 1958 devastatingly reviewed by Gerschenkron, 1959.) Malenkov's fall in 1955 was the occasion for the reassertion of this principle. But it was sharply questioned a few years later. It is obvious, argued a critic, that if the technical means of saving in the use of capital and of intermediate goods existed, and so of increasing the share of final goods in total output, it would be absurd to forgo this possibility. Conversely, a high rate of increase in the volume of producers' goods relatively to final consumable output may well be due to wasteful practices, errors of planning. The point, to cite another critic, is obviously to 'obtain the maximum final social product with the most progressive productive structure'. (Arzumanyan, *Pravda*, 24 and 25 February 1964 and Yefimov, *PKh*, 1964, No. 5, p.14.) Waste can arise out of rewarding managers for output of intermediate goods and services (e.g. tons of steel, ton-kilometres of transportation), and this point was noted by Brezhnev in his 25th party Congress speech. The effect of any such waste is to expand the output of department I.

The dogma was therefore formally abandoned, and replaced by the reasonable proposition that one should minimize costs incurred in obtaining the desired final output. It then becomes a consequence of one's efficiency in doing so, and also of the nature of technological changes, whether or not in fact department I expands faster than department II.

However, all the above discussion had and has one aspect not yet touched upon, and very important in an economy often beset by shortages: the principle of the administrative priority of those branches of heavy industry which make producers' goods. This expresses itself in many ways: higher pay for those engaged, allocation of better-quality materials, better transport facilities, more research effort, and so on. This reflects a widespread attitude of the entire planning system, and such a view has been criticized: at the 25th party Congress (1976) Brezhnev deplored the view that consumers' goods and services are 'of secondary importance'. This, however, has no connection with Marx or Lenin. It may represent a high valuation set on building the future, as against consuming in the present. It may also reflect the planners' anxieties about inputs: if supplies are short, one can always argue that supply bottlenecks in fuel, steel and cement have cumulative negative effects throughout the economy, whereas delay in the production of shoes or cabbages has far fewer such effects.

A last remark relates to the treatment in such analyses of the output of the defence industries. As we have seen, Strumilin suggested that they constitute a category of their own, which he called 'means of annihilation'. Needless to say, the large volume of military hardware makes a significant difference to the division between A and B. Judging from the published breakdown of the content of B, defence hardware must be in A. (*NKh*, 1973, pp.207–8.) But naturally its presence must distort any quantitative analysis designed to trace a relationship between the level of output of producers' goods and economic growth

CHAPTER 13

SOURCES, STATISTICS, EVIDENCE

THE PRESS AS A WHOLE

The preceding chapters endeavoured to present an objective account of the Soviet economic system, its structure, its problems. Inevitably some elements of personal judgement and interpretation have affected the presentation. (Even authors are human.) But what of the factual, empirical base? What solid evidence is there of actual preformance? Are published statistics reliable? How much that actually occurs is concealed? To take one example, no strikes are ever reported. This *could* show that there were no strikes, or, more probably, that the censor has been at work. Workers are presented by the media as enthusiastic (see almost any issue of *Pravda* and its smiling steelmen or builders on page one). The typical émigré presents them as apathetic, much given to work-avoidance and pilfering. Once again, we cannot confidently strike (sorry!) the right balance. But this means that, in a chapter on labour problems, we *may* be omitting something of relevance and significance. Similarly, we know little about the scale of unrecorded transactions, some semi-legal, some illegal. The press does not report accidents, epidemics, racial or national conflicts (except, of course, in capitalist countries). Crimes, whether economic or just criminal, are reported only very selectively, and no statistics on crime or on the prison population ever appear. Salaries of ministers and party officials are secret. If goods shortages exist, they are seldom referred to: thus a joke current recently asserted that 'it has been decided to declare Sverdlovsk a hero-city, because its citizens have seen no meat for ten years'. Whatever the truth about the supply of meat to Sverdlovsk, the press (including any published in Sverdlovsk) is very unlikely to tell us.

So the student of the Soviet economy or society must never overlook the fact that many events and attitudes will simply not find any reflection in the press, or else the reflection will be that of a distorting-mirror. This is *not* to say that no negative or critical material appears. A great deal of it appears, and has been utilized in this book. The observant reader of the Soviet newspapers, books and periodicals will soon learn to identify what can and what cannot be critically discussed, and the selective way in which certain critical material is allowed to be presented. To take a few examples, if Armenians protest about job discrimination in Georgia this will not be printed. Corruption in Georgia, though notorious, remained undisclosed until the Party decided on a major clean-up. But there may be quite widespread reports (in Georgia, or anywhere) on failures to repair tractors, roofs that leak, poor-quality footwear, delays in receiving supplies of components, planning errors of many kinds. Some of these criticisms would appear even under Stalin, though usually with qualifying phrases such as: 'not everywhere are tractors kept repaired', or addressing the criticism to one low-level manager or official. Now, however, we do frequently encounter serious discussions, especially in the learned journals, of the basic causes of deficiencies, with real debate concerning the advantages and disadvantages of possible remedies. One cannot challenge directly the party line, or pronouncements by senior party leaders, that goes without saying. But there is scope for the appearance of a good deal of critical material.

Indeed it has sometimes been possible to criticize party policy, though obliquely. A good example was the appearance, usually in literary journals, of material on agriculture and the peasants which drew attention to the negative consequences of some of Khrushchev's 'campaigns' when Khrushchev was still in command (see Nove, 1964, Chapter 8.) But it must be emphasized that this is rare.

AVAILABILITY OF STATISTICS

In the period from the end of the thirties until 1956 the publication of normal economic statistics ceased altogether. Not a single volume of statistics was published, and secrecy covered such elementary data as the size of population, the level of wages, the output in physical terms of most products (though the appearance of occasional percentage data enabled the observant reader to calculate the output of, for instance, steel, by adding the percentage to the prewar base). Economists did not dare to make calculations of their own, or editors to publish them. As a result, if a new figure did appear in a signed article, say in *Voprosy ekonomiki*, it could be treated as official: the author must either have been told to publish it or had cleared it with high-officialdom.

Now the situation is, in these respects, much better. The statistical annual for 1973, for instance, runs to 880 pages. As will be pointed out, some important items are still missing, but the statistical 'ration' is incomparably larger than it was twenty years ago. Also Soviet economists, sociologists and demographers have been able to undertake valuable research, in which they present their own calculations, their own interpretations of official data, their disagreements with one another. All this is still subject to limitations, in some fields very severe limitations. None the less, valuable information can be gleaned from the work of scholars and of institutes. By 'valuable information' I do not mean a catalogue of negative phenomena; one believes in the reality of achievements, which do exist, more readily if the source is seen to be honestly also reporting defects. (There are the famous lines from Beaumarchais: *'sans la liberté de blâmer il n'y a pas d'éloge flatteur'*.)

Let us now look more closely at the availability of statistical information, and then at its reliability.

At the present time it is easier to list the items which are *not* published, under main headings. These are:

(a) *Industrial output*. No physical-output data on non-ferrous metals. None at all on ships, aircraft, most electronics, or anything remotely connected with weapons. All-union statistics omit alcoholic beverages, though some republics publish figures. Some items are over-aggregated, a few appear and then disappear from statistical reports.

(b) *The labour and wages statistics* have many gaps. The 1959 census gave data on the size of the armed forces, but this was secret again when the 1970 census was published. Little appears about actual earnings of different categories of workers in different industries, or about income differentials. One cannot, for instance, compare the pay of managers in any or all industries with that of labourers or clerks, or find the take-home pay of medical practitioners, primary school teachers, professors, or police officials. Basic rates may be found for some of these categories, but not actual earnings. As already mentioned, salaries of high officials are secret. Rural and urban income comparisons are lacking. (Perevedentsev, 1975, p.137.) Nothing appears which could enable one to compare earnings of men and women. One has to search hard and long to find anything about differentials within agriculture, or between the better-off and worse-off *kolkhozy*. As we shall see, there are gaps and ambiguities with regard to private earnings of peasants, and nothing on incomes from other forms of private activity.

(c) *Social* statistics are patchy. Information is hard to find on average levels of pensions. None is published about industrial accidents. Data on nationalities contain gaps: thus one may have income and education data on Uzbekistan, but not on Uzbeks (which may make a sizable difference with many Russians in the urban population).

(d) *Financial* statistics are also incomplete. As we noted in Chapter 9, there are no published tables of rates of turnover tax. Agricultural subsidies are, as a rule, hidden from view. The coverage and breakdown of allocations to the national economy and also defence are unclear in important particulars, giving rise to much guesswork among Western specialists (see Chapter 9).

(e) There is a regrettable lack of clear *definitions* of categories and coverage also in other spheres, although the short explanatory notes at the back of the statistical annuals are better than nothing.

(f) *Foreign trade* data contain one anomaly, or unexplained gap. Let me illustrate this by the figures for 1974. Total exports to 'developing countries' is given in the annual *Vneshnaya torgovlya SSSR* as 3389 milliard roubles, the figure for imports from this same category of countries as 2384 milliards. If one adds together the statistics for every such country (the list is almost all-inclusive), the sum of the imports adds up to very nearly the total given. Not so exports: the gap in 1974 was 1540 milliard roubles. Of what does this consist, and where does it go? A possible clue is contained 'negatively' (remember Sherlock Holmes: the point was that the dog did not bark), in another omission. The prewar trade statistics included two items, listed under classes 28 and 31, defined respectively as 'objects of gold and precious stones' and 'pyrotechnical materials'. (*Vneshnaya*, 1918–60, pp.28–9.) These two classes are simply left out of the postwar listings. If 'pyrotechnical materials' can be assumed to stand for armaments, it would seem that Soviet arms sales are listed as going to no country, and are 'dumped' statistically into the residual of exports to developing countries. (It seems unlikely that exports of gold as such are included in commodity exports, and anyhow gold is sold mostly in the West.) No explanation has been found, despite repeated attempts. If the above hypothesis is correct, the published trade balance with countries which buy Soviet arms is seriously distorted.

STATISTICS OF PHYSICAL OUTPUT

Few indeed are those who believe that Soviet output statistics are invented. The consensus is that they represent the data which the planners and statisticians themselves use, though of course with omissions. Indeed some of the omissions, when they occur, reinforce this view. Thus there have been occasions when an item suddenly disappears from the annual statistical report. When, later, it is reinstated, it can be seen that its output had declined. So selective concealment, not outright invention, is the practice (though, in fairness, figures showing declines are sometimes published also). A considerable number of émigrés have worked in economic-statistical offices, and not one has alleged that two sets of books are kept. (E.g. Tretyakova and Birman, 1976.) The same conclusion was reached by Grossman in a carefully researched work (1960b). Therefore, say, if it is claimed that 710 million pairs of footwear have been produced, this is what the records show in the Central Statistical Office. One must, of course, watch definitions carefully: is it *leather* footwear, and how is leather footwear defined; these things can alter.

One must, of course, always keep definitions in mind, especially in international comparisons. Thus electricity output in some countries excludes power used in the electricity industry, some include it. Coal figures sometimes (as in the USSR) include low-calorie lignite, or are sometimes quoted in hard-coal equivalent. Fertilizer data in the USSR are given in two ways: gross weight and in terms of standard nutrient content. Railway goods wagons are still quoted in terms of 'four-axle equivalent'. Meat in the USSR includes offal and poultry, which others may omit. None of this is at all illegitimate, and in their own published international comparisons Soviet statisticians will usually make the necessary adjustments.

Statisticians have to rely on reports from enterprises, and it is elementary prudence to bear in mind that these reports could be incorrect, and not only in Russia. Much depends on the interests of those who report, and on the ability and desire of the statistical agency to check on the reliability of the reporting. It is important for managers to claim they have fulfilled output plans. Might they not therefore 'inflate' production?

This is quite possible, but two points must be borne in mind. The first is that what is reported as produced must usually be delivered to some specified customers, so that falsification is likely to be detected. Secondly, it sometimes 'pays' to conceal output, either to carry it over to the following plan-period (to make life easier in the future) or to divert it to the so-called parallel market, i.e. to use it illegally or just steal it. More serious is another kind of distortion: the production of goods of inadequate quality or the wrong specification, but that raises different questions; referring back to the previous example, the 710 million pairs of shoes would indeed exist, but perhaps many millions are of inferior design, the range of choice is small, some of the leather defective. This raises still other questions, already touched upon in Chapter 11, to which we will return in a moment in connection with the measurement of rates of growth. One should also recall the 'law of equal cheating'. This 'law' states that exaggerated output reporting cannot affect the rate of growth unless the *extent* of the exaggeration changes. I see no evidence of this, although presumably there must be some variation in different industries and at different periods, with changing regulations and priorities. (One must not forget that no country has perfect statistics, and that non-communists are perfectly capable of concealing the truth from their statisticians!)

SOME SPECIAL ISSUES IN AGRICULTURE

Agriculture has been a special case. From 1933 until 1953 statistics of the grain harvest were expressed in so-called 'biological' yield; this purported to measure the crop on-the-root, instead of in the barn, but there were also good reasons for wishing to exaggerate the on-the-root crop, as the farms' delivery obligations would then be increased, especially that part which was nominally paid for the services of the Machine Tractor Stations, an amount which was a proportion of the nominal harvest. In this instance it was the state that pressed for exaggeration, while the *kolkhozy* were interested in concealment. In fact it is because it 'paid' to understate the true harvest that 'biological yield' was introduced. This led to massive overstatement of the real harvest. It is much to the credit of the late Dr N. Jasny to have been the first to have shown the large scale of the consequent exaggeration. His estimate of the real harvest in 1937 was within 1 per cent of the official revised estimate, published a decade later. Corrected data for almost all years may be found elsewhere. (Nove, 1969a.) It is enough here to quote one instance. The 1952 harvest was reported to have been 130 million tons, according to Malenkov's speech to the 19th party Congress in October of that year. The revised figure that now appears in the official statistics is 92 million tons, showing an inflation greater than critics in the West believed possible. After a few years of statistical silence, grain harvests reappeared, with the lower 'barn yield' figures. However, suspicions of exaggeration again crept in. Under Khrushchev unripe maize for silage was counted as grain (not any longer). More important, there is persistent suspicion that there is insufficient allowance for foreign bodies and excess moisture in the grain, which is not in fact 'barn yield' but the weight in the combine-harvester *(bunkerny ves)*, and also that losses in transport and storage are large, so that to obtain the utilizable harvest one needs to subtract an unknown number of millions of tons from the reported total. Some unutilizable grain is included in all countries' harvest statistics, but it is thought that the discount is larger in the USSR than elsewhere. One reason is the very serious lack of storage facilities, a defect now being corrected: the tenth five-year plan (1976–80) includes construction of grain elevators of a capacity of 30 million tons.

Opinions differ, however. Thus Dr W. Klatt, a stern critic of communist agriculture, has argued (1976) that, faced with a bad harvest in 1975, many farms under-reported the size of the grain crop in order to keep as much of it as possible. By contrast in 1973 some of the over-abundant harvest could not be transported or stored, and losses were unusually large, and the motive for under-reporting was absent, or at least less urgent.

The point is that grain, unlike (say) steel or cloth, has numerous uses at the producing enterprise (seed, feed, food, and it can be marketed at higher prices in town); only a portion of total output is delivered to the state. It follows that both the motive for falsification and the means of its detection are different in agriculture as compared with industry.

Finally, there are grounds for doubt about any figures relating to the output of the private plots. These figures are in any case few and far between. The share of private output is likely to be understated because a proportion of the livestock raised by peasant families is acquired by *sovkhozy* and *kolkhozy* and delivered to the state as their own, so it counts in the total of state and collective production. This has several causes: firstly, numbers of private livestock are limited by law, so that some calves, piglets, etc. have to be disposed of. Secondly, administrative pressures and shortage of fodder have at times compelled the peasants to sell. (This was notoriously the case during Khrushchev's unhappy campaign to overtake America in the production of meat.) (R. & Zh. Medvedev, 1975.) Thirdly, with high bonus prices now paid for over-plan deliveries to the state from the farms, they and the peasants alike find it worth while to sell in this way (and no doubt quietly to divide the proceeds), as we have already seen in Chapter 5.

Perhaps for this sort of reason, or more probably because of its undesirable ideological associations, the output of the private sector hardly ever appears as such in any statistical source. It must be genuinely difficult to identify the precise proportions of output of this sector. The same difficulty is encountered in other countries too. For instance, in Hungary some of the so-called collective production is in fact undertaken by peasant families on a semi-private basis.

Labour input statistics in agriculture are deficient in most countries, peasant countries especially, because of part-time and seasonal work. Soviet practice for calculating the labour input on *kolkhozy* is particularly inadequate: 'the average annual number of *kolkhozniki* undertaking collective work is determined by dividing by 12 the total number of *kolkhozniki* working in each month . . . regardless of the number of days worked'. It therefore follows that a statistical increase in labour inputs in *kolkhozy* could be recorded 'with no increase in work participation, even if there is a reduction. It is enough that as many peasants as possible (whether able-bodied, aged, or juveniles) work just one day a month.' As *sovkhozy* calculate labour inputs on the basis of actual employment, there is a 'statistical' reduction in labour participation if a *kolkhoz* is turned into a *sovkhoz*. (Korchagin and Filippov, *PKh*, 1974, No. 8, p.135.) Since most peasants spend some time on the private plots, it is evidently incorrect simply to add this to the total period allegedly worked on *kolkhozy* (incidentally, official data on time spent in private agricultural activity are extremely scarce). (For a debate on this see Cohn et al., 1965.)

Perhaps it will now become clear that any conclusions as to the relative labour productivity of state versus collective versus private agriculture are liable to be of doubtful validity.

EMPLOYMENT AND UNEMPLOYMENT

A point to bear in mind, in all countries, is that definition and coverage vary and are ambiguous. Thus who works in the motor industry? Does one include those who are engaged in the manufacture of components, storemen, loaders, clerical staffs at the factory, cleaners, etc. etc.? The answer to such questions can vary not only between countries but even between different firms in the same industry in the same country. Thus in Britain the answer is affected by the degree of vertical integration, and also by whether a given activity is undertaken by employees of the car firm or by an outside firm on contract. This whole area abounds in pitfalls for the careless (or even the careful!) statistical researcher. The Soviet employment figures for particular industries (which are surprisingly sparse) are qualified by the words 'industrial productive personnel', but not otherwise defined.

We have already noted that unemployment is said not to exist, though there must be some individuals between jobs. The materials of the 1970 census, according to a Soviet source, show that 'over half of those engaged in domestic and private auxiliary economy were a potential source of labour on condition that measures are taken which would enable them to participate in social production (more kindergartens . . . part-time work, work near place of residence, work of their qualification, etc.)'. (Korchagin and Filippov, *PKh*, 1974, No. 8, p.137.) But, of course, unemployment is a much more serious problem in the West.

INDICES OF ECONOMIC GROWTH

However, the most important and probably the most interesting issues arise when one looks at the reliability, meaning and international comparability of Soviet growth indicies. These play an important part in the argument about the effectiveness of the Soviet industrialization model. There are several issues involved, which are too easily confused. Let us try carefully to distinguish between them.

There is, first, the 'normal' index number problem. If n commodities are produced in 1950 and in 1970, and their relative quantities and prices have changed unequally, as is of course always the case, then one has different growth rates according to which prices one uses. In the Soviet case, the prices of 1926/7 were used right through to 1950.

It has been noted, especially in the work of Alexander Gerschenkron, that the use of early-year price-weights gives higher growth rates than weights pertaining to a later date. This is logical: thus the items whose production is most likely to increase will tend to be relatively scarce and dear at the earlier date, and so the use of those prices assigns a higher weight to the rapidly growing items. This is particularly noticeable when there is rapid structural change. Gerschenkron (1951) pointed out that American machinery output increased fifteen-fold from 1899 to 1939 in 1899 prices, but only doubled in 1939 prices. Without suggesting that the disparity is necessarily as large as this, the difference is certainly substantial. Bergson (1961), in his computations for the period 1928–37, also showed that growth is much more rapid with 1928 than with 1937 weights.

There is nothing 'wrong' in an index being computed in the prices of 1926/7, but their continued use during a long period of drastic change in output and prices imparted a strong upward bias in the index of growth, and the figures through 1950 were never revised or corrected, but merely 'chained' onto later figures computed in more recent prices. Any Soviet recomputation of the 1928–50 figures in prices other than those of 1926/7 has remained unpublished. We can be certain that it showed much lower growth rates. (Incidentally, this suggests that some of the slowdown in growth which occurred after 1950 is due to a change in weights.)

But this is only the beginning of the story, since so far we have made the quite unrealistic assumption that the commodities produced in our chosen years 1950 and 1970 were identical in type and specification, and that no new ones appeared. In practice, many of the items made in 1950 were not made in 1970, and vice versa. Some items, produced in both years, altered in design. Very few machines, vehicles, clothes, etc. etc., remain the same over twenty (or even two) years. Therefore, an output index comes to depend greatly on how unlike is compared with unlike: thus how many DC3's (made in 1950 but not 1970) equal one DC9 (made in 1970 but not in 1950)? How does one value electronic calculators, which did not exist at all in 1950? How many mini-skirts make the equivalent of a longer 1950 skirt? What value should be attached, in '1950 prices', to a machine-tool not made in 1950, or in 1970 prices to a 1950 machine not made in 1970?

This, clearly, is *not* at all the same as the index number problem. There is usually no precise solution, in any country. How does one deflate by a price index, when non-comparability stands in the way of devising such an index for the category in question? To use a price index applicable to other goods is hardly proper, bearing in mind that prices change by different percentages for this or that good. It should also be recalled that physical-output measures are, as a rule, aggregations of many different types. If we know that output of foot-wear, tractors or bread has exactly doubled (in pairs, units and tons respectively), it tells us little, since there are many kinds of footwear, tractors and bread, of different qualities, and so the real volume may have risen by more, or less, than this.

It may be asked: if the problem is universal, why is this a cause of specifically *Soviet* exaggeration? To this there is one basic answer: it is that the interest of the reporting agencies is involved in the USSR, and much less so in the West. Thus when calculations were made in 1926/7 prices, new products were notionally valued in these prices, in which plan-fulfilment was also calculated. It then became a matter of great importance for managers to persuade the planners to adopt high '1926/7-price'-equivalents, which really had very little to do with what were, or could have been, the prices of the real year 1926/7. There was no reason for the central planners and statisticians to be unduly tough, since high growth rates pleased the leadership. (See Nove, 1957, for details and documentation.) No such inducement to inflate growth statistics exists in the West (at grassroots levels at least. There the aim is profit).

'The prices of 1926/7 are history,' someone might say. But unfor-tunately, though in less acute form, an inducement to exaggerate exists still today. A key success indicator, as we have seen, is 'sales' *(realizatsiya)*, expressed in roubles. Another is labour productivity per head. It 'pays' to show that one's output and sales have gone up. In calculating the extent of any increase, it is in the interests of the management to claim that prices have not risen, for the obvious reason that this will present *their* growth index in a more favourable light. We have already seen in Chapters 6 and 9 how prices of many goods rise, when they are replaced with a different and allegedly improved model. The choice of product mix to some extent depends on how the choice affects the statistical measurement. Sometimes the design is just sufficiently 'new' to qualify as a different product, thereby justifying a price which, it is claimed, is not really an increase on the old one, because the goods are not comparable. When this happens, the value of the output in roubles goes up, but as a rise in prices has been disguised, the price-index used as a deflator is too low, so the volume index is accordingly too high.

In Poland, as well as the USSR, the view is freely expressed, also among economists (though in private) that the official price index understates the real price rises. The figures for machinery are par-ticularly doubtful. Thus the Soviet indices look like those in Table 31. Given the higher prices for materials and fuels, this seems inherently improbable. But it is precisely machinery which abounds in new products. No doubt the price index used as a deflator is greatly influenced by the prices of those machines that were being first intro-

Table 31   *Prices indices (1949 = 100)*

	1950	1970	1978
Fuel industries	76	132	131
Ferrous metallurgy	60	90	93
Machinery and metal-working	41	39	31

(*Source*: NKh, 1978, p.138.)

duced at the beginning of the period and are now genuinely cheaper to produce, and this index is (to my mind illegitimately) extended to the entire range of machinery produced, much of it new.

It is important to note that what we have just described is neither lying nor cheating. It is the effect of playing to the rules, by managers and ministries which seek to present in the best possible light the results of their work, under conditions in which no precise 'truth' can exist; comparing unlike with unlike is not exact and scientific and cannot be. But if, for reasons of self-interest in impressive growth statistics (and evasion of price controls), they all try to choose the upper end of the range of permissible variants of measuring growth, the total will be significantly shifted upwards in the process of aggregation; whereas in the West the inevitable inexactitude of such calculations has, in all probability, a random effect, since no one is particularly interested in growth statistics, except perhaps a few economists.

Some interesting conceptual problems arise, already touched upon in Chapter 10. Let me illustrate them with a simple example. Let us suppose that we have the following information: between 1950 and 1970 the output of bread has risen by 30 per cent in tons and by 60 per cent in value, i.e. the price seems to have risen by 23 per cent. This could be quite consistent with a shift towards higher-quality well-baked white bread, and it may well be that no prices in fact increased; citizens simply prefer to pay more for more of the better bread. But suppose the prices and quantities are exactly the same, but the new assortment is 'obligatory': the citizens would prefer the cheaper bread and cannot get it in the accustomed quantity. Then there *has* been an increase in price. I do not suggest that this has actually happened with bread, but evidence is strong that such things occur frequently in many branches of both heavy and light industry, and especially where (unlike bread) new products can be designed.

When all is said, however, there is a general consensus among Western scholars that there has been much less 'inflation' of the growth index since 1950 than before. Also it is only fair to add that, whereas in the thirties there was a widespread deterioration of quality, there has been a considerable improvement in more recent years.

It should be recalled that gross industrial output indices are affected by the extent of multiple-counting involved in adding together all the outputs of all enterprises. Gross agricultural output also involves much double-counting, and the index of *net* output, if we had it, would certainly be lower, since the relative share of inputs in total value has undoubtedly risen with increased mechanization and use of fertilizer.

It must again be emphasized that the scepticism about aggregate *indices* of national income and industrial production does not extend to the physical output magnitudes already discussed.

If one speaks of exaggeration of growth indices, on what scale is it? There have been a number of Western recomputations, which are either based on aggregating the available physical quantities, or proceed by calculating price-deflators. Interested readers are referred to the works of Bergson (e.g. 1961), and to Nutter (1962), Moorsteen (1962) and others. In my view, despite their undoubted merits (no one can do better with the evidence available), one should hesitate before simply substituting them for the Soviet official index. The reason, as their authors well know, is that we cannot confidently overcome the statistical difficulties and ambiguities listed on the preceding pages, and in addition many Soviet physical-output data are themselves aggregations of a varied product mix (pairs of shoes, tons of steel, etc.). So when Seton has industrial output rising twelve-fold from 1913 to 1955, and Nutter opts for a five-and-a-half-fold increase for the same period, we must note that both are far below the incredible official claim that industrial output was twenty-one times higher, but without being able to judge between them.

An example of an impossible official claim relates to the national income for that period. The official figures claim a seventeen-fold rise for 1913 to 1955. But the Russian Empire in 1913 had a national income approximately a fifth of that of the United States, according to estimates accepted also in the Soviet Union. After making due allowance for (the slower) US growth in the same period, one is forced to the conclusion that the USSR had reached the United States national income by 1955, an absurd conclusion, even allowing for all the peculiarities of index numbers. In any event, gross agricultural output is said to have risen by only 70 per cent in the same period, and so a phenomenally low weight for agriculture is needed to arrive at a seventeen-fold increase in national income (this is, needless to say, national income in its Soviet definition, as described in Chapter 12).

All of which is not to deny that the Soviet economy grew rapidly over these years, nor that it is still growing (though at more modest rates) today. Though our statistical picture of reality is imperfect, with gaps and uncertainties, we do know enough to attempt an assessment of the performance and prospects of the Soviet system, in relation to the West and to the developing world, and to this task we will turn in the next and final chapter.

Statistical censorship has been increasing. Thus Soviet foreign trade statistics after 1977 no longer include figures on imports of any fuel, non-ferrous metals, rubber, and much of the data on physical quantity have disappeared too. So have statistics on infant mortality (which had been rising).

An article by V. Krasovsky (*Voprosy ekonomiki*, 1980, No. 1) expresses strong scepticism concerning the validity of the price index for machinery. It must, in his view, be based on an unrepresentative sample. In fact prices have been rising quite steeply. This supports the author's interpretation of these statistics.

CHAPTER 14

ASSESSMENT

HOW DOES ONE PROCEED?

What should this final chapter look like? What ought one to be assessing? Presumably it is accepted that, though at heavy cost, the Soviet system has created a mighty industrial power, but one which in a number of respects is backward still. By reference to what standards does one, can one, measure its achievements? Or the cost of these achievements? Are the pockets of backwardness part of the cost of the priority of modernization? How much could be ascribed to the despotic excesses of Stalinism? Is the system, designed for the ultra-rapid creation of a heavy-industrial base, able to cope with the task of operating a mature and sophisticated economy? How can one compare the efficiency of systems, bearing in mind the different levels of development, resource endowment, policy objectives, political culture, multiple inter-relationships of cause and effect, some 'systemic' and others not?

It would be neat, tidy and satisfying to be able to say: *this* is the optimum, the standard of efficiency, the production-possibilities frontier, and the Soviet system falls short of it by a specified percentage. Unfortunately, absolute standards of efficiency are not definable, production possibilities frontiers never visible except in the pages of the more abstract textbooks of economics. Can one measure the gap which separates the USSR or its allies from the most developed Western countries and attribute this gap to the system of state ownership and directive planning? Or derive far-reaching conclusions from the fact (the undeniable fact) that the USSR over the past thirty years has grown faster than the United States? What of the conflicts and contradictions, economic, political, social, that threaten to upset the functioning of the systems which we may be wishing to compare?

Many questions. There could be many more. Few precise answers. This is because the evidence is often ambiguous, contradictory, inconclusive, unquantifiable with any pretence at precision. So the reader may be dissatisfied. He or she might say: 'I recall a fable which asserted that if one lays a hundred economists end to end they would never reach a conclusion; evidently the author is one such.' The author is guilty, but with extenuating circumstances. My object here is to draw attention to what is relevant to an assessment of performance, and to draw attention also to the many pitfalls and blind-alleys that await the analyst. In the end (as Brezhnev would probably say, and rightly) history will judge: in the year 2000 we may know which system has the highest survival-value, and adaptability. Extrapolation of present-day trends, even if we can agree about what they are, will get us nowhere. Of course, survival-value is not the same as efficiency, but, after all, it will be the survivors who will write history, and describe the social-economic system which will exist a quarter of a century hence, warts and all.

REALISTIC CRITERIA

These lines are being written in Great Britain in 1976. Anyone who is not blind can see before his or her eyes many signs of serious disarray, in at least this Western country. Some would argue that this is largely a British disease, others that the whole Western economic (and social-political) system is in a fundamental crisis, that its economic efficiency and social acceptability are very seriously challenged. It is not in this book that one would expect to find confirmation or denial of such diagnoses as these. But one should never lose sight of the point made right at the beginning: we ought not to compare Soviet economic performance and efficiency with the idealized world of the textbook, whether a 'bourgeois' textbook or one expressing the Utopian hopes of a neo-Marxist enthusiast. Criteria of judgement applied to the real world, whether in the Soviet Union or anywhere else, should relate to the possible, and to the place and time (for admittedly the area of the possible alters). There could, needless to say, be differences of opinion and interpretation as to what is or is not feasible in given circumstances, but it is often the case that the more closely one studies a given situation, the more conscious one becomes of the limitations of effective action. The cost of the proposed action may be too high, in terms of the conflicts or confusions which it might cause. Alternatives which might appear attractive may in fact be impossible. One should also mentally distinguish between at least three very different kinds of 'impossible':

(a) 'It is impossible for the party leadership to allow freedom of private trade'; or a rabbi *cannot* eat ham.
(b) 'It is impossible for the Polish army to repulse a determined attack from the greatly superior enemy'.
(c) 'It is impossible to have your cake and eat it' (and all the variations on this theme).

In the case of (a), the actions in question are not *physically* impossible, but rather are unthinkable for a Soviet communist leadership (or a rabbi) to consider, because they are what they are. The second example is a matter of power relations. The Polish army could not (for instance) cope with the German invasion of 1939. Or the supporters of certain kinds of reform cannot overcome the overwhelming strength of the opposition. The third is in quite another category. No amount of power and determination can get a quart into a pint pot, or fulfil an unbalanced and unfulfillable output plan, or combine self-managed enterprises with a centralized non-market economy.

There were some things which the Bolsheviks could not do because they were Bolsheviks, though others would have done them: for instance, rely on a prosperous market-oriented private peasantry. For rather different reasons, they could not escape from the consequences of Russian history and climate. They could not, even if they had wished, reproduce in Russia the special features of Japanese economy and society, or turn the Russian peasant into an American farmer, or industrialize without sacrifices. All this is *not* intended to imply that whatever happened *had* to happen, by a sort of historic necessity or inevitability. There were choices. But a number of developments *could not* have occurred in the USSR, and it is pointless to 'blame' Stalin or Brezhnev for not doing that which they could not do.

THE HISTORICAL CONTEXT: AN INDUSTRIALIZATION MODEL

While the Soviet economic model has not only a developmental connotation, few indeed can doubt that both the chosen strategy and the organizational forms were deeply affected by the fact that Stalin's Russia was engaged in a process of rapid industrialization. Therefore in examining this strategy, and the role within it of economic criteria, it is useful to try to situate Soviet experience wthin the controversies of development economics. This might well assist the reader in thinking more clearly both about that experience and these controversies.

There is by now a massive literature on economic development. There is a wide range of opinions expressed in this literature, and any generalizations are therefore dangerous. However, a considerable number of development economists (Myrdal, Lewis, Hirschman, Higgins, Perroux, to name a few) would probably agree with the following set of propositions. Development is about rapid structural change, very often without the political, social and economic preconditions which would make the process 'organic' or smooth. There are disequilibria, strains, potential or actual disorder. The so-called 'demonstration effect' gives rise to expectations and aspirations which are bound to be disappointed. In countries with national or tribal divisions the social and economic strains can cause disruption and even chaos. Very often the new forces of industralism conflict with an older power-structure (as they did in Tsarist Russia). The threat to public order leads to, or reinforces the need for, strong government. There is a search for a mobilizing ideology, in the name of which to generate enthusiasm, impose sacrifices, organize the national effort.

Development very often is a matter of (or is thought to require) *purposive* planning, i.e. a consciously directed change in the existing structures. For this purpose, almost by definition, the conventional Western market criteria are not sufficient, may be positively misleading. In Hirschman's words, 'in these basic types of investment decisions, it is, therefore, not sufficient to supplement, qualify and otherwise refine the usual investment criteria. We must evolve entirely new aids to thought and action in this largely uncharted territory of efficient sequences and optimal development strategies.' (Hirschman, 1958, p.79.) One seeks leading sectors, growth points, and, far from looking for equilibrium or optimum allocation of the conventional kind, priority may be given to sectors which, in the words of Francois Perroux (1958), *'excercent un exceptionnel pouvoir déstabilisant'*, which are change-inducing.

Political-social factors, class relations, the role of the state, the problem of imposing sacrifices in the name of an ideology, all enter into realistically defined development economics. It is not primarily concerned with optimum allocation of resources by conventional static criteria; one is faced by problems of development *strategy*. This requires different criteria, and these are very hard to define.

While it is both true and important that the Russian Empire in 1913 was partly developed (with some modern industries, a rail network, a good educational system), it was none the less predominantly a peasant country still, and therefore the transformation of such a country into a mighty industrial state naturally interests many in today's developing countries. The USSR is seen, and rightly seen, as having raised itself by her own boot-straps, industrializing very largely by its own efforts. It is undeniable that Western machinery and credits helped, but it remains a fact that the Soviet model is one in which ownership remained firmly in the hands of the state, in which foreign investment and the activities of Western firms played a restricted role. Given the large and generally hostile literature in developing countries on dependency and the multinational corporations, it is noteworthy that the USSR was able to invest in her own development while avoiding such undesirable entanglements, or at least minimizing them.

Inefficiencies, sacrifices, oppressive government, the collectivization disaster, if recognized, can be played down. Perhaps, so it can be held, inefficiencies are part of the cost of learning, sacrifices in the name of an ideology are inevitable, and as for oppression, what country industrialized with consensus; did anyone ask the British population if they wanted the industrial revolution? How many developing countries today are democratic? Many believe that an industrializing despotism is the only effective way forward. Finally, the long Soviet experience of centralized planning is of evident interest for anyone desirous of planning industrial development; one can learn what to do, and what not to. This last point is accepted also by the more intelligent Soviet thinkers on development problems. Thus, in urging more attention to economic rationality in the third world, Shmelev commented: 'Development of socialist countries moved along an uncleared path, and many things became evident only in process of practical experience. . . . ' Shmelev, *MEMO* (1968, No. 8, p.61 – with thanks to A. Erlich for the reference.) In other words, learn from our mistakes.

These arguments help to explain the appeal of the Soviet model and particularly of the Stalinist phase, with all its crudities and cruelties. The present USSR, in the stage of so-called 'developed socialism', a country already largely industrialized, in many respects conservative, challenged by a militantly revolutionary China, is a less attractive model because less relevant to the stage which many developing countries have reached, being less revolutionary, no longer concerned with structural transformation.

There is much more that could be said about the impact of Soviet experience, and how it is understood abroad. Perhaps more immediately relevant to our main theme is what we can learn from the theory and practice of economic development to help explain certain features of the Soviet system. One understands better the restricted role of the price mechanism and the market, the perplexities over investment criteria. 'In fact,' wrote Myrdal (1957, p.89), 'a large part of the economic process . . . has to be directed by changing costs, prices and profit rates through modifying the conditions under which the price system functions.' The role of apparently irrational economic-political campaigns, which serve the purpose of mobilizing the people and also providing a goal and success indicators for the controlling apparatus itself, becomes functional, despite the waste it occasions. One becomes conscious of the inadequacy, in the context of rapid development, of merely indicative or paper planning: many so-called development plans look impressive but have no effect on what actually happens. The USSR's plans are sometimes unreal, are often underfulfilled, but they are operational, and great investment projects are, as a rule completed, even if behind schedule.

One learns, too, of the pitfalls involved in using the word 'rationality', in the context of development strategy, in the Soviet Union as elsewhere. Political and social objectives have a logic of their own, which can contradict *economic* rationality narrowly understood. To borrow an example from Myrdal (1957, p.75), suppose in some country the spirit of nationalism is a vital mobilizing and unifying factor; then in such a country it may seem necessary to take measures to restrict foreign firms, measures which in themselves may actually harm development. In the West during the war, centralized planning was adopted, to concentrate resources for the waging of war. The resultant network of bureaucratic regulations produced a multitude of micro-irrationalities. Yet these are best seen as part of the *cost* of a necessary degree of centralization. No one would seriously argue, I trust, that the most efficient way of waging war would have been achieved by restoring the market mechanism, in the interests of rational resource allocation, in (say) 1943.

The parallel with a war economy is an apt one. Thus Oskar Lange once described the traditional Soviet system as a 'war economy *sui generis'*, and a leading development economist, Benjamin Higgins (1959, p.453), saw that 'total war, like planning of development of poor and stagnant economies, involves marked and discontinuous structural changes, and resource allocation without reference to the market'. The same author also wrote: 'Nor are the required adjustments strictly marginal. In such countries growth itself must be managed, and sectoral planning is necessary. The various rates at which heavy industry, light industry, agricultural improvements, transport and communications, housing and the like are to be pushed becomes a matter of conscious policy. Planning of this kind involves a calculus, involving a cost benefit comparison, but it is no longer a purely marginal calculus.' (Higgins, 1959, p.451.)

Readers unfamiliar with the controversies surrounding development economics must be warned that this whole approach has been challenged. It is not our task to enter into disputes about this. The above views are simply quoted to show that, though not derived from a study of the Soviet system, they evidently have some features which any student will recognize as bearing also on the Soviet economic experience. It underlines the fact that the USSR has been a developing country, and that it has shared in some of the problems common to such countries, not least of which is to identify and utilize criteria for economic efficiency in the context of consciously directed structural change.

This entire argument should not be seen as an essay in sophisticated apologetics. Soviet economic history (not to mention political history) abounds in spectacular waste, excesses, crimes indeed (such as forcible collectivization), and it would be quite illegitimate to argue that this multitude of errors and coercion were somehow 'necessary', let alone justified *ex post* by growth statistics or success in war. But it is plainly essential to appreciate that the Soviet system arose in a historical developmental context, continuing a process of industrialization begun under the Tsars, and that not only is its experience of interest for developing countries, but the theory and practice of economic development helps us understand better the economic history and problems of the USSR.

Including those of the present day? Yes, because the *structure* of Soviet planning was designed, under Stalin, in a period of ultra-rapid industrialization. The lopsided process of unbalanced growth which characterized Soviet economic history has now brought into being a system which Soviet theorists call 'developed' or 'mature socialism' *(razvity sotsializm)*. Yet in some sectors, agriculture especially, but also services and many non-priority industries, the USSR remains backward, the least developed of the big industrial economies. Furthermore, to use Marxian terminology, there exists a contradiction between the forces of production and the relations of production, between the modern industrial economy which has been built (with so much blood, sweat and tears) and the centralized structure of control, exercised through the party-state hierarchy. It is to the consequences of this contradiction that a great many pages of this book have been devoted.

HOW TO COMPARE THE EFFICIENCY OF SYSTEMS?

If this were a textbook on comparative economic systems, how would one go about comparing systems effectiveness? A whole book could be devoted to this topic, which is of challenging complexity. It will only be possible here to indicate the principal issues involved, and perhaps to suggest lines along which solutions might be sought.

The historic dimension is vital, and one returns to the theme of realistic criteria, touched upon in the opening of this chapter. The revolution occurred in Russia. A social and political breakdown, in the midst of a destructive war, eventually led to the retention of power by the Bolsheviks, with the elimination of capitalists and landlords. Whether the revolution was itself 'inevitable' in this form it is unnecessary for us to discuss here. Once it had happened, evidently the state became the only basis upon which capital accumulation and industrializing investment could rest. Whether the Russian Empire, already in the throes of industrialization, could have grown into a mighty power without any revolution we shall never know. Quite possibly it could, given its very large natural resources, but on the assumption of political stability and therefore also of the ability of the Tsarist political and social system to adapt to modern needs. One must also assume the absence of World War I, the continued flow of foreign capital, the emergence of a strong native bourgeoisie. It might be an agreeable exercise of the imagination to re-write Russian (and European) history on these lines. It seems also a futile exercise.

Yet the effect of the *system* on the performance of the Soviet economy could only be measured if we could compare present achievement with what *would* have been achieved in Russia under another system. Otherwise we may be unable to identify other important causes affecting performance, ranging from the human element to natural resource endowment.

A Polish economist once said (in private conversation): 'Our economic-reform model is much superior to the East German, but East German performance is far superior to ours.' He attributed the difference to the much more highly developed work ethic among Germans, workers and managers alike. To take a less serious (?) but equally relevant example: if Britain were a socialist country and France were capitalist, it might be tempting to attribute French restaurants' superiority in cooking to private enterprise, but we would surely not be wrong in suspecting that social-traditional factors were even more important. In Eastern Europe, Hungarian restaurants and retail-trade establishments are notably superior to the Polish and Russian varieties, but perhaps tradition as well as economic reform should be 'blamed' for this. In the Soviet Union itself, agriculture and services are much more efficient in Estonia than in the adjoining Russian areas, and output per head in Central Asia is far below that of the Baltic states and of central Russia, for reasons which, we would surmise, are again mainly historical-cultural in character. The same observations would apply to comparison between Western countries: thus if Italy or Great Britain are much less 'efficient' than the United States, this is not evidence of superior or inferior 'system', but is a result of a complex of causes, to which sociological and historical analyses are certainly at least as relevant as that of economics.

This brings one to resource endowment. Thus Soviet agriculture is handicapped by large areas of poor soil and, in areas of fertile soil, by recurrent drought. Transport costs (and thus efficiency) would be much lower if rivers did not flow into the Arctic ocean or in inland Caspian sea, and did not freeze in winter, or if iron ore and coking coal could be found close together instead of a thousand miles apart. It would be easier and cheaper to build roads if the great Russian plain were provided with rocks. A recent study of the coal industry, to cite one more example, showed Soviet labour and capital productivity very far behind the United States, but much of the difference was evidently due to the nature and convenience of the coal seams. These and other handicaps affect factor productivity, and yet it would be absurd to pronounce that they have anything to do with 'systemic' inefficiencies.

What, then, can we conclude from the statement that the Soviet national income, or factor productivity, is (say) 40 per cent of that of the United States? Approximately this figure follows from the careful study of Abram Bergson (1968), using data for 1960, this being the rough average of the different weights used. Such information is, of course, of interest. But only an unknown portion of the difference is due to the superiority of the US *system*. The historical dimension, furthermore, is also relevant here: if, for reasons with roots in the past, Russia could not have effectively adopted the US system, then the comparison is only of limited meaning also for that reason. Japan's remarkable performance seems to be conditional, to a degree we cannot measure, upon being peopled by Japanese; it is pointless to assert that Tsar Nicholas or Stalin, or Harold Wilson, 'should' have adopted the Japanese model of development.

One must carefully define not only such words as 'rationality' but also 'efficiency'. Not, this time, because of the problem of 'efficiency for what', but 'efficiency in relation to what'. Let us take an example. Finnish agriculture is less productive than that of the United States. It is, however, quite remarkably efficient in overcoming climate-and-soil handicaps. If one were to measure efficiency simply in terms of performance, this would be obscured. In terms of ability to cope with the natural environment, the vote should probably go to the Finns. For all these reasons, care is needed in interpreting international efficiency comparisons, including those between the United States and the USSR.

Should dynamic efficiency be measured by growth statistics? This is another useful indicator, but suffers from many limitations. Some of these were already mentioned in Chapter 11, in the context of the criteria by which one judges the success of economic reform. More is not necessarily better. Quantitative output targets encourage the chase after quantitative results. Improvements in quality seldom receive the statistical 'credit' they deserve. Output and national-income statistics measure remunerated activity ('productive' activity in the Soviet definition), whether or not it is socially desirable or economically rational. Some humourist once said that a possible way of increasing GNP is to breed mosquitoes and then very efficiently expand the output of mosquito-nets and insect-repellent sprays. More seriously, it is hardly necessary again to stress that the 'command' system plus fixed prices can give rise to production of goods of indifferent quality which fail to match user requirements but which are included in the statistics all the same, at officially fixed prices. I have argued elsewhere (Nove, 1964, pp.286–99), that wasteful investment decisions can, paradoxically, 'count' as national income, and they can give rise to productive activities which may as such be 'efficient' but are unnecessary: an example is wrong location, which generates additional transportation, which calls for the production of more steel rails, goods wagons, rail services, in all of which there could be high productivity, yet part of this extra output could and should have been avoided. In relation to the volume of investment, or of the output of producers' goods, the growth of final output would be unnecessarily small. This would be the sort of outcome mentioned in Chapter 12 above, in the discussion on the superior growth of department I over department II. Unnecessary investment counts as GNP, but increases the capital-output ratio, the share of investment in national income, the relative magnitudes of A as against B goods.

There is also the argument advanced by W. Brus: to measure efficiency with growth statistics is 'too simplified, an example of the characteristic fanaticism of growth ("growthmanship")'. There may come a time when 'the positive effects of economic growth cease to outweigh the negative ones'. What about more leisure, protection of the environment, and so on? (Brus, 1975, p.23.) It must be admitted that the elusive concept 'the quality of life' finds little reflection in aggregate growth indices. This said, it must also be admitted that a superior growth rate sustained over a long period does establish the presumption that productive capacity and material living standards are advancing faster, and Soviet analysts quite understandably stress the importance of this point.

There is still another aspect of inter-system comparisons, dynamically interpreted, and this concerns the disruptive influences of social and class conflict, inflation, cyclical fluctuations. Whether or not we are about to witness the 'final crisis of capitalism', few will deny that the postwar confidence of being able to avoid depressions and unemployment has been seriously shaken. The relationship of the developed West with primary-producing countries has also undergone a major transformation, and the shock given to the whole system by OPEC (the quadrupling of the price of oil) could be repeated for some other commodities. This may prove to be connected with the gradual exhaustion of natural resources. One need not be a 'doomster' to realize that, despite the ingenuity of man in devising substitutes, the earth and the riches thereof is (are) finite. The 'cod war' between Britain and Iceland is one by-product of this. It may be said, truly, that this puts paid to the naive-Marxist vision of worldwide abundance, since quite plainly the standard of living of (say) a French worker cannot possibly be extended to the Asian masses without running into impossible supply constraints. But one might well argue that this Marxian or pseudo-Marxian abundance is a matter of faith or religion, and that the real issue is the ability of systems to cope with the difficulties of the real world. The Western system, if it can be so called, is not performing well by this criterion. There are forces making for disintegration, both at the level of international trade and payments and within the countries concerned, as social stresses lead to internal troubles, which react inevitably upon economic performance.

Then there is the consequence of the unregulated spread of automation upon employment, and the economic and social consequences of this, already visible in the United States. Combined with low growth rates and/or cyclical fluctuations this could be an explosive mixture. The political and social-economic pressures which have surely contributed to inflation may well have a lasting disruptive effect. Few can doubt that a high degree of uncertainty as to the future course of prices, interest rates, foreign exchange, plus a high risk of civil commotion, are inconsistent with rational economic management in any economy, but particularly a free-enterprise economy. In such circumstances, even a demonstrable superiority in its micro-economic model would scarcely be relevant. It would be analagous to claiming a superior menu, with a wide range of choice, in the restaurant of a sinking ship.

It may be objected that all this silently assumes that the Soviet 'ship' is seaworthy, that its economic and social system is free of irreconcilable conflicts and contradictions. The objection is a valid one. Much of this book has been concerned with analysing various weaknesses and strains in the Soviet economic system, and more will be said about them in a moment. Furthermore, it could well be that political-social stresses of potentially disruptive kinds are concealed by the Soviet censorship: local nationalisms, workers' discontent, even conflicts within the party or with the military, *may* erupt, and, if they do, this will have adverse effects also on the economy. The point I was trying to make was simply that the stability and coherence of the entire complex of productive and social relations must not be taken for granted, and that if (repeat *if*) the Soviet Union is better able to maintain stability, in an increasingly unstable world, then this is a matter of vital importance in inter-system comparisons.

New technology can not only create a dangerously high level of unemployment, it provides new challenges and opportunities in the whole field of economic organization and management; Systems analysis, with stress on interdependencies and complementaries, will surely soon replace the conventional Western stress on marginalism, increments and the profit-maximizing separateness of economic units, linked together conceptually only with general-equilibrium models and perfect (or imperfect) markets. It is true, as we have seen, that the Soviet system in its present form is poor at handling technical progress, especially its diffusion through the economy. Much in the great bureaucracy rejects the mental and institutional flexibility required for such diffusion. Critics such as Academician Sakharov have been pointing to the consequences, in this field, of imposed conformism and the dead hand of party control. Yet we must note that the party leadership is very much alive to the existence and importance of the scientific-technical revolution. Brezhnev laid great stress on it in his speeches both to the 24th and the 25th party Congresses (1971 and 1976). The theme has been repeated in countless books and articles. Authoritative texts speak of 'a fundamental transformation of science and technique and of their linkages and social functions, leading to a universal revolution in the structure and dynamic of the productive forces of society, in the sense of a change in the role of man in the system of productive forces on the basis of the complex technological application of science as a direct productive force, penetrating all the component parts of human life . . . Only socialism can fully realize and utilize it.' (Kedrov and Shukhardin, 1973.)

Can it? Soviet-type economies have not so far been able to 'realize and utilize' their potential in this field, but an attempt is being made, and probably Brezhnev would agree that much depends on the success of this highly necessary process of adaptation. Given the strength of conservatism and inertia in the USSR, there are no very strong grounds for anticipating success. This is not a book of prophecies, neither is its author a prophet. Difficulties and strains are inevitable on both sides, that seems clear. The aim is to draw attention to a key element in the future evolution of economic systems.

Twenty or even ten years ago it was common to see, and to write, such phrases as that 'the Soviet system is unsuitable and inappropriate for a modern industrial society'. One's confidence in the validity of the above judgement is affected by a growing feeling that the Western system is not so appropriate either. Perhaps a future historian (if the human race has a future) might conclude that the development of technique, computers, weapons, etc., far outran the capacity of human beings and institutions to handle them.

SOME KEY WEAKNESSES AND THEIR REMEDIES

Turning now from the highly general to the more detailed particular, what conclusions can be drawn as to the health and ailments of the Soviet-type economy of today?

Most of the weaknesses which we have been discussing relate in some way to diseconomies of centralized scale. In a model which Brus has called 'etatist socialism', i.e. in which the state, acting on behalf of society, determines what is needed, what should be produced, how and by whom, the volume of decision making and information processing *enormously* exceeds the capacity of the centre. No amount of reorganization can change this basic fact. We have seen that this has two profound consequences: the centre itself becomes divided ('centralized pluralism'), and a very large number of decisions become dependent *de facto* on the actions of subordinate officials, in enterprises and elsewhere. They have to fill *lacunae* in the plans, they disaggregate agregated plan targets, they make proposals and provide (or conceal) information which forms the basis of central orders, they have to cope with inconsistencies and breakdowns, e.g. in supply of inputs. Improvements in quality, the introduction of new designs, the diffusion of technological innovation, depend greatly on management at intermediate and local levels. Yet they lack any criteria for operational decision making, other than the necessarily incomplete and aggregated plan-orders received from above. Lines of responsibility are further confused by the intervention of party organs, and by the lack of coherence between ministerial lines of subordination and the actual production and investment processes, a consequence of the immense organizational complexity. A price system designed to facilitate evaluation of performance and control over expenditures fails to provide economic information, to management and planners alike. The incentive system is too often producing paradoxical results. It has been impossible to devise success indicators which would stimulate and reward the actions which planners and party leaders evidently desire, but which they are incapable of defining operationally: quality, conformity to user requirements, and so on. They are 'incapable' not through mental inadequacies, but because an operationally effective definition, in most of the economy, simply cannot be found.

This complex of problems is linked with another: the consequence of the political system and the censorship upon the flow of information. In the period of the Stalin terror very serious losses were caused simply by fear: a proposal emanating from a high level could not be queried, even by those who knew (as the authors of the proposal might not have known) that it contained grave errors. Stalin is dead, and businesslike discussions and practical suggestions are now much more common. However, there are still many examples of central 'restriction and manipulation of the information system', and 'arbitrary assumptions and one-sided arguments' at the top, to cite Brus (1975, pp.192–3), who argues strongly for 'democratism in the political system as an essential condition for a change in this state of affairs'.

It is hard not to agree with the proposition that democratization can affect not only decisions on priorities, but also the flow of more reliable information and the attitude to their work of both the workers and the managerial strata. At the same time, it must be stressed that goodwill, while valuable, does not resolve the bulk of the problems of Soviet micro-economics, which, as we have seen, are not due fundamentally to negative human attitudes. With the best will in the world no official can decide what to do unless he or she possesses not only information as to what is best but also the means to act. The means (and power) to act are usually placed in the upper reaches of the bureaucracy not because (or not only because) of power-seeking and vested interest; it is only at these higher levels that the full consequences of the proposed course of action can be compared with alternatives, these consequences weighed, the necessary resources provided.

We have also seen that mathematical or programming models, while useful tools for planners, do not and cannot resolve the basic problems here discussed. Optimization is, of course, an *optimum optimorum* never achieved in real life, but even to define what it is one should be

maximizing presents one with a question with no operationally meaningful answer. It has also proved very difficult indeed, for the analyst
as well as the planner, to define and devise a clear 'optimizing' criterion
for managers. This is closely connected with the fact that the centre
usually has no micro-economic objectives of its own, and that consequently it does not know exactly what it is that the management
should be rewarded for doing – other than fulfilling some (usually
aggregated) plan-indicators, based in the main on past performance,
i.e. on extrapolation.

The party, or rather its senior full-time officials, appear to desire
both the efficient operation of the economy in an age of technological
revolutions *and* the maintenance of its control over the appointment
and actions of economic management at all levels, and also over
information flows, the media, policy priorities and the scale and recipients
of rewards. This, so it is widely believed, represents a major obstacle to
the reform of a system designed to achieve drastic structural change
in a backward country, and which has been, literally, outgrown.

At the same time, attentive readers of the preceding pages will have
been cured (I hope) of the naive notion that reform is a simple matter,
barred only by ideological fervour and/or vested interest. The limitations of the market mechanism, particularly in the absence of a capital
market, must be admitted. So must the inadequacy of any (even so-
called 'rational') prices as a guide to long-term investment decisions.
Market forces do have some negative as well as positive consequences:
the dangers of unemployment, duplication of effort, excessive income
differentiation, conflicts within a mixed economy between the planned
and the unplanned, all these are legitimate causes of worry, among
socialists especially. Yugoslavia's experience, for all its immense
interest and considerable achievements, is not reassuring. 'A combination of high unemployment, high emigration, high inflation, a
heavy negative balance of payments . . . and much duplicative investment.' (Granick, 1976, p.468.) Hungarian reform experience also shows
that difficulties can and do arise.

This has led some 'new-left' commentators into simply rejecting the
market-reform solution, without being able to put anything coherent
in its place. It seems to me that Brus has the correct formulation: 'the
model of a planned economy using a regulated market mechanism'
represents a feasible solution. He distinguishes between 'fundamental
macro-economic decisions' and 'current operating problems', within
a context in which households are free to decide their place of work,
expenditure patterns, etc. Current production and utilization decisions
would rely on a market mechanism, subject to rules and parameters
laid down by the centre. (Brus, 1975, p.74.) Coexistence of plan and
market will throw up problems, expose the system to dangers. But one
cannot reject the very possibility of such coexistence without denying

at the same time the possibility of effective socialist planning in a modern economy, except on quite unreal assumptions ('abundance', i.e. the absence of economic problems) or on the basis of religious faith ('Marx said so').

COSTS AND BENEFITS OF SYSTEMS

The beginning of wisdom in real-world economics is to appreciate that all things have a cost, and this includes both economic systems and any measures of reform. One does not, as a rule, get something for nothing. It is a feature of the two extremes – the 'Pareto-optimizers' and perfect-marketeers on the one hand, the millenarians of the far left on the other – that the real problems of the real world are overcome by definition, with the conflicts and contradictions of economic and social life reconciled also by definition. The perfect-marketeers usually ignore structure, so that conflict (for instance) between centralization and decentralization never appears. The millenarians attribute conflict to capitalism or élites. Yet the problem is inescapable. At the centre one sees many things, many inter-relationships, but at a distance, darkly. At the periphery one sees the details clearly, but the wider consequences of one's actions will be much less clear. 'Externalities' arise. Consequently, in any economic system, a move towards or away from decentralization will incur a cost. Presumably, proceeding by trial and error, one attempts a cost-benefit analysis and hopes that the disadvantages will be outweighed in each case by the advantages.

To let people choose, in their capacity as managers, consumers, farmers, means that they may choose wrongly, can get in each others' way, can duplicate or frustrate each others' actions. If editors are free of censorship they may produce rubbish or pornography. Yet the imposition of censorship (as the experience of the USSR abundantly shows) has its own cost, direct and indirect. A control apparatus designed to prevent actions judged undesirable – by managers, farmers, consumers, editors – can and usually does develop bureaucratic habits, and again there is a cost: that of the apparatus itself and the frustrations which it engenders. If the Yugoslav model of workers' self-management develops a sense of participation, reduces the sense of alienation, adds to the vigour with which workers deploy their skills, these would be advantages to set against the undeniable defects of the model. As the readers have surely guessed, my own preference is for a model similar to that which was tried out in Hungary in 1968, but it too has its cost.

Continuing this line of thought, and relating it rather more directly with inter-system comparison, let us look at unemployment of human and material resources, a common feature of Western economics, and full or even over-full resource utilization, commonly encountered in the 'East'. (Let us leave aside how far this is due to overmanning and hoarding of labour in certain sectors and areas.) In the West, with some resources unused, it is usually difficult to sell. In the east it is usually difficult to buy. Both these circumstances give rise to negative phenomena, impose costs on the economy and on society. Lack of 'slack' impedes flexible adjustment to requirements, lack of competition for custom plus ease of selling makes for indifference to these requirements and for all the familiar phenomena associated with a sellers' market. Citizens (and managers) have to stand and wait, and take what they are given rather than what they really want or need. The scene is set for privileged access to scarce goods and services, black markets, etc. No wonder the Hungarian economist Kornai insists that this is a deplorable state of affairs, when the suppliers are in so strong a position.

However, suppose it is difficult to sell. This can lead to massive expenditure on advertising and packaging, the encouragement of 'consumerism', the undesirable phenomena associated with commercialization. Also unemployment is demoralizing and wasteful, yet without it the market system lacks the flexibility and the discipline it needs: the unsuccessful competitor *should* go bankrupt. We in the West see the negative features of our own system, but we may be unaware of the cost of alternatives. Conversely, many 'Eastern' economists, dismayed by the inefficiencies they see around them, have tended to underplay the deficiencies of a Western competitive market economy, with which they were unfamiliar.

Conceptual problems arise if one tries to evaluate, or weight, positive and negative characteristics of system. Thus suppose that the USSR does not suffer from unemployment, but does suffer from the discomforts, delays and frustrations of Soviet shopping, *and* (as suggested above) these positive and negative features are causally linked. If the West has unemployment but a much superior distribution system, which is 'better'? By what criteria? How does one even attempt the task of measurement?

Despite this, let us attempt an evaluation of strength and weakness, bearing in mind also their potential: thus the identification of *remediable* defects also identifies possibilities of improvement.

Central planning enables large-scale investment plans to be made with less uncertainty, and we have noted that it is lack of knowledge of the future, rather than detailed price-and-rate-of-return calculations, that are the source of most of the conspicuous waste in this field. The system also facilitates the maintenance of a steady *rate* of investment, since it becomes dependent upon decisions by the political planning authority, and not on the autonomous decisions of corporate and private savers. The volume of investment can be adjusted to the production programme of investment goods. True enough, these advantages are by no means always realized in practice. We have noted in

Chapter 6 that there are in fact large fluctuations in the rate of increase of investment in most East European countries; for example, Poland doubled its investments in the four years ending in 1975, and plans an increase in the next few years of little more than zero per cent, as a consequence of the resultant strains and stresses. The link between investment plans (including their financial aspects) and the production of investment goods has also often been faulty. There are grave deficiencies in what could be called the micro-economics of investment and innovation, much discussed in Chapter 6, above. But the system does seem here to possess some solid advantages, which it may be learning to realize.

It can be argued that the system is better able to take care of environmental and other externalities. Again, it is easy to demonstrate that it has not been successful in doing so in the past. But the reason could be that the centre, whose job it is, has simply not bothered with such matters. Now, however, pollution and environment are in the public eye in the Soviet Union also, as is conservation. After much criticism of wasteful and over-lavish utilization of such resources as forests, fresh water, metal ores, energy, a greater consciousness of the need to conserve is already affecting plans. The system is at least *potentially* capable of handling such problems, probably better than one based on private enterprise.

Since Soviet planning has been most particularly 'geared' to the enforcement of centrally determined priorities, its advantages are obvious if one desires to concentrate resources on objectives which would not be indicated by any spontaneous market forces, such as defence, or if the object is rapid structural change. Control over relative incomes prevents the diversion of human skills into areas judged less important (and it could be argued that much ingenuity is misused in the West on such non-essentials as advertising, the stock market, commercial pop and much else).

Despite all the qualifications mentioned (indeed stressed) in Chapter 9, the fact remains that the controls over prices and incomes are more effective than in the West, and the social conflicts inevitable in any modern society are more successfully resolved or suppressed. As usual, there is a cost. Price control is, as we have seen, unmanageably clumsy and generates misleading signals. Wage differentials are wide open to criticism and are only partially effective. The suppression of conflict by censorship and police measures has negative effects, for the economy also. So there is a trade-off. Inflation-prone economies in the West can be so distorted that (it can be argued) a considerable price is worth paying to avoid these distortions. Or, to put the point in a very different way, it may be that the Western liberal philosophy of 'negative freedom', with each person and group seeking their own advantage, leads not to an optimum or even a tolerable compromise, but to increasingly disruptive conflict. Which brings one back to the point we were at at the beginning of this chapter.

Turning now to defects, it is unnecessary to repeat the point about the cause of so many of them: the system's functional logic requires an impossible centralization. Most of the weaknesses are to be found in the micro-economic realm: the transmission of user demand, quality, innovation, initiative, long-term responsibility, misleading prices, lack of objective criteria for choice, all these are problem areas which have been discussed at length in earlier chapters. They are 'systemic', deeply embedded in the essence of the centralized 'directive-planning' system, highly resistant to partial reform, or to any cure which does not tackle the nature of the system itself, including its political organization. The effects of these weaknesses on productivity, the numerous examples of unintended inefficiency, misallocation, waste, inconsistent plans, contradictory or confusing incentives, should be familiar to the reader of this book, as they are to the Soviet leader-ship. The latter is, I suspect, bewildered by its own inability to put these matters right. It is not enough for them to urge the need for intensive methods, effectiveness and quality. It is a basic problem of *directive*-planning that so much must depend on the directive, its con-tent, its enforceability. Experience shows only too clearly that it is far easier to draft an instruction containing an order to produce 10,000 tons of widgets (an imaginary commodity) than to achieve 'efficiency' or 'quality'. There is no difficulty at all in talking about greater effi-ciency and higher quality, but they are far less comprehensible (and enforceable) than the more traditional quantitative instruction. So many well-meaning orders come to resemble imprecise exhortations. The West's superiority in the general area of micro-economics seems beyond dispute. Centralization leads to grave diseconomies of scale.

Some would stress also the lack of goodwill, the failure of the middle-grade management and workers to identify with the aims of the plan, or with the remote Authority that drafts the orders they are supposed to obey. Undeniably these are important matters, which have been touched upon on several occasions. Human attitudes, labour relations, affect efficiency, quality and information flows. However, the question is often the inability of those concerned to identify the right thing to do, rather than a conscious reluctance to do it. In any event, labour relations appear to vary widely in different countries in both systems, and indeed as between industrial sectors in the same country. This is a subject on which solid or quantifiable information is scarce. How, for instance, can we divide up the 'blame' for the lower productivity of the British compared with the West German car industry between managerial inefficiency, underinvestment, negative work attitudes, obsolete trade union organization, and so on? Where a given statistic-ally measurable result is affected by a number of causal factors, the weighting of each of these factors can only be arbitrary.

Then there is the way in which the two kinds of economy identify and correct mistakes. 'One of the few things that can be said with certainty about planning is that there will be errors', said an American corporation official, referring also to plans made by firms in the West. (Grove in Khachaturov, 1976, p.426.) Corrective action must depend in large degree on feedback, i.e. the speed with which information reaches the decision maker. Soviet experience suggests that views which imply that a party-state decision is mistaken are likely to be discouraged or blocked. We do not know, however, how many autocratic and wilful company chairmen discourage constructive criticism by *their* subordinates. Similarly, while one can criticize the selection process by which managers are appointed in the 'East', the process of appointment in the West has its own oddities and distortions. One can surmise, however, that errors and bad management are more likely to be punished in a competitive economy.

How do economies adjust to the unexpected? When the shock is very big, it may be too big for the market to adapt itself smoothly, and quite big enough to cause the supreme managers of a centrally planned economy to respond, even if prices fail to reflect the new scarcities. A good example of this is the response of the two systems to the oil crisis. In the West, prices of oil rose dramatically, giving a stimulus to oil-saving measures, and to increased investment in other kinds of fuel and in oil exploration. There were also administrative measures in a number of affected countries, to save oil or to strengthen an ailing balance of payments. In the USSR prices of fuels altered little. However, the planners were well aware of the large potential earnings of hard currency from sales of oil in the West, and therefore of the high opportunity-cost of increased domestic consumption. The tenth five-year plan (1976–80) therefore provided for a cutback in the use of fuel-oil, increased investments in natural gas and nuclear fuel generation, a sharply reduced rate of growth of production of motor vehicles, a speed-up in oil prospecting, in other words very much the sort of thing which a 'capitalist' Russian economy would be doing under the impact of a drastic change in relative prices.

Indeed it has been argued that the Western economies have been excessively extravagant in their use of energy, and even the increase in oil prices is failing to restrain them. The USSR or China, by contrast, possesses, at the top, planners who have to take the long view, thinking in operational terms about 1990 and beyond. The time-horizon of our corporation executives is shorter, made even more so by inflationary uncertainties and high interest rates.

There is an apparent contradiction here, and the last pages of the book will be devoted to unravelling it. In earlier chapters we often found clumsy bureaucracy failing to respond to change and to opportunity, as well as showing a tendency to concentrate on short-run objectives to the detriment of the long view; we also laid stress on the losses which arise out of the lack of rational crieria, the abundance of irrational price-relationships, and so on. Yet there is no real contradiction. The Soviet-type model is, almost by definition, able to focus upon those questions which, of their nature, are capable of being handled by the centre. These are not just the broad macro-economic categories, but also the development plans of basic industries and sectors. As already argued in Chapter 6, big long-term investment decisions are everwhere taken by reference to forecasts, which include estimates of future demand in quantitative terms. Large and durable changes in supply, technique, cost, can be incorporated into the analysis even if one's own prices and exchange rates are highly deficient, as the example of oil shows. (Conversely, errors such as overinvestment in British electricity supply in the seventies were not due to the deficiencies of the price system, but to an incorrect estimate of future demand.) The Soviet system *is* capable of developing a long-term policy for fuel and power, and, though error is certainly possible, this is unlikely to be due to the system as such.

It is in micro-economic matters that the troubles accumulate. There short-sightedness rules, because what matters is always the fulfilment of the plan now current, and there is little sense of longer-term responsibility. There are grave deficiencies both in the signalling apparatus (success indicators, prices, etc.) and in the possibilities of conveying, and responding to, user demand. Whenever the efficient functioning of factories or farms, or the design of new and better machines, depends on low-level initiative, as most of it must, error and distortion abound. Activities, sectors, types of decision, can be analysed in terms of 'central planability', always bearing in mind that 'the centre' itself is really plural, and that it has a limited information-absorbing and directive-giving capacity. Where, as in agriculture and in many branches of industry, local conditions vary greatly and adjustment to them and to requirements of customers *must* be the *de facto* responsibility for those on the spot, the system is particularly inefficient. And since the big 'macro' magnitudes are the result of a multitude of actions in the micro-economic sphere, one sees the end-result in low productivity and misallocation.

However, as has been pointed out, differences not due to system, and inadequacies of the statistical expression both of output and of waste, make it impossible to measure the comparative effectiveness or ineffectiveness of the Soviet-type economy in a rapidly changing and alarming unstable world. I just hope that the reader who has got this far has been made aware of the issues and complexities involved, and will be encouraged to read more, argue, criticize, and try to reach his own independently thought-out conclusions.

REFERENCES

A. Abouchar (ed.): *The Price Mechanism in the Socialist Economy*, Duke University Press (forthcoming).

F. A. Abramov (1963): 'Vokrug da okolo', Neva, No. 1, translated as 'The Dodgers', 1973, London.

A. G. Aganbegyan and K. K. Valtukh (eds) (1969): *Problemy narodnok-hozyaystvennogo optimuma*, Moscow.

V. Andrle (1976): *Managerial power in the Soviet Union*, London.

O. K. Antonov (1965): *Dlya vsekh i dlya sebya: o sovershenstvovanii pokazateley planirovaniya sotsialisticheskogo promyshlennogo proizvodstva*, Moscow.

Maria Augustinovics (1975): 'Integration of mathematical and traditional methods of planning' in M. Bornstein (ed.), *Economic Planning East and West*, Cambridge, Mass.

S. Ausch (1971) in Vajda and Simai (1971).

B. Balassa (1973) in Bornstein (1973).

E. Barone in Nove and Nuti (1972).

A. Bergson (1961): *The real national income of Soviet Russia* (Harvard).

A. Bergson (1968): *Planning and productivity under Soviet socialism* (New York).

L. Ya. Berri (ed.) (1968): *Planirovaniye narodnogo khozyaystva SSSR*, Moscow.

C. Bettelheim (1969): *Calcul économique, catégories marchandes et formes de proprieté*, Paris.

C. Bettelheim (1971): 'The Dictatorship of the Proletariat', *Monthly Review*, Vol. 22, No. 6.

A. M. Birman (1967): 'Talant ekonomista', *Novy Mir*, No. 1.

M. Bornstein (ed.) (1973): *Plan and Market*, New Haven.

A. Bose (1975): *Marxian and post-Marxian Political Economy: an introduction*, Harmondsworth, Penguin.

A. Ya. Boyarsky (1962): *Matematiko-ekonomicheskiye ocherki*, Moscow.

W. Brus (1973): *The Economics and Politics of Socialism*, London.

W. Brus (1975): *Social's ownership and political systems*, London.

P. G. Bunich (1973) in Fedorenko and Bunich (1973).

L. Burmistrov (1968): *Nalogi i sbory s naseleniya v SSSR*, Moscow.

D. E. Carr (1975): 'The Lost Art of Conservation', *Atlantic Monthly*, Vol. 236, No. 6.

A. A. Chukhno, I. G. Sayapin, V. G. Likhodey (1968): *Voznagrazhdeniye za trud pri sotsializme*, Kiev.

S. H. Cohn, M. Feshbach and A. Nove (1965): 'Comment on "$2\frac{1}{2}$ per cent and all that",' *Soviet Studies*, Vol. XVI, No. 3.

G. D. H. Cole (1933): introduction in K. Marx, *Capital*, London.

J. M. Collette (1968): *Politique d'investissement et calcul économique: l'expérience sovietique*, Paris.

W. J. Conyngham (1973): *Industrial management in the Soviet Union*, Stanford.

CPSU Congress 1971: *Materialy XXIV sezda KPSS*, Moscow.

B. Csikos-Nagy (1969) in Friss (1969).

B. Csikos-Nagy (1971) in Vajda and Simia (1971).

B. Csikos-Nagy (1975): *Socialist Price Theory and Price Policy*, Budapest.

K. C. Davis (1976): 'Soviet-Japanese trade and economic relations', Unpublished Ph.D. thesis, University of Birmingham.

I. I. Dmitrashko (1966): *Vnutrikolkhozniye ekonomicheskiye otnosheniya*, Moscow.

N. Ye. Drogichinsky (1973) in N. P. Fedorenko and P. G. Bunich (1973).

N. Ye. Drogichinsky and V. G. Starodubrovsky (eds) (1971): *Osnovy i praktika khozyaystvennoy reformy v SSSR*, Moscow.

E. P. Dunayev (1974): *Obyedineniya predpriyatiy kak forma obobshchestvleniya proizvodstva*, Moscow.

I. S. Dvornikov and V. L. Nikitinsky (1957): *Novy poryadok rassmotreniya trudovykh sporov*, Moscow.

S. S. Dzarasov (ed.) (1974): *Nauchnyye osnovy upravleniya sotsialistcheskoy ekonomikoy*, Moscow.

M. Ellman (1973): *Planning problems in the USSR*, Cambridge.

A. Emmanuel (1969): *L'échange inégal*, Paris.

F. Engels (1936): *Anti-Dühring*, London.

N. V. Faddeyev (1974): *Sovet ekonomicheskoy vzaimopomoshchi*, Moscow.

N. P. Fedorenko (1964) (ed.): *Planirovaniye i ekonomiko-matematicheskiye metody*, Moscow.

N. P. Fedorenko (1967) (ed.): *Sovershenstvovaniye planirovaniya i upravleniya narodnym khozyaystvom*, Moscow.

N. P. Fedorenko (1968): *O razrabotke sistemy optimal'nogo funktsionirovaniya ekonomiki*, Moscow.

N. P. Fedorenko (1973) in N. P. Fedorenko and P. G. Bunich (1973).

N. P. Fedorenko and P. G. Bunich (eds) (1973): *Mekhanizm ekonomicheskogo stimulirovaniya pri sotsializme*, Moscow.

I. Friss (ed.) (1969): *Reform of the Economic Mechanism in Hungary*, Budapest.

O. Gado (ed.) (1972): *Reform of the Economic Mechanism in Hungary: Development 1968–1971*, Budapest.

V. F. Garbuzov (1974): *O gosudarstvennom byudzhete na 1975 god i ob ispolnenii gosudarstvennogo byudzheta SSSR za 1973 god*, Moscow.

V. F. Garbuzov (1980): *Zadachi dalneishego ukrepleniia ekonomiki i finansov kolkhozov i sovkhozov*, Moscow.

G. Garvy (1966): *Money, Banking and Credit in Eastern Europe*, New York.

L. M. Gatovsky (1967) in N. P. Fedorenko (1967).

V. Z. Gerashchenko (1970): *Denezhnoye obrashcheniye i kredit SSSR*, Moscow.

A. Gerschenkron (1951): *A Dollar Index of Soviet Machinery Output*, Santa Monica.

A. Gerschenkron (1959): Review of A. I. Pashkov (1958) in *American Economic Review*, Vol. 49, No. 4.

J. Goldmann (1964): 'Fluctuations and Trend in the Rate of Economic Growth in some Socialist Countries', *Economics of Planning*, Vol. 4, No. 2.

Gosplan SSSR (1974): *Metodicheskiye ukazaniya k razrabotke gosudarst-vennykh planov razvitiya narodnogo khozyaystva SSSR*, Moscow.

A. Gozulov (ed.) (1967): *Statistika sel'skogo khozyaistva*, Moscow.

D. Granick (1976): *Enterprise guidance in Eastern Europe*, Princeton.

G. Grossman (1960a): 'Soviet Growth: Routine, Inertia and Pressure', *American Economic Review*, Vol. L. No. 2.

G. Grossman (1960b): *Soviet Statistics of Physical Output of Industrial Commodities: their compilation and quality*, Princeton.

S. A. Gusarov (1971) in Drogichinsky and Starodubrovsky (1971).

P. Havas in *Public Finance*, No. 2, 1971.

J. N. Hazard, I. Shapiro, P. B. Maggs (1969): *The Soviet Legal System*, revised edition, New York.

B. Higgins (1959): *Economic Development*, New York.

A. O. Hirschman (1958): *The Strategy of Economic Development*, New Haven.

A. O. Hirschman (1970): *Exit, Voice and Loyalty: Responses to Decline in Firms, Organisations and States*, Cambridge (Mass.).

H. H. Höhmann, M. C. Kaser and K. C. Thalheim (eds) (1975): *The New Economic Systems of Eastern Europe*, London.

F. D. Holzman (1955): *Soviet Taxation*, Harvard.

J. F. Hough (1969): *The Soviet Prefects: the local party organs in industrial decision-making*, Cambridge (Mass.).

Hungarian Central Statistical Office (1974): *Statistical Yearbook, 1972*, Budapest.

Ye. Kapustin (1964): *Kachestvo truda i zarabotnaya plata*, Moscow.

Ye. Kapustin (1974) in A. Volkov (1974).

A. Katsenellenboigen (1977): 'Coloured Markets in the Soviet Union' *Soviet Studies*, Vol. XXIX, No. 1.

A. Kaufman (1953): 'The Origin of the "Political Economy of Socialism",' *Soviet Studies*, Vol. IV, No. 3.

B. Kedrov and S. Shukhardin in *Nauchno-tekhnicheskaya revolyutsiya i obshchestvo*, Moscow, 1973, quoted by T. H. Rigby and R. F. Miller *Political and Administrative Aspects of the Scientific and Technical Revolution in the USSR*, Canberra, 1976.

M. Keren (1973a) in Bornstein (1973).

M. Keren (1973b): 'The New Economic System in the GDR: an Obituary', *Soviet Studies*, Vol. XXIV, No. 4.

T. S. Khachaturov (1968) (ed.): *Voprosy izmereniya effektivnosti kapital'nykh vlozenii*, Moscow.

T. S. Khachaturov (1976) (ed.): *Methods of Long-term Planning and Fore-casting:* Proceedings of a conference held by the International Economic Association at Moscow, London, 1976.

T. S. Khachaturov (1980): *Effektivnost' sotsialisticheskogo obshchestvennogo proizvodstva*, Moscow.

W. Klatt (1976): 'Reflections on the 1975 Soviet harvest', *Soviet Studies*, Vol. XXVIII, No. 4, October 1976, p.485.

A. N. Komin (1971): *Problemy planovogo tsenoobrazovaniya*, Moscow.

J. Kornai (1959): *Overcentralisation in Economic Administration*, London.

J. Kornai (1971a): *Anti-Equilibrium: on economic systems theory and the tasks of research*, Amsterdam.

J. Kornai (1971b): *Pressure and suction on the market*, Amsterdam.
A. N. Kosygin (1965) in Nove and Nuti (1972).
V. M. Kozlov (1969) in S. A. Trifonov (1969).
V. P. Krasovsky (ed.) (1970): *Intensifikatsiya i rezervy ekonomiki*, Moscow.
V. P. Krasovky (1980): *Ekonomicheskie problemy i fondootdachi*, Moscow.
Constance Kruger (1974): 'A note on size of subsidies . . .', in *ACES Bulletin*, Fall.
S. Kuznets (1953): *Economic Change: selected essays in business cycles, national income, and economic growth*, London.
O. Kyn (1975) in Höhmann *et al.* (1975).
O. Lange (1938): *On the Economic Theory of Socialism*. Reprinted in Nove and Nuti (1972).
Lazarczik (1974) in United States Congress (1974).
B. M. Lazarev (1967): *Upravleniye sovetskoy torgovley*, Moscow.
M. Ya. Lemeshev (1973) in L. Ya. Berri (1973).
W. Leontief (1960): 'The Decline and Rise of Soviet Economic Science', *Foreign Affairs*, Vol. 38, No. 2.
G. Leptin (1975) in Höhmann *et al.* (1975).
M. Lewin (1974): ' "Taking Grain": Soviet Policies of Agricultural Procurements before the War' in C. Abramsky and B. J. Williams (eds) *Essays in honour of E. H. Carr*, London.
E. G. Liberman (1971): *Economic Methods and the Effectiveness of Production*, White Plains.
A. Lindbeck (1971): *The Political Economy of the New Left: an outsider's view*, New York and London.
G. Lisichkin (1966): *Plan i rynok*, Moscow.
J. Löwenhardt (1974): 'Scientists-entrepreneurs in the Soviet Union', *Survey*, Vol. 20, No. 4.
M. McAuley (1969): *Labour Disputes in Soviet Russia, 1957-1965*, Oxford.
H. Machowski (1975) in Höhmann *et al.* (1975).
Ye. Z. Maiminas (1976) in Khachaturov (1976).
A. N. Malafeyev (1964): *Istoriya tsenoobrazovaniya v SSSR (1917-1963)*, Moscow.
E. Malinvaud, see Khachaturov 1976.
M. Markovic (1974): *The contemporary Marx*, Nottingham.
F. S. Massarygin (1974): *Kreditnaya Sistema SSSR*, Moscow.
V. S. Mavrishchev (ed.) (1970): *Ekonomika sotsialisticheskoy promyshlennosti*, Minsk.
L. I. Mayzenberg (1973) in Fedorenko and Bunich (1973).
R. and Zh. Medvedev (1975): *Khruschev, gody u vlasti*, Columbia University Press and Xerox University microfilms.
R. Moorsteen (1962): *Prices and Production of Machinery in the Soviet Union, 1928-1958*, Cambridge (Mass.).
I. Motyashov (1968): 'Tverdaya tochka', *Moskva* 1968, No. 8.
Mozhayev (1966): 'Iz zhizni Fedora Kuzkina', *Novy mir*, 1966, No. 7.
G. Morovkin (1973) in L. Berri (1973).
G. Myrdal (1957): *Economic Theory and Underdeveloped Regions*, London.
V. S. Nemchinov (ed.) (1959): *Primeneniye matematiki v ekonomicheskikh issledovaniyakh*, Moscow.
A. Nove (1951): 'The Kolkhoz – some comments on Dr Schlesinger's

Article', *Soviet Studies*, Vol. III, No. 2.

A. Nove (1953): 'Rural Taxation in the USSR', *Soviet Studies*, Vol. V, No. 2.

A. Nove (1957a): 'Soviet industrial reorganisation', *Problems of Communism*, Nov–Dec 1957.

A. Nove (1957b): '1926/7 and all that', *Soviet Studies*, Vol. IX, No. 2.

A. Nove (1964): *Was Stalin Really Necessary?*, London.

A. Nove (1969a): *An Economic History of the USSR*, London.

A. Nove (1969b): 'Internal economies', *Economic Journal*, Vol. 79, No. 4.

A. Nove (1972): 'Market socialism and its critics', *Soviet Studies*, Vol. XXIV, No. 1.

A. Nove (1973): *Efficiency Criteria for Nationalised Industries*, London.

A. Nove and J. A. Newth (1967): *The Soviet Middle East, a Model of development?*, London.

A. Nove and D. M. Nuti (eds) (1972): *Socialist Economics: Selected Readings*, Harmondsworth.

V. V. Novozhilov (1959) in V. S. Nemchinov (1959).

V. V. Novozhilov (1967): *Izmereniye zatrat i rezul'tatov*, Moscow.

G. W. Nutter (1962): *Growth of Industrial Production in the Soviet Union*, Princeton.

OECD (1969); *Science Policy in the USSR*, Paris.

Ya. L. Orlov and V. Shimansky (1970): *Reforma i torgovlya*, Moscow.

A. I. Pashkov (1958): *Ekonomichesky zakon preimushchestvennogo rosta proizvodstva sredstv proizvodstva*, Moscow.

V. I. Perevedentsev (1966): *Migratsiya naseleniya i trudoviye problemy Sibiri*, Novosibirsk.

V. I. Perevedentsev (1975): *Metody izucheniya migratsii naseleniya*, Moscow.

G. V. Perov (1973) in L. Ya. Berri (1973).

F. Perroux (1958): *La coexistence pacifique*, Paris.

N. Ya. Petrakov (1966): *Nekotoryye aspekty diskussii ob ekonomicheskikh metodakh khozyaystvovaniya*, Moscow.

N. Ya. Petrakov (1971): *Khozyaystvennaya reforma: plan i ekonomicheskaya samostoyatel'nost*, Moscow.

T. M. Podolski (1972): *Socialist banking and monetary control*, Cambridge.

Ye. A. Preobrazhensky (1926): *Novaya ekonomika*, Moscow. Translated by B. Pearce as *The New Economics*, Oxford, 1965.

P. Rebrin (1969): 'Glavnoye zveno', *Novy Mir*, 1969, No. 4.

G. B. Richardson (1971): 'Planning versus competition', *Soviet Studies*, January 1971.

L. A. Rotshteyn (1971) in Drogichinsky and Starodubrovsky (1971).

O. Rybakov (1975): *Ekonomicheskaya effektivnost' sotrudnichestva SSSR s sotsialisticheskimi strananni*, Moscow.

Ya. A. Sapel'nikov (1969) in S. A. Trifonov (1969).

G. Schroeder (1972): 'The Reform of the Supply System in Soviet Industry', *Soviet Studies*, Vol. XXIV, No. 1.

E. Rychlewski (1976) in English summary of *Ekonomista* No. 1, Warsaw.

R. Selucky (1973): 'Marxism and self-management' in *Critique*, No. 3.

G. L. Shagalov (1973): *Problemy optimal'nago planirovaniya vneshneekonomicheskikh svyazey*, Moscow.

S. Shkuro (1974) in A. Volkov (1974).

A. Shuster (1968) in T. Khachaturov (1968).

O. Šik (1967): *Plan and Market under Socialism*, Prague.

L. Skvortsov (1972): *Tseny i tseno-obrazovaniye v SSSR*, Moscow.

B. M. Smekhov (1968): *Perspektivnoye narodno-khozyaystvennoye planiro-vaniye*, Moscow.

N. N. Smelyakov (1975): *S chego nachinayetsa rodina*, Moscow.

Hedrick Smith (1976): *The Russians*, London.

J. V. Stalin (1952): *Economic Problems of Socialism in the USSR*, Moscow. Relevant parts reproduced in A. Nove and M. Nuti (1972).

S. G. Stolyarov (1969): *O tsenakh i tsenoobrazovanii v SSSR*, Moscow.

R. Stojanovic in Khachaturov 1976.

S. Strumilin (1964) in N. P. Fedorenko (1964).

A. K. Suchkov (1949): *Gosudarstvennyye dokhody SSSR*, Moscow.

B. M. Sukharevsky (1974) in A. Volkov (1974).

P. Sweezy (1971): 'The Transition to Socialism', *Monthly Review*, Vol. 23, No. 1.

P. Sweezy and C. Bettelheim (1970): 'The Transition to Socialism', *Monthly Review*, Vol. 22, No. 7.

L. Szamuely (1974): *First Models of the Socialist Economic Systems: Principles and Theories*, Budapest.

H. H. Ticktin (1974): 'Socialism, the Market and the State. Another View: Socialism vs. Proudhonism', *Critique*, No. 3.

V. Tikhonov (1978): *Razvitie mezhotraslevykh sviazei sel'skogo khoziaistva*, Moscow.

V. Treml *et al.* (1972): *The Structure of the Soviet economy*, New York.

A. Tretyakova and I. Birman (1976): 'Input-Output Analysis in the USSR', *Soviet Studies*, Vol. XXVIII, No. 2.

S. A. Trifonov (ed.) (1969): *Ekonomicheskaya reforma i sovershenstvovaniye torgovli*, Moscow.

D. I. Tsarev (1971) in Drogichinsky and Starodubrovsky (1971).

M. Tugan-Baranovsky (1918): *Osnovy politicheskoi ekonomii* (5th edn), Petrograd.

Ye. Tyagay (ed.) (1956): *Ekonomika promyshlennosti SSSR*, Moscow.

V. S. Tyukov (1969) in S. A. Trifonov (1969).

United States Congress (1974): *Reorientation and Commercial Relations of the Economies of Eastern Europe*: a Compendium of Papers submitted to the Joint Economic Committee, Congress of the United States. ·

I. Vajda and M. Simai (eds) (1971): *Foreign Trade in a Planned Economy*, Cambridge.

K. K. Val'tukh (1969) in A. G. Aganbegyan and K. K. Val'tukh (1969).

K. K. Val'tukh (ed.) (1973): *Problemy narodnokhozyaystvennogo optimuma*, Novosibirsk.

J. Vanek (1970): *The General Theory of Labour-Managed Market Economies*, New York.

A. L. Vaynshteyn (ed.) (1967): *Statistika narodnogo bogatstva, norodnogo dokhoda i natsional'nyye scheta: ocherki po balansovoy statistike*, Moscow.

Vneshnyaya torgovlya SSSR za 1918–1940, Moscow, 1960.

P. Volin (1969): 'Lyudi i ekonomika', *Novy Mir*, 1969, No. 3.

A. P. Volkov (ed.) (1974): *Trud i zarabotnaya plata v SSSR*, Moscow.

B. Ward (1967): *The Socialist Economy: a study in organizational alternatives*.

P. Wiles (1976): *On the Prevention of Technology Transfer*, NATO, Brussels 17–19.3.76 – to be published.

A. A. Yakobi (1973) in L. Ya. Berri (1973).

Yu. V. Yakovets (1974): *Tseny v planovom khozyaystve*, Moscow.

A. Yashin (1956): 'Rychagi', *Literaturnaya Moskva*, 1956, 2nd issue.

V. A. Yevdokimov (1974): *Kontrol' za ispolneniyem gosudarstvennogo byudzheta SSSR*, Moscow.

L. N. Yurovsky (1928): *Denezhnaya politika sovetskoy vlasti (1917–1927)*, Moscow.

A. M. Zagorodneva (1968) in L. Ya. Berri (1968).

A. Zauberman (1960): 'New winds in Soviet planning', *Soviet Studies*, Vol. XII, No. 1.

A. Zauberman (1975): *The mathematical revolution in Soviet planning*, Oxford.

A. Zauberman (1967): *Aspects of Planometrics*, London.

J. G. Zielinski (1973): *Economic Reforms in Polish Industry*, London.

N. A. Zotova (1969): *Torgovla mezhdu stranami SEV v usloviyakh khozyay-stvennykh reform*, Moscow.

A. Zverev (1970): *Natsional'ny dokhod i finansy SSSR*, Moscow, 2nd edn.

BIBLIOGRAPHY

A full bibliography would require a volume in itself. What follows is a short list of some of the more important books on specific subjects in English. Large numbers of books and periodicals in Russian are referred to in the text, which should serve as a guide to any reader wishing to dig deeper into original sources. In those cases in which the author's name is followed only by the date, the books have already appeared in the References. Articles and periodicals in Western languages are so numerous that no attempt is made to list them here. Some of the most important for the student appear in the two books of Readings listed at the end of the bibliography.

HISTORICAL BACKGROUND

E. H. Carr: *A History of Soviet Russia* (London and Harmondsworth, many volumes).
M. Dobb: *Soviet Economic Development Since 1917* (London, 1966).
A. Nove: *An Economic History of the USSR* (Harmondsworth, 1969).
N. Spulber: *Soviet Strategy of Economic Growth* (Bloomington, 1964).

POLITICS

A. H. Brown: *Soviet Politics and Political Science* (London, 1974).
M. McAuley: *Politics and the Soviet State* (Harmondsworth, 1977).
Roy Medvedev: *On Socialist Democracy* (London, 1975).
L. B. Schapiro: *The Government and Politics of the Soviet Union* (London, 1973).

GENERAL WORKS ON SOVIET-TYPE ECONOMIES

A. Bergson: *The Economics of Soviet Planning* (Yale, 1964).
W. Brus (1973).
W. Brus (1975).
R. Campbell: *Soviet-type Economies* (London, 1974).
M. Ellman: *Socialist Planning* (Cambridge, 1979).
P. Gregory and R. Stuart: *Soviet Economic Structure and Performance* (New York, 1974).
M. Kaser: *Soviet Economics* (London, 1970).
M. Lavigne: *The Socialist Economies* (London, 1974).
H. Sherman: *The Soviet Economy* (Boston, 1969).
B. Ward (1967).
P. Wiles: *The Political Economy of Communism* (Oxford, 1962).

PLANNING, MANAGEMENT, REFORMS

V. Andrle (1976).
J. Berliner: *Factory and Manager in the USSR* (Harvard, 1957).

M. Bornstein (ed.): *Plan and Market* (Yale, 1973).
D. Granick: *Managerial Comparisons of Four Developed Countries* (MIT, 1972).
J. Marczewski: *Crisis in Socialist Planning* (New York, 1974).
B. Richman: *Management in the Soviet Union* (East Lansing, 1967).
O. Šik (1967).
N. Spulber: *Socialist Management and Planning* (Bloomington, 1971).
V. Treml *et al.* (1972).

(Eastern Europe)
R. Bicanic: *Economic Policy in Socialist Yugoslavia* (Cambridge, 1973).
B. Csikos-Nagy: *Socialist Economic Policy* (Budapest/London, 1973).
I. Friss (1969).
O. Gado (ed.) (1972).
D. Granick (1976).
D. Milenkovich: *Plan and Market in Yugoslav Economic Thought* (Yale, 1971).
R. Selucky: *Economic Reforms in Eastern Europe* (New York, 1972).
J. Wilczynski: *Socialist Economic Development and Reforms* (London, 1972).
P. J. D. Wiles: *Economic institutions compared* (Oxford, 1977).
J. G. Zielinski (1973).

MATHEMATICAL METHODS IN PLANNING

M. Ellman (1973).
L. Kantorovich: *The Best Use of Economic Resources* (Oxford, 1967).
J. Kornai: *Mathematical Planning of Structural Decisions* (Budapest 1975).
O. Lange: *Optimal Decisions, the Principles of Programming* (Oxford, 1971).
V. Nemchinov (ed.): *The Use of Mathematics in Economics* (Edinburgh, 1964).
R. Porwit: *Central Planning: evaluation of variants* (Oxford, 1967).
A. Zauberman: *Mathematical Economics in the Soviet Union* (Oxford, 1976).

LABOUR, WAGES, TRADE UNIONS

Janet Chapman: *Real Wages in Soviet Union since 1928* (Harvard, 1963).
A. Kahan and B. A. Ruble (eds): *Industrial Labour in the USSR* (New York, 1979).
Mary McAuley (1969).
P. Wiles: *Distribution of Income, East and West* (Amsterdam, 1974).

PRICES AND PUBLIC FINANCE

B. Csikos-Nagy (1975).
R. W. Davies: *Development of Soviet Budgetary System* (Cambridge, 1958).
G. Garvy (1966).
F. Pryor: *Public Expenditure in Communist and Capitalist Countries* (Homewood, 1968).

INVESTMENT AND TECHNICAL PROGRESS

J. Berliner: *The Innovation Decision in Soviet Industry* (MIT, 1976).
H. Fiszel: *Investment Efficiency in a Socialist Economy* (Oxford, 1966).
OECD (1969).

AGRICULTURE

T. Bergman: *Farm Policies in Socialist Countries* (Westmead, 1975).
W. A. Douglas Jackson (ed.): *Agrarian Policies and Problems* (Seattle/London, 1971).
J. Millar (ed.): *The Soviet Rural Community* (Illinois, 1971).
E. Strauss: *Soviet Agricultural in Perspective* (London, 1969).
K.-E. Wädekin: *The Private Sector in Soviet Agriculture* (Berkeley, 1973).

INTERNAL TRADE

M. Goldman: *Soviet Marketing* (London, 1963).
P. Hanson: *The Consumer in Soviet Society* (London, 1968).
P. Hanson: *Advertising and Socialism* (London, 1974).

INDUSTRY

R. A. Amman, J. M. Cooper and R. W. Davies: *The Technological Level of Soviet Industry* (New Haven, 1977).
R. Campbell: *The Economics of Soviet Oil and Gas* (Baltimore, 1968).
D. Granick: *Soviet Metal Fabricating* (Madison, 1967).
J. D. Park: *Oil and Gas in Comecon Countries* (London, 1978).

FOREIGN TRADE

A. Boltho: *Foreign trade criteria in socialist economies* (Cambridge, 1971).
A. Browne and E. Neuberger: *International Trade and Central Planning* (Berkeley, 1968).
F. Holzman: *Foreign Trade under Central Planning* (Harvard, 1974).
M. Kaser: *Comecon* (London, 1965).
I. Vajda: *The Role of Foreign Trade in a Socialist Economy* (Cambridge, 1971).
J. Wilczynski: **The Economics and Politics of East-West Trade** (London, 1969).
P. Wiles: *Communist International Economics* (London, 1966).

STATISTICS AND GROWTH

A. Becker: *Soviet National Income, 1958–64* (Berkeley, 1969).
A. Bergson: *The National Income of Soviet Russia since 1928* (Harvard, 1961).
R. Clarke: *Soviet Economic Facts, 1917–70* (London, 1972).
V. Treml and J. P. Hardt: *Soviet Economic Statistics* (Durham, N. Carolina, 1972).

REGIONS

V. Bandera and Z. Melnyk (eds): *The Soviet Economy in Regional Perspective* (Praeger, NY, 1973).

TRANSPORT

H. Holland Hunter: *Soviet Transport Experience* (Washington, 1968).
L. Symons and C. White: *Russian Transport* (London, 1975).

ENVIRONMENT

M. Goldman: *The Spoils of Progress* (MIT, 1972).
P. R. Pryde: *Conservation in the Soviet Union* (Cambridge, 1972).

BOOKS OF READINGS

M. Bornstein and D. Fusfeld: *The Soviet Economy* (4th edn, 1974).
G. Feiwel: *New Currents in Soviet-Type Economies* (Scranton, 1968).

INDEX

Abramov, F. A. 129
Academy of Sciences 38
accumulation fund 337
administration, expenditure on 245
Afghanistan, military intervention in 12.
    292
Aganbegyan, A. G. 79–80, 168
agricultural joint enterprise 153; rising
    costs 152; tax 240–1; transport and
    storage, lack of 152
agriculture 124–53; autonomous work
    unit 152; campaigns 131–4; choice of
    crops 132–3,150–1; harvest size 358;
    in the Hungarian model 297, 300; in
    the Yugoslav model 304; inefficiency
    in 134–52; natural conditions 135;
    organisation of 28–32, 142–4; output
    28, 136, 333–5, 358–60; planning
    130–5; Polish 312; private sector
    126–30, 252; production costs 153;
    productivity in 128; specialisation
    150–1; state procurements 130–1, 150;
    statistics 358–60; techniques 127; *see
    also* prices, agricultural
agrogorod 220
agro-industrial complexes 143–4, 150–1
allocation (of inputs) 38–9, 63–4, 319;
    at republican level 67; redistribution
    of 75
all-union ministries 22–8
American embargoes 292
amortization fund 246–8
Andrle, V. 114
Antonov, O. K. 53, 96, 110
arbitration tribunals 112
Arzumanyan, A. 352
Augustinovics, M. 57, 318
Ausch, S. 281, 287
automation 375–6
Autonomous Soviet Socialist Republics
    23
Azerbaydzhan 69

Bachurin, A. 317
balance of payments 279
bank credits 247–9

Barone. E. 19
barter; for supplies 104. 253; in foreign
    trade 275. 284
Bergson, A. 361. 364
Berri. L. Y. 55. 56. 57
Bettelheim, C. 307. 312. 321. 323–4
beznaryadnoye zveno 153
Bezrukov. V. 56
Birman, A. M. 113. 314
birth rate 222, 226
black market 192, 253
bond sales 239
bonuses 314; managerial 89–90. 106–7.
    108; for white collar workers 209–10;
    in agriculture 197; profit related 300;
    workers' 208
Bose. A. 267
bourgeoisie. the 320
Boyarsky, A. 58
Brezhnev, L. 61. 86. 98. 133. 134. 176.
    233, 256. 266. 320. 325. 352. 375–6
Brus, W. 25. 233, 309. 375, 377, 378.
    379
budget 234–41; payments into 89; plan-
    ning and 35, 234; republic and local
    expenditures in 234–5. 245–6. 268;
    surplus 245
budgetary revenue 32. 234–41; from
    foreign trade 240; redistribution of
    69; *see also* specific taxes
Bukharin. N. I. 164, 338
Bulganin, N. A. 206
Bunich. P. 93. 106–7. 110, 247–8
bureaucracy 318, 372; problems of 48;
    responsibilty and 50–1
Burmistrov. L. 239, 240

capital equipment 161. 163
capital output ratio 162–3. 374–5
capitalism 32. 345. 348
Carr, D. E. 172
Carter. President James 12
censorship 365, 378. 380, 382
Central Asian Republics 69–70. 142
Central Mathematical Economics Insti-
    tute 90. 183, 313, 317